AF413842

TRANSLATION AND TRANSFER OF KNOWLEDGE IN ENCYCLOPEDIC COMPILATIONS, 1680–1830

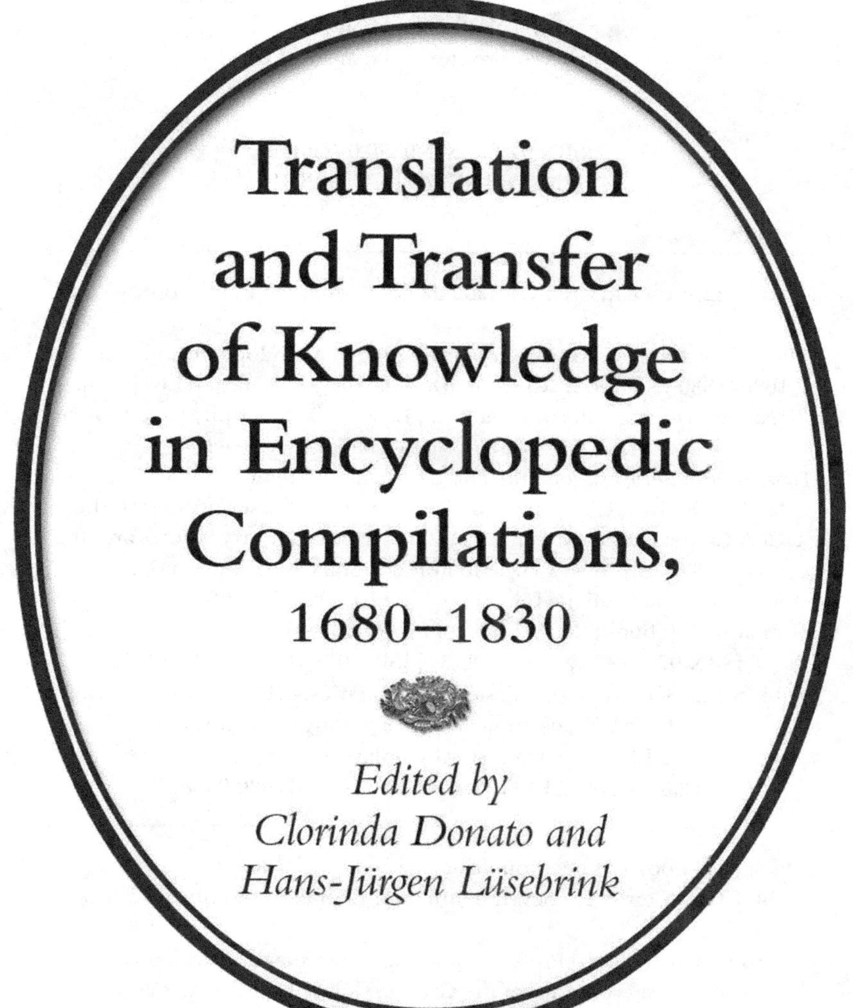

Translation and Transfer of Knowledge in Encyclopedic Compilations, 1680–1830

Edited by
Clorinda Donato and
Hans-Jürgen Lüsebrink

Published by the University of Toronto Press in association with the UCLA Center for Seventeenth- and Eighteenth-Century Studies and the William Andrews Clark Memorial Library

ISBN 978-1-4875-0890-6 (cloth)
ISBN 978-1-4875-3927-6 (EPUB)
ISBN 978-1-4875-3926-9 (PDF)

Library and Archives Canada Cataloguing in Publication

Title: Translation and transfer of knowledge in encyclopedic compilations,
1680–1830 / edited by Clorinda Donato and Hans-Jürgen Lüsebrink.
Names: Donato, Clorinda, editor. | Lüsebrink, Hans-Jürgen, editor.
Series: UCLA Clark Memorial Library series.
Description: Series statement: The UCLA Clark Memorial Library series |
"Published by the University of Toronto Press in association with the
UCLA Center for Seventeenth- and Eighteenth-Century Studies and the
William Andrews Clark Memorial Library" | Includes index.
Identifiers: Canadiana (print) 20210145706 |
Canadiana (ebook) 20210146354 | ISBN 9781487508906 (hardcover) |
ISBN 9781487539276 (EPUB) | ISBN 9781487539269 (PDF)
Subjects: LCSH: Encyclopedias and dictionaries – History and criticism. |
LCSH: Translating and interpreting – History. |
LCSH: Learning and scholarship – History.
Classification: LCC AE1.T73 2021 | DDC 030.9–dc23

This book has been published with the help of a grant from
the UCLA Center for Seventeenth- and Eighteenth-Century Studies.

University of Toronto Press acknowledges the financial assistance to its
publishing program of the Canada Council for the Arts and
the Ontario Arts Council, an agency of the Government of Ontario.

Contents

Contents

Acknowledgments

The editors are grateful to the many people who invested their time and energy into the publication of this volume and the organization of the UCLA Clark Library conference "Translation and Transfer of Knowledge in Encyclopedic Compilations 1680–1830," out of which the volume grew. We wish to acknowledge the generous support offered by the UCLA Center for Seventeenth- and Eighteenth-Century Studies, the UCLA William Andrews Clark Memorial Library, the Deutsche Forschungsgemeinschaft (DFG), and the California State University, Long Beach George L. Graziadio Center for Italian Studies that brought scholars far and wide together to exchange the views that have now been made concrete and lasting in this collection of essays. Special thanks are due to the former directors of both the UCLA Center and the Clark Library, Barbara Fuchs and Helen Deutsch, for promoting the conference and recommending the manuscript for inclusion in the UCLA Clark Memorial Library Series, published by University of Toronto Press. We extend heartfelt thanks to University of Toronto Press acquisitions editor Mark Thompson, who expertly guided us through all stages of manuscript preparation and review. This project would not have been brought to completion without the editorial assistance of Carla Dalbeck, research assistant in Romance Cultural Studies and Intercultural Communication, Universität des Saarlandes, and Manuel Romero, associate director of the Clorinda Donato Center for Global Romance Languages and Translation Studies at California State University, Long Beach. We would also like to recognize the UCLA Center and Clark Library staff for making the conference a success, for good conferences make good volumes. We are therefore indebted to any number of those who make the Center and the Clark such pleasant sites of intellectual endeavour, in particular, Kathy Sanchez, Candis Snoddy, Erich Bollmann, Jeannette LaVere, and Alastair Thorne.

TRANSLATION AND TRANSFER OF KNOWLEDGE IN
ENCYCLOPEDIC COMPILATIONS, 1680–1830

Introduction

CLORINDA DONATO AND HANS-JÜRGEN LÜSEBRINK

The contributions collected in this volume represent the forefront of eighteenth-century research and thinking about the ubiquitous albeit systematically overlooked translated encyclopedias and encyclopedic dictionaries that kept the printing presses of numerous publishing houses throughout Europe running at breakneck speed during the second half of the eighteenth century. So plentiful are these compilations that it has been difficult to even assemble a comprehensive list of them. Yet we know, for example, of some thirty different compilations within the Italian market alone, thanks to the painstaking work of bibliographers and book historians, not to mention the equally florid Dutch market, which is documented in no fewer than three of the contributions to this volume, those of Baggerman, Paul, and Baggerman/Donato. And while the study of so many compilations might appear to be a daunting and perhaps somewhat tedious undertaking, a cursory look at the scholarship offered by our contributors will certainly be more than adequate to the task.

But why now? What is the relevance of these multiple editions of encyclopedic works that were slated to appeal to new markets, constituencies, and reading publics? One of the most compelling arguments in this regard comes from the discipline of economic history in the form of a series of studies over the past fifteen years that have singled out encyclopedias as reliable indicators of economic expansion and precursors to the most prosperous centres of nineteenth-century industrial activity as the Industrial Revolution developed. These arguments have been articulated by Joel Mokyr in two books that have appeared over the past nineteen years: *The Gifts of Athena: Historical Origins of the Knowledge Economy* (2002) and *A Culture of Growth: The Origins of the Modern Economy* (2016). The latter returns to the evidence of the eighteenth-century knowledge economy constituted by encyclopedias to reflect upon their ubiquitous presence and unrelenting production in the second half of the eighteenth century in Europe:

> European encyclopedias are emblematic of a main theme of the Industrial Enlightenment in that they were explicitly meant to reduce access costs and make useful knowledge available to those who could make use of it. By organizing large bodies of knowledge in single publications, they showed their eagerness to distribute the knowledge to the curious and to those who might want to use it. Yet such compendia also contained conservative elements, because they present a snapshot of present accumulated knowledge, unless they were constantly updated and replaced. European encyclopedias, it was universally realized, went out of date almost as soon as they were published, and hence they were quickly replaced [...] To sum up: the knowledge revolution in the eighteenth century was not just the emergence of new knowledge; it was also better access to knowledge that made the difference.[1]

Mokyr's provocative analysis of the role of encyclopedic compilations in the industrial growth economy of the eighteenth century offers a refreshingly practical rationale for their continual production and application across national as well as regional markets throughout Europe, adding an important analytical perspective to the more traditional history of ideas/history of the book analyses such as those promoted by Robert Darnton through the prism of the French book trade.[2] Yet for all of the attention paid to encyclopedic compilations in eighteenth-century studies, the transnational, transcultural, and intercultural dimensions have been largely overlooked. This is surprising, if we consider the number of eighteenth-century encyclopedias that were translated, rewritten, or adapted to reflect evolving intercultural perspectives by translation specialists who were valued for their ability to render particular cultural contexts from one language into another.

One of the aspects that Mokyr has downplayed in his economic analysis of the eighteenth-century knowledge industry is that of national pride and the need to own and promote the knowledge of one's nation or region. The increasingly national character of encyclopedic compilations coincides with the rise of the concept of the nationstate in the second half of the eighteenth century. Indeed, knowledge and knowledge transfer that took place in the language of the nation suddenly assumed an important practical and symbolic value. It was practical, on the one hand, in response to the explosion of knowledge in the eighteenth-century world of commercial and colonial competition; it was also symbolic, as control of the world through language became a powerful tool in the forming of perceptions both local and global. At the end of the eighteenth century, new encyclopedic projects were launched to correct, through translation and adaptation, how a particular nation, people, and cultural entity were perceived. Thus compilations and their role in knowledge transmission constitute an overlooked source for understanding the intercultural dynamics of the global Enlightenment. Europeans were not the only ones to realize the importance of reference books. Indeed China, since the beginning of the Ming period (fourteenth to seventeenth centuries), had developed an intense production of encyclopedias before their Western equivalents that reached impressive dimensions in terms of number of volumes and contributors. As Burke (2000, 175) points out, "the early fifteenth-century *Yongle dadian* involved some 2,000 contributors and ran more than 10,000 volumes, making it too expensive to print and too difficult to preserve." Chinese encyclopedic compilations differed greatly from their European peers in their extremely limited production runs destined, as they were, for the most elite and royal citizens as static documents of erudition and intended for very specific purposes. As Burke underlines, "as early as the Tang dynasty, encyclopedias were produced primarily to serve the needs of the candidates in the examinations which led to posts in the imperial bureaucracy. The examinations took the form of essays, and the works of reference consisted mainly of quotations arranged by topic, allowing candidates with good memories to lard their answers with appropriate references to the literary classics" (175).

The same phenomenon can be observed in Japan, where the introduction of a Western tradition of encyclopedic writing at the end of the eighteenth century constituted a sharp contrast with traditional Japanese concepts of collecting knowledge in encyclopedic genres. The first encyclopedia based on a Western model was the translation and adaptation of Noël Chomel's *Dictionnaire œconomique* (first edition in 1709), which used as source texts the Dutch translations of Chomel (1743, third revised translation in 1786–93) that were brought to Japan through the Dutch trading post in Nagasaki at the end of the eighteenth century. The Japanese translation of Chomel's economic encyclopedia was undertaken at the beginning of the nineteenth century in the imperial town of Edu, where a group of learned persons worked on the sixty volumes between 1811 and 1839 (Proust 2001, 2005). In contrast to early modern non-Western traditions, the modern Western tradition consisted in a constant updating of knowledge, in which a fundamentally critical attitude towards traditional knowledge and the need for its constant renewal plays a central role. A comparison of the successive editions of encyclopedias illustrates that their editors and publishers renewed and rewrote numerous articles, generally quite frequently, in order to bring the knowledge they contained up to date. When Abraham Rees conceived his *Proposals* (1778) for revising Chambers's *Cyclopædia* he "emphasized his intention to exclude obsolete science, to retrench superfluous matter" (Burke 2012, 150). The translation and transfer of knowledge from other cultures, which in the eighteenth century embraced not only a European but also a more and more global dimension, represent important elements in this fundamental cultural dynamic, a marked characteristic of Western knowledge cultures since the Age of Enlightenment.

While such an intercultural dimension is evident in most areas of knowledge represented in a given encyclopedic compilation, geographical and historical articles of translated encyclopedias are the most extensively adapted and rewritten. The relationship between these two disciplines became very close in the eighteenth century when culture and politics advanced as areas to be included under the rubric of geography in encyclopedic compilations. They are therefore the areas that most dramatically exemplify the intercultural dynamic at work. As each of the essays making up this volume demonstrates, knowledge mobility, fluidity, adaptability, and repurposing through the vehicle of translation in knowledge transfer moved and reshaped knowledge.

While England and Spain controlled the colonial world, France dominated intellectually that world's description in Western cultures in the Age of Enlightenment. The desire to change the French narrative manifests itself in the form of the translated encyclopedias considered in this volume.

Just as there is an attempt to preserve cultural diversity in our globalized world of today through the rendering of texts, through translation, into the language or languages of the nation in question, so too in the eighteenth century was there a sense that translation could become a source of power and nation building.

Indeed, the perception of language as a national treasure in Europe became manifest during the sixteenth and seventeenth centuries, in particular, when in 1583 the Italian Crusca Academy was founded to promote and protect the Italian language. The Italian case is unique and emblematic, for at the time the Italian Academy was created, there was no Italian nation. Yet the founders of that academy knew that Italy's identity lay in her cultural and linguistic heritage, both of which would be evoked time and time again as a means of exhorting the Italians to form, finally, their nation as a unified political entity as well. As late as 1772 Girolamo Tiraboschi, author of the thirteen-volume *Storia della letteratura italiana* (1772–82), the first history of Italian literature, defined those writers to be addressed in his compendium in the following way: "Nostri diciamo tutti coloro che vissero in quel tratto di paese che or dicesi Italia" (We refer to as ours all of those who lived in that expanse of country that is now known as Italy).[3]

The thirst for knowledge drove the flourishing book trade in eighteenth-century Europe. The quick turnaround of best-selling or highly anticipated texts drove a dizzying production of translations, compilations, and translations of compilations that in many cases were commissioned by several publishing houses at the same time, with the aim of being the first to hawk a particular translation at the twice-annual book fair in Leipzig. A perusal of the Leipzig book fair catalogues over a number of years shows that multivolume compilations such as dictionaries and encyclopedias were the number-one sellers. Publishers of dictionaries, encyclopedias, and compilations of every kind required not only a first-tier set of writers and editors, but also second- and third-tier literary figures who worked in teams to compose, translate, shift, copy, and adapt text in response to market demand across Europe as a whole, and within discrete pockets of demand for specific literary products. Leah Price's discussion of anthologizing as a genre in the eighteenth century provides a cultural history of the excerpt, its power, and growing sphere of influence as the reading public sought to consume constantly increasing amounts of printed knowledge. Enter the translator, who multiplied and moved these texts into ever-expanding and shifting contact zones.[4]

The eighteenth century marked the birth of a number of new sciences and technologies whose terminology lexicographers attempt to codify. Among these burgeoning fields, geography and travel exploration occupied a central position. Both of them are highly important when it comes to the discussion of compilations, for much innovation in culture, science, and the arts came from geographical exploration. But who was doing all of these translations? The essays in this volume identify for the first time the organization of translation work for encyclopedic projects and the multilingual abilities of so many authors, compilers, publishers, and book dealers involved in the realization of these enterprises. While previous studies have informed us about the translation of travel literature in the periodical press, such as the work of Yasmine Marcil (2006), author of *La fureur des voyages: Les récits de voyage dans la presse périodique* (1750–89), and her carefully compiled statistics, we now know far more about the reception of translation and what drove translation into or from particular languages at certain times in the eighteenth century. Marcil has also remarked in her work that the format of travel literature was reduced for easy transport and reference by those who used such literature as guidebooks for their own travels. In-folio editions were now reserved for encyclopedias and books on art and architecture, which were intended for use in personal libraries or scholarly *cabinets.*

The Enlightenment period constitutes the actual moment in which modern genres arose and blossomed. At the centre of such projects sits research on translation. Transfer and intercultural reception of the genre in other cultures and cultural spaces, like those examined here, illustrate the cultural and scientific dynamics of translation processes. Translations of encyclopedic works position themselves in a special way as critical correctives to the originals, whose completion is achieved through new rounds of research, revision, and scientific advancements, most of which are recorded in the translated editions that always appear after the original source editions.

This dynamic can be illustrated through a certain number of examples that will be systematically analysed in the contributions to this volume. Just as the *Encyclopédie* of Diderot and d'Alembert was developed originally as a translation of Ephraim Chambers's *Cyclopaedia* (1728, eighth edition 1751–2), the work of translation, which immediately revealed gaps in knowledge, develops its own dynamic whose results illustrate the full influence and richness of this work and its potential in other contexts. Encyclopedias evolved at the same time as newspapers and gazettes, together with other literary forms such as salon discussions and philosophical novels, as outstanding media for constituting knowledge and its dissemination during the Enlightenment. But no other genre embodies more fully the goals of the Enlightenment.

Although encyclopedias had already emerged in several European languages in the seventeenth century thanks to the spread of the printing press, the genre acquired new dimensions and functions during the Enlightenment period. The new spirit of enlightened criticism, which Reinhart Koselleck analysed in 1959 in his pioneering study *Kritik und Krise: Eine Studie zur Pathogenese der bürgerlichen Welt* (Critic and crisis: Enlightenment and the pathogenesis of modern society), was grounded indeed in a constant movement of questioning the "pro" and "contra" (akin to the program of action adhered to by the Abbé Prévost in his critical journal *Le Pour et contre*, which vetted social, religious, and political phenomena, convictions, and beliefs). Indeed, the stance of critique, which engendered the dynamic of the Enlightenment, is based on the suspicion that all inherited knowledge should be constantly re-examined and requestioned on the basis of rational criteria, by means of the confrontation of different sources and various opinions, through critical comparison as well as by means of empirical evidence drawn from the opposing of fact and fiction.

What can we say about the translations themselves, and what are the criteria for translation in the eighteenth century? The rush to get knowledge to the marketplace and to shape it to cohere to criteria of national expression and identity meant that very often, these translations constituted compilations whose articles were made up of several sources. Here translators often became compilers, cutting and pasting from other sources so as to complete, update, and modernize their work. Several indications of how to interpret and analyse these translations and their goals are found in forewords, footnotes, addenda, supplements, and appendices. This paratextual material brought the translated compilation into its new context, introducing it to its new public. Even the titles of translated encyclopedias provide general indications regarding the strategies of creative adaptation and transformation of the very template of the encyclopedic genre itself in the translation process. Thus, the English translation of Noël Chomel's *Dictionnaire œconomique* of 1725 indicates that it is "Revised and recommended"; two years later a new edition appeared in Dublin "with considerable alterations and improvements." The subtitle of the 1778 Dutch translation of Fortunato Bartolomeo De Felice's economic encyclopedia states that "more than half" had been improved upon with respect to the original.

The English and Spanish translations of Moréri's *Grand Dictionnaire historique*, first published in French in 1674, are important in this regard. The editor of the English translation, published in 1694, clearly states that his is not a "bare translation" but rather his own edition of the work: "I call it an Edition, because the Reader should not think it a bare Translation; there being Abundance of Collections added in entire Paragraphs by themselves with a * prefix'd to distinguish them,"[5] while the Spanish edition, published much later, in 1753 (and constituting the first Spanish encyclopedia in the modern sense), clearly indicates in its title that it will be providing the best of Spain in its pages of corrected text.[6] As a side note, the story of this particular translation and its translator is fascinating, as he understood the need for Spain to enter the market-place of ideas that had been kept from it for so long. The partial and very selective German and English translations of Noël Chomel's voluminous *Dictionnaire œconomique, Contenant divers Moyens pour augmenter son bien, et de conserver sa santé* (1710) reflected already in their titles, in a quite programmatic way, the orientation of the translation and its logic of selection and adaptation. Whereas the English translation, made by Richard Bradley, transformed Chomel's encyclopedia into a "family dictionary," as the title indicates (*Dictionnaire œconomique: or, the Family Dictionary*), the German translation underscored its genuine encyclopedic dimension, but also its function of making both "rulers" and their "subjects" "happy" by increasing their pragmatic knowledge (*Die wahren Mittel Länder und Staaten glücklich, Ihre Beherrscher mächtig, und die Unterthanen reich zu machen* [...] *oder Grosses und vollständiges oeconomisch- und physicalisches Lexicon* [The true means to make countries and states happy, their rulers powerful, and the subjects rich [...] or great and complete economic and physical lexicon]) (Leipzig 1750–7).

The preface of the 1734 English translation of Bayle's *Dictionnaire* reveals the logic of selection and creative appropriation by which it is characterized. Written by the those who carried out the translation, Reverend John Peter Bernard, Reverend Thomas Birch, and John Lockman (1698–1771; an independent, autodidactic scholar and translator), the preface of the first volume points out that the translation would generally respect Bayle's work, but would nevertheless contain omissions on the one hand and numerous additions and corrections on the other hand. The omissions concern the geographical articles, considered "as being foreign to a Work of this kind."[7] The additions aim predominantly at integrating essential knowledge of British history and culture in the dictionary, including knowledge of the British empire, by means of some nine hundred additional biographical articles most of which concerned Englishmen, and by articles on Oriental history written by George Sale. This new focus on British national history and biography, which made this translation the "first important ancestor" of the British *Dictionary of National Biography*,[8] is rooted in an ostensible patriotic discourse: "We believe," write the authors and editors of the translation in the preface of the first volume, "it may be justly affirmed, that no nation boasts of a greater number of valuable Authors in every branch of Learning than our own; and yet no people have been less careful of doing justice to their memory."[9] Nevertheless, upon closer inspection, this translation goes far beyond a mere national British appropriation of a French encyclopedic dictionary by introducing factual corrections. It also contains numerous very critical remarks concerning Bayle's philosophical skepticism, which border on censorship. The authors of the preface introduce this perspective as follows:

> It may perhaps be expected, that we should take notice of the objection which has been made to Mr. BAYLE'S Work by some great and good Men, on account of the vein of unbounded Scepticism, and the sallies of a loose imagination, which he has indulged in several Articles. But as this relates to that Author only, whose Work we have no right to retrench any part of, we can only condemn whatever is obnoxious in it, and should have taken the liberty of making some observations of our own upon those passages.[10]

The translation of such media, as well as their use and implications, are an area of translation studies that has received relatively little attention, despite the fact that compilations are among the most widely used resources where translation has been employed as one of the primary tools enabling knowledge transfer. As the thirteen essays making up this collection demonstrate, translated compilations are overlooked sources for better understanding the intercultural dynamics of the global Enlightenment, especially with regard to the transmission and circulation of the cultural, economic, and anthropological knowledge embedded in their geographical writings. They not only fill in egregious gaps in our knowledge with research on representative mediating figures, such as translators, publishers, and editors, but they also offer analysis of exemplary translations, and their incumbent transfer and adaptation processes.

The chapters that follow explore the large field of encyclopedic translations and adaptations in the Age of Enlightenment in various and complementary ways. The creative process of transfer, translation, and adaptation of encyclopedias moving between different cultural areas is addressed in the contributions of Hans-Jürgen Lüsebrink, Ina Ulrike Paul, Arianne Baggerman/Clorinda Donato, and Clorinda Donato. As these different contributions illustrate, such processes lead to some forms of national "appropriation" of "foreign" encyclopedic models, reflecting a rather paradoxical connection between transcultural translation and cultural nationalization that can also be observed in other fields. A second field of investigation within this volume concerns the function and dimension of the translation processes themselves within specific encyclopedias, like the *Encyclopédie Méthodique* analysed by Kathleen Hardesty Doig or the Dutch encyclopedias studied by Ina Ulrike Paul. A third focus examines the circulation of knowledge between different genres (historiography, travelogues, encyclopedias) as analysed by Susanne Greilich, Karen Struve, Luigi Delia, Iwan-Michelangelo D'Aprile, and Ulrich Johannes Schneider. These studies explore additional knowledge fields ranging from juridical discourses to ethnographic and anthropological knowledge of the non-European world. Alain Cernuschi's chapter on the transfer of knowledge about theatre offers a provocative look at a discipline whose lines of information transfer and adaptation did not cohere as thoroughly to those of geography and history, reminding us of the importance of considering the history and evolution of particular disciplines when tracing them in encyclopedic compilations.

By placing the processes of transfer and translation at the centre, this volume transculturalizes while at the same time denationalizing the study of early modern encyclopedias. The examination of new sources forces us to reconsider a genre that for almost two centuries reflected the rise of nationalism and the domination of national cultures. While the intention of early encyclopedists had been to construct the compilation as a symbol of a universal knowledge without boundaries and to create a genuine incarnation of cosmopolitism embracing the ideals of the Enlightenment, national perspectives on knowledge proved to be inevitable, spawning corrective reactions that required a reappropriation of knowledge telling and transfer. Thus, since the late eighteenth century monumental symbols of nations and national cultures emerged, as each nation desired to have its own (or sometimes several) "national encyclopedias," like the German *Brockhaus Conversations-Lexicon*, the *Encyclopedia Britannica*, the *Grand Larousse* in France, or the *Encyclopedia Americana* in the United States. The recent evolution of the interplay between universal knowledge and nationalizing trends may be seen by the rise of Wikipedia in English, with an ever-growing number of translated and adapted Wikipedia articles in a vast range of languages. Thanks to the low cost of online publication, we now find any number of geographical and cultural articles in local dialects and *patois* that serve to maintain cultural and linguistic relevance and preservation. As a case in point, we cite the article "Imèr," written in "Diałeto primierot," which is the language spoken in the Primiero Valley in the Trentino region of Italy.[11] As all multilingual Wikipedia users know, an article that is pertinent to a particular cultural or linguistic group will receive far more nuanced treatment in the language of local provenance of the particular person or phenomenon in question. These new forms of transcultural and encyclopedic cosmopolitanism find their roots in the compilations presented here. They reflect very similar endeavours for inclusion and distinction that certainly characterized the early modern purveyors of knowledge transfer across platforms of collection and compilation that are encyclopedias, no matter what their format might be.

NOTES

1 Joel Mokyr, 2016, *A Culture of Growth: The Origins of the Modern Economy*, Graz Schumpeter Lectures (Princeton: Princeton University Press), 322.

2 Robert Darnton, 1971, "Reading, Writing, and Publishing in Eighteenth-Century France: A Case Study in the Sociology of Literature," *Daedalus* 100(1): 214–56; Darnton, 2007, "'What Is the History of Books ?' Revisted," *Modern Intellectual History* 4(3): 495–508.

3 Girolamo Tiraboschi, 1772–1782, *Storia della letteratura italiana* (Modena: La Società Tipografica), 1:viii, Clorinda Donato's translation.

4 Leah Price, 2000, *The Anthology and the Rise of the Novel* (Cambridge: Cambridge University Press), 5.

5 Louis Moréri and Edmund Bohun, 1694, *The great historical, geographical and poetical dictionary: being a curious miscellany of sacred and prophane history: containing, in short, the lives and most remarkable actions of the patriarchs, judges ... heresiarchs ... emperors ... and all those who have recommended themselves to the world ... together with the establishment and progress both of religious and military orders ...; [with] The genealogy of several illustrious families in Europe; The fabulous history of the heathen gods and heroes; The description of empires, kingdoms.* London: Printed for Henry Rhodes ... [and 3 others], vol. 1, "The Preface," 3–4.

6 Louis Moréri, 1753, *El gran diccionario historico, o Miscellanea curiosa de la historia sagrada y profana, que contiene en compendio la historia fabulosa de los dioses y de los heroes de la antiguedad pagana: las vidas y las acciones notables, de los patriarchas, jueges, y reyes de los Judios ... El establecimiento y el progresso de las ordenes religiosas y militares; y la vida de sus fundatores. Las genealogias de muchas familias ilustres de España, de Portugal, y de otros paises. La descripcion de los imperios, reynos republicas, provincias, ciudades, islas ... La historia de los concilios generales y particulares, con el nombre de los lugares donde se celebraron. Traducido del frances de Luis Moreri. Con amplissimas adiciones y curiosas investigaciones relativas à los reynos ... de España y Portugal . .. por Don* Joseph de Miravel y Casadevante ..., Paris y Leon: Hermanos de Tournes.

7 Pierre Bayle, 1734–41, *A General Dictionary Historical and Critical: in Which A New and Accurate Translation of the Celebrated Mr. Bayle, with the Corrections and*

Observations printed in the late Edition at Paris, is included; and interspersed with several thousand LIVES never before published. The whole containing the History of the most illustrious Persons of all Ages and Nations, particularly those of Great Britain *and* Ireland, distinguished by their Rank, *Actions, Learning and other Accomplishments. With Reflections on such Passages of Mr. BAYLE, as seem to favour* of Scepticism *and the* Manichee *System.* By the Reverend Mr. John Peter Bernard; The Reverend Mr. Thomas Birch; Mr. John Lockman; and other Hands. And the Articles related to Oriental History by George Sale, Gent. London: Printed by James Bettenham, for G. Strahan, vol. 1, "The Preface," 3.

  8 James Marshall Osborn, 1938, "Thomas Birch and the General Dictionary (1734–41)," *Modern Philology* 36, no. 1 (August 1938): 25.

  9 Bayle, *General Dictionary,* "The Preface," 3.

10 Bayle, *General Dictionary,* "The Preface," 4.

11 Accessed 10 May 2020, https://vec.wikipedia.org/wiki/Dia%C5%82eto _primierot.

Selected Bibliography

This section lists the works that have been of the greatest use in the writing of this chapter.

Burke, Peter. 2000. *A Social History of Knowledge,* vol. 1: *From Gutenberg to Diderot.* Based on the first series of Vinhoff Lectures given at the University of Groningen, Netherlands. Cambridge UK: Polity.

– 2012. *A Social History of Knowledge,* vol. 2: *From the "Encyclopédie" to Wikipedia.* Cambridge: Polity.

Candaux, Jean-Daniel, Alain Cernuschi, Clorinda Donato, and Jens Häseler, eds. 2005. *L'Encyclopédie d'Yverdon et sa résonance européenne: Contextes – contenus – continuités.* Geneva: Slatkine.

Charle, Christophe, Hans-Jürgen Lüsebrink, and York-Gothart Mix, eds. 2017. *Transkulturalität nationaler Räume in Europa (18. bis 19. Jahrhundert). Übersetzungen, Kulturtransfer und Vermittlungsinstanzen. La transculturalité des espaces nationaux en Europe (XVIIIe –XIXe siècles). Traductions, transferts culturels et instances de médiations.* Göttingen: V&R Unipress.

Chevrel, Yves, Annie Cointre, and Yen-Maï Tran-Gervat, eds. 2014. *Histoire des traductions en langue française, XVIIe et XVIIIe siècles, 1610–1815.* Paris: Verdier.

Darnton, Robert. 1971. "Reading, Writing, and Publishing in Eighteenth-Century France: A Case Study in the Sociology of Literature." *Daedalus* 100(1): 214–56.

– 2007. "'What Is the History of Books ?' Revisted." *Modern Intellectual History* 4(3): 495–508.

Denny, Joseph, and Paul M. Mitchell. 1994. "Russian Translations of the *Encyclopédie*." In *Notable Encyclopedias: Nine Predecessors of the* Encyclopédie, edited by Frank A. Kafker, 335–86. Oxford: Oxford University Studies in the Enlightenment.

Donato, Clorinda. 1997. "Übersetzung und Wandlung des enzyklopädischen Genres: Johann Georg Krünitz' *Oeconomische Encyclopädie* (1771–1858) und ihre französischsprachigen Vorläufer." In *Kulturtransfer im Epochenumbruch. Frankreich/Deutschland 1770–1815*, edited by Hans-Jürgen Lüsebrink/Rolf Reichardt with the collaboration of Annette Keilhauer and René Nohr 2:539–65. Leipzig: Leipziger Universitätsverlag.

– 2005. "La *Encylopedia Metódica*: Transfer and Transformation of Knowledge about Spain and the New World in the Spanish Translation of the *Encyclopédie Méthodique*." In *Das Europa der Aufklärung und die außereuropäische koloniale Welt*, edited by Hans-Jürgen Lüsebrink, 74–112. Göttingen: Wallstein-Verlag.

Eybl, Franz M., Wolfgang Harms, Hans-Henrik Krummacher, and Werner Welzig, eds. 1995. *Enzyklopädien der Frühen Neuzeit: Beiträge zu ihrer Erforschung*. Tübingen: Niemeyer.

Goulemot, Jean-Marie. 1989. "Écriture de la possession du monde et philosophie des Lumières." In *Le Temps de la Réflexion* 10: 67–75.

– 1998. "Bibliothèque, encyclopédisme et angoisses de la perte: L'exhaustivité ambiguë des Lumières." In *Le pouvoir des bibliothèques. Les mémoires des livres en Occident*, edited by Marc Baratin and Christian Jacob, 285–98. Paris: Albin Michel (Coll. Histoire).

Kafker, Frank A., and Loriot-Raymer, Gisèle. 1992. "Les traductions de l'Encyclopédie du XVIIIe siècle: quelle fut leur influence?" In *Recherches sur Diderot et l'Encyclopédie, 12*, 165–73.

Koselleck, Reinhart. 1959. *Kritik und Krise. Eine Studie zur Pathogenese der bürgerlichen Welt*. Freiburg/München: Verlag Karl Alber. Translated into English as *Critique and Crisis: Enlightenment and the Pathogenesis of Modern Society*, Oxford: Berg, 1988.

Leca-Tsiomis, Marie, ed. 2006. "Presentation." In *Dictionnaires en Europe*, special issue of *Dix-huitième siècle*, edited by Marie Leca-Tsiomis, 38, no. 1: 4–16.

Lüsebrink, Hans-Jürgen. 2002. "Trilateraler Kulturtransfer. Zur Rolle französischer Übersetzungen bei der Vermittlung von Lateinamerikawissen im Deutschland des 18. Jahrhunderts." In *Französisch-deutscher Kulturtransfer im Ancien Régime*, edited by Günter Berger and Franziska Sick, 81–97. Tübingen: Stauffenberg Verlag.

– 2004. "Wissen und außereuropäische Erfahrung im 18. Jahrhundert." In *Macht des Wissens: Die Entstehung der modernen Wissensgesellschaft*, edited by Richard van Dülmen and Sina Rauschenbach with the collaboration of Meinrad von Engelberg, 629–53. Vienna, Weimar: Böhlau.

– 2015. "Histoire des traductions et littératures 'nationales' à l'époque des Lumières et des Révolutions (1680–1820). Questionnements, défis et voies d'approche." In *Histoire des traductions et histoire littéraire*. Special issue of *Lendemains*, edited by Carolin Fischer, 158/9, no. 40: 184–98.

Marcil, Yasmine. 2006. *La fureur des voyages. Les récits de voyage dans la presse périodique (1750–1789)*. Paris: Honoré Champion.

Meulleman, Machteld. 2016. "Les traductions de l'Encyclopédie: L'in(ter)compréhension manquée ?" In *L'Encyclopédie, 250 ans après, la lutte continue*, edited by Véronique Le Ru. Reims: Presses Universitaires de Reims, 109–54.

Mokyr, Joel. 2002. *The Gifts of Athena: Historical Origins of the Knowledge Economy*. Princeton: Princeton University Press.

– 2016. *A Culture of Growth: The Origins of the Modern Economy* (Graz Schumpeter Lectures). Princeton: Princeton University Press.

Proust, Jacques. 2001. "Voie de passage de l'Encyclopédie vers le Japon: La Hollande." In *L'Encyclopédie. Du réseau au livre et du livre au réseau*, edited by Robert Morrissey and Philippe Roger, 103–14. Paris: Honoré Champion.

– 2005. "Sur la route des encyclopédies: Paris, Yverdon, Leeuwarden, Edo (1751–1781)." In *L'Encyclopédie d'Yverdon et sa résonance européenne: Contextes, contenus, continuités*, edited by Jean Daniel Candaux, Alain Cernuschi, Clorinda Donato, and Jens Häseler, 443–68. Geneva: Slatkine.

– 2006. "De quelques dictionnaires hollandais ayant servi de relais à l'Encyclopédisme européen vers le Japon." In *Dictionnaires en Europe*, special issue of *Dix-Huitième Siècle*, edited by Marie Leca-Tsiomis, 38, no. 1: 17–38.

Schneider, Ulrich Johannes, ed. 2006. *Seine Welt wissen: Enzyklopädien in der Frühen Neuzeit*. Darmstadt: Wissenschaftliche Buchgesellschaft.

Stockhorst, Stefanie, ed. 2010. *Cultural Transfer through Translation: The Circulation of Enlightened Thought in Europe by Means of Translation*. Amsterdam/New York: Brill.

chapter one

The Savary des Bruslons'
Dictionnaire universel de commerce:
Translations and Adaptations

HANS-JÜRGEN LÜSEBRINK

Published in 1723, the *Dictionnaire universel de commerce* represents the first universal dictionary of commerce in European cultural history. The Abbé Morellet, who in 1789 conceived the publication of a new dictionary to succeed the *Dictionnaire universel de commerce* – probably at the instigation of Jean-Charles Trudaine, the then French minister of finance – underlined in his "Prospectus" the innovative character of the publication and pointed out with some pride that the project had been carried out in France: "We have the advantage of having preceded other nations in the effort to deposit in a huge publication the part of human knowledge that has become, since the middle of the century, an increasingly important object of the reflections and speculations of the Philosophers and the content of a great number of writings."[1] Jacques Peuchet, author of a new *Dictionnaire universel de la géographie commerçante* published at the end of the century, one of the co-authors of the *Encyclopédie méthodique,* and the editor of the posthumous edition of the *Histoire des deux Indes* of Guillaume-Thomas Raynal published in 1826,[2] pointed out in his long introduction to the latter ("Discours préliminaire") the novelty of the Savary des Bruslons' project, suggesting that it had anticipated and largely surpassed similar English publications:

Nous avons déjà remarqué que quoique les Anglais aient, de bonne heure, traité les questions d'économie politique relatives au commerce, ni eux, ni aucuns des États commerçans de l'Europe n'avaient entrepris un ouvrage qui, comme le *Dictionnaire du commerce de Savary*, présentât la réunion de diverses branches de commerce et l'exposition des moyens employés, soit dans la pratique, soit dans la banque par les commerçants.

(We have noticed that even though the English had, early on, addressed questions of political economy as it relates to commerce, neither they, nor others from among the trading nations of Europe, have ever undertaken a work that, like the *Dictionnaire de commerce de Savary*, presented the different branches of commerce in the same work, together with a discussion of the means that were employed both in practice and in the bank for traders.)[3]

Initiated at the beginning of the eighteenth century, the *Dictionnaire universel de commerce* was "invented" and compiled by two brothers, Jacques Savary des Bruslons (1657–1716) and Louis-Philémon Savary (1654–1727), whose professional activities were closely linked to it. The elder brother, Jacques, was nominated in 1686 by Minister François Michel Le Tellier de Louvois, General Inspector of the Royal Manufactures at the Customs of Paris (Inspecteur Général des Manufactures, pour le Roy, à la Douane de Paris), whereas the younger brother, Louis-Philémon, was canon of the Royal Church of Saint-Maur-des-Fossés, one of the main fonts of late seventeenth-century and early eighteenth-century erudition, particularly since 1733 and the publication of a new literary history of France, the *Histoire littéraire de la France*.

The economic dictionary of the brothers Savary des Bruslons was inspired on the one hand by the book *Le parfait négociant*, a handbook published in 1675[4] by their father Jacques Savary (1622–1690), who practised the profession of "négociant-commerçant" (merchant and trader); and on the other hand by practical concerns and professional observations. The *Dictionnaire universel de commerce* thus gave a new dimension to their father's relatively small handbook. As an alphabetic and encyclopedic dictionary of several volumes treating concrete questions related to trade and commerce, like their father's *Le parfait négociant*, the *Dictionnaire universel de commerce* was initially devoted to very pragmatic issues. In the late 1680s, after his nomination as "Inspecteur des manufactures à la douane de Paris," Jacques Savary des Bruslons started a notebook entitled *Manuel Mercantile* in which he wrote down the definitions of the numerous types of merchandise he was inspecting, their mode of manufacture or collection, and their quality, prices, and origins. Also included was information concerning their value in different currencies and their weight in different systems of measurement. Drawing mainly on commercial prints, royal decrees, and official reports, like the *Mémoires des Intendants*, and correspondence of the royal trade companies, Jacques Savary des Bruslons completed these materials by means of personal observation, informal information given by colleagues, systematic research, and even interviews.

His handbook, which was never published and existed only in manuscript form, fulfilled a strictly personal, professional function, yet it comprised the core material for the project of a printed dictionary, which he conceived together with his younger brother, probably in the very last years of the seventeenth century. Encouraged by three important functionaries – the royal minister of finance, Claude Le Pelletier; Marc-René de Voyer de Paulmy d'Argenson, Lieutenant de police de la ville de Paris;[5] and Royal Chancellor Henri François d'Aguesseau, who gave him access to the royal archives concerning the international trade of the Kingdom of France – the project developed from a personal manual into a huge compilation that integrated personal observations and material mentioned above with archival and printed material extracted from a large number of sources and publications (dictionaries, travelogues, manuals, etc.). The first edition was finally published in 1723 in two in-folio volumes, by the younger brother, seven years after the death of Jacques Savary des Bruslons and two years before his own death in 1727. Carried on by their editor Jean Estienne in new editions published in 1741 and in 1748, and illegally reprinted in 1726–32 in Amsterdam, the *Dictionnaire universel de commerce* continued being published in French until 1765, through three other editions published in four volumes in 1742 and 1750 in Geneva and in five volumes in 1759–65 in Copenhagen.

Regardless of the form it would take in further editions and appropriations and as a result of translations, adaptations, and the needs of different reading publics, the *Dictionnaire universel de commerce* initially represented, in the first Paris edition of 1723, both a pragmatic and an almost official publication. Closely related to the new mercantilist economic policy conceived and realized by Jean-Baptiste Colbert, its combined official and pragmatic functions are underlined in the introduction to its last edition published in 1759: "this dictionary has the benefit of satisfying the public and of demonstrating to the court the success of one of the most important supports for the manufacturies of France."[6]

The Savary des Bruslons' *Dictionnaire universel de commerce* was not only based on original, unedited, first-hand materials, but also on the extensive use of pre-existing print materials from which the authors selected and compiled excerpts, which they then rearranged and placed within a new structural and generic context, often with substantially different forms of commentary. Louis-Philémon Savary indicated in his preface to the dictionary that he and his brother had used treatises and numerous travelogues, "a kind of library of all the books of commerce printed in France and in foreign countries" that his brother Jacques had initially assembled in order to "increase considerably his *Manuel Mercantile*."[7] In the forewords of the different editions of the *Dictionnaire universel de commerce*, we also find precise indications of the printed works the authors compiled for their dictionary; in the preface of the 1723 edition fully fifty printed books are quoted. This number would grow with the publication of subsequent editions.[8] For the articles on Africa, for example, they compiled in particuliar the *Relation des Costes d'Afrique, appellées Guinée* (1669) by Nicolas Villaut de Bellefont and the travelogues by Etienne de Flacourt (*Histoire de la grande isle Madagascar*, 1658) and Urbain Souchu de Renefort (*Relation du premier voyage de la Compagnie des Indes orientales en l'isle de Madagascar ou Dauphin*, 1688). The articles on South America were essentially based on first-hand information gathered by their nephew Edme, who was a merchant in Buenos Aires, and on a series of printed material, mainly translations of Spanish historical works and travelogues like the *Historia del descubrimiento y conquista del Perú* (1577; French transl. *Histoire de la découverte et de la conquête du Pérou*, 1706) by Augustín de Zárate; the *Descripción de las Indias Occidentales*[9] by Antonio de Herrera (1601–15; French transl. *Description des Indes occidentales, qu'on appelle aujourd'huy le Nouveau Monde … translatée d'espagnol en françois*);[10] the *Historia de la conquista de México* by Francisco López de Gómara; the *Historia de la Florida* by Inca Garcilaso de la Vega; and the travelogues of Lahontan and Thomas Gage, as well as the *Description géographique et historique des côtes de l'Amérique septentrionale, avec l'histoire naturelle de ce pays* (1671) by Nicolas Denys.

When describing their treatment of the printed sources, and consequently their concept of creative compilation, the authors of the *Dictionnaire universel de commerce* use the following terms and notions: they speak of "tiré de" (taken from), "pris" (taken), "pris quelques morceaux de" (taken some pieces from), and "emprunté" (borrowed); but they also underscore their critical attitude in using the term "méfiance" (distrust) and "juger" (judge) with regard to any manuscript and printed source, indicating a fundamentally critical position of judgment and examination. In the preface published by the editors of the 1759 edition of the *Dictionnaire universel de commerce*, other sources are mentioned that had been integrated into this new and final edition of the dictionary: articles and information drawn from the *Encyclopédie* by Diderot and d'Alembert; the *Journal Économique*; the *Gazette de Commerce*, published in Copenhagen;[11]

"Mémoires très instructifs sur le Commerce de l'Allemagne, du Dannemarc, de la Suède & de la Russie" (Very instructive memoirs on the commerce of Germany, Denmark, Sweden, and Russia), which resulted in "different particuliar researches" by which the "mistakes" of the previous editions would be repaired.[12] As the commercial archives of Nantes explored in the 1920s by Léon Vignols prove, these printed materials were only some of the sources used in the dictionary; the others being first-hand materials that were used in every edition of the dictionary. The Archives de la Chambre de Commerce de Nantes, for example, contain several letters written by the Royal French contrôleur des finances, Philibert Orry, that are addressed to the Chamber of Commerce of Nantes, which was one of France's leading commercial harbours at the time. Orry asks them to carefully read the articles in the *Dictionnaire universel de commerce* that deal with their own activities and to send their observations, criticisms, and any supplementary information for the new edition of the *Dictionnaire* to be published in 1741 in Paris:

> Comme le bien du commerce exige, Messieurs, qu'il soit fait un supplément au Dictionnaire du Commerce, il paraît nécessaire de rassembler toutes les observations qui peuvent fournir ce supplément. Vous êtes plus en état que personne de faire ces observations sur les articles qui sont défectueux dans ce dictionnaire et sur ceux qui, y manquant, doivent composer le supplément.[13]

The Savary des Bruslons' *Dictionnaire universel de commerce* enjoyed considerable editorial and commercial successes in France and among the French reading public outside France. The four different editions published in Paris in 1723, 1741, 1748, and 1750 in two volumes and then in three volumes, with a supplement added in 1741, and three other editions published in Amsterdam in 1726, in Geneva in 1742 and 1750, and in Copenhagen between 1759 and 1765, in four volumes and then, for the last edition, in five volumes, made of the *Dictionnaire* an indispensable reference work for the economic and commercial world of the eighteenth century. While the French editions of the *Dictionnaire* reflected the economic policies of France, the corresponding Swiss, Dutch, and Danish editions (1742–65) clearly defended a physiocratic viewpoint, incorporating articles from the *Encyclopédie* written by Quesnay, Turgot, and Véron de Forbonnais.[14] The fact that the Savary des Bruslons' *Dictionnaire* was very well received and commonly appropriated by Diderot and d'Alembert in the *Encyclopédie* and by Guillaume-Thomas Raynal in the *Histoire des deux Indes* demonstrates the *Dictionnaire*'s status as a reference work at least until the 1780s. Yet the borrowing also moved in the opposite direction, for Diderot and d'Alembert's *Encyclopédie* would become a source for the last Copenhagen edition of the *Dictionnaire universel de commerce* (1759).

In June 1769 the Abbé Morellet announced a new dictionary of commerce partially based on and intended to replace the Savary des Bruslons' *Dictionnaire*. However, he never succeeded in completing the project or publishing it.[15] In presenting his own project of a new commercial encyclopedia – finally realized thirty years later by Jacques Peuchet with the support of Lucien Bonaparte, minister of the interior[16] – he severely critized the *Dictionnaire*, especially its numerous mistakes and inaccuracies and the fact that it focused too heavily on French trade and commerce, contractory to its apparently "universal" objectives. Jacques Peuchet, author of the *Dictionnaire universel de la géographie commerçante*, which was published in five in-folio volumes in 1799–1800 and can be considered the successor to the *Dictionnaire universel de commerce* in the French-speaking world at that time, viewed his predecessor's work as somewhat out of date. But he still paid homage to this pioneering collection, emphasizing that it was the first dictionary in Europe that "presented a joining of diverse branches of commerce and an exposition of the means employed, whether in practice or in the financial sector by the merchants."[17]

Transfers and Translations

Like the *Parfait négociant* of their father, the *Dictionnaire universel de commerce* by the brothers Savary des Bruslons was translated into several languages and gained European-wide diffusion and reception, in addition to the spread of the French editions partly published – and distributed – outside of France, in Amsterdam, Geneva, and Copenhagen. As Jean-Claude Perrot has pointed out, 71 per cent of the 327 suscribers of the 1759–65 five-volume Copenhagen edition of the *Dictionnaire* came from northern Europe (France, Germany, Scandinavia, Russia), whereas the subscribers from France and Switzerland represented 9 per cent and 7 per cent respectively.[18] The predecessor of the *Dictionnaire universel de commerce*, the *Parfait Négociant*, had been translated into German, English, Dutch, and Italian, but also adapted and imitated in different manners and in various versions. Peuchet talks about this in his *Dictionnaire univer-sel de la géographie commerçante*:

> *Le Parfait négociant* was not the only one to be translated into foreign lan-guages; the *Dictionnaire du commerce* also had this honour; it even had imita-tors, especially in England. Actually, we have seen several works modelled on those by *Savary*, especially in England. Among them we find the dic-tionaries of *Postlethwayt, Rolt*, and *Mortimer*. The first was published in two volumes *in-folio*, in 1751; the second in one volume *in-folio*, in 1761; and the one by *Mortimer* in 1765, also in two volumes *in-folio*.
>
> (*Le Parfait négociant* n'a pas été seul traduit en langues étrangères; le *Diction-naire du commerce* a eu cet honneur; il a eu même des imitateurs, surtout en Angleterre. En effet, on vit paraître dans ce pays plusieurs ouvrages sur le modèle de celui de *Savary*. De ce nombre sont les Dictionnaires de *Postleth-wayt*, de *Rolt*, de *Mortimer*. Le premier fut imprimé en deux volumes *in-folio*, en 1751; le second en un volume *in-folio*, en 1761; et celui de *Mortimer* en 1765, également en deux volumes *in-folio*).[19]

We can suppose that the translations of the *Dictionnaire* reached a read-ing public that did not read French fluently, but they also fulfilled other functions. The Savary des Bruslons' *Dictionnaire* was, in fact, translated into six languages in the eighteenth century, counting as one of the most intensively translated encyclopedic dictionaries of that century throughout Europe. In Germany, a first translation was released between 1741 and 1743 in Leipzig under the conspicuously baroque title *Allge-meine Schatz-Kammer der Kauffmannschaft, oder vollständiges Lexikon aller Handlungen und Gewerbe, sowohl in Deutschland als auswaertigen König-reichen und Ländern*. The translation was done and coordinated by Carl Günther Ludovici, professor at the University of Halle and co-editor of Zedler's *Universal-Lexicon*. This translation was re-edited in a trans-formed and enlarged version between 1752 and 1756 under the title *Eröffnete Academie der Kaufleute: oder vollständiges Kaufmanns-Lexicon* and contained a supplement that announced a "Compendium of a com-plete system for merchants" (*Grundriß eines vollständigen Kaufmanns-Systems*). A third German edition edited by Moses Israel finally came out in 1809 in a largely adapted version[20] under the title *Universal-Lexicon der Handlungswissenschaften*.[21] A review appearing in the periodical *Göttin-gische Gelehrte Anzeigen* in 1810 noted that this economic encyclopedia (of which only the first volume was ultimately published),[22] would be of interest to a readership of merchants and traders ("mercantilischen Publicums").[23]

In England a first translation of the Savary des Bruslons' *Dictionnaire* was published between 1749 and 1755 in two volumes in London by Malachy Postlethwayt (1707–1767) under the title *Universal dictionary of trade and commerce: Translated from the French of the celebrated Monsieur Savary ... with large editions and improvements* and was re-edited and enlarged three times in the ensuing fifteen-year period in 1757, 1766, and 1774. The *New dictionary of trade and commerce, compiled from the information of the most eminent merchants, and from the works of the best writers on commercial subjects, in all languages*, published by Richard Rolt in 1761 and prefaced by Samuel Johnson, is partly based on the Savary's *Dictionnaire* but is in fact a compilation extracted and adaptated from different dictionaries and commercial treaties. Thomas Mortimer's *New and complete dictionary of trade and commerce* published in 1766,[24] a compiled adaptation of the *Dictionnaire*, can be considered as the last translation – in a wider sense of the term – of the *Dictionnaire universel du commerce* in England. Peuchet judged it, in his *Dictionnaire de la géographie commerçante* of 1799, as "far superior to the others" and admitted to have integrated, in translation, several articles from Mortimer's dictionary into his encyclopedia of commerce.[25]

An Italian translation came out in Venice in 1770–1 under the title *Dizionario di commercio, di signori Fratelli Savary ... tratti dall' Enciclopedia, e delle memorie dell' accuratissimo Mr. Garcin.*[26] As early as 1747, a Russian translation (in fact an extract) was published in Saint Petersburg. A second, more complete Russian translation by Vasily Alekseevitch Levshin (based on either the French original or the German translation) came out in 1787 during the reign of Empress Catherine II, who promoted and supported several translation and encylopedic projects for Western cultures.[27] A Greek translation was partly realized between 1815 and 1817 by Nicolas Papadhópoulos, who published four of the seven anticipated volumes of his dictionary *Hermès the God of Profit or commercial Encylopedia.*[28] The first two volumes of this first Greek economic encyclopedia (which was also well known by merchants and traders in Bulgaria in the beginning of the nineteenth century)[29] represent an adapted translation of the Savary's *Dictionnaire*, whereas volumes three and four were based on its French successor, the *Dictionnaire universel de la géographie commerçante* by Jacques Peuchet. The Greek translator and editor was apparently slow to discover Peuchet's *Dictionnaire*. Finally, a partial and adapted Portuguese translation with numerous supplementary examples from the Portuguese world of trade[30] by Alberto Jacqueri de Sales (1723–1800), an economist of Swiss origin during the reformist ministery of the Marquess of Pombal (1750–1777), remained unpublished and is conserved at the National Library of Portugal in Lisbon as a manuscript.[31]

To this series of entire or complete translations should be added a list of translated extracts published separately, like the *Historische Nachricht von den Spiegelglasmanufakturen in Frankreich. Aus der Herren Savary Dictionnaire universel de Commerce* [...] *übersetzt* or *Die Art das ungarische Leder zuzurichten, aus der Herren Savary Dictionnaire Universel de Commerce*, published in the 1760s and concerning specific techniques of handicraft described in extensive articles in the Savary des Bruslons' *Dictionnaire.*[32]

In general, the translations of the *Dictionnaire universel de commerce* show two converging tendencies: first, the tendency to adapt the dictionary to the economic, geographic, and political realities of the receiving culture by adding numerous articles and by transforming others; and second, related to this, the tendency to show, by an inherent logic of "emulation" based on national competition between different European societies and their governments, that the translation of the *Dictionnaire* was not only superior to the original, but could also serve as a striking example of the excellence or even (in the case of England) the presumed superiority of the relevant translating culture and economy in comparison with France.

Transcultural Appropriations: From Adaptation to Autonomy

Most of the translations of the *Dictionnaire* went far beyond mere translations. They represented, in fact, intercultural adaptations or forms of productive reception of a translated version of the Savary des Bruslons' encyclopedic dictionary and developed particular and significant transcultural dynamics. National competition and national emulation were, indeed, important factors in the self-representation of the Savary des Bruslons' dictionary itself and consequently also of their translators and adaptors. Jacques Peuchet, for example, emphasizes in the foreword to his *Dictionnaire universel de la géographie commerçante* that even if the English nation, as the dominant commercial nation in Europe, had dealt very early with matters of political economy, the honour of publishing the very first economic encyclopedia undoubtedly went to the French nation.[33] In his introduction, the Italian editor of the Savary des Bruslons' dictionary, Giambattista Pasquali, pointed out that he gave "in substance" ("in sostanza") a translation of the whole dictionary, but that he had also "eliminated" articles that seemed "not useful" to him for "we other Italians" ("noi altri italiani"), because they had to do with French

regulations and commercial laws. But this "Italianization" of the dictionary also involved the addition of numerous articles related specifically to
the political economy of Italy: "My intention is," wrote Pasquali, "to give
to Italy a compiled new Dictionary of Commerce" that would meet the
particular interests of Italian merchants.[34] The introduction written by
Malachy Postlethwayt to the third edition of his English translation of the
Dictionnaire universel de commerce, published in 1766, three years after the
end of the Seven Years' War and the Treaty of Paris, which had "made a
great alteration in the state of the British trade and territories in America
and Africa,"[35] pointed out the direct links between the English translation and adaptation of the Savary des Bruslons' dictionary ("the first of
its kind that was ever published in Great Britain"),[36] the rise of British
trade and commerce, and the sharp political and economic competition
with France, referring explicitly, in its second edition published during
the Seven Years' War (1756–63), to the underlying patriotic aim of his
enterprise:

> The political knowledge of commerce throughout this work, being chiefly
> grounded on the practical knowledge thereof, is a plan which has not been
> attempted, to my knowledge, in the comprehensive manner of this work,
> in any nation whatsoever: and, as the dictionary form has been found, by
> the great success of Mon. Savary's work throughout all Europe, to be most
> acceptable both to men of business and gentlemen, for immediate refer-
> ence, we have judged it best to follow his example in this respect: and,
> as likewise that gentleman's performance was calculated chiefly for the
> commercial prosperity of France, so are these our labours, for the lasting
> prosperity, we humbly hope, of Great-Britain; the author desiring to live
> no longer, than he can be useful to mankind in general, and to his native
> country in particular.[37]

While the general idea of Savary's economic dictionary was ultimately
superceded, the basic lexematic structure of the original was reproduced
and large parts of most of the articles were translated. Nevertheless,
numerous modifications and points of amplicification may be identified
through comparison, for example, with the 1748 and 1759 French editions of the dictionary, the German edition of 1743, and the 1766 English
translation published in London.

Postlethwayt's translation/adaptation of Savary's dictionary was
intended not only to serve the interests of the British empire and of
British patriotism, but also to reinforce its pragmatic dimension, as was

underlined in the preface: "As to the knowledge of merchants, remitters, insurers, and insured, wholesale dealers, tradesmen, factors, warehousemen, manufacturers, and mechanics, there never was so great a compass of useful matter, and that so suitably methodized for immediate reference, made public to the world before."[38] The basic structure of the Savary's *Dictionnaire* was generally adopted in translations like the English one. That structure had eight major elements: (1) the definition of the term treated (with, optionally, its etymology); (2) additional details (provided in numerous articles by statistics, diagrams, tables, and cross-references to other articles in the dictionary); (3) the term's historical background; (4) philosophical discourses; (5) examples of letters, accounts, and the like ("templates" that the reader could use as examples); (6) "laws and regulations" of the different countries; (7) "summaries of legal cases where some of these laws have been applied"; and (8) "instructions on how to do specific things, e.g. various types of calculations etc."[39]

The article on Canada, for example, which comprised 19,600 characters in the 1748 French edition, was increased to 28,700 in the 1758–65 Copenhagen edition, showing the growing importance of New France for French trade before the Seven Years' War. In particular, the enlarged version provided more ethnological and anthropological details about the lives of Native Americans, their customs, languages, demography, and social structure, referring to the growing importance the editors of the *Dictionnaire universel de commerce* attached to the social, cultural, and psychological factors of international trade.[40] In contrast, the German-adapted translation published by Heinsius in Leipzig in 1741 contains only one very short article on Canada totalling no more than eleven lines and four hundred characters, though two other short articles on the subject were added to the supplement (twenty-two and eight hundred signs long respectively) concerning Canada as a territory and the "Canada" – or Saint Lawrence – River. The extent to which the expansion or reduction of an article in the translation directly followed the geo-political and geo-economic interests of the readership is shown by the translated and adapted 1766 English version of the article "Canada," which totalled 56,400 characters and reflected a completely new and reoriented British imperial view of Canada. Appearing just after the Treaty of Paris, it assigned the territories of New France to the Kingdom of Great Britain. The author stated in his "Remarks" at the end of the article that by "the definitive treaty of 1763, having annexed CANADA and all its DEPENDENCIES to the crown of GREAT BRITAIN, and also Florida and

Louisiana [...] the whole face of the commerce of our British American colonies will be changed, and all those fears and apprehensions we so justly had of the power and machination of our FRENCH rivals here be dissipated."[41] But the authors also recognized, in some aspects, a French superiority, not with regard to the number of their colonists or their soldiers in North America – which was far inferior to those of the British – but regarding their anthropological and local knowledge, and their relationship with the Indigenous peoples, which is seen as providing an example that the British should follow:

> Though the French in Canada have never exceeded us in numbers, nor the rest of their countrymen in bravery, nevertheless it is certain that they have gained upon us for many years past. Nor will this seem any matter of wonder, to one who seriously reflects on the constitution and form of their government, and the encouragement they have from the crown of France, and their dexterious way of managing the Indians.[42]

The evolution of the Savary des Bruslons' pioneering economic dictionary reflects both an intracultural and a transcultural dynamic. The dictionary initially presented the written and printed transcription of oral commercial knowledge.[43] It was then rapidly developed in various successive, enlarged, and modified French editions between 1723 and 1765 in tandem with the expansion of commerce, international trade, and colonialism, becoming one of the foremost reference works in the field of commerce and international trade until the 1780s. Its status as a salient reference work was also recognized outside of France, particularly in the German-speaking countries and in south-east Europe until the beginning of the nineteenth century. The transfer and translation of the dictionary to other cultural spheres was related to the parallel process of commercial development, a reciprocal process that also opened up new dimensions, representing both a transfer of knowledge and the transfer of a specific pattern that each time produced a completely new commercial dictionary reflecting multiple forms of adaptation. In this case as in others, the translation and transfer process often operated through the dynamics of distancing, domesticating, and autonomization, whereby translation established a new original, source text, one that integrated itself into a new, culturally different national tradition. The translations and creative appropriations of the *Dictionnaire universel de commerce* thus illustrate, in a paradigmatic way, the important cultural dynamics produced by translations and the transcultural transfers they generated in the long eighteenth century.

NOTES

1 Abbé Morellet, 1769, *Prospectus d'un Nouveau Dictionnaire* (Paris: Frères Estienne), 9: "Nous avons donc l'avantage d'avoir devancé les autres nations dans le soin de déposer dans un grand Ouvrage cette partie des connoissances humaines, qui, depuis le milieu du siècle, est devenue un objet plus fréquent des spéculations des Philosophes, et la matière d'un grand nombre d'écrits." Unless otherwise indicated, translations into English are the author's.

2 Guillaume-Thomas Raynal, 1820–1, *Histoire philosophique et politique des établissemens et du commerce des Européens dans les deux Indes. Nouvelle édition, précédée d'une notice biographique et de considérations sur les écrits de Raynal, par M. A. Jay, et terminée par un volume supplémentaire contenant la situation actuelle des colonies, par M. Peuchet* (Paris: A. Costes), 12 vols. + atlas. On Peuchet, see Ethel Goffier, 2009, *Un encyclopédiste réformateur: Jacques Peuchet (1758–1830)* (Quebec City: Presses de l'Université de Laval).

3 Peuchet, "Discours préliminaire," in *Dictionnaire de la géographie commerçante,* vol. 1 (Paris: Blanchon), xviii.

4 Peuchet, "Discours préliminaire," xix, offers the following details: "Retiré du commerce dès 1658, il fut appelé à la commission chargée de rédiger le *code marchand* ou ordonnance de 1673. Les travaux qu'il fut obligé de faire, comme membre de cette commission, le portèrent à travailler au *Parfait négociant,* qu'il fit imprimer, pour la première fois, en 1675; il l'augmenta considérablement dans les éditions suivantes. *Le Parfait Négociant* fut traduit en Allemand et imprimé à Genève en 1696, avec le Français à côté; il le fut également en Anglais, en Italien et en Hollandais, peu de tems après qu'il parut en France; ce qui fait connaître qu'il n'y en avait point de semblable en aucune de ces langues. … , Outre son *Parfait négociant,* il donna encore au Public, deux ans avant sa mort, ses *Parères, ou Avis et conseils sur les plus importantes matières du commerce;* c'est un recueil de décisions consulaires et de lois et usages du commerce." (Retired from his commercial activities since 1658, he was nominated in the commission in charge with the composition of the *Code marchand* [code or order for merchants]. The works he was forced to accomplish, as member of this commission, lead him to work on his *Parfait Négociant,* which was printed, for the first time, in 1685; he extended it considerably in the following editions. The *Parfait Négociant* was translated into German and printed in Geneva in 1696, together with

the French version; it was also translated into English, Italian, and Dutch,
shortly after its publication in France, which shows that there was nothing
similar in any of these languages ... Beside his *Parfait négociant*, he gave
also to the public, two years before his death, his book *Parères*, or *Avis et
conseils sur les plus importamtes matières de commerce* [Customary business rules,
or advice and guidance on the most important materials of commerce],
which constitues a collection of consular decisions and of laws and customs
referring to trade.) See also Henri Hauser, 1925, "'*Le Parfait négociant*'
de Jacques Savary. *Revue d'Histoire Économique et Sociale* 13, no. 1: 1–28.
The different editions (on the whole thirty-three in French and different
translations between 1675 and 1800) of this very influential and widespread
manual are listed in Jochen Hoock and Pierre Jeannin, eds., 1991, *Ars
mercantoria. Handbücher und Traktate für den Gebrauch des Kaufmanns. Manuels
et traités à l'usage des marchands, 1470–1820. Eine analytische Bibliographie. Mit
einer Einleitung in deutscher und französischer Sprache* (Paderborn: Schöningh),
2:488–97.

5 Peuchet, "Discours prélimiaire," xviii: "Il [Jacques Savary des Bruslons]
 trouva dans le Gouvernement, des encouragements et des secours pour
 terminer son entreprise. Il les dut à M. d'*Argenson*, alors lieutenant de
 police de Paris [en 1702] qui n'épargna rien pour lui témoigner l'intérêt
 qu'il prenait au succès d'un ouvrage qui devait être utile à la France.
 C'était le caractère des ministres sous Louis XIV de voir ainsi les choses en
 hommes d'État, et la postériorité a su apprécier ce véritable patriotisme."
 (He [Savary des Bruslons] found in the government encouragement
 and assistance in order to accomplish his project. He owed this to Mr.
 d'*Argenson*, police chief of Paris [in 1702], who spared nothing in order to
 underline the interest he took in the success of a publication that should
 be useful for France. This way of considering these affairs as statesmen
 characterized the ministers under Louis XIV, and posterity knew how to
 appreciate this true patriotism.)

6 "Préface historique," in Jacques Savary des Bruslons and Philémon-
 Louis Savary, eds., 1759–65, *Dictionnaire universel de commerce: contenant
 tout ce qui concerne le commerce qui se fait dans les quatre parties du
 monde, par terre, par mer, de proche en proche, et par des voyages de long
 cours, tant en général qu'en détail. L'Explication de tous les termes qui ont
 trait au Négoce, les Monnayes de Comptes qui servent à y tenir les livres et
 écritures des marchands* ... Nouvelle édition, exactement revue, corrigée
 (Copenhague, chez les Frères Cl. and Ant. Philibert, 1759) (hereafter
 cited as *Dictionnaire universel de commerce*), 1:xv: "[L]'avantage de satisfaire
 le Public, & en même temps d'assurer à la cour la réussite d'un des plus

importants desseins qu'on eût jusques-là entrepris pour l'utilité des
Manufactures de France, & que Monsieur Colbert lui-même avoit crû trop
difficile pour oser le tenter." (The advantage to satisfy the public, and at the
same time to ensure the court of the success of one of the most important
projects undertaken until then for the usefulness of the manufactures of
France, and which Mr. Colbert himself had considered as too difficult and
riskful to be tried.)

7 "Préface historique," xv: "Excité ensuite par l'utilité qu'il en retiroit
  presque'à chaque moment, il se fit une espèce de Bibliothèque de tous les
  Livres de Commerce imprimés en France & dans les Païs étrangers qu'il put
  ramasser, & qui lui fournirent de quoi augmenter considérablement son
  MANUEL MERCANTILE, comme il avoit coutume de le nommer."

8 Léon Vignols, 1929, *Le Dictionnaire universel du commerce de Savary des
  Bruslons. L'opinion des négociants nantais en 1738, etc.* (Rennes: Oberthur)
  (Extrait des *Annales de Bretagne*, vol. 38, no. 4), 3.

9 The precise title of the book is *Historia general de los hechos de los castellanos en
  las Islas y Tierra Firme del mar Océano que llaman Indias Occidentales* (1601–15,
  4 vols.).

10 Subtitle: *Qu'on appelle aujourd'hui le Nouveau Monde [Texte imprimé], par
   Antoine de Herrera, … translatée d'espagnol en françois. A laquelle sont adjoustées
   quelques autres descriptions des mesmes pays, avec la Navigation du vaillant
   capitaine de mer Jacques Le Maire et de plusieurs autres* (Amsterdam: E. Colin,
   1622).

11 Sources cited by Jacques Savary des Bruslons and Philémon-Louis Savary,
   eds., 1759–65, *Dictionnaire universel de commerce … Nouvelle édition, exactement
   revue, corrigée* (Copenhague: chez les Frères Cl. and Ant. Philibert), vol. 1
   [1759], "Avis des Libraires," n.p. (i): "Le célèbre *Dictionnaire Encyclopédique.
   & le Journal Œconomique*, renferment des richesses dont nous nous sommes
   fait un devoir de profiter" (The famous *Dictionnaire Encyclopédique & le
   Journal Œconomique*, which contains a wealth that we make it our duty to
   take advantage of). On the relations between the *Encyclopédie* and Savary des
   Bruslons' *Dictionnaire*, see Ryuji Kojima, 2014, "Le *Dictionnaire universel de
   commerce* des frères Savary," *Les sources de l'*Encyclopédie, Édition Numérique
   Collaborative et CRitique de l'*Encyclopédie*, http://enccre.academie.sciences.fr.

12 *Dictionnaire universel de commerce*, vol. 1 [1759], "Avis des Libraires," (i): "À
   ces secours, nous avons joint différentes recherches particulières, qui nous
   ont procuré des Mémoires très instructifs sur le Commerce de l'Allemagne,
   du Dannemarc, de la Suède & de la Russie, articles fautifs & foiblement
   traités dans les précédentes Éditions; mais sur lesquels nôtre établissement
   dans cette Capitale nous a mis en état de répandre un grand jour." (To this

purpose we have undertaken particuliar investigations drawn from very instructive memoirs on the commerce of Germany, Denmark, Sweden, and Russia, containing faulty and weak articles in the previous editions that our establishment in this capital has allowed us to spread out in broad daylight.) See also "Préface historique," vi–x.

13 See the letter of the contrôleur général des finances, Orry, to the Chambre de Commerce de Nantes, from 20 January 1738, quoted by Vignols, *Dictionnaire universel de commerce*, 3–4. I translate the quotation as: "Sirs, profitable commercial advantage calls for the creation of a supplement to the Dictionary of Commerce, and in order to do so it would be necessary to collect all of the observations that might constitute this supplement. You, more than any other entity, are disposed to furnish these observations about the articles that are defective in this dictionary as well as those that are absent and should make up the supplement."

14 Melanie Mamroth-Brokman, 1908, *Das* Dictionnaire universel de Commerce *der Gebrüder Savary als Spiegelbild des Übergangs der ökonomischen Theorien vom Merkantilismus zum physiokratischen System* (Wittenberg: Herrosé & Ziemsen), 24, 32, 41–3, 56, 61.

15 Abbé André Morellet, 1769, *Prospectus d'un nouveau "Dictionnaire de Commerce." En cinq volumes in-folio. Proposés par souscription* (Paris: Frères Étienne), 15. See on this project Hans-Jürgen Lüsebrink, 2021, "(Re)Inventing a New Economic Encyclopedia: The Stranding of the Abbé Morellet's Ambitious *Nouveau Dictionnaire de Commerce* (1769)," in *Stranded Encyclopedias, 1700–2000*, ed. Linn Holmberg and Maria Simonsen, 73–97. New York: Palgrave Macmillan.

16 [1786–1805] 1994, *Lettres d'André Morellet*, edited and annotated by Dorothy Medlin and Jean-Claude David with the collaboration of Paul Leclerc (Oxford: Voltaire Foundation), 2:265, note 4 (= lettre no. 364 to Jacques Peuchet).

17 Peuchet, "Introduction," xviii: "le *Dictionnaire de commerce de Savary*, présentât la réunion des diverses branches de commerce et l'exposition des moyens employés, soit dans la pratique, soit dans la banque par les commerçants."

18 Jean-Claude Perrot, 1981, "Les dictionnaires de commerce au XVIIIe siècle," *Revue d'Histoire Moderne et Contemporaine* 38: 41. The numbers of subscribers, which may have totaled approximately eight hundred to one thousand, show the success of this last edition of the *Dictionnaire universel de commerce*. The list of subscribers is published under the title "Liste générale de Messieurs les souscripteurs. Sa Majesté le Roi de Dannemark et de Norvège, etc. etc. etc. S.A.R. Monseigneur le Prince Royal. 3 avril 1765," *Dictionnaire universel de commerce, d'Histoire Naturelle, & des Arts et Métiers* … Ouvrage posthume du Sieur Jacques Savary des Bruslons … Continué sur les Mémoires de l'Auteur, et donné au public par Monsieur

Philémon-Louis Savary … Nouvelle édition, exactement revûe, corrigée, et considérablement augmentée. Copenhagen: Chez Claude Philibert, 1765, 5: n.p. (four pages at the end of the volume).

19 Peuchet, "Discours," xix. Peuchet is referring here to the dictionaries of Richard Rolt (1756 [2nd ed. 1761], *A New Dictionary of Trade and Commerce, compiled from the information of the most eminent merchats,* London: n.p.) and of Thomas Mortimer (1766, *A New and Complete Dictionary of Trade and Commerce,* 2 vols., London: n.p.), and to the English translation of the Savary des Bruslons' *Dictionnaire* made by Malachy Postlethwayt and published in 1751 in London. Mortimer's *Dictionary* was in fact published in 1766 and not in 1765, as Peuchet stated.

20 This is indicated by the subtitle: "Bearbeitet nach Savary" (adapted from Savary) and also underlined in some reviews of this dictionary, for example in *Göttingische Gelehrte Anzeigen,* 97, 18 June 1810, 966: "indem es das bekannte Werk von Savary […] nicht sowohl übersetzt, als vielmehr zum Leitfaden gewählt hat … " (having not translated the well-known work of Savary, but much more used it as a guideline).

21 Moses Israel, Friedrich Heusinger, and Casar Ihling, eds., 1809, *Universal-Lexicon der Handlungswissenschaften, bearbeitet nach Savary* (Leipzig: Heinrch Gräff), 1 vol., in-4°, 603 pages.

22 The other volumes had probably not been published because of the economic crisis related to the end of the Napoleonic era, which made it extremely difficult to edit and publish a very ambitious encyclopedia whose envisioned size was some twelve volumes and seventy-five hundred pages.

23 Thomas Mortimer, 1766, *A New and Complete Dictionary of Trade and Commerce containing a distinct explanation of the general principles of commerce, an accurate definition of its terms … a particular description of the different productions of art and nature which are the basis and support of commerce, particularly distinguishing the growth, products and manufactures of Great Britain and its colonies* (London: the author, printed by S. Crowder, J. Coote, J. Fletcher), 2 vols.

24 "Universal-Lexicon der Handlungswissenschaften; bearbeitet nach Savary." In *Göttingische Gelehrte Anzeigen,* 97, 18 June 1810: 965–7: "haben die Verfasser den ungeteilten Dank des mercantilischen Publicums" (the authors have the undivided gratitude of the public interested in economic affairs).

25 Peuchet, "Discours préliminaire," xix: "Ces trois Dictionnaires (Postlethwayt, Rolt, Mortimer) n'ont point un mérite égal. Celui de *Mortimer* est de beaucoup supérieur aux deux autres, et nous avons transporté dans le nôtre divers articles sur la grande Bretagne qui s'y trouvent traités avec méthode et clarté." (These three dictionaries [Postlethwayt, Rolt, Mortimer] do not have the same merit. The one by

Mortimer is far superior to the two others, and we have transferred to our one various articles on Great Britain that are treated there with method and clearness.)

26 1770–1 (Venice: Press Giambatista Pasquali), 2 vols.

27 Jacques Savary des Bruslons, 1747, *Экстракт Савариева лексикона о комерции*, ed. Sergei Savvich Volchkov (St. Petersburg: Akademie der Wissenschaft), in-4°; Savary des Bruslons, 1787–92, *Словарь коммерческий* [...], ed. Vasily Alekseevich Levshin, 4 vols. (Moscow: Тип. Комп. Типогр), in-8°. See also Perrot. "Les dictionnaires de commerce," 42.

28 Translation of the original Greek title. For further details about this translation, see Ivan Roussev, 2005, "Les premiers manuels de commerce bulgares et les influences européennes au XIXe siècle," *Revue des études slaves* 76, no. 4: 475–6.

29 Roussev, "Les premiers manuels de commerce bulgares," 475: "Il semble que l'encyclopédie de Nicolas Papadhópoulos ait été bien connue par des Bulgares, véhiculant les idées des auteurs français Savary et Peuchet; elle était dans toutes les bibliothèques d'école." (It seems that the encyclopedia of Nicolas Papadhópoulos was well known by the Bulgarians, conveying the ideas of the French authors Savary and Peuchet; it could be found in every school library.) See also Triantafyllos E. Sklavénitis, 1986, "Les manuels de commerce parus pendant l'occupation vénitienne et l'occupation turque," in *Économies méditerranéennes. Équilibres et intercommunications, XIIIe–XIXe siècles*, Actes du IIe colloque international d'histoire, Athens, 18–25 Septembre 1983 (Athens: n.p.), 3:174–5.

30 Cláudia Maria das Graças Chaves, n.d., "As aulas de comércio no Império luso-brasileiro: O ensino prático profissionalizante," Accessed 21 April 2020, www.humanas.ufpr.br/portal/cedope/files/2011/12/As-aulas-de-comércio -no-Império-luso-brasileiro-Cláudia-Maria-das-Graças-Chaves.pdf.

31 Alberto Jacqueri de Sales, *Diccionario do commercio* (manuscript), 4 vols., enc.; in-34 cm, accessed 4 April 2021, Biblioteca Nacional de Portugal, Digital, https://purl.pt/13945/4/.

32 1763, "Historische Nachricht von den Spiegelglasmanufakturen in Frankreich. Aus der Herren Savary Dictionnaire universel de Commerce. Th. II,. S. 658 u.f. übersetzt," in *Gemeinnütziges Natur- und Kunstmagazin oder Abhandlungen zur Beförderung der Naturkunde, der Künste, Manufacturen und Fabriken* (Berlin: Arnold Wever), 1(3): 292–339; 1763, "Die Art das ungarische Leder zuzurichten: aus der Herren Savary *Dictionnaire universel de Commerce*. Th. 1. S. 1290 u.f. der neuesten Genever Ausgabe," in *Gemeinnütziges Natur- und Kunstmagazin*, 1(1): 100–4; 1763, "Aufrichtige und vollständige Beschreibung der Art, wie die Zitsen in Indien gemacht

warden (et)c. Aus der Herren Savary *Dictionnaire universel de Commerce.* Th. IV. S. 798 u.f. der neuesten Genever Ausgabe," in *Gemeinnütziges Natur- und Kunstmagazin,* 1(1): 29–47; 1763.

33 Peuchet, "Discours préliminaire," vol. 1, xviii: "Nous avons déjà remarqué que quoique les Anglais aient, de bonne heure, traité les questions d'économie politique relatives au commerce, ni eux, ni aucun des États commerçans de l'Europe n'avaient entrepris un ouvrage … comme le *Dictionnaire de commerce de Savary.*" (We have already noticed that even if the English people had very early treated the questions of political economy related to commerce, neither they nor any of the trading nations in Europe had ever undertaken a work … like the *Dictionnaire de commerce de Savary.*)

34 1770. *Dizionario di commercio dei Signori Fratelli Savary, Che comprende la cognizione delle Merci d'ogni Paese; Accresciuto di vari importantissimi Articoli, tratti dall' Enciclopedia, e dalle Memorie dell'accurattissimo Mr. Garcin.* Edizione prima italiana (Venice: Presso Giambattista Pasquali), 1, "Giambattista Pasquali a chi legge," iii: "Io intesi, ed intendo di dare all'Italia un compiuto Dizionario di Commercio: Sicchè faceva di mestieri l'abbracciare tutto quello, che sì nel *Savari,* che nella *Enciclopedia* ha relazione ad esso Commercio, e lasciare d'inserirvi tutte quelle Leggi, Statuti, e Regolamenti, che sono moltissimi, ed ampiamente distesi, che sono fatti per la Francia, son particolari ad essa sola, e che a nulla servono per i Mercatanti d'altri Domini, e singolarmente per noi altri Italiani." (I have the intention to give to Italy a perfect Dictionary of Commerce that embraces all the activities that are treated in Savary's dictionary and in the *Encyclopédie,* and related to Commerce, but to leave aside all the Laws, Statutes, and Rules, which are very numerous and extensive, but only made for France and particular to this country, and which are of no use for the merchants of other countries, and especially for our Italian fellow countrymen.)

35 *The Universal dictionary of trade and commerce: translated from the French of the celebrated Monsieur Savary … with large editions and improvements, adapting the same to the present state of British affairs in America, since the last treaty of peace made in the year 1763. With great variety of new remarks and illustrations incorporated throughout the whole: together with everything essential that is contained in Savary's Dictionary; also, all the material laws of trade and navigation relating to these kingdoms, and the customs and usages to which all traders are subject,* 3rd ed. (London: H. Woodfall, 1766), "Introduction," 1:iii.

36 *Universal dictionary,* iii.

37 *Universal dictionary,* 2nd ed. (London: John Knapton, 1757), "Of the usefulness of this work; with the general contents more particularly delineated", 1: xiii.

38 *Universal dictionary*, 2nd ed., 1: V.: 229.
39 Sven Tarp and Theo J.D. Bothma, 2013, "An Alternative Approach
    to Enlightenment Lexicography: The Universal Dictionary of Trade
    and Commerce," *Lexicographia – International Annual for Lexicography/
    Internationales Jahrbuch für Lexikographie* 29, no. 1: 241.
40 1748, *Dictionnaire universel de commerce*, vol. 2, art. "Canada," 510–18; 1765,
    Dictionnaire universel de commerce, vol. 5, art. "Commerce du Canada," cols.
    1471–8. The article was written during the Seven Years' War and remained
    in the section of the dictionary concerning the commerce of the French
    colonies in America, in spite of the fact that Canada became British in
    1763, as a footnote remarks: "Nous laissons subsister ici cet article quoique
    le Canada en entier soit cédé aux Anglois par le Traité du 3 Nov. 1762, art.
    II & toutes les Isles dans le Golfe du fleuve de S. Laurent, sans restriction"
    (col. 1471, note a) (We leave here this article even if Canada has been given
    up, without restriction, to the English by the Treaty of 3 November 1762,
    art II, as well as all the islands in the Gulf of the Saint Lawrence river). On
    this point see also Lüsebrink, "Émergences encyclopédiques du Canada.
    La *Nouvelle France* dans les Encyclopédies de la première moitié du XVIIIᵉ
    siècle," in *Inventing Canada – Inventer le Canada*, ed. Klaus-Dieter Ertler/
    Martin Löschnigg (Frankfurt am Main: Peter Lang) (Coll. "Canadiana.
    Literaturen/Kulturen – Literatures/Cultures – Littératures/Cultures,"
    vol. 6), 295–307.
41 *Universal dictionary*, 3rd ed. (1766), vol. 1, art. "Canada," n.p. (col. 9).
42 *Universal dictionary*, 3rd ed (1766), vol. 1, art. "Canada," n.p., col. 7.
43 On this point see Monique Aubain, 1984, "Par-dessus les marchés: Gestes
    et paroles de la circulation des biens d'après Savary des Bruslons," *Annales
    E.S.C.* 39, no. 4: 820–30.

Bibliography

Primary Sources

1763. "Aufrichtige und vollständige Beschreibung der Art, wie die Zitsen
    in Indien gemacht warden [etc.]. Aus der Herren Savary *Dictionnaire
    universel de Commerce*. Th. IV. S. 798 u.f. der neuesten Genever Ausgabe." In
    *Gemeinnütziges Natur- und Kunstmagazin oder Abhandlungen zur Beförderung der
    Naturkunde, der Künste, Manufacturen und Fabriken*, 1(1): 29–47. Berlin: Arnold
    Wever.
1763. "Die Art das ungarische Leder zuzurichten: Aus der Herren Savary
    Dictionnaire universel de Commerce. Th. 1. S. 1290 u.f. der neuesten Genever

Ausgabe." In *Gemeinnütziges Natur- und Kunstmagazin oder Abhandlungen zur Beförderung der Naturkunde, der Künste, Manufacturen und Fabriken*, 1(1): 100–4. Berlin: Arnold Wever.

1763. "Historische Nachricht von den Spiegelglasmanufakturen in Frankreich. Aus der Herren Savary Dictionnaire universel de Commerce. Th. II, S. 658 u.f. übersetzt." In *Gemeinnütziges Natur- und Kunstmagazin oder Abhandlungen zur Beförderung der Naturkunde, der Künste, Manufacturen und Fabriken*, 1(3): 292–339. Berlin: Arnold Wever.

1770–1. *Dizionario di commercio, dei signori Fratelli Savary … tratti dall' Enciclopedia, e delle Memorie dell' accuratissimo Mr. Garcin.* 4 vols. Venice: Press Giambatista Pasquali.

Herrera, Antonio de. 1601–15. *Historia general de los hechos de los castellanos en las Islas y Tierra Firme del mar Océano que llaman Indias Occidentales.* 4 vols.

Israel, Moses, Friedrich Heusinger, and Casar Ihling, eds. 1809. *Universal-Lexicon der Handlungs-wissenschaften, bearbeitet nach Savary.* 1 vol., in-4°, 603 pp. Leipzig: Heinrch Gräff.

Morellet, Abbé André. 1769. *Prospectus d'un Nouveau Dictionnaire.* Paris: n.p.

– 1769. *Prospectus d'un nouveau "Dictionnaire de Commerce." En cinq volumes in-folio. Proposés par souscription.* Paris: Frères Étienne.

– 1994 [1786–1805]. *Lettres d'André Morellet.* Edited and annotated by Dorothy Medlin and Jean-Claude David with the collaboration of Paul Leclerc. Oxford: Voltaire Foundation.

Mortimer, Thomas. 1766. *A New and Complete Dictionary of Trade and Commerce containing a distinct explanation of the general principles of commerce, an accurate definition of its terms … a particular description of the different productions of art and nature which are the basis and support of commerce, particularly distinguishing the growth, products and manufactures of Great Britain and its colonies.* London: the author, printed by S. Crowder, J. Coote, J. Fletcher. 2 vols., in-folio.

Peuchet, Jacques. 1798–9. *Dictionnaire de la géographie commerçante.* 4 vols. Paris: Blanchon.

Raynal, Guillaume-Thomas. 1820–1. *Histoire philosophique et politique des établissemens et du commerce des Européens dans les deux Indes. Nouvelle édition, précédée d'une notice biographique et de considérations sur les écrits de Raynal, par M. A. Jay, et terminée par un volume supplémentaire contenant la situation actuelle des colonies, par M. Peuchet.* 12 vols. + atlas. Paris: A. Costes.

Sales, Alberto Jacqueri de. *Diccionario do commercio* (manuscript). 4 vols., enc.; in-34 cm. Accessed 21 April 2020. http://catalogo.bne.es/uhtbin/cgisirsi /x/0/0/5/?searchdata1=433063440.

Savary des Bruslons, Jacques. 1747. *Экстракт Савариева лексикона о комерции.* Edited by Sergei Savvich Volchkov. In-4°. St. Petersburg: Akademie der Wissenschaft.

– 1787–92. *Словарь коммерческий* […]. Edited by Vasily Alekseevich Levshin. 4
 vols. in-8°. Moscow: Тип. Комп. Типогр.
Savary des Bruslons, Jacques, and Philémon-Louis Savary, eds. 1759–65.
 Dictionnaire Universel de Commerce … New edition, revised and corrected. Vol. 1
 [1759]. Copenhagen: chez les Frères Cl. and Ant. Philibert.
– 1759–65. *Dictionnaire universel de commerce: Contenant tout ce qui concerne le
 commerce qui se fait dans les quatre parties du monde, par terre, par mer, de proche en
 proche, et par des voyages de long cours, tant en général qu'en détail. L'Explication
 de tous les termes qui ont trait au Négoce, les Monnayes de Comptes qui servent à y
 tenir les livres et écritures des marchands …* Nouvelle édition, exactement revue,
 corrigée [1759]. Copenhagen: chez les Frères Cl. and Ant. Philibert.
"Universal-Lexicon der Handlungswissenschaften; bearbeitet nach Savary."
 Göttingische Gelehrte Anzeigen 97 (18 June 1810): 965–7.

Secondary Sources

Aubain, Monique. 1984. "Par-dessus les marchés: Gestes et paroles de la
 circulation des biens d'après Savary des Bruslons." *Annales E.S.C.* 39, no. 4:
 820–30.
Goffier, Ethel. 2009. *Un encyclopédiste réformateur: Jacques Peuchet (1758–1830)*.
 Quebec City: Presses de l'Université de Laval.
Graças Chaves, Cláudia Maria das. n.d. "As aulas de comércio no Império luso-
 brasileiro: O ensino prático profissionalizante." Accessed 21 April 2020. www
 .humanas.ufpr.br/portal/cedope/files/2011/12/As-aulas-de-comércio-no
 -Império-luso-brasileiro-Cláudia-Maria-das-Graças-Chaves.pdf.
Hauser, Henri. 1925. "'*Le Parfait négociant*' de Jacques Savary." *Revue d'Histoire
 Économique et Sociale* 13, no. 1: 1–28.
Hoock, Jochen, and Pierre Jeannin, eds. 1991. *Ars mercantoria. Handbücher
 und Traktate für den Gebrauch des Kaufmanns. Manuels et traités à l'usage des
 marchands, 1470–1820. Eine analytische Bibliographie. Mit einer Einleitung in
 deutscher und französischer Sprache.* Vol. 2. Paderborn: Schöningh.
Kojima, Ryuji. 2014. "Le *Dictionnaire universel de commerce* des frères Savary." *Les
 sources de l'*Encyclopédie, Édition Numérique Collaborative et Critique de
 l'*Encyclopédie*, http://enccre.academie.sciences.fr.
Lüsebrink, Hans-Jürgen. 2008. "Émergences encyclopédiques du Canada.
 La *Nouvelle France* dans les Encyclopédies de la première moitié du XVIIIe
 siècle." In *Inventing Canada – Inventer le Canada*, edited by Klaus-Dieter Ertler
 and Martin Löschnigg, 295–307. [Coll. "Canadiana. Literaturen/Kulturen
 – Literatures/Cultures – Littératures/Cultures," vol. 6]. Frankfurt am Main:
 Peter Lang.

Lüsebrink, Hans-Jürgen. 2021. "(Re)Inventing a New Economic Encyclopedia: The Stranding of the Abbé Morellet's Ambitious *Nouveau Dictionnaire de Commerce* (1769)." In *Stranded Encyclopedias, 1700–2000*, edited by Linn Holmberg and Maria Simonsen, 73–97. New York: Palgrave Macmillan.

Mamroth-Brokman, Melanie. 1908. *Das* Dictionnaire universel de Commerce *der Gebrüder Savary als Spiegelbild des Übergangs der ökonomischen Theorien vom Merkantilismus zum physiokratischen System.* Wittenberg: Herrosé & Ziemsen.

Perrot, Jean-Claude. 1981. "Les dictionnaires de commerce au XVIIIe siècle." *Revue d'Histoire Moderne et Contemporaine* 28, no. 1: 36–67.

Roussev, Ivan. 2005. "Les premiers manuels de commerce bulgares et les influences européennes au XIXe siècle." *Revue des études slaves* 76, no. 4: 473–83.

Sklavénitis, Triantafyllos E. 1986. "Les manuels de commerce parus pendant l'occupation vénitienne et l'occupation turque." In *Économies méditerranéennes. Équilibres et intercommunications, XIIIe–XIXe siècles* (Actes du IIe colloque international d'histoire, Athens, 18–25 September 1983), 3:173–6. Athens: n.p.

Tarp, Sven, and Theo J.D. Bothma, eds. 2013. "An Alternative Approach to Enlightenment Lexicography: The Universal Dictionary of Trade and Commerce." *Lexicographia – International Annual for Lexicography/ Internationales Jahrbuch für Lexikographie* 29, no. 1: 222–84.

Vignols, Léon. 1929. *Le Dictionnaire Universel du Commerce de Savary des Bruslons. L'opinion des négociants nantais en 1738, etc.* [Extract from *Annales de Bretagne*, vol. 38, 4]. Rennes: Oberthur.

chapter two

The Cultural and Esthetic Challenges of Translating English and German Articles on the Performing Arts in French Eighteenth-Century Encyclopedias

ALAIN CERNUSCHI

Our understanding of the articles on theatre and the performing arts in enlightenment encyclopedias has much to gain from the kind of comparative and genealogical research that the tools of translation and transfer of knowledge analysis can provide. Such research forms the framework of this study, which examines a corpus of articles related to theatre and performance compiled from three encyclopedias: Chambers's *Cyclopædia* (1728); the *Encyclopédie*, edited and managed by Diderot and d'Alembert (1751–65); and the *Encyclopédie* d'Yverdon, the rewritten Protestant edition published in the 1770s by Fortunato Bartolomeo De Felice.

Generally speaking, these three corpuses are of interest because translation has played a significant role in their creation. As we know, the English-language articles of Chambers's *Cyclopædia* formed the basis for the great French *Encyclopédie*. Indeed, the query about entries related to theatre to be pursued here stems from the relationship between the two encyclopedias that links them through translation, and is formulated in the following research question: In the field of theatre arts, did the translation of Chambers's texts into French allow for a transfer of knowledge about the English theatre scene for French readers? In order to study this question thoroughly, we must consider the original contributions of certain collaborators to the *Encyclopédie* that thoroughly bypassed the articles in the *Cyclopædia*, relying instead on other sources that they often translated and incorporated into their articles. For the field of theatre analysed here, then, the work of the Chevalier de Jaucourt is of particular interest. Well versed in English literature, Jaucourt wrote numerous articles for the *Encyclopédie* whose purpose was to familiarize his French readers with English poetry. Was it his intention to offer French readers the same level of familiarity with English theatre? Pertinent to the issue of knowledge transfer in the realm of theatre with regard to the *Encyclopédie* d'Yverdon, we note that a significant number of the articles in that work that address the arts were sourced in large measure from Sulzer's German dictionary on the beaux arts, *Die Allgemeine Theorie der Schönen Künste* (1771–4). Did the translation of the texts from Sulzer's dictionary occasion in any way a transfer of theatre knowledge from this German source, and thus, the German context overall?

These are the principal questions that will inform the three parts of this contribution. While the results of this research may appear to be minimal, they are revelatory nonetheless, for they enable us to formulate some hypotheses about the role of encyclopedias in the transfer of knowledge about theatre and other areas of study that, like theatre, may follow a somewhat different pattern and itinerary of sources, and movement among them. Furthermore, these results remind us how important it is to ponder the collective set of the references and sources from which the encyclopedists drew during the course of their work – indeed, a reference set that evolves a great deal between the beginning and end of the eighteenth century.

For enlightenment encyclopedias, everything begins in London in 1728 with the publication of Chambers's *Cyclopædia*. The two in-folio volumes comprising the original edition, counting some 2,500 pages in all, offer an erudite synthesis of scientific, philosophical, and literary knowledge in the form of a dictionary. By contrast, factual data on history and geography are not included.

The corpus of *Cyclopædia* articles on the art of performance readily reveals Chambers's horizon of reference. This corpus is made up of 120 articles, which is not much when you consider that the two volumes of the *Cyclopædia* combined include more than 30,000 articles. The 120 articles in our corpus gravitate around two poles: theatrical architecture (for example "Amphitheatre," "Coliseum," or "Stage") and dramatic poetics (such as "Catastrophe," "Episodic," "Manners in Poetry," "Polymythy"). Within these two categories, antiquity constitutes the dominant reference.[1]

A perusal of all the names of authors mentioned by Chambers in this corpus reveals an unbalanced and disproportionate representation among theatrical figures, with a marked preference for theoreticians over dramaturges. Chambers mentions in passing some twenty playwrights, more than half of whom were active in antiquity, yet he refers to some sixty critics and theoreticians, with a slight advantage this time given to the modern poeticians who wrote during the Renaissance and a particular focus on those who were active during the Classical Age. Chambers clearly privileged their doctrines, poetical theories, and the debates surrounding them, which he offers in synthetic summaries. Two poeticians receive the bulk of his attention: Aristotle, not surprisingly, and René Le Bossu, a Frenchman upon whom Chambers lavishes high praise in the numerous references made to him.[2]

In his treatment of theatre, Chambers clearly favoured the presentation of theoretical knowledge over the more historical data about the authors and their works, both of which appear to be secondary in his estimation. Without exception, only the great playwrights of antiquity, Sophocles in particular, benefit from repeated mentions. As far as the moderns are concerned, we detect only the rarest of allusions to the French creators of theatre, Racine and Molière, as well as Perrin, inventor of the opera in France, with a few references to the English dramatists Shakespeare, Johnson, Fletcher, Otway, Lee, and Congreve, peppered throughout the volumes.[3]

This small corpus extracted from the *Cyclopædia* confirms a pattern of representation that I have developed elsewhere: Chambers's articles still reflect the Renaissance and classical periods of the Republic of Letters, which scholars and *philosophes* throughout Europe, heirs of the ancients, collectively and cumulatively promoted as the foundations upon which they endeavoured to create new knowledge; this they in turn promoted as universal knowledge.[4] The rupture with the Renaissance and classical traditions that Chambers espouses through the publication of his encyclopedic dictionary occurs, in fact, at the level of access and communication: by proposing a dictionary in English instead of an *erudite summa* in Latin, Chambers in his *Cyclopædia* clearly opens up humanistic and scientific knowledge to a much larger readership. However, this rupture of access didn't much modify the set of references and sources from which it drew. Consequently, one notes that the French translation of those articles, done during the 1740s in preparation for the *Encyclopédie*, doesn't in reality generate knowledge transfer. Aristotle and Le Bossu constitute shared references for Chambers's and for Diderot and d'Alembert's encyclopedists alike.

Nonetheless, it the field of theatre, we can find about a dozen articles by Chambers in which a more specifically English purview of sources can be perceived. It is interesting to examine how the French encyclopedists dealt with these English-sourced articles, with responses running the gamut from complete and total rejection to all-encompassing incorporation, moving through degrees of adaptation.

The article "Humour" from the *Cyclopædia* constitutes the most remarkable case, as it is the only one of the corpus to thematize what it describes as a particularly English characteristic: "*Humour* is usually look'd on as peculiar to the *English* Drama; at least, our Comic Poets have excell'd therein, and carry'd it beyond those of any other Nation: Ours is perhaps the only Language that has a Name for it" (1:263). And later on, Chambers mentions an eminent English critic: "A very great Judge, the Duke of *Buckingham*, makes *Humour* to be all: Wit, according to him, should never be us'd, but to add an Agreeableness to some proper and just Sentiment, which, without some such Turn, might pass without its Effect" (1:263). This article cannot be found in the *Encyclopédie*, which offers a different, unsigned article entitled "Humour" in its place, one that addresses the art of English humour in more general terms – "les Anglois se servent de ce mot pour désigner une plaisanterie originale, peu commune, & d'un tour singulier" (the English use this word to indicate an original, uncommon joke, characterized by a particular turn of phrase)[5] – and considers Swift to be the foremost proponent of English humour.[6]

Other articles by Chambers containing English theatre references are adopted when they serve to illustrate a general purpose or when they can be used to attribute value to the classical rules of theatre. With no changes or modifications, the French article "Soliloque" reproduces Chambers's entry "Soliloqy" (2:95) (spelled in this way as the headword, yet spelled "soliloquy" in the article itself), including the six lines of verse by the Duke of Buckingham, who condemns the usage of the monologue at the theatre.[7] Another example can be found in the subentry "Scene," in which Chambers discusses the unity of place. This subentry has been included under the article "Scène" (*Littérature*), with the addition of examples taken from Racine's tragedies. The excerpt on the attitude of English playwrights who take a great deal of liberty with the notion of the *unity of place* is preserved: but we observe that Chambers took a critical stance, in support of those English dramaturges who made the effort to respect this unity ("*the more judicious and accurate of our Writers are very moderate in the Use of this Licence,*" 2:29). The final criticism of Shakespeare has also been reproduced ("*The great Shakespeare is exceedingly faulty in this Respect, in almost all his Plays,*" 2:29; which in the Parisian translation becomes: "Shakespeare n'a pas beaucoup respecté la règle de l'unité de *scène*, il ne faut que parcourir ses ouvrages pour s'en convaincre," *Enc.*, 14:753 [Shakespeare hardly respected the unity of *scene*, one merely has to read through his works to be convinced of it]).[8]

If the fortune of the articles translated from Chambers has varied so greatly, it is due to the way in which the *Encyclopédie* was produced, which differed from how the *Cyclopædia* was published. A collective work that appeared progressively over a number of years, the *Encyclopédie* was a polyphonic and evolving product. Each collaborator defined for himself his own way of addressing the subject matter he was going to tackle, not to mention the ongoing changes taking place among the editorial team during the course of the enterprise. Additionally, the project took on proportions that were completely new. The *Cyclopædia* proposed a formal, unified synthesis of knowledge in 2,500 pages, while the *Encyclopédie* presented itself as a disparate *summa* of more than 16,000 pages, in seventeen volumes.

These general characteristics of the *Encyclopédie* are reflected in thematic corpuses of articles. Thus for the theatre and the performing arts, one can pull together almost 350 articles from the French volumes (three times more than in the *Cyclopædia*), with signed articles written by eighteen different authors.[9] Thirteen of these authors are occasional contributors, such as Duclos on the "Déclamation des Anciens" or Grimm about the "Poeme lyrique." Then at the centre of the theatre corpus we find five important collaborators: the abbé Mallet, Cahusac, Marmontel, Diderot, and Jaucourt.

In this field, the strong suit of the abbé Mallet, author of *Principes pour la lecture des poëtes* (1745), was dramatic poetics. He based the bulk of his entries on Chambers's articles; however, in 1755 he died in the middle of the enterprise. Next comes the librettist Cahusac, who supplies numerous articles on all technical and spectacular aspects of theatrical representation, including dance and opera, but he too dies mid-production. We also note a dozen developed contributions by Marmontel, which complete and expand the brief articles written by Mallet, and at times appear to have been written to replace them. Diderot himself intervened in some twenty of those articles, which had also originated in Chambers and were linked to *Histoire ancienne*, such as "Amphithéâtre," "Chorages," and "Course du cirque." Finally, of course, there is the Chevalier de Jaucourt – without whom the *Encyclopédie* would have never been completed. Jaucourt is the author of 132 articles of which all or a part are related to the theatre. It is to him especially that we owe the numerous biographical notices related to European dramaturges that had been inserted into the articles carrying the designation *Géographie moderne*, a topic to which I will return later on in this essay.

Each of these five contributors develops his own style of presenting knowledge, and thus each operates from within a frame of reference that is particular to his expertise and experience. From this perspective, it is interesting to compare Cahusac and Marmontel. Cahusac mentions French references almost exclusively, dropping here and there the rare mention of antiquity or Italy. In fact, in certain articles he lobbies for reforming the French musical scene. In addition, he openly seeks to promote French culture by drafting extensive articles on the celebrations of the court and the big cities of France.[10] His contribution is thus clearly inscribed within the French cultural space, which constitutes, at the same time, the scope of his source material. Marmontel instead pushes himself to expand his pool of references, integrating some English playwrights into his examples. Thus, at the beginning of his long article "Comédie," when he defines the distinctive traits of comedy as a genre in opposition to tragedy, he balances French examples from Molière at that point with some references from Shakespeare or Addison as well. However, the use of these examples is somewhat limited, while the references to antiquity dominate above all. Also, when he attempts to provide a history of the genre in the modern period, his commentary becomes extremely theoretical; through the use of general stereotypes that are highly simplistic in their referencing of national customs and traits, he first tries to define what elements make up the comic in Spanish, Italian, French, or English. Nevertheless, when compared with that of Cahusac, his set of references is always European.

In fact, it is primarily thanks to Jaucourt that we are able to link the theatrical corpus from the *Encyclopédie* to the topic of this volume. For it is to Jaucourt, far more than to Chambers, that we owe the presence of numerous references to English literature in the Paris *Encyclopédie*. This is due in part to Jaucourt's Anglophilia (he had spent time in Cambridge) and in part to his working habits, which were essentially those of a compiler. We know, for example, of his admiration for the Scottish poet James Thomson, for he slips long passages from Thomson's *Seasons* into articles where one might least expect to find them, availing himself of a recently published translation of the poem by Madame Bontemps.[11] But at times he foregoes the translation, directly citing authors in English. Thus, he includes excerpts from Dryden's poem *The Iron Age* (which is actually the translation into English of a passage from Ovid's *Metamorphoses*), quoted in the article "Fer, (*Age de*) *Myth*"; Jaucourt also includes the same excerpt in French. At times, he even skips the French translation of the excerpts of his quotes, as in the article "Imitative, phrase, (*Gram. & Poésie*)," which ends with a few lines of Dryden's verses describing the Cyclopes, extracted, this time, from his translation of Virgil's *Aeneid*.

Let us turn our attention to theatre. For this subject, Jaucourt cites English playwrights far less frequently. But there are a number of divergent, interesting exceptions. The most important of them can be found in the article "Tragédie" where, after having defined the genre with Aristotle and Corneille and retraced the long history of its birth and development in ancient Greece, Jaucourt evokes the "two rival theater nations"[12] with the help of biographical notices presenting first a few French tragedians (Jodelle, Garnier, Hardy, and Corneille), in less than one page, followed by almost three pages of English tragedians: Shakespeare, Johnson, Otway, Congreve, Rowe, and "l'illustre Addison." The first and the last are recognized with a detailed presentation, providing the opportunity for further citations. With regard to Shakespeare, Jaucourt follows Voltaire's perspective, inserting Voltaire's very free translation of Hamlet's famous monologue, as found in his *Lettres philosophiques*. Jaucourt devotes an entire page of relatively original content to Addison's tragedy *Caton*. He begins by borrowing his remarks from Chauffepié's *Nouveau Dictionnaire historique et critique*, but he quickly departs from that content to quote and offer commentary on the English excerpts he provides, including Steele's praise and a rebuttal to Voltaire's critique of the tragedy. In this article, Jaucourt presents *Caton*, as "the most beautiful [play] ever represented on any stage" and its author as "one of the most pristine writers of Great Britain," referring to him also as "the poet of wise men."[13] In this article, we can see the extent to which Jaucourt has branched out, drawing from new sources that decentred the French perspective on theatre in the *Encyclopédie*.

To be sure, this effort certainly belongs to a more overriding intention on Jaucourt's behalf, and it may well be that he agreed to his overarching role of encyclopedist who filled in the gaps in multiple disciplines in the *Encyclopédie* precisely with the intention of introducing a general idea, or vision, of what we might define as a cultural geography of Europe. At times Jaucourt has been derided for the apparent lack of logic in his placement of innumerable biographical notices into geographical articles written to describe cities or regions. Of course, this practice made it difficult to consult the *Encyclopédie* as one might consult a biographical dictionary, since, for example, you need to look for the biography of Philip Massinger in the article "Salisbury (*Géog. mod.*)," or the article on William Wycherley under the entry for "Shropshire (*Géog. mod.*)." But we know that enlightenment encyclopedias, starting with Chambers, sought to differentiate themselves from biographical dictionaries by proposing a new model of knowledge organization that followed the more philosophical logic of liaison among the branches of knowledge, rather than adhering to the historical model of presentation. Thus the liaison among branches of knowledge, and therefore the connections among different facts, now lie at the heart of the project. It is in this sense that we must interpret Jaucourt's "gesture" that inscribes his presentation of great men, and in particular artists, within a geographical space; in this way he suggests that we no longer imagine the Republic of Letters as an abstract and universal zone, but rather that we view it through a variegated cartography where nations and cultural differences play an important role.

Let us again return to the theatre, keeping in mind the example of the English references. Jaucourt wrote a dozen biographical notices about English playwrights, among them Addison, Hughes, Johnson, Lee, Massinger, Otway, Rowe, Shakespeare, and Wycherley, never hesitating, at times, to repeat the developments found in the article "Tragédie" already mentioned. In the article "Westminster," where we find, for example, Ben Johnson, he devotes quite a long notice to a famous actor of the London scene, Thomas Betterton. For French readers, the merging of this data opened windows of access to a different cultural horizon, bringing in all sorts of details, often anecdotal, about London's theatrical life, but also about certain authors and their works with which the French were less familiar. In the article "Stratford" the long biographical notice reserved for Shakespeare mentions *A Midsummer Night's Dream, Henry the Fourth, The Merry Wives of Windsor, Julius Caesar, Macbeth, Hamlet* (where he copies for a second time Voltaire's version of Hamlet's monologue), *Coriolanus, All's Well that Ends Well,* and *Timon of Athens,* at times with lengthy quotations.

But we have to put Jaucourt's work on the English theatre into perspective, because the biographical notices he includes were not written by him. Jaucourt didn't draft them directly from the primary English sources either. When we reconstitute the materials he used, we immediately realize that his work consisted of synthesizing and reorganizing the information he had at the ready from the *Nouveau Dictionnaire historique et critique* by Chauffepié, which had appeared in Amsterdam in four volumes between 1750 and 1756.[14]

It is particularly important to remember that some of the new articles from this Chauffepié edition came from an English translation of Bayle's *Dictionnaire historique et critique,* published between 1734 and 1741, an edition that had been augmented to include numerous English biographies, for example articles on Betterton, Johnson, Otway, and Shakespeare, which Jaucourt compiles directly.[15]

With regard to the transfer of knowledge in the field of theatre, it is clear that the real transfer took place *before* the *Encyclopédie*, during the history of translation and expansion of Bayle's *Dictionnaire historique et critique*, passing through England and then returning to France. Thus, by using Chauffepié as a source, Jaucourt offers a synthetic selection, picking only a few excerpts from the previous work that was far more extensive and complete. To state it differently and somewhat provocatively, we can provisionally claim that in some specific disciplinary cases, such as the theatre under review here, the encyclopedias of the Enlightenment were not, perhaps, the most privileged mediums for the massive transfer of knowledge. At times, then, it was by the very virtue of their position "at the pinnacle of the pyramid," when it came to offering syntheses of the masses of documentation produced and stockpiled in the eighteenth century, that they found themselves to be beyond the wholesale processes of transfer through translation from one compilation to the other. In the case of Jaucourt's writings on theatre in the *Encyclopédie*, we find a far more nuanced process of transfer through translation, one that ultimately allowed certain encyclopedists, like him, to construct profitable lessons from these processes.

We can nevertheless wonder if we might not further qualify this reflection to encompass the changes that would take place in the last decades of the eighteenth century, during the course of which encyclopedic enterprises would multiply. Among the many such encyclopedic enterprises that flourished during the second half of that century, I will discuss only the *Encyclopédie* d'Yverdon, although there would be much to say about the *Encyclopédie méthodique* as well, as other contributions to this volume can amply attest. Before considering the *Encyclopédie* d'Yverdon, we must first underscore the fact that De Felice, an Italian refugee in francophone Switzerland, managed and directed this new edition of the Paris encyclopedia with the idea of creating a European project. Indeed, he frequently critiqued the Franco-centrism of Diderot and d'Alembert's *Encyclopédie*. His correspondence confirms his concern with balancing the content of his edition with a European readership in mind. For example, he severely reprimands his Swiss collaborator, Gottlieb Emanuel von Haller, son of the great Albrecht von Haller, whose entries bespeak an excess of "Helvetism": "We should not measure the interest of an article by the interest that we personally attach to it [...]. We are creating a work that should be of commensurate interest to all nations. The Parisians have made a work of which at least half is of interest only to France; I say down with all of these national *misères*; indeed, I do not wish to be reproached for having substituted French articles with

Swiss articles."[16] We are therefore not surprised that De Felice's edition eliminates, for example, all of Cahusac's articles on French royal celebrations and French cities.[17]

One of the innovative aspects of the Yverdon edition is the introduction of biographical articles. Generally speaking, they were compiled from the most recently published dictionaries, including the *Nouveau Dictionnaire historique portatif*, which went through a number of editions between 1760 and 1770. All of these biographical articles are classified under the designation of *Histoire Littéraire*. One finds entries on Addison, Hughes, Johnson, or Shakespeare appearing in alphabetical order in the Yverdon encyclopedia as separate, stand-alone entries, rather than encountering them within the geographical articles of the *Encyclopédie*. Thus, the *Encyclopédie* d'Yverdon contains more entries about English dramaturges, including William Congreve, John Denham, John Dryden, John Fletcher, Richard Savage, and John Steele, than Jaucourt had covered. In any case, all of the articles dedicated to writers are constructed according to the same conventions adopted by the biographical dictionaries of the period, whose texts the *Encyclopédie* d'Yverdon merely reproduces.

We note here a surprising exception (which, of course, confirms the rule), bound to the Germanic domain, in the article "Gottsched, *Jean Christophle*, (N), *Hist. Litt.*," which carries the initials designating as author the naturalist pastor Elie Bertrand, a correspondent of Voltaire and one of De Felice's closest collaborators. The article is well developed and takes a clear position regarding the classical ideas of the German poet, to which Bertrand fully subscribes.

Let us consider how he introduces Gottsched's education and training: "[Gottsched] began learning French at an early age so as to form his taste on the great models of the Age of Louis XIV. Soon he was teaching eloquence and poetry in this city [Königsberg], laying early on the foundations for the revolution in literary taste to which he would so thoroughly contribute with his precepts, works, and example."[18]

However, Bertrand adopted a more neutral tone on the topic of Gottsched's views of the theatre:

Il jugeoit que le théâtre allemand, encore informe, devoit être épuré et perfectionné: il s'y appliqua, soit en traduisant avec liberté des pièces françoises et étrangères, soit en composant lui-même des pièces régulières. Il fit aussi une *Poétique*, à la tête de laquelle il plaça une *traduction en vers* de la *Poétique d'Horace*: il finit chaque chapitre par les *préceptes* de Boileau. Son *Caton d'Utique* fut reçu avec applaudissement.[19]

Regarding the polemical reactions that Gottsched's ideas provoked, the
Yverdon encyclopedist Bertrand included some interesting thoughts
about the cultural specificity of the Germanophone region in his article:

> Il [Gottsched] eut cependant des démêlés littéraires à soutenir avec plu-
> sieurs écrivains Allemands de diverses contrées, qui vouloient chacun soute-
> nir leur idiome. Les littérateurs Zuricois même voulurent entrer dans la lice.
> La langue françoise n'a eu qu'un centre, formé de la réunion d'autorité des
> écrivains de la capitale, des courtisans de Versailles et des académiciens:
> de-là doivent partir des oracles décisifs. Il n'en est pas ainsi de l'Allemagne:
> autant d'Etats et de capitales indépendantes, autant de temples du goût, où
> l'on prétend rendre des oracles sûrs.[20]

But the most original part of this article comes at the end when Bertrand offers a personal account, thus adding first-hand information to
his article on Gottsched:

> J'ai été long-tems en correspondance de lettres avec M. *Gottsched*, et il
> s'efforça de me prouver que les différentes langues n'ont point un génie
> propre, ou un caractère essentiel distinctif; mais que la différence des
> langues vient de celle du génie des écrivains qui les employent; de la dif-
> férence des idées, du goût, du caractère, des préjugés ou des connoissances
> des auteurs; que la méchanique des langues est bien différente, mais qu'elle
> n'influe que peu sur le caractère et le génie de la langue même; et qu'avec
> des instrumens d'une forme un peu différente on peut parvenir à faire des
> ouvrages également parfaits. Il s'étoit occupé pendant un tems à adoucir
> la prononciation de plusieurs mots allemands, et à imaginer les moyens de
> rendre cette prononciation uniforme par-tout: c'est ce qu'il m'écrivoit peu
> d'années avant sa mort, arrivée en 1767.[21]

Compared with the three sparse lines that Jaucourt wrote about Gottsched and his spouse in the Paris *Encyclopédie* (article "Konigsberg,"
9:134b), the three pages written by Bertrand are a testimony to the interest that the Yverdon edition takes in the Germanophone region. But it
is hardly in the biographical entries that this interest is best seen, for
De Felice banned the writing of articles on living scholars and literary
figures in the *Encyclopédie* d'Yverdon, as his letter to G.E. von Haller from
19 March 1771 explains: "We need to settle for talking about those who
have already died, for any discussion of those who are still alive might
expose us too greatly."[22]

In order to expand the horizon of reference for his encyclopedia, De Felice preferred compiling directly and borrowing heavily from recent non-French sources that he commissioned for translation. In the case of the discipline that interests us here, the most widely exploited source is Sulzer's *Allgemeine Theorie der Schönen Künste,* a dictionary of two volumes published in 1771 and 1774 respectively. Apparently, it was De Felice's correspondent and collaborator from Berlin, Jean Henri Samuel Formey, who provided him with the French translation of a certain number of Sulzer's articles.

It is interesting to draw attention here to a methodological difficulty. The *Encyclopédie* d'Yverdon never mentions the sources from which its articles have been compiled. It is therefore necessary to patiently work one's way through the volumes in order to find the borrowings. In the course of previous research conducted in this manner, I have been able to reconstruct a list of forty-four articles that were borrowed from Sulzer's German-language dictionary,[23] among which we find "Comédie," "Spectacles," and "Tragédie."[24] The research conducted for this chapter yielded five more articles that have some links to the theatre.[25]

Thanks to Sulzer, the *Encyclopédie* d'Yverdon is the most up-to-date work on the German theatrical scene, since its article "Scène, (R), *Littérat.*", in the sixth volume of the *Supplément* (published in spring 1776), refers to the very recent play by the young Goethe, *Götz von Berlichingen,* which had appeared in 1773. In this historical drama, the twenty-four-year-old Goethe broke with the unities of place, time, and action with militant purpose in the name of the fledgling Sturm und Drang esthetic, which sought creative liberation against classical conventions.

However, if we examine the article in question a little more closely, we might have doubts about whether or not the translated paragraph of Sulzer, where this reference is found, constitutes a real transfer of knowledge. First, Sulzer is esthetically in disagreement with the esthetic orientation in question, even though Goethe's play is presented as "a remarkable piece."[26] Certainly, Sulzer lays bare the intention that motivates Goethe's breaking with classical convention; but, at the same time, he reduces the work to those known as "pièces à tiroirs," that is, plays consisting of embedded, episodic elements, with no central plot or denouement in this instance; we also note that the term is written in French in the German article. Sulzer pointed out that the model of embedded narratives in plays should not be followed. Finally, in the *Encyclopédie* d'Yverdon the reference is faulty and incomplete; it is faulty because the title has been oddly Frenchified to *Gôze de Berlichingen;* it is incomplete because in the German text, Sulzer doesn't provide the author's name, which would have been obvious to the German public in 1774. There is no way, then, for the French reader to connect it with Goethe's text.

The same kind of analysis can be made for all of the non-French references, which through Sulzer's dictionary have been imported into the *Encyclopédie* d'Yverdon. In the article "Terreur, (R), *Beaux-Arts*" (translated from the article "Schreken, Schreklich"), which focused on dramatic poetry, Sulzer developed a theoretical, indeed prescriptive aim, whose mentions of Eschyle and Shakespeare are nothing more than allusive reference points that engage no set of real references whatsoever. The final cross-references to "Fuessli's designs" ("dessins de Fuessli") and to the description of Judas Iscariot's death by Klopstock are more interesting. However, in the absence of a quote or explanation, they are merely simple allusions with little to say. The article "Vraisemblance, (R), *Beaux-Arts*" (translated from the article "Wahrscheinlichkeit") contains another passage, a bit more developed, that is dedicated to Klopstock and that may entice readers to seek out the complete work. But the *Encyclopédie* d'Yverdon suppresses Sulzer's quote, especially the note that invites the reader to look at the German poet's work, *Der Messias.*

On the whole, it is true that in the *Encyclopédie* d'Yverdon, the transfer of the translated Sulzer articles is direct (they do not undergo the filtering and synthesizing performed by Jaucourt, for example, in the *Encyclopédie*) and includes texts in French that were conceived of in a non-francophone cultural space; this creates a defamiliarizing effect on the French reader. Nonetheless, the effect of knowledge transfer in this case doesn't appear to have been truly triggered in the absence of a textual apparatus of commentary and notes. Such an apparatus would make all of the foreign references decodable and convincing for the French reader. In this case, we have doubtless encountered one of the limitations of the encyclopedic enterprise that De Felice faced as managing editor in charge of all aspects of production. The accelerated mode of production, linked to the economic obligations incurred by De Felice's publishing house, meant that the viability of the enterprise relied on the simple act of compiling. This made his *Encyclopédie* d'Yverdon directly dependent on his sources, thus impeding, more often than not, any effort of adaptation. But in the case of the arts addressed here, we can easily imagine that De Felice was most interested in the theoretical level of Sulzer's *Allgemeine Theorie der Schönen Künste,* which made the general scope of his articles readily accessible, regardless of differences in cultural background.

In conclusion, despite the variety of ways in which the encyclopedias of the Enlightenment developed over the course of the eighteenth century, their universalist vocation remains, in the final analysis, their dominant feature. Indeed, this feature may well be responsible for having distanced these great, generalist compilations from the authentic process of knowledge transfer that was characteristic of the period. Nevertheless, we note that these compilations succeeded in profiting from the processes of knowledge transfer in their own distinct way.

NOTES

1 It's noteworthy that these articles are rarely developed in depth. Only twelve of them are longer than a column, and eight of them are part of broader topics encompassing epic poetry and dramatic poetry: "Action, in Poetry," "Character, in Poetry," "Epic *Poem*," "Fable," "Hero," "Machine," "Poetry," and "Probability, in Poetry." The only long articles contained in this corpus are "Chorus, in Dramatic Poetry," "Comedy," "Gladiator," and "Tragedy."

2 The *Traité du poème épique* by Le Bossu was published in 1675 and appears to have fascinated Chambers. Le Bossu is the only theoretician whom he praises in the articles making up our corpus. Here is one of many examples one could cite in praise of Le Bossu: "*The accurate F. Bossu* […] *that excellent Critic*" (in the article "Comedy," Chambers, *Cyclopædia* [London, 1728], 268).

3 Corneille and Dryden are equally present, but Chambers only refers to them as theoreticians. He mentions Corneille in the article "Comedy" and Dryden in the articles "Catastrophe" and "Peripetia."

4 See Cernuschi, 2013, "Les encyclopédies des Lumières comme génératrices d'une circulation des connaissances par dessus les frontières," in *Europa in der Schweiz – Grenzüberschreitender Kulturaustausch im 18. Jahrhundert*, ed. Heidi Eisenhut, Anett Lütteken, and Carsten Zelle (Göttingen: Wallstein), 43.

5 All translations are Clorinda Donato's. I am deeply grateful to her for her very careful translation work in this chapter.

6 *Enc.*, 8:353. Another example of rejection can be found in the short article "Rant," illustrated in the tragedies by Lee and in a quote taken from Ben Johnson's *Cataline.*

7 The addition of a paragraph of a lexicographical nature can be found at the end of the article; it reveals a rather imperfect mastery of the material: "Nous n'employons en France que le terme de *monologue*, pour exprimer les discours ou les scenes dans lesquelles un acteur s'entretient avec lui-même,

le mot de *soliloque* étant particulierement consacré à la théologie mystique
& affective. Ainsi nous disons les *soliloques* de saint Augustin, ce sont des
méditations pieuses" [In France, we only use the term 'monologue' to
explain the discourses or scenes in which an actor speaks to himself, while
the word 'soliloquy' is used in particular for discourses that are gauged
towards mystical and affective theology. Thus, we refer to the soliloquies
of Saint Augustin, which are pious meditations]" (15:323–4). Logically,
Chambers's article should have been placed under the entry "Monologue"!

 8 For other examples of integration or adaptation, see "Prologue" and
"Representation".

 9 Sixty-three of them are not signed.

10 "Fête, (*Beaux-Arts*)" (6:576–9); "Fêtes de la Cour de France" (6:580–5);
"Fêtes de la Ville de Paris" (6:585–8); "Fêtes des grandes Villes du Royaume
de France" (6:588–93); "Fêtes des Princes de France" (6:593–8).

11 Thomson, 1759, *Les Saisons. Poëme Traduit de l'Anglois de Thompson*
(translation in prose: Marie-Jeanne de Chatillon Bontemps), Paris,
Chaubert et Hérissant.

12 "[D]eux nations rivales du théâtre" (*Enc.*, 16:518).

13 In French: "La plus belle qui soit sur aucun théatre" (517); "un des plus
purs écrivains de la Grande-Bretagne," "le poëte des sages" (518).

14 The complete title is: *Nouveau Dictionnaire historique et critique pour servir de
Supplément ou de continuation au Dictionnaire historique et critique de Mr. Pierre
Bayle, par Jaques George de Chauffepié.*

15 *A General Dictionary, Historical and Critical: in which A New and Accurate
Translation of that of the Celebrated Mr. Bayle* [...], By the Reverend Mr.
John Peter Bernard; The Reverend Mr. Thomas Birch [etc.], London, 10
vol., 1734–41. (There had been a prior English translation by Pierre Des
Maizeaux in 1710, which also appeared in the following second edition: *The
Dictionary Historical and Critical of Mr Peter Bayle*, 5 vols., 1734–8 [London:
n.p.])

16 Original text of the letter dated 12 November 1771: "Nous ne devons
pas mesurer l'intérêt d'un article par celui que nous y attachons nous-
mêmes [...]. Nous faisons un ouvrage qui doit intéresser toutes les nations
également. Les Parisiens en ont fait un dont la moitié au moins n'intéressait
que la France; je fais main basse sur toutes ces misères nationales; or je
ne voudrois pas qu'on nous reprochât qu'à la place des articles François
nous y en avons substitué des Suisses." De Felice's active and passive
correspondence has recently been the subject of a scientific edition
(thanks to a grant made to the author from the Fonds national suisse de
la recherche scientifique). The edition of this correspondence, edited by

Léonard Burnand, is open to the public at the site of the University of Lausanne: www.unil.ch/defelice. The letters appear as pdf documents that have been organized in rubrics under the name of each correspondent on the site. My citations of De Felice's correspondence have been taken from this edition. About the interest of this correspondence, see the dossier of articles published in *Recherches sur Diderot et sur* l'Encyclopédie 49, no. 1 (January 2014): 87–143.

17 In their place we find an important, sixteen-page article written by the pastor and philosopher Gabriel Mingard: "Fête, (R), *Hist. anc. Religion Polit.*" (18:692–708; in this *Encyclopédie*, "(R)" indicates that the article has been rewritten). It is an extremely significant article for understanding the orientation of the Yverdon enterprise. The article offers a reflection on "the crowd's relishing of celebration," starting with a historical overview, leading to the issue of the usefulness of public celebrations and spectacles that are held in the interest of maintaining social bonds; he addresses, as well, their long evolution and inherent dangers, such the abuses to which celebration may lead, combined with a critique of Catholicism.

18 The article from which these citations have been taken can be found in volume 21 of the *Encyclopédie* d'Yverdon. The French text reads: "[Gottsched] s'appliqua de bonne heure à la langue françoise, pour se former le goût, sur les grands modèles du siècle de Louis XIV. Bientôt il se mit à donner des leçons d'éloquence et de poésie, dans cette ville, jettant déja les fondemens de cette révolution dans le goût de la littérature, à laquelle il devoit contribuer si efficacement par ses préceptes, son exemple et ses ouvrages" (796).

19 "He judged German theater, still amorphous, to be in need of purging and perfecting. He applied himself to this task by loosely translating French and foreign plays, as well as by composing his own regular plays, that is, plays written in compliance with the three classical unities. He also wrote a *Poetics* that opened with a *translation in verse* of Horace's *Poetics*, while each chapter ended with Boileau's *precepts*. His *Caton d'Utique* was received with great acclaim" (797).

20 "He [Gottsched] nevertheless ended up entering into a number of literary disputes with any number of German writers from a variety of regions, each of whom wanted to promote their local dialects and styles. Even the writers from Zurich wanted to jump into the fray. The French language, by contrast, has had just one centre, formed by the conjoined authority of resulting writers from the capital, courtiers at Versailles, and academicians; whence should emerge definitive oracles. The German situation is quite different: so many different States and independent capitals, so many temples of taste that claim to promulgate precise and correct judgments" (797).

21 "I conducted a long epistolary exchange with M. *Gottsched*, who strove to prove to me that different languages do not possess their own particular creative genius, nor, for that matter, do they possess an essentially distinctive characteristic; instead, the difference among languages comes from the creative genius of the writers who use them, the difference in ideas, taste, character, and biases or the amount of knowledge each author possesses; he explained that the mechanics of languages may be quite different, but that these differences have scant influence on the character or creative genius of the language itself; and with instruments of a different kind, one can succeed in creating literary works that are equal in perfection. During a certain period of time he took it upon himself to soften any number of German words and to imagine the means for standardizing German pronunciation everywhere. That is what he wrote to me only a few years prior to his death in 1767" (797).

22 "Il faut [se contenter] de parler des morts; car nous ne saurions nous meler des vivans sans trop nous exposer." www.unil.ch/defelice/files/live/sites/defelice/files/shared/DF_HALLER_GEv.pdf.

23 See the section "Le dictionnaire des beaux-arts de Sulzer dans l'*Encyclopédie* d'Yverdon," in Léonard Burnand and Alain Cernuschi, 2006, "Circulation de matériaux entre l'*Encyclopédie* d'Yverdon et quelques dictionnaires spécialisés," *Dix-huitième siècle*, 38:254–60 and the appendix, 266–7.

24 "Tragédie, (R), *Art dramatique*," 41:166–80, and in the *Supplément* of *Encyclopédie* d'Yverdon, the articles "Comédie, (R), *Art dramatique*" (2:703–15), and "Spectacles, (N), *Invent. anc. & mod.*" (6:127–37); "(N)" indicates that the article is a new one.

25 "Terreur, (R), *Beaux-Arts*" (40:515–17) and "Vraisemblance, (R), *Beaux-Arts*" (42:588–91); and in the *Supplément*, "Force, (R), *Beaux-Arts*" (3:555–8), "Prose, Prosaique, (R), *Art d'écrire*" (5:458–9), and "Scene, (R), *Litterat.* et *Théat.*" (6:3–6).

26 It is presented as such in the *Encyclopédie* d'Yverdon article, where it is referred to as "un morceau remarquable," for Sulzer's text differs on this point, stating instead that Goethe's play is the most recent example of the kind of drama he is talking about. In German it is referred to as "die neueste Probe."

Bibliography

Primary Sources

1734–41. *A General Dictionary, Historical and Critical: in which A New and Accurate Translation of that of the Celebrated Mr. Bayle* [...], By the Reverend Mr. John Peter Bernard; The Reverend Mr. Thomas Birch [etc.]. 10 vols. London.

Chambers, Ephraim. 1728. *Cyclopædia; or An Universal dictionary of arts and sciences*. 2 vols., in-fol. London: Knapton.

Chauffepié, Jacques-Georges de. 1750–6. *Nouveau Dictionnaire historique et critique pour servir de Supplément ou de continuation au Dictionnaire historique et critique de Mr. Pierre Bayle, par Jacques-Georges de Chauffepié*. 4 vols. Amsterdam: Pierre de Hondt.

Des Maiseaux, Pierre. 1734–8. *The Dictionary Historical and Critical of Mr Peter Bayle*. 2nd ed. 5 vols. London: Printed for J.J. and P. Knapton.

Diderot, Denis, and Jean-Baptiste le Rond d'Alembert, eds. 1751–80. *Encyclopédie, ou dictionnaire raisonnée des sciences, des arts et des métiers*. 35 vols., in-fol. Paris, Neuchâtel: Briasson.

Felice, Fortunato Bartolomeo de. 1770–80. *Encyclopédie, ou Dictionnaire universel raisonné des connoissances humaines*. 58 vols, in-4°. Yverdon: n.p.

Thomson, James. 1759. *Les Saisons. Poëme Traduit de l'Anglois de Thompson.* [Translation in prose: Marie-Jeanne de Chatillon Bontemps.] Paris: Chaubert et Hérissant.

Secondary Sources

Burnand, Léonard, and Alain Cernuschi. 2006. "Circulation de matériaux entre l'*Encyclopédie* d'Yverdon et quelques dictionnaires spécialisés." *Dix-huitième siècle*, 38: 254–67.

Cernuschi, Alain. 2013. "Les encyclopédies des Lumières comme génératrices d'une circulation des connaissances par dessus les frontières." In *Europa in der Schweiz – Grenzüberschreitender Kulturaustausch im 18. Jahrhundert*, Proceedings of the 3rd Trogener Bibliotheksgespräch, Trogen, 10–13 June 2009, edited by Heidi Eisenhut, Anett Lütteken, and Carsten Zelle, 41–57. Göttingen: Wallstein.

chapter three

Camels in the Alps? Translation, Transfer, and Adaptation in Dutch Encyclopedias and Their European Predecessors

INA ULRIKE PAUL

Camels were not an unknown species in eighteenth-century Europe. For as long as people could remember, preachers in the pulpits had been evoking caravans of camels from the Holy Land, and they were an integral part of cultural memory in the eighteenth century. The Bible spoke of the beautiful Rebecca who brought camels water to drink, the Three Wise Men from the East who arrived on the backs of camels, and the proverbial phrase that "it is easier for a camel to go through the eye of a needle than for a rich man to enter the kingdom of God."[1] However, while camels may have been familiar in the context of cultural history, little was known about how camels lived in their natural habitat. Most readers therefore did not laugh when in 1709, in the first German-language Enlightenment encyclopedia (*Allgemeines Historisches Lexicon*, or the "Leipziger Lexikon" as it was also known), it was stated that "a large number of deer, bears, and camels" lived in the Swiss mountains.[2] Perhaps no one bothered to read the entry on Switzerland very closely?

The Swiss editors working on the first genuinely Swiss encyclopedia, which would come to be known as the "Basler Lexikon," did notice this entry, however, and they of course recognized the camel as something foreign to Switzerland. After this book came out in 1726–7 in Basel, the publisher Johann Brandmüller then had to deny accusations of plagiarism brought against him by Thomas Fritsch, the publisher of the Leipziger Lexikon. The accusations were all too justified: to minimize costs, the Swiss publisher had relied on the most recent edition of the Leipziger Lexikon as a source for his own encyclopedia, which he then tailored to the Swiss book market. Although this was not permissible, it was nevertheless very common at the time, and Brandmüller thus avoided the financial costs of translating other sources.[3] The Leipzig encyclopedia was therefore edited for Swiss German and only certain parts were newly typeset – excerpts from the original Leipzig edition on Switzerland were thoroughly revised and partially rewritten, as had been promised in the title and preface of the Basler Lexikon.[4] Incidentally, while making these revisions, the editors of the Basler Lexikon discovered that, in the Leipzig encyclopedia the French (and English) word "chamois" had been erroneously translated as "camel" (*chameau* in French), as they informed their readers in the preface with obvious delight.

This faulty translation exposed the German-language Leipziger Lexikon as itself having a French source. Like the incriminated Swiss encyclopedia, the German encyclopedia was thus also a compilation of sorts. By its own admission, the Leipziger Lexikon was based on the following: (1) the three revised editions from France, England, and the Netherlands of Moréri's encyclopedia, of which the majority of the articles had been translated; (2) the *Dictionnaire historique et critique* (1697) by Pierre Bayle; and (3) Barthélemy d'Herbelot's *Bibliothèque orientale* (1697).[5] The publisher Fritsch from Leipzig had attempted to repeat the successful book sales of Moréri's encyclopedia in the German-speaking regions of the empire, and for this purpose had obtained the assistance of the respected theologian and orientalist Johann Franz Buddeus from Jena as an academic figurehead and editor.[6] The publisher Brandmüller from Basel used this method in turn for his encyclopedic endeavour for the German-speaking cantons of Switzerland, securing the help of the scholar Jakob Christoph Iselin.

It is notable that the antagonistic dyad of *Le Grand Dictionnaire Historique* by the Catholic cleric Louis Moréri and the *Dictionnaire historique et critique* by the reformed liberal philosopher Pierre Bayle were two of the source texts for the Leipziger Lexikon as well as the Basler Lexikon. As is generally known, Bayle had originally merely intended to correct the numerous mistakes, fallacies, and unverified facts in Moréri's *Dictionnaire Historique* by creating his own version of the encyclopedia as a project for which he had already received advance funding from a Dutch publisher. As a result of his revisions, however, he had incidentally created his own work of extraordinary importance.[7]

But what do the camels and chamois found in these European encyclopedias have to do with the Dutch encyclopedias that would later follow in their footsteps? Moréri, Bayle, and Buddeus would later form the triad of encyclopedic authorities on which the Dutch encyclopedists (and others) would expressly rely in the middle of the eighteenth century; they would also prove to be the root cause of the camel/chamois faux pas.

With this in mind, three major Dutch-language encyclopedias – respectively edited by Abraham George Luïscius; David van Hoogstraten, Matthæus Brouërius van Nidek, and later Jan Lodewijk Schuër; and Egbert Buys – offer us valuable insight into the intercultural, transnational, and economic dimensions of encyclopedic endeavours in the eighteenth century. For the sake of discussing processes of translation across languages and cultures – in other words, knowledge transfer – I am posing two simple questions: Who were the "makers" of the three Dutch encyclopedias? And why did they pursue these encyclopedic projects from which only Dutch readers would be able to profit?

I will begin by taking a closer look at the protagonists of the three Dutch encyclopedias: the editors, authors, publishers, and booksellers who published these works. What networks of acquaintances or colleagues were they able to rely on? To what extent did their own scholarly production play a role in the encyclopedic project that they were promoting? Did they personally profit from the project financially? Did their later careers benefit from it? Second, I will concentrate on how and where in the encyclopedias the authors, editors, publishers, and booksellers expressed the value and significance of their encyclopedic projects, arguing that this is where translation across languages and cultures of encyclopedias into Dutch is presented most authentically. These statements by the Dutch encyclopedists are made all the more important by the fact that educated Dutch readers would have been able to read the French, German, or English works on which these compilations were based in the first place. Finally, I discuss possible answers to these questions by connecting the producers of the encyclopedias and their shared intentions to those elements of transfer that resulted in a "national" adaptation *avant la lettre* of the encyclopedias to the Dutch book market.

The Protagonists: The Publishers, Editors, Authors, and Their Networks

In the early stages of the Enlightenment from 1680 to 1715, a climate of tolerance and open-mindedness evolved in the United Provinces of the Netherlands, which was the largest Protestant republic in northwestern Europe. This solidified the Netherlands' role as a "great ark" (Pierre Bayle) for religious and political dissidents, and it fostered the development of the sciences and arts beyond the "Golden Age."[8] The country's urbanization (40 per cent of all inhabitants lived in cities) had reached a remarkable level. The rate of literacy of the population was high, the number of educated people was above the European average, and the Dutch market for printed materials, whether books or periodicals, had an international focus, all of which created a fertile ground for the wide acceptance of the encyclopedic movement.

The success story of encyclopedias in the national languages of Europe had begun in 1674 with the already mentioned *Le Grand Dictionnaire Historique* by the priest Louis Moréri.[9] This work was imitated, translated, and adapted more often than any other encyclopedia (with the exception of Diderot's and D'Alembert's *Encyclopédie,* discussed below), spawning its own family of encyclopedic "offshoots" in many European languages. Adaptations of Moréri's work were first published in England, Italy, and Germany before the 1720s and 1730s, when Swiss and Dutch adaptations were published, followed, finally, by a Spanish translation in 1754.

In the following, I will focus on the editors, authors, publishers, and publishing booksellers (as well as their personal networks) of the three first Dutch encyclopedias. I will also take into account the paratexts (prefaces, dedications, and so forth) and how these provided "reception instructions" for the encyclopedias.

The First Dutch Encyclopedia

In 1724, the first of eight volumes of the *Het Algemeen Historisch, Geographisch en Genealogisch Woordenboek* (The general, historical, geographical, and genealogical dictionary) was published by the booksellers Pieter Husson from The Hague and Reinier Boitet from Delft.[10] The first encyclopedia in Dutch, whose title made it obvious that it was an adaptation of Moréri, boasted that it was a one-man enterprise by the then thirty-one-year-old legal scholar and historian Abraham George Luïscius.[11] The completion of the eight-volume encyclopedia took thirteen years and probably ruined him financially. Luïscius was born in Xanten in the Duchy of Cleves near the border of the United Netherlands. He studied law at the University of Duisburg, where he enrolled as a student when he was ten years old, then later in Leiden (Leyden). His first book was published in 1713 and was a translation from English into Dutch of a history of the House of Brunswick-Lüneburg. He became such a well-known scholar, outside the Netherlands as well, that he was appointed a foreign member of the Royal Prussian Academy of Sciences in Berlin in 1734. Other members at the time included Philippe Joseph von Jariges, Anders Celsius, and Pierre-Louis Moreau de Maupertuis. During his time as a member, Luïscius also held representative political offices. He most likely earned the necessary income for financing his encyclopedia from his position as Prussian resident and special envoy to the States General in The Hague starting in 1732. However, he was dismissed in 1739 due to embezzlement, and he lost all of his academic and public offices, dying the following year.

As to others involved in Luïscius's *Algemeen Woordenboek*, there is no mention in the encyclopedia of any associates. However, it is possible that Luïscius used personal funds to pay anonymous contributors, just like Louis de Jaucourt, the editor of the *Encyclopédie*, had done. While Pieter Husson and Reinier Boitet are listed as the publishers on the baroque title page, only Pieter Husson – along with the booksellers Johannes van Duren, Thomas Johnson, and Charles le Vier – wrote the preface, thus describing the encyclopedic project's genesis, the time pressure involved, and the many incidents that are always likely to occur during such a large endeavour.[12]

Whether merely a word of goodwill or an early form of a modern advertisement for the author and his book, a poem of praise for the "encyclopedia … by Luïscius" was written by the court poet Hendrik Schim. He concluded his laudation by calling on all Dutch people to show their appreciation to the much-deserving Luïscius for his scholarly fervour – or, in Schim's words, "to hand him the laurel wreath."[13] Among the addressees of this appeal were the remarkable number of subscribers – their names filled five folio pages – who had supported this Dutch-language encyclopedic endeavour. If we are to believe the printer's preface in the eighth and last volume from 1737, most of the subscribers remained loyal to Luïscius's "library in a single book" (*een bibliotheek in een enkel boek*) down to the last volume. This meant that they also purchased the work, although they were only morally obligated to do so, because the subscription was not a kind of advance payment.[14] No costs were spared concerning the beauty and value of this work – neither the quality of the engravings, typeset, or paper nor the exactness of the corrections. The printer informed subscribers that, as with many other encyclopedias of this type, this particular one would also come with a supplement containing entries not included in the regular volumes.

The Second Dutch Encyclopedia

The second Dutch encyclopedia was entitled *Groot Algemeen Historisch, Geographisch, Genealogisch, en Oordeelkundig Woordenboek* (Great universal, historical, geographical, genealogical, and critical dictionary).

It was introduced on the Dutch market in 1725, only one year after Luïscius's *Algemeen Woordenboek*. From the beginning, this encyclopedia set out to replace Luïscius's work, a mission for which it was very well positioned with its similar title, which began with *Groot Algemeen* instead of *Het Algemeen*.[15] For one thing, it was supported by a consortium of several booksellers from Amsterdam, Utrecht, Leiden, and The Hague who were able to put significant pressure on the encyclopedia's authors and associates, thus guaranteeing the punctual publication of the volumes.[16] They also engaged a prominent national historian, committing him to yearly contracts and preventing him from revealing materials to their competitor, Luïscius, who also tried to win him over.[17] Second, famous figures were responsible for the content. One author was the poet, writer, and physician David van Hoogstraten,[18] who had fought a spectacular poet's war with Jean Le Clerc,[19] one of Moréri's compilers who lived in Amsterdam. His pupil and friend, the wealthy law scholar, writer, and specialist on the history of the Netherlands Matthæus Brouërius van Nidek, was his co-author.[20] Despite their friendship, the two prima donna scholars had a serious dispute while working on their joint endeavour – possibly because in the same year as the publication of the first volume of the new encyclopedia, Brouërius also appeared on title pages of competing encyclopedic works as an editor.[21] For example, Brouërius completed the first genuine Dutch adaptation of Moréri, the encyclopedia *Tooneel der Vereenigde Nederlanden* (which translates loosely as "Theater of the United Netherlands"), which he took over from François Halma, a bookseller and cartographer who had died three years previous. Unlike other European adaptations of Moréri, the *Tooneel* was not a nationalized encyclopedia, but rather an encyclopedia that specialized in the Netherlands à la Moréri. It was gorgeously decorated with maps and engravings.[22] In addition to this work, Brouërius also edited two commentated collections of engravings about the history of the Netherlands in 1725.[23] A very productive scholar, he was the head of the Dutch sections of the *Groot Algemeen Woordenboek* – especially for antiquity and ancient times (*Oudheden*), history and geography, and all other specialized fields of expertise regarding the Netherlands. How he ultimately integrated the three other projects he was working on (and doubtless others) into the *Groot Algemeen Woordenboek* would require closer analysis of the selected entries. Concerning elective intertextual affinities as well as transfer processes, it should be remembered that the authors of encyclopedias often borrowed from their own works that had already been published or from works they were simultaneously writing and editing in order to speed up the progress of the encyclopedic project.

Other collaborators deserve our attention in addition to the numerous aforementioned associates: translators from French and German into Dutch, and the main editors van Hoogstraten and Brouërius, who edited the entries for the letters "A" and "B." These include the famous preacher Hermannus van der Wall from Amsterdam and the preacher and rector Gerard Outhof from Kampen, both of whom contributed numerous historical, theological, clerical, geographical, and genealogical articles, at least in the beginning.[24] Two other contributors – Johannes Haverkamp and the preacher and rector of a Latin school in Gouda, Arnold Henrik Westerhof, who was of German descent, also edited the entries for the letters "A" to "D."[25]

Already in the early stages of this second Dutch encyclopedia, a scholarly collaboration grew between Westerhof and van Hoogstraten's successor, Jan Lodewijk Schuër. They would later translate the already famous *Dictionnaire Œconomique* by the French agronomist Noël Chomel into Dutch in 1743 as the *Huishoudelyk woordboek*.[26] This Dutch edition would reach Japan via "la route des encyclopédies" (Jacques Proust), where it was held in high regard;[27] a copy of the *Huishoudelyk woordboek* was found in the library of the scholar and collector Yoshio Kōsaku, who was an influential figure in "Hollandology" (or *rangaku* as it was called in Japan).[28] Schuër's and Westerhof's translation of Chomel's work was still so successful a century later that the reform-oriented politician, inventor, and scholar Sakumana Shōzan first learned Dutch by studying an edition of the *Huishoudelyk woordboek*, which he had acquired in 1844. He then proceeded to familiarize himself with the techniques of glass manufacture and the usage of magnets, thermometers, and other technical devices with it.[29]

Before they cooperated on the Dutch translation of Chomel, Schuër and Westerhof had both gained experience translating encyclopedic works by the German educationalist and encyclopedist Johann Hübner, to whom Schuër was related on his mother's side. While still working on the *Groot Algemeen Woordenboek*, Schuër published a Dutch translation of Hübner's *Lexicon Genealogicum Portatile* in 1727, the same year as the original was published.[30] Westerhof, for his part, translated the first German popular encyclopedia (*Konversationslexikon*) a few years later, which included a preface by Johannes Hübner and was entitled *Reales Staats-, Zeitungs- und Conversationslexikon*.[31] These personal and professional relationships between Schuër, Outhof, and Hübner demonstrate another aspect of scholarly culture of the eighteenth century, which profoundly fostered the interweaving of translated "scholarly" encyclopedias (and popular encyclopedias [*Konversationslexika*]) across linguistic and cultural borders until there was a rhizome of protagonists and a mycelium of seemingly unconnected editions of encyclopedias.

The successful conclusion of the *Groot Algemeen Woordenboek* was put in jeopardy by van Hoogstraten's death in the same year the first volume was published. He was only sixty-six years old at the time, his death the result of an accident.[32] The situation was made worse by the fact that Brouërius did not get along with Lodewijk Schuër, who replaced van Hoogstraten. Schuër was a skilled translator and compiler from Amsterdam and, according to the preface of the encyclopedia, he was also a well-known, talented expert in history and geography – the very areas for which, up to then, Brouërius had been solely responsible.[33] Consequently, Brouërius left the editorial team of the *Groot Algemeen Woordenboek* in 1726. The work thus lost both of its original figureheads – not an easy blow for the project's public image and sales. The consortium quickly found a remedy, however: van Hoogstraten's name would remain on the title page of all the remaining volumes, placed even before his successor Schuër's, who was the actual editor and who turned out to be an excellent choice on the part of the booksellers' consortium. Schuër, in fact, managed to finish all ten volumes of the encyclopedia within eight years. After the successful completion of the encyclopedic project *Groot Algemeen Woordenboek*, Schuër went on to publish several historical and political works in quick succession, including a short history of the city of Gdansk, a history of the Netherlands from 1621 to the Peace of Utrecht in 1713, and a chronicle of unusual events of the last two centuries.[34] It is still thought today that he died before September 1740, which would indicate that the last of his publications appeared posthumously.

The Third Dutch Encyclopedia

As with Schuër, we only know date of birth and death as well as the publications of Egbert Buys, the essayist and encyclopedist behind the third Dutch encyclopedia, *Nieuw en Volkomen Woordenboek der Konsten en Wetenschappen* (New and complete dictionary of the arts and sciences) – a work with ten volumes that was launched in 1769, roughly thirty-five years after Luïscius's *Algemeen Woordenboek*.[35] Buys had made a name for himself in the 1740s as an editor and writer of moral weeklies, and in the 1760s he published several multivolume works on art history and history in general.[36] Judging from his complete works, Buys was a scholar who also initially worked as a merchant, and his professional contacts most likely opened doors for him in diplomatic and political circles. In 1745 he became a privy councilor to the king elect, Augustus II of Saxony and Poland, and in 1763 he also became privy councilor to August II's victorious opponent, the Prussian king Frederick the Great. Like Luïscius before him, Buys resided in The Hague, which was the seat of the Stadtholder (steward). He was conscious of his status, and he is listed on the front page of his *Nieuw en Volkomen Woordenboek* as the "privy councilor to the Polish and Prussian majesties."[37] What little we know of Buys's life can be found in a printed account of the war of roses between him and his wife Alida, which provides a perspective (albeit not a daily one) on the life of an encyclopedist. Alida had accused him of fraudulent bankruptcy, and he immortalized her (like Messalina and Xantippe) as one of those "women with a hideous character" (*een afgryzelyk caracter*).[38]

The ten volumes of Buys's *Nieuw en Volkomen Woordenboek* were published between 1769 and 1778 by the bookseller Steven Jacobus Baalde in Amsterdam. Unlike the previous two Dutch encyclopedias, however, this project began after the encyclopedic paradigm shift, brought on by the *Encyclopédie, ou Dictionnaire raisonné des sciences, des arts et des métiers* by Denis Diderot and Jean le Rond d'Alembert, had occurred. Following the lead of this encyclopedia, Buys's encyclopedia also explicitly focused on trades along with science and the arts. Buys wrote on the title page that the particular strength of his encyclopedia was the "useful knowledge" (*nuttige kennis*) provided by the descriptions and illustrations of modern machines, tools, and devices, as well as the study of nature and geography. He added that the foundations had been laid by "the best writers in all languages," which was entirely in the encyclopedic tradition of claiming to provide comprehensive knowledge.

Like Luïscius, Buys's financial circumstances were precarious, and like van Hoogstraaten, he died in the first year of publication of his grand encyclopedic project. The further editing and supervising of the authors recruited by Buys was probably taken over by the bookseller Baalde, who mentions this in the tenth and last volume in 1778 but does not specify his own name.[39] In 1772 a second round of subscriptions was organized for the work, which was still published under Buys's name. The majority of subscribers in this second round were booksellers, as the six-page-long list reveals.[40] All in all, the endeavour was apparently ill fated, however. As the publisher wrote, not only Buys but other associates (not named here) also died later while working on the *Nieuw en Volkomen Woordenboek*, continually postponing the work's publication. Furthermore, the planned number of volumes had risen from eight to ten during the nineteen years of working on the encyclopedia. In the end, the encyclopedia cost the steep sum of sixty guilders. Still, the publisher optimistically announced that a supplement would complement the previous volumes and bring them up to date. He planned to rely for this on the new French *Encyclopédie* d'Yverdon and the *Deutsche Encyclopädie*, which was published in Frankfurt am Main beginning in 1778.[41] Interested readers as well as subscribers, the latter of whom had since aged two decades, never did warm up to this idea, however. Regardless of the reason, the planned supplement was never published.

Media of National Self-Portrayal: Paratextual Elements as Compared to Predecessors from Other Nations

The elaborately printed title pages and frontispieces of encyclopedias from the enlightened eighteenth century are striking. The German philologist Paul Michel from Switzerland has pointed out the significance of the frontispieces of encyclopedias. He argues that they contain "statements that form a kind of metalanguage" about the work, "just as in other paratexts or in advertisements." This was apparently intentional, because they also acted as advertisements of sorts for the works in question, especially if they were made by an outstanding contemporary artist and bore witness to the encyclopedia's exquisite features.[42] The twin goals of advertising and informing are even more prominent in the Baroque, most often multicoloured title pages that provided information not only about the editor and publisher, but also about the core themes and scope of general knowledge, while also announcing the work's special qualities that made it recommendable for the educated public of the country where it was produced.[43]

Luïscius's *Algemeen Woordenboek*

At first glance, the frontispiece of Luïscius's *Algemeen Woordenboek* (figure 3.1) seems to imply not so much a specific transfer of knowledge as a collection of knowledge. In it, a "great multitude which no man could number, from every nation, from all tribes and peoples and tongues" (Rev. 7:9) crowds around a group of allegorical personifications of Genealogy, Mnemosyne, and Historiography, who are writing the history of humanity with the help of companions. They are also flanked by

3.1. Copperplate engraving by Bernard Picart illustrating the copious
text on the opposing title page of Luïscius's *Algemeen Woordenboek*.
Niedersächsische Staats- und Universitätsbibliothek Göttingen.

allegories of the four known continents at the time. Adam and Eve and the founders of the three major religions of the book rise above the multitudes of the past generations, joined by secular and clerical princes, war heroes, philosophers, and "most serene highnesses," all marching from the distant past into the present. In the foreground of the scene, the personifications of science and the arts, recognizable by their attributes, are occupied with solving the most fundamental questions of humanity. The representation and composition are so rich with figures and references that they are accompanied by an explanatory text. This magnificent engraving by Bernard Picart, who like William Hogarth was one of the most famous engravers of his time, also illustrates the copious text on the opposing title page of Luïscius's *Algemeen Woordenboek*.[44] This text finishes with a paragraph of superlatives praising the two "unique selling points" of this first Dutch encyclopedia: that it is "compiled from the very best dictionaries [encyclopedias] of other nations" and that it represents the very latest knowledge and is therefore more up to date than all other works currently being used.[45]

In addition to the encyclopedia's relevance, Luïscius and his publisher also stressed its Dutch focus, arguing that one could find more articles on the Netherlands in it than in any other encyclopedia. It was thus a truly Dutch encyclopedia, and not merely one written in Dutch. This appeal to readers' political and cultural sense of identity reverberated in many encyclopedias in various national languages, and it anticipated a special interest on the part of educated readers willing to purchase these books in the countries where they were published. This trend was expressed for the first time in 1709 on the title page of Buddeus's *Leipziger Lexikon*, and it appeared again on the title pages of the two first encyclopedias in the Netherlands, then immediately afterwards on the title page of the *Basler Lexikon*, and later also in encyclopedias in Spain (*por lo que mira à España*), Italy, Poland, and Sweden.[46]

One would expect the "Dutch" quality of this first Dutch encyclopedia to be most clearly detectable in the entries devoted to the Netherlands. Luïscius's main article on the Netherlands was first mentioned in 1727 under "D" (for *Duytschland*) in a cross-reference to "Lower Germany" (*Neder-Duitschlandt*) but was then later forgotten and left out. In the last volume of the encyclopedia, the printer wrote a statement, saying that overlooking one entry or two was inevitable in a project of such size. The main keyword "Netherlands" (*Nederlanden*) was also not included until the supplement (*Aanhangsel*) to the last volume was published in 1737. It should be noted that this article was also based on an encyclopedia by Thomas Corneille from 1708, which had been little revised and had already served as the source of information on the Netherlands in editions of Moréri's work. Corneille's encyclopedia was itself based on an even older reference work by the French diplomat and geographer Jean-Baptiste d'Audriffret. These facts undermined the claim Luïscius had made on the dedication page regarding the originality of the articles, especially those on the Netherlands.[47] The entry on the "Union of Utrecht" (*Unie van Utrecht*) from 1597, which was the founding event of the United Netherlands, was also only to be found in the supplement, where interested readers could in addition find a list of recent publications by the publishing booksellers involved in the encyclopedic project.[48]

As previously mentioned, in Luïscius's dedication to the acting grand pensionary (prime minister) of Holland and West Friesland, Isaac van Hoornbeek, he stressed that history was a compass, especially for statesmen, for future actions regarding domestic and foreign policy.[49] As to why he became involved in the encyclopedia in the first place, he points out that he took on this work solely because at the time nothing like it existed "in our Dutch language" (*in onze nederlandse taal*). He thus devoted himself to studying the history of his mother country and "based his work on many sources" (*geschept uit hondert bronnen*), meaning it was compiled from similar encyclopedias from other nations, the quality of which he guaranteed but the names or details of which he did not mention here or elsewhere. In this way, Luïscius referred back to the promise on the title page, which was also explained in more detail in the consortium of booksellers' preface for readers.

The publishing booksellers also integrated subtle product placement in several entries in the encyclopedia, thereby introducing readers to their extensive publishing catalog. This included works by excellent encyclopedists from the time before Luïscius's *Algemeen Woordenboek* that were selected according to scholarly as well as financial criteria. Not only were Bayle, Furetière, Moréri, and other authors associated with particularly successful encyclopedias that had been reprinted several times included, but these individuals were also in-house authors, meaning their works were published by the same publishing bookseller and printers of Luïscius's *Algemeen Woordenboek*. The article on Pierre Bayle, which was eighteen pages long and thus much longer than any comparable entry, concluded with references advertising the new edition of his *Dictionnaire historique et critique* "beautifully printed in folio format" as well as the third edition, which was published in 1720.[50] Because the *Dictionnaire Universel* by Antoine Furetière was also published by the same booksellers, there was an entry for this encyclopedia as well.[51] Finally, there also was a long entry on Louis Moréri, whose *Le Grand Dictionnaire Historique* was much criticized but still lived up to its great reputation.[52] It is astonishing that no mention whatsoever is made of the English *Lexicon Technicum* by the Anglican cleric and mathematician John Harris, which came out in 1704–8, or the already mentioned *Allgemeines Historisches Lexicon* (Leipziger Lexikon) by the Protestant theologian Johann Franz Buddeus, from 1709, which was the German offshoot of the great family of Moréri adaptations – just like Luïscius's encyclopedia was the Dutch adaptation. The competing encyclopedia, van Hoogstraten's *Groot Algemeen Woordenboek*, on the other hand, put special emphasis on Buddeus.

Van Hoogstraten's *Groot Algemeen Woordenboek*

The three main figures Historiography, Genealogy, and Mnemosyne in the frontispiece (figure 3.2) of the *Groot Algemeen Woordenboek*, edited by van Hoogstraten, do not have the same artistic quality as in Luïscius's encyclopedia. This frontispiece also shows an allegorical personification of enlightened science, crowned with an aureole, who is writing the names "Moréri," "Bayle," and "Buddeus" in the open book presented to the spectator. This artistic representation, together with the opposing title page of the *Groot Algemeen Woordenboek*, sends the message that these three famous predecessors were an inspiration to this new work, with its contemporary focus on Dutch interests for the first time.

The particular significance of this encyclopedic endeavour for the Dutch public is underlined by the fact that the consortium of booksellers dedicated it to Jan Trip van Berkenrode the acting regent of Amsterdam since 1709.[53] Like Luïscius, they argued that the French, the British, and the Germans had their own encyclopedias in their national languages (*in zyne vaderlandsche sprake*), and "only the Dutch" (*Alleen onze landgenoten*) were missing such an "excellent means of promoting the sciences" (*uitmuntend hulpmiddel tot bevordering der wetenschappen*). It was this gap the encyclopedia intended to fill. Ignoring Luïscius's encyclopedia, which had begun publication the previous year, it claimed to be the first work of its kind to be published in the Netherlands. According to the encyclopedia, it was also based not only on other "foreign" works but on "our own [i.e., Dutch] scholars" for issues concerning the Netherlands. "We have no doubt," they concluded, "that this work will be useful and delightful for our fellow countrymen and fellow Dutch speakers."[54]

3.2. The frontispiece of the *Groot Algemeen Woordenboek* alludes to the famous predecessors Moréri, Bayle, and Buddeus and illustrates the title of Hoogstraten et al.'s encyclopedia. Artist unknown, Stiftung Johannes a Lasco Bibliothek Emden.

As already mentioned, such a standard patriotic formulation could be found in many "national" adaptations of the extensive Moréri family. The title page of the Basler Lexikon, for instance, stressed that Swiss authors had written all of the articles on Switzerland.

The booksellers – in their role as publishers – wrote not only the dedication but also the preface. There, they declared all encyclopedic works since antiquity as precursors of this new, enlightened way of alphabetically organizing knowledge that Louis Moréri had first presented. They stated that the translations and revisions of Moréri's work that had evolved in France, the Netherlands, England, and Germany, and of which Jean Le Clerc's edition was the most excellent, lent Moréri's original work new glamour. In addition, they listed the great Pierre Bayle's "excellent" (*overheerlyk*) encyclopedia and the supplementary volumes of Moréri's work published by Jacques Bernard in Amsterdam as important sources for their own work.[55] It is therefore clear that they regarded the process of knowledge transfer – through translating, editing, and compiling similar works, in addition to specialized literature – as an enrichment for the original work, and not as the revision of old and antiquated knowledge.

Also in the preface, they wrote that in order to facilitate their long-cherished plan of publishing a grand encyclopedic work "in our mother tongue" (*in onze moedertale*), the translation of articles from the most recent and best editions of these works had been entrusted to top-notch scholars. Because of this new concept, this encyclopedia therefore surpassed its predecessors in two ways: not only did it include the historical, geographical, and genealogical features of France, Germany, and England – meaning adaptations made for the respective languages and book markets – of the encyclopedias before it, it also offered quite a large number of new articles that had been written especially for Dutch readers.

If we compare the entries concerning the Netherlands in this second Dutch encyclopedia by van Hoogstraaten, the main keyword he chose was "United Provinces" (*Vereenigde Provincien*), which meant that the article about the Netherlands did not appear until the very last volume. Interested readers and subscribers therefore had to wait some time before they could read it. However, this entry – which is extraordinarily long, with twenty-two columns (in folio!) – includes all the essential facts about the organization of the Dutch state, its political and economic circumstances, and its history. It is not a compilation based on Moréri, Bayle, and Buddeus, but was indeed written solely for this purpose.[56]

Buys's *Nieuw en Volkomen Woordenboek*

As to the third encyclopedia, Buys's *Nieuw en Volkomen Woordenboek* physically distinguishes itself from its two previous Dutch encyclopedias from the 1720s and 1730s. Unlike the two older Dutch encyclopedias, which were printed in the encyclopedic folio format, the *Nieuw en Volkomen Woordenboek* was published in octavo format, which was common for the convenient popular encyclopedias (*Konversationslexika*). The frontispiece (figure 3.3) can be described as rather modest artistically, especially in comparison to the other two. In it, a female figure, whose attributes identify her as the antique goddess of wisdom, Athena, holds an open book in her lap, in which we can decipher the words "Buys" and "Woordenboek." She seems to be giving a lesson to a young man, dressed fashionably in the style of the eighteenth century, leaning intently next to her. She and the young man can be seen in front of a plinth on which a lion – the symbol of the States-General – sits with his head turned toward the sea and his right paw resting on a globe, thus demonstrating the claims of a maritime power. To the left of the plinth, we see the sail of a ship behind a barrel and boxes next to which two putti are standing and kneeling, the larger of whom appears to be explaining a technical drawing to the smaller one.

Like the other frontispieces, Buys's tells us quite a bit about the content of the encyclopedia. The technical drawing refers to the detailed descriptions of machines, tools, and devices emphasized in the book's title. Similarly, the plants and fruit in the foreground can be seen as a reference to the classification of animals, plants, and minerals according to Linné, whose *Systema Naturae* had been published in Leiden in 1735. Political geography rounds off the entire picture.

On the title page, the encyclopedia (like its two predecessors) stresses that the entire content had been compiled by the best writers in all languages and supplemented by a significant amount of new articles by none other than Egbert Buys himself.[57] Like his anonymous source, the English encyclopedist Croker (discussed below), had done before him with the *Encyclopédie,* Buys added a new dimension to the "patriotic self-promotion" on which the first two Dutch encyclopedias had also relied by placing the sciences and arts on the same footing as trades and the new natural sciences. Furthermore, Buys did not include the dedications and prefaces usually written by the publishers or booksellers. Instead, he wrote a short preface for readers, which he signed with his own name, place, and date: "'s-Hage den 4 October 1768, E. Buys."

3.3. Frontispiece of Buys's *Nieuw en Volkomen Woordenboek*. engraving, artist unknown. De Digitale Bibliotheek voor de Nederlandse Letteren (DBNL): www.dbnl.org/tekst/buys003nieu01_01/index.php.

As to the sources and materials on which his work was based, Buys revealed little more than the fact that "knowledgeable and educated friends" had supported him, that the works he had cited were too numerous to list, and that he had "used [them] with the greatest liberty" (*met de grootste Vryheid gebruikt*).[58] While he had shortened several entries, he made others more elaborate than in the art encyclopedias from which they originated, one of which Buys himself had translated from English into Dutch. As to the new articles included in the work, he stated that their focus was on commerce, science, and natural history. Buys then presented a committed argument for using systematic cross-references, whose logic and utility he demonstrated on the entry for "Animal." With his own professional experience in mind, he wrote that references were like the double-entry bookkeeping done by a merchant; they guaranteed harmony, unity, and order within a work.

In place of a wordy introduction to his encyclopedia, he instead chose to include a schematic tree of knowledge, arguing that "that way we could guide our course through the expansive ocean of the sciences as if using a compass pointing north." Buys stressed that his *arbor scientiæ ex objectis desumpta* (division of the sciences according to their subjects) fundamentally differed from Ephraim Chambers's tree, which he regarded as too "school masterly and abstract" (*te schools en afgetrokken*). Anticipating criticism from modern philosophy, he added that even the tree by the "great [Francis] Bacon," which had been improved by the authors of the French *Encyclopédie*, tested the limits of practicability with its "abundance of materials" (*te zeer opgehoopt*). Buys confidently claimed that he was doing no less than introducing a new system of order for the "human sciences" that was superior to all others, because not only was it "constructed to be simpler and more natural, but also more complete and precise."[59] By introducing this schematic epistemological system of order, Buys's encyclopedia distinguished itself fundamentally from the two Dutch encyclopedias that came before it. However, the ideas behind this did not originate from Buys: he borrowed them from another encyclopedia, which he vaguely referred to as "the English work" and which was "an especially rich source of articles."[60] While this English work served Buys as the actual basis for his "truly Dutch" encyclopedia, he claimed it was merely a source and criticized it for not referring to Dutch and German works because of a lack of knowledge of these languages. This English precursor – and the original source of Buys's translations, revisions, and adaptations – was in fact *The Complete Dictionary of Arts and Sciences* by Temple Henry Croker, Thomas Williams, and Samuel Clark, which was published in London only a few years before Buys's own encyclopedia.[61] The very first anonymous "advertisement" written in the "we" form inside this English reference work referred to its own original sources – including Ephraim Chambers's *Cyclopædia* "and other Works of that Kind," the *Encyclopédie* by Diderot and d'Alembert, as well as "original authors."[62] Buys's encyclopedia therefore profited not only directly from secondary encyclopedic sources, but also indirectly from these two well-known works (which had been published too recently to have played a role for the older two Dutch encyclopedias). It is interesting to note that, instead of a tree of knowledge, Croker's *Complete Dictionary* has a table of four columns for the "various Branches of Literature" with sixty terms – from "A" for "Agriculture" to "T" for "Theology." Buys adopted and integrated this hierarchy into his tree of knowledge, relying on, and including excerpts from, the introductory remarks in the *Complete Dictionary* in his own preface, as he himself pointed out.[63]

As to the articles in Buys's *Nieuw en Volkomen Woordenboek*, these differ from the two older Dutch encyclopedias in their seemingly modern conciseness and choice of themes – for example, the power of the Netherlands and her European competitors in maritime trade is mentioned as important in the articles on Africa, America, and Asia. The main, more general keywords for these continents are also accompanied by more specific keywords relating to the commodities and colonies of the respective areas ("Americaansche Waaren," "Europische Waaren"). The style of the *Nieuw en Volkomen Woordenboek* reminds us of the popular encyclopedias (*Konversationslexika*, which had developed alongside the more scholarly encyclopedias since the beginning of the eighteenth century. With the nationalization, specialization, and growing acceptance of general knowledge, the popular encyclopedias (*Konversationslexika* continued to acquire more and more influence until they eventually became dominant in the age of revolutions, ultimately taking over the term "encyclopedia" itself. True to the logic of this transformation, Buys integrated "Dutch elements" in as many keywords as possible, and he stressed the economic aspect of all the keywords referring to the Netherlands. The keyword "Dutch Commodities" gave him the opportunity to refer to his motherland as the "depot and warehouse of the entire world," which compensated for its lack of natural resources.[64] He recycled this phrase almost verbatim in the content-rich article on "The United Netherlands," which stands out in comparison with the two older Dutch encyclopedias and Moréri editions from roughly the same time, in terms of both content and systems employed.[65] The article was based primarily on a Dutch translation of the eleven-volume encyclopedia *Neue Erdbeschreibung* (A new system of geography) by the Prussian theologian and geographer Anton Friedrich Büsching, which was first published in 1754, then in many successive editions.[66] The article, which is over ten columns long and is filled with cross-references, has a "Dutch" ending, in a patriotic sense. The anonymous author who compiled the article concludes with three "basic principles" (*Grondbeginzelen*) for the welfare of the Dutch republic: the continual growth of wealth, maintaining peace in balance with freedom, and steadfast loyalty. No other entry devoted to a European power is as long and targets its Dutch readership as intensely.

Conclusion

When discussing knowledge transfer processes in encyclopedias, it is helpful to address the "entangled histories" of Europe's enlightened encyclopedias of the eighteenth century. From the beginning, the mode of production of enlightened encyclopedias meant that the latest encyclopedias published in national languages necessarily integrated the content of the encyclopedias that came before them, interweaving it into their own. While technically not allowed, reprinting, translating across languages and cultures, and compiling of text collages to create articles for encyclopedias was common practice.

The connections shared by the various encyclopedias written in national languages enhanced the transnational popularization of the latest knowledge within the enlightened societies of Europe. Thus, those who were unwilling, or unable, to read Moréri's *Le Grand Dictionnaire Historique* in the French original at the turn of the century would be able to find a translation of the latest edition in their own language, tailored towards their own country. Within this development, the "makers" – the editors, authors, publishers, and publishing booksellers – played a central role.[67] While some had more educational ambitions, others guarded their economic interests. Together they shared a clearly patriotic desire to see – written in their own language and by their own scholars – what their neighbours in Europe had long been boasting of: encyclopedic works written for their own nations that presented comprehensive and reliable encyclopedic knowledge in a politically and religiously "correct" way. When one such encyclopedia attributed wild drinking as a national trait of Germany, this was not denied in a newer German encyclopedia, but simply written off as an outdated practice. Similarly, the entries for "language" in works from England, France, and Italy stated that each national language was best suited for poetry and science, while in a Spanish encyclopedia, it was written that God had spoken to Moses in Spanish. Finally, concerning the religious differences in Europe, Moréri's "la Religion Pretenduë Reformée" became "die Reformirte Religion" (the reformed religion) in the encyclopedias from the Protestant towns of Leipzig and Basel, while it remained "la Religione pretesa riformata" in an encyclopedia from Catholic Venice.[68]

The publishers, publishing booksellers, editors, and authors who planned the alphabetized encyclopedias in their own languages were generally well-connected scholars. In their endeavours, they tended to follow the model of already existing works. The different languages in Europe may have been homogenous, hence isolated, areas, but they were also open book markets for all kinds of cultural and scholarly transfer processes. The makers of the encyclopedias had the intellectual, personal, and financial capacity to successfully realize elaborate book projects, such as multivolume encyclopedias, either by themselves or in cooperation with like-minded colleagues. Regarding their social status, they were all roughly the same age – for example, the team working on the second encyclopedia in Dutch were all born in the 1660s and 1670s. They came from similar backgrounds, and their careers as students and scholars were very alike. They all spoke several languages, and they were either theologians, (national) historians, or scholars of law or medicine. They were all also writers and translators. Finally, when writing their dedications, these "producers" took care to include instructions regarding the reception of the encyclopedias. They thus provided an abundance of information about the works in question. Not only did they explain their encyclopedic projects in these dedications, which had the character of announcements, but they put them in a context with previous works, on whose scientific validity they also commented. They took stock of revisions and the resulting improvements as well as the goals of each specific work and its presumed target audience. The readers could (and still can) also read about contributing authors, project delays, subscription rates, and sales prices.

Not only the frontispieces with engravings designed and executed by artists, but also the elaborately printed title pages, dedications, and prefaces all focused on wooing readers and informing them about the breadth and themes of the general knowledge presented. As such, these paratexts directed readers' attention toward those new aspects that made each new encyclopedic work valuable to the educated public of its native country. While Luïscius – as well as van Hoogstraten, Brouërius,

and Schuër – proudly heralded their "improved and expanded" rendi-
tions of Moréri, Bayle, and Buddeus, Buys criticized his predecessors
respectfully but boldly, making his own intellectual achievements clear.
For all of them (and the general public), the process of knowledge transfer through the translating and editing of works from one language and
culture to another – integrating comparable works, and enriching the
basic text created in this manner with specialized literature on the history
of the country – enriched the original works rather than simply revising
what was already known.

Although the editors and authors of these encyclopedias consistently
stressed on their title pages the affinity between their new works and the
encyclopedias before them – "look, these are our famous forerunners,
which we have improved significantly!" – the overlapping content shared
by the different encyclopedic projects was not at first obvious due to
their clearly visible "national" differences. As can be illustrated with the
example of the Moréri "family" of German, Swiss, Dutch, English, and
other translations, this overlapping was instead a tangle of roots below
the surface that constantly produced new offshoots. The translation of
already published encyclopedias into the different national languages
primarily meant revising excerpts and adapting the content for each new
country to various degrees. A retranslation into the original language
would not have reproduced the original book. Instead, the adaptation,
revision, and enrichment of the original articles created an entirely new
work and new reality of knowledge. While the Leipziger Lexikon from
1709 may have been wrong about camels being native to Switzerland, one
Swiss camel – in the form of the mascot of the Zunft zum Kämbel (guild
of the camel), founded in the fourteenth century in Zurich – lives on to
this day.

Translated by Michelle Miles and Ingo Maerker

NOTES

1 The allegory of the camel and the eye of the needle is recorded in the three
   synoptic gospels (Matthew 19:24; Mark 10:25; Luke 18:25), but there are
   also variations in the Babylonian Talmud and the Koran.

2 Entry for "Schweitz/Schweitzerland" (Switzerland), in *Allgemeines Historisches
   Lexicon*, preface by Johann Franz Buddeus (hereafter referred to as the
   "Leipziger Lexikon"), 1st ed. (Leipzig, 1709), vols. 3–4 (in one volume),
   401–2. For more on criticism of the false "camels," see *Neu-vermehrtes*

Historisch und Geographisches Allgemeines Lexicon, preface by Jacob Christoph Iselin (hereafter referred to as the "Basler Lexikon") (Basel, 1726–7), vol. 3 (1726), preface, 12.

3 The second edition of the Leipziger Lexikon was published as *Allgemeines Historisches Lexicon … andere und vermehrte Auflage,* preface by Johann Franz Buddeus, 4 vols. (Leipzig, 1722).

4 The first edition of the Basler Lexikon was published in 1726–7 and included a preface by the theologian Jakob Christoph Iselin (1681–1737), who taught history and from 1711 dogmatics at the University of Basel. He was also the director of the university library. The second edition included four volumes and two supplemental volumes (Basel, 1728–44). The third edition consisted of six volumes (1742–4). Special emphasis was put on the fact that the content of the encyclopedia had been "rewritten and expanded upon, especially in regard to the issues concerning Switzerland, its towns and regions, and the neighbouring countries." In this context Johann Rudolf von Waldkirch (1678–1757), an expert in constitutional law from Bern, played a huge role. See Ina Ulrike Paul, 2007, "Niemals ohne Gewähr. Über die Quellen nationaler Eigen- und Fremdbilder in europäischen Enzyklopädien und Universallexika," in *Allgemeinwissen und Gesellschaft,* ed. Paul Michel, Madeleine Herren, and Martin Rüesch (Aachen), 195–225, e-book, www.enzyklopaedie.ch/kongress/publikation.htm.

5 In his preface to the first edition of the Leipziger Lexikon, Buddeus referred to the ninth edition of the *Le Grand Dictionaire Historique* in four volumes (Amsterdam, The Hague, 1702), which contains the following addendum: "Neuvième Édition où l'on a mis le Supplément dans le même ordre Alphabetique, corrigé les fautes nsure [*sic*] dans le Dictionnaire Critique de Mr. Bayle & grand nombre d'autres & Ajouté Plus De 600 Articles et Remarques." Buddeus particularly praised the "Dutch" editions of Moréri, especially the sixth and seventh editions, which had been supervised by Jean Le Clerc, and the eighth, in which Pierre Bayle had taken part. See Pierre Bayle, 1697, *Dictionnaire Historique et Critique,* 2 vols. (Rotterdam, 1697); and Barthélemy d'Herbelot de Molainville, *Bibliothèque orientale, ou Dictionaire universel …* (Paris).

6 The name "Buddeus" was the Latinized version of the family name "Budde."

7 The new edition of Bayle's *Dictionnaire* was published at the same time as the ninth edition of Moréri's *Le Grand Dictionnaire Historique* was published in Amsterdam, in 1702. The latter had the addendum "corrigé les fautes censurées dans le Dictionnaire Critique [*sic*] de Mr. Bayle."

8 For more on this, see Wiep van Bunge, 2003, "Netherlands: An Overview," in *Encyclopedia of the Enlightenment,* vol. 3, ed. Alan Charles Kors (Oxford),

163–9; van Bunge, 2003, "Introduction: The Early Enlightenment in
the Dutch Republic, 1650–1750," in *The Early Enlightenment in the Dutch
Republic, 1650–1750*, ed. van Bunge (Leiden), 1–16; and Madeleine Van
Strien-Chardonneau, 1997, "Hollande," in *Dictionnaire européen des lumières*,
ed. Michel Delon (Paris), 547–50. The quotation is from Pierre Bayle,
Dictionnaire européen des lumières, ed. Delon, 550.

 9 Arnold Miller, 1981, "Louis Moréri's Grand dictionnaire historique," in
*Notable Encyclopedias of the Seventeenth and Eighteenth Centuries: Nine Predecessors
of the Encyclopédie*, ed. Frank A. Kafker, vol. 194 of *Studies on Voltaire and the
Eighteenth Century* (Oxford), 13–52.

10 Abraham George Luïscius, 1724–37, *Het Algemeen Historisch, Geographisch, en
Genealogisch Woordenboek …*, 8 vols. (The Hague, Delft), hereafter referred to
as "Luïscius's *Algemeen Woordenboek*."

11 The law scholar and lexicographer Abraham George Luïscius (born in 1693
in Xanten, died after 1740) was enrolled in the register of the University of
Duisburg on 24 September 1703. He probably also studied at the University
of Leiden (Leyden). Luiscius published a Dutch translation of *The History
of the Most Serene House of Brunswick-Lunenburgh*, which had been published
anonymously by David Jones, under the title *Historie des doorluchtigste Huize
van Brunswyk-Lunenburg … Uit het Engelsch vertaald, uitgebreid en vermeerdert
door A. G. Luiscius* (Amsterdam, 1716). On 24 June 1734 he became a
foreign member of the Royal Prussian Society (Academy) of the Sciences in
Berlin; from 1732 to 1739 he was a Prussian resident and special envoy to
the States General in The Hague as well as Royal Prussian domain council.
In 1739, he was dismissed due to embezzlement. He attempted suicide and
lost all of his offices. For more on the Royal Prussian Society (Academy)
of the Sciences in Berlin, see www.bbaw.de (under "Vorgängerakademien"
[previous institutions]). See also Abraham Jacob van der Aa, 1865,
Biographisch Woordenboek der Nederlanden, vol. 11 (Haarlem), 718–19, www
.dbnl.org/tekst/aa__001biog13_01/aa__001biog13_01_1512.php#ll496.

12 "Report of van de Boekverkoopers," in Luïscius's *Algemeen Woordenboek*, vol. 1
(1724), n.p.

13 "O Nederlanders! Komt, doet nu en grote stap, / In 't huis der wetenschap,
/ En reikt Luïscius een krans van Lauwerlover / Voor zynen yver over."
Those are the four last verses of Schim's laudation "Op het Algemeen,
Historisch, Geographisch en Genealogisch Woordenboek, door den Heere
A.G. Luïscius, Rechtsgel." For more on Hendrik Schim (1695–1742), see
www.dbnl.org/auteurs/auteur.php?id=schi017 (accessed 27 July 2020).

14 "Berigt [*sic*] van den Drukker," in Luïscius's *Algemeen Woordenboek*,
vol. 8 (1737), n.p. A methodological and theoretical evaluation

of the lists of subscribers is discussed by Alexander Sigelen,
2002, "Freunde und Mäzene, Vermittler und Rezipienten –
Subskribenten- und Pränumerantenverzeichnisse als Quellen zur
Sozial- und Rezeptionsgeschichte der Volksaufklärung," in *Jahrbuch
für Kommunikationsforschung* 4: 52–103; Reinhard Wittmann, 1977,
"Subskribenten- und Pränumerantenverzeichnisse als lesersoziologische
Quelle," in *Buch und Leser. Vorträge des ersten Jahrestreffens des Wolfenbütteler
Arbeitskreises für Geschichte des Buchwesens, 13./14. Mai 1976*, ed. Herbert
Göpfert, vol. 1 of *Schriften des Wolfenbütteler Arbeitskreises für Geschichte des
Buchwesens* (Hamburg), 125–59.

15 David van Hoogstraten, Matthæus Brouërius van Nidek, and Jan Lodewyk
Schuër, 1725–33, *Groot Algemeen Historisch, Geographisch, Genealogisch, en
Oordeelkundig Woordenboek …*, 10 vols. (Amsterdam). The first volume of the
Groot Algemeen Woordenboek came out in 1725 after its initiator, the poet and
writer David van Hoogstraten (1658–1724), who was a physician by trade,
had already died. The second editor, the law scholar and poet Matthæus
Brouërius van Nidek (1677–1742), quit his position as editor after the
second volume was published. The trained historian and editor, translator,
and compiler Jan Lodewijk Schuër (roughly 1698–1740) took over the role
of sole editor under Brouërius's supervision.

16 "Voorreden van de Boekverkopers aan den Lezer," in van Hoogstraten/
Brouërius, 1725, *Groot Algemeen Woordenboek*, 1: n.p. The consortium of
booksellers included Brunel, Weststein, Waesberge, de Coup, and Humbert
from Amsterdam; Willem van de Water from Utrecht; Samuel Luchtmans
from Leiden (Leyden); and van Dole, Vaillant, and the widow A. Moetjens
in The Hague.

17 1733, "Aanspraak van Jan Lodewyk Schuër tot den bescheiden Lezer," in
Groot Algemeen Woordenboek, 10: n.p.

18 David van Hoogstraten (1658–1724) was born in Rotterdam, studied
medicine in Leiden, and initially practised as a physician in Dordrecht.
That his practice was not very successful made it easier for him to pursue
his passion for literature, and he became a teacher at the local Latin school.
After moving to Amsterdam, he was vice rector of the local Latin school
until 1721–2. A poet and writer himself, he also worked as a translator,
editor, and biographer of Dutch neo-Latin poets. This became the cause of
a strident intellectual dispute (1713–16) between van Hoogstraten and Jean
Le Clerc (1657–1736), accessed 22 February 2013, www.dbnl.org/auteurs
/auteur.php?id=hoog002. See also Gijsbert Rutten (met medewerking van
Michiel Roscam Abbing), 2005, "De biograaf gebiografeerd: De vele levens
van David van Hoogstraten (1658–1724)," in *Voortgang: Jaarboek voor de*

neerlandistik, 23: 145–76, accessed 27 July 2020, www.dbnl.org/tekst
/_voo004200501_01/_voo004200501_01_0006.php.

19 The Remonstrant theologian and philosopher Jean Le Clerc (1657–1736)
was born in Geneva and taught in Amsterdam. He was in charge of the sixth
and seventh editions of Moréri's *Grand Dictionnaire* (Amsterdam, The Hague,
Utrecht, 1694). He also published *Histoire Des Provinces-Unies Des Pays-Bas* …,
4 vols. (Amsterdam, 1723–28). Johann Franz Buddeus (1667–1729), the
(Protestant) editor of the Leipziger Lexikon from 1709, specifically refers to
these "Dutch editions," which he held in high regard. See Buddeus, 1709,
Allgemeines Historisches Lexicon, vols. 1 and 2 (A–G) (Leipzig), preface, n.p.

20 Bert Kolkman has written an excellent online biography (including an
annotated bibliography) of the scholar Matthæus Brouërius van Nidek, who
also worked as a barrister for the admiralty in Amsterdam; accessed 27 July
2020, www.historischetopografie.nl/brouerius/levensloop3a.pdf; www
.historischetopografie.nl/brouerius/levensloop.htm; J.D. van der Giesens
Biographie, www.historischetopografie.nl/brouerius/levensloop3a.pdf; and
http://oldcowz.nl/De-Brou-rius-van-Nidek-Dynastie/.

21 According to Kolkman the two accused each other of several faults,
including supposed breaches of copyright ("inbreuk op octrooien").

22 Frans Halma, 1725, *Tooneel der Vereenigde Nederlanden, En Onderhorige
Landschappen, …, Algemeen, Historisch, Genealogisch, en Staatkundig
Woordenboek, Vervolgt door M. Brouërius van Nidek* (Amsterdam). In his
preface to the *Tooneel*, Brouërius writes that Halma had begun to write an
encyclopedic work in alphabetical order about twenty years before Moréri's
work had become a model for this: "Den yvren [= ijverigen] François
Halma, geen der minste letterkundigen zyner eeuwe, heeft het voor ruim
twintigh jaren gelust, hier van eenen proef te nemen naar den reex van
't A B C, op het spoor, by andere volken loffelyk ingeslagen, inzonderheit
heeft hem hier toe het algemeen, historisch en geographisch Woordenboek
van Lodewyk Moreri, in de fransche tale ontworpen, de aanleidinge
gegeben en aangemoedigt" (2). (A score of years ago, the assiduous
François Halma, a by no means unimportant scholar in his day, took it
upon himself to attempt this in the order of the A, B, C after the manner
meritoriously adopted by other nations, in which task Louis Moreri's Great
Historical, Geographical and Poetical Dictionary served him particularly
for model and encouragement). Halma finished the work up to the letter
W, and Brouërius completed it and published it. Brouërius also wrote a
detailed biography of Halma (1653–1722). For more on Halma, accessed 20
July 2020, www.dbnl.org/auteurs/auteur.php?id=halm002 and www.dbnl
.org/tekst/hait001repe01_01/hait001repe01_01_0304.php and https://
www.dbnl.org/tekst/bran038biog01_01/bran038biog01_01_1702.php.

23 In 1725 alone, Brouërius published two other works in Amsterdam in
    addition to the *Groot Algemeen Woordenboek*. These were *Analecta medii aevi:
    Ofte oude en nooit voorrheen gedrukte Nederlandsche geschiedenis boeken, 1. deel,
    waar in gevonden worden Sicke Beninga Chronickel der Vriescher landen; Sybe
    Jarichs korte cronyck, tracteerende van de herkomste der Vreesen; Eens onbekenden
    schryvers Cleyne cronica van de Groninger omlanden; Tjalling Aykema's Cronyske
    vaan de ommelanden; Opgezamelt en uitgegeven / door Matthaeus Brouërius van
    Nidek* and the book of engravings *Het verheerlykt Watergraefs- of Diemer-Meer
    by de Stadt Amsterdam vertoont in verscheide vermakelyke Gezichten … / Geteekent
    door Daniel Stopendael en beschreven door Matthaeus Brouërius van Niedek.* The
    latter work was republished as a new edition in 1727 in Amsterdam, with
    an elaborate text by Brouërius, under the title *Kabinet Van Nederlandsche En
    Kleefsche Outheden … En in 300 verscheide printtafereelen vertoont door Abraham
    Rademaker.* It also included Dutch, English, and French subtitles for the
    etchings.
24 "Voorreden van de Boekverkopers aan den Lezer," in van Hoogstraten/
    Brouërius, 1725, *Groot Algemeen Woordenboek*, 1: n.p. For more on
    Hermannus van de Wall (1672–1733), accessed 27 July 2020, www.dbnl
    .org/tekst/molh003nieu05_01/molh003nieu05_01_1343.php. For more on
    Gerardus Outhof (1673–1733), accessed 27 July 2020, www.dbnl.org/tekst
    /aa__001biog17_01/aa__001biog17_01_0540.php.
25 Johannes (Jan) Haverkamp, accessed 25 January 2014, www.dbnl.org
    /auteurs/auteur.php?id=have011; and Arnold Henrik Westerhof (sometime
    before 1700, roughly 1737), accessed 20 July 2020, www.dbnl.org/auteurs
    /auteur.php?id=have011.
26 *Huishoudelyk woordboek, vervattende vele middelen om zyn goed te vermeerderen,
    en zyne gezondheid te behouden …, door M. Noel Chomel, Priester en Pastoor der
    Parochie van St. Vincent te Lyon. In 't Nederduits vertaald, in orde geschikt, en
    vermeerderd met nuttige Artikelen, door de Heeren Jan Lodewyk Schuër Uitgever
    van 't Groot Algemeen Woordboek, A. H. Westerhof, V.D.M. en Rector der Latynse
    Scholen te GOUDA, en zeker Liefhebber, En met Kunstplaten verrykt,* 2 vols.
    (Leiden, Amsterdam: 1743), accessed 27 July 2020, www.dbnl.org/tekst
    /chom003huis01_01/chom003huis01_01_0001.php.
27 Jacques Proust, 2005, "Sur la route des encyclopédies: Paris, Yverdon,
    Leeuwarden, Edo (1751–1781)," in *L'Encyclopédie d'Yverdon et sa résonance
    européenne: Contextes, contenues, continuités,* ed. Jean Daniel Candaux,
    Alain Cernuschi, Clorinda Donato, and Jens Häseler, vol. 7 of *Travaux
    sur la Suisse des Lumières* (Geneva), 443–68. Proust is able to prove that
    the Japanese encyclopedists deliberately chose the Dutch Chomel
    edition and none of the extended editions by Jacques Alexandre de
    Chalmot (452f). For more, see Jacques Proust, 2001, "Voie de passage de

l'Encyclopédie vers le Japon: La Hollande," in *L'Encyclopédie. Du réseau au livre et du livre au réseau. Textes réunis et présentés par Robert Morrissey et Philippe Roger* (Paris), 103–14.

28 See Wikipedia article on Yoshio Kōsaku (1724–1800), accessed 27 July 2020, http://de.wikipedia.org/wiki/Yoshio_K%C5%8Dsaku.

29 See Wikipedia article on Sakumana Shōzan (1811–64), accessed 27 July 2020, http://en.wikipedia.org/wiki/Sakuma_Sh%C5%8Dzan. For more on this (especially Chomel and Jacques-Alexandre de Chalmot, who later published Chomel's *Huishoudelyk woordboek*), see J. MacLean, 1974, "The Introduction of Books and Scientific Instruments into Japan, 1712–1854," *Japanese Studies in the History of Science* 13: 22ff.

30 In 1727, Schuër translated Johann Hübner's *Lexicon Genealogicum Portatile: Das ist: Ein Verzeichnis aller itzt-lebenden Hohen Häupter in der gantzen Welt, Welches man allezeit bey sich tragen kann,* 1st ed. (Hamburg, Frankfurt, Leipzig: Felginer, 1727) into Dutch as *Johan Hubner de Jonge, Beknopt genealogisch woordenboek, behelzende alle thans in leven zynde keizere, koningen, keur- en andere vorsten … van de gehele wereldt, … Uit het Hoogduitsch overgezet, en uit de overgezondene berechten van … Johan Hubner … en eigene aantekeningen tot dezen tydt vervolgt* (Amsterdam: Bos, 1727).

31 A.H. Westerhovius, 1732, *De Staats- en Koeranten-Tolk of Woordenboek der Geleerden en Ongeleerden … in het Hoogduitsch uytgegeeven; en met en Voorrede verzelt door den Heere Johannes Hubner … En nu volgens den twaalfden druk vertaalt,* 2 vols. (Leiden). The second volume consists of the *Kunstwoordenboek* attributed to Hübner, which was probably a translation of Paul Jakob Marperger's encyclopedia, which Johann Hübner had published: *Curieuses Natur- Kunst- Gewerk- und Handlungs-Lexicon* (Leipzig, 1712).

32 David van Hoogstraten fell into an inner-city canal in the fog in Amsterdam, probably Geldersekade today. For more on this, see Kolkman's online Brouërius biography, www.bertkolkman.nl/brouerius/brouerius.htm.

33 Jan Lodewijk Schuër (born in Hamburg 1698, died sometime after 1743) lived in Amsterdam in 1724 with his father and married a woman from Amsterdam. When he became a citizen of Amsterdam on 11 January 1725, he stated "translator" as his profession. E.O.G. Haitsma Mulier and G.A.C. van der Lem, 1990, *Repertorium van geschiedschrijvers in Nederland 1500–1800* (The Hague: Nederlands Historisch Genootschap), accessed 26 July 2020, www.dbnl.org/tekst/hait001repe01_01/hait001repe01_01_0688.php. For more on the collaboration between Brouërius and Schuër, see Kolkman's online Brouërius biography, www.bertkolkman.nl/brouerius/brouerius.htm.

34 Jan Lodewijk Schuër, *Beknopte beschrijving van Dantzig* (Amsterdam, 1735); *Algemeene Nederlandsche geschiedenissen, zedert het Twaalfjarige bestandt van het*

jaar 1621 tot de Uitrechtse Vreede in 't jaar 1713 gesloten, 3 vols. (Amsterdam, 1742); and *Nederlands merkwaardigste gebeurtenissen sedert bijna twee eeuwen, beginnende in 1555 en eindigende met den dood van Willem IV van Oranjen*, 3 vols. (Amsterdam, 1752; 2nd ed. Utrecht, 1767).

35 Egbert Buys, 1769–78, *Nieuw en Volkomen Woordenboek van Konsten en Weetenschappen: Bevattende alle de Takken der Nuttige Kennis …*, 10 vols. (Amsterdam). Buys (roughly 1725–69) had already died when the first volume came out. That volume was reviewed in *Historisches Journal von Mitgliedern des Königlichen Historischen Instituts zu Göttingen* 700: 7 (1776), accessed 27 July 2020, https://reader.digitale-sammlungen.de/de/fs1/object/display/bsb10738204_00005.html.

36 For more on the two moral weeklies by Buys – *De Algemeene Spectator* (Amsterdam, 1748; reprinted Utrecht, 1775), and *De Hollandsche Wysgeer* (Amsterdam, 1759–63) – see Hugo Sebastiaan Okel, 2004, *Der Bürger, die Tugend und die Republik. "Bürgerliche Leitkultur" in den Niederlanden im 18. Jahrhundert im Spiegel der Moralischen Wochenschriften*, PhD diss., University of Bonn. See also *De waereld in 't klein, of De spoedige reiziger, geevende een beknopt verhaal van al het geene in alle landen, nuttig … is* (The Hague, 1762; 2nd ed. 1770); *Historie van het doorluchtig huis van Brunswyk*, vol. 1 (Amsterdam, 1762); and *Volkomen Konstwoordenboek, bevattende eene genoegzame verklaring van alle woorden, ontleend van de Grieksche, Spaansche, Fransche, Hoogduitsche en Nederduitsche Talen, die men gebruikt om eenige Konst, Wetenschap, Gewoonten, Ziekten, Geneesmiddel, Plant, Bloem, Vrugt, Gereedschap, Werktuig enz. te benoemen*, 2 vols. (Utrecht, 1768).

37 For more about Buys's life, see Mulier and van der Lem, *Repertorium*, www.dbnl.org/tekst/hait001repe01_01/hait001repe01_01_0137.php.

38 Egbert Buys, 1753, *Verhaal der procedures tusschen Alida van der streng en Egbert Buys* (Amsterdam: Jacobus Haffman; Utrecht: H. van Kamen) (bound with *Memorie van rechten en de zelfsverdedigin van Mr. Carel Philip van Cuylenborgh*, 2nd ed., and *Egbert Buys Ontmaskert*, part 1 [Utrecht: Anzelmus Muntendam, 1754]).

39 "Bericht van den Uitgeever," in Buys, *Nieuw en Volkomen Woordenboek*, vol. 10 (1778).

40 The alphabetic list of names of those who took part in the second subscription comprises six pages. "Alphabetische Naam-Lyst der Heeren, Welke Deel genomen hebben in de Tweede Inschyving van dit Werk," in Buys, *Nieuw en Volkomen Woordenboek*, vol. 4 (1772), III–VIII.

41 Heinrich Martin Gottfried Köster and Ludwig Julius Friedrich Höpfner (and Johann Friedrich Roos, starting with vol. 18), 1778–1804, *Deutsche Encyclopädie oder allgemeines Real-Wörterbuch aller Künste und Wissenschaften*, 23 vols. (A–Ky) (Frankfurt am Main).

42 Paul Michel and Ruth Affolter-Nydegger, "Frontispizien von Enzyklopädien,"
    accessed 16 February 2021, www.enzyklopaedie.ch/fronti/frontispizien
    _hauptseite.html. The website is marked with the initials P[aul] M[ichel]
    and was created in 2007 and last updated 14 October 2020. For information
    about the interdisciplinary research project *Allgemeinwissen und Gesellschaft.*
    Enzyklopädien als Indikatoren für Veränderungen der gesellschaftlichen Bedeutung
    von Wissen, Bildung und Information, project "Allgemeinwissen und
    Gesellschaft," see www.enzyklopaedie.ch (accessed 27 July 2020).

43 The example here is the title page of Luïscius's *Algemeen Woordenboek.*
    The title lists the encyclopedia's key elements as general knowledge,
    historiography, geography, and genealogy. The topics presented can be
    seen in the long list of keywords on the title page – like "secular and
    church history," the "history and geography of countries," "genealogy,"
    and, finally, "customs and traditions." The last sentence mentions the
    "unique selling point" of this work and can be loosely translated as: "All
    content was assembled (meaning compiled) from the best encyclopedias
    of other nations in alphabetical order and supplemented with a great
    number of new articles that could not be found in any other encyclopedia.
    These expanded the areas of historiography, chronology, and geodesy
    with sources and publications by the most excellent [alleruitmuntendste]
    authors."

44 The credit for finding the name of the artist Bernard Picart (1673–1733)
    goes to Karin Gludovatz, professor of early modern European art history
    (fourteenth to eighteenth centuries) at the Freie Universität Berlin. She
    also helped me find the engraving entitled *Allegorie waarin Geschiedenis de*
    historie schrijft as a separate print (1726), as well as the records on it in the
    collections of the Rijksmuseum Amsterdam, www.rijksmuseum.nl/nl
    /collectie/RP-P-OB-77.758. Prof. Gludovatz pointed out that at least one
    French edition existed (apparently also a separate print for the French
    market) whose inscription differs from the Dutch (e-mail message to the
    author, 7 February 2014). For more on Picart, see Cornelia Logemann
    and Ulrich Pfisterer, 2012, "Götterbilder und Götzendiener in der Frühen
    Neuzeit: Bernard Picarts 'Cérémonies et coutumes religieuses de tous
    les peuples du monde' und das Konzept der Ausstellung," in *Götterbilder*
    und Götzendiener in der Frühen Neuzeit. Europas Blick auf fremde Religionen,
    exhibition catalogue, University of Heidelberg, ed. Maria Effinger,
    Cornelia Logemann, and Ulrich Pfister in cooperation with Margit
    Krenn (Heidelberg), 9–21; and Lynn Hunt, Margaret Jacob, and Wijnand
    Mijnhardt, eds., 2009, *Bernard Picart and the First Global Vision of Religion* (Los
    Angeles).

45 "Alles na de orde van het Alfabet uit de allerbeste Woordenboeken van andere natien zamengesteld, en met een grote menigte van Artikels, voornamely ten opzicht van de zaken van deze Nederlanden, in gene andere Woordenboeken te vinden, uit echte Berichten en Bewyzen vermeerdert," Luïscius's *Algemeen Woordenboek*, vol. 1 (1737), title page.

46 For more on this, see Ina Ulrike Paul, 2013, "'Dieses Universallexicon hat seines Gleichen nicht' – oder doch? Zedlers enzyklopädische Vorläufer in Europa," in *Die gesammelte Welt. Wissensformen und Wissenswandel in Zedlers Universal-Lexicon*, ed. Kai Lohsträter and Flemming Schock, vol. 19 of *Schriften und Zeugnisse zur Buchgeschichte* (Wiesbaden), 9–16. The quote "*por lo que mira à España*" can be found in Juan de la Serna, 1750, *Diccionario Geographico* (Madrid), vol. 1, title page.

47 Thomas Corneille, 1708, *Dictionnaire Universel, Géographique et Historique ...*, 3 vols. (Paris), here the entries for "Pays-Bas out Germanie Inférieure," and "Provinces Unies," vol. 3 (70–1, 180–2); Jean-Baptiste d'Audiffret, 1694, *Histoire et Géographie Ancienne et Moderne, Tome Second, Qui contient La France, Les Pays-Bas, Les Provinces-Unies, La Suisse, & la Savoye* (Paris: Chez Jean-Baptiste Coignard), 525–78.

48 The book *Annales des Provinces-Unies* (The Hague, 1726) by the Protestant scholar Jacques Basnage de Beauval (1653–1723), who immigrated to the Netherlands after the Edict of Nantes, was published by Charles Le Vier. The work referred to here, *État présent de la Republique des Provinces-Unies, et des pais qui en dependent* (The Hague, 1729), by the French writer and translator François Michel Janiçon (1674–1730), was published by Johannes van Duren. For more on Janiçon, accessed 27 July 2020, https://zs.thulb .uni-jena.de/receive/jportal_person_00015651?XSL.q=Janicon.

49 Isaac van Hoornbeek (1655–1727) held the highest office in the government of the republic of the United Netherlands from 1720 to 1727 as the grand pensionary (prime minister) of Holland and West Friesland.

50 Entry for "Bayle, Pierre," in Luïscius's *Algemeen Woordenboek*, vol. 2 (1725), 160–81. The *Dictionnaire* is commented on as follows: "Dit woordenboek is niet algemeen, gelyk andere woordenboeken, Bayle heeft uit de oude en nieuwe vermaarden eenigen uitgekipt, en met wydlopige aanmerkingen en aanhalingen, meest in zyne noten onder de artikelen, verrykt" (180). (This dictionary is not general, similar to other dictionaries, Bayle has picked out a few from the old and the new famous ones, and enriched with a lot of remarks and citations, mostly in his notes under the articles.)

51 Antoine Furetière (1619–1688), *Dictionnaire universel, contenant généralement tous les mots françois* (The Hague/Rotterdam: Leers 1690); and *Dictionnaire universel ..., Corr. et augm. par Henri Basnage de Beauval. Nouvelle éd. revû,*

corr. et considérablement augm. par Jean Baptiste Brutel de la Rivière, 4 vols. (The Hague, 1727).

52 "Moréri, Lodewyk," in Luïscius's *Algemeen Woordenboek*, vol. 6 (1732), 485. What speaks against the idea of self-promotion, however, is that the Venetian cartographer Vincenzo Maria Coronelli OFM, with his *Bibliotheca universale sacro-profana*, 7 vols. (A–Caque) (Venice, 1701–06), was not one of the in-house authors, but still had an entry: "Coronelli, Vincentius," Luïscius's *Algemeen Woordenboek*, vol. 3 (1726), 96. Along with Moréri's *Dictionnaire*, Coronelli's *Bibliotheca* is one of the earliest encyclopedias in a national language and was originally planned to have forty-five volumes.

53 "De Compagnie Boekverkopers, Uitgevers van dit Woordenboek (Amsterdam, den 15 October 1725): Opdragt aan den edelen grootachtbaren Here Mr. Jan Trip, Here van Berkenrode ...," in Hoogstraten/Brouërius, *Groot Algemeen Woordenboek*, vol. 1 (1725), 6 pages (n.p.). Jan Trip van Berkenrode (1664–1732) was the regent of Amsterdam until 1727.

54 "[N]aardien wy den arbeitdt van die uitheemsche schriften in het volvoeren van dit werk te bate genomen, en gebouwd hebben op de gronden, die andere gelegd hadden, de byzonderheden, die alleen ons landt raken, daar by doende uit onze eigene schryvers / Wy twyffelen niet, of dat werk zal onze land-en taal-genoten aangenaam zyn, ter oorzake van zyne nutheit" (As we have made use of foreign texts in accomplishing this work and built on foundations laid by others [and] taken the peculiarities that affect our country alone from our own writers / we have no doubt that this work will be both useful and pleasing to our fellow countrymen and Dutch speakers) ("De Compagnie Boekverkopers, Uitgevers van dit Woordenboek).

55 Jacques Bernard, 1716, *Supplément Aux Anciennes Editions Du Grand Dictionnaire Historique De Mre. Louis Moreri* [...], 2 vols. (Amsterdam: Pierre Brunel, R. & G. Wetstein, David Mortier, Pierre De Coup; The Hague: Adrian Moetjens, L.& H. Van Dole; Utrecht: Guillaume van de Water).

56 Article on "Vereenigde Provincien, (De)," in van Hoogstraten/Schuër, 1733, *Groot Algemeen Woordenboek*, 10: 47–59.

57 The text on the title page of the *Nieuw en Volkomen Woordenboek* reads "Alles verzameld uit de beste Schryvers in alle Taalen, en met een menigte van nieuwe Artykelen vermeerdt, door Egbert Buys" (Everything was compiled by the finest writers of all languages and enriched with many new articles by Egbert Buys).

58 Buys, "Voorreden," in *Nieuw en Volkomen Woordenboek*, vol. 5. Buys lists only different types of sources – including encyclopedias, treatises, memoirs, and language dictionaries – saying these had all contributed "materials"

(*Materialen*) for constructing the "new building," which is why he says he does not mention them here, but in the articles themselves.

59 Buys, "Voorreden," in *Nieuw en Volkomen Woordenboek*, vol. 6: "als zynde niet alleen eendvoudiger [*sic*] en natuurlyker, maar ook volkomener en naauwkeuriger uitgewerkt."

60 Buys, "Voorreden," in *Nieuw en Volkomen Woordenboek*, vol. 7: "Het tot hier toe gezegde is hoofdzakelyk den Inhoud der Inleiding van het Engelsch Werk, dat ons allerbyzonderst, een ryke Stoffe van Artykelen verschaft heeft."

61 Temple Henry Croker, Thomas Williams, and Samuel Clark, 1764–6, *The Complete Dictionary of Arts and Sciences*, 3 vols. (London, Cambridge, Dublin). I thank Jeff Loveland for generously pointing out this encyclopedia to me in April 2013. See his "Two Partial English-Language Translations of the *Encyclopédie*: The Encyclopedias of John Barrow and Temple Henry Croker," in *British-French Exchanges in the Eighteenth Century*, ed. Kathleen Hardesty Doig and Dorothy Medlin (Cambridge, Newcastle, 2007), 168–87.

62 Advertisement in Croker, Williams, and Clark, *Complete Dictionary*: "It is not, however, our Intention to depreciate the Works of others in order to recommend our own; but we will venture to promise, that every thing valuable in Mr. Chambers' Cyclopedia, and the other Works off [*sic*] that Kind, particularly the Encyclopedie published at Paris, shall be contained in this Dictionary of Arts and Sciences, that we have extracted the greater Part of our Articles from Original Authors; being sensible that the Authority of any Work of the Writers from whom it is collected; And our Readers may be assured, that in such Articles as are extracted from Foreign Authors, all the Difficulties and Obscurities that occur in the Original will be removed and explained in their respective Translations" (n.p.).

63 Buys, "Voorreden," in *Nieuw en Volkomen Woordenboek*, vol. 7: "Het tot hier toe gezegde is hoofdzakelyk den Inhoud der Inleiding van het Engelsch Werk, dat ons allerbyzonderst, een ryke Stoffe van Artykelen verschaft heeft." (That which has been said thus far is principally the contents of the introduction to the English work that provided us with particularly rich material in the way of articles.)

64 Entry for "Hollandsche Waaren" in Buys, *Nieuw en Volkomen Woordenboek*, vol. 5 (1773), 279.

65 "Nederlanden, (De Vereenigde)," in Buys, *Nieuw en Volkomen Woordenboek*, vol. 7 (1775), 655–60.

66 *Nieuwe geographie, of aardrijksbeschrijving, door Antoni Fredrik Busching; naar den vierden druk en de medegedeelde nadere vermeerderingen en verbeteringen van den beroemden schrijver, uit het Hoogduitsch vertaald door Jacobus de Jongh Junior* (The Hague, Amsterdam, Utrecht, 1761–n.d.).

67 For more on the typology of authorship in English, French, and German
   encyclopedias, see Jeff Loveland, 2010, "Varieties of Authorship in
   Eighteenth-Century Encyclopedias," *Das Achtzehnte Jahrhundert* 34, no. 1:
   81–102; Hans de Waardt, 2003, "Academic Careers and Scholarly Networks,"
   in *The Early Enlightenment in the Dutch Republic, 1650–1750*, ed. Wiep van
   Bunge (Leiden), 19–38.
68 See "Provincie Unite" in Gianfrancesco Pivati, *Nuovo dizionario, scientifico
   e curioso,* […] (Venice, 1746–51), vol. 7 (1749), 645–6 (after referring to
   Calvinism as "la Religione pretesa riformata"): "Con tutto ciò si è lasciata
   ai Cattolici un ampia libertà di coscienza […]. Evvi innoltre gran numero
   d'altre Religioni o Sette, che vengono tollerate nell'estensione delle
   Terre della Repubblica." (In spite of this, Catholics are given considerable
   latitude of conscience […]. There are, in addition, a large number of other
   religions or sects that are tolerated throughout the republic.)

Bibliography

Primary Sources

Audiffret, Jean-Baptiste d'. 1694. *Histoire et Géographie Ancienne et Moderne, Tome
Second, Qui contient La France, Les Pays-Bas, Les Provinces-Unies, La Suisse, & la
Savoye,* Paris: Chez Jean-Baptiste Coignard.

Bayle, Pierre. 1697. *Dictionnaire Historique et Critique.* 2 vols. Rotterdam: Reinier
Leers.

Bernard, Jacques. 1716. *Supplément Aux Anciennes Editions Du Grand Dictionnaire
Historique De Mre. Louis Moreri* […]. 2 vols. Amsterdam: Pierre Brunel, R. & G.
Wetstein, David Mortier, Pierre De Coup; The Hague: Adrian Moetjens, L.&
H. Van Dole; Utrecht: Guillaume van de Water.

Buddeus, Johann Franz. 1709. *Allgemeines Historisches Lexicon* […].1st ed.
4 vols. Vol. 3–4 in one vol. Leipzig/Frankfurt: Thomas Fritsch. (Second
edition: 1722, *Allgemeines Historisches Lexicon ... andere und vermehrte Auflage,*
preface by Johann Franz Buddeus, 4 vols. Leipzig.)

Busching, Antoni Fredrik. 1761–n.d. *Nieuwe geographie, of aardrijksbeschrijving,
door Antoni Fredrik Busching; naar den vierden druk en de medegedeelde nadere
vermeerderingen en verbeteringen van den beroemden schrijver, uit het Hoogduitsch
vertaald door Jacobus de Jongh Junior.* The Hague/Amsterdam/Utrecht: n.p.

Buys, Egbert. 1753. *Verhaal der procedures tusschen Alida van der streng en Egbert Buys.*
Amsterdam: Jacobus Haffman; Utrecht: H. van Kamen. (Bound with *Memorie van
rechten en de zelfsverdedigin van Mr. Carel Philip van Cuylenborgh,* 2nd ed.)

– 1754. *Egbert Ontmaskert.* Part 1. Utrecht: Anzelmus Muntendam.

– 1762. *Historie van het doorluchtig huis van Brunswyk.* Vol. 1. Amsterdam.
– 1762. *De waereld in't klein, of De spoedige reiziger, geevende een beknopt verhaal van al het geene in alle landen, nuttig* [...] *is.* The Hague. (2nd ed. 1770.)
– 1768. *Volkomen Konstwoordenboek, bevattende eene genoegzame verklaring van alle woorden, ontleend van de Grieksche, Spaansche, Fransche, Hoogduitsche en Nederduitsche Talen, die men gebruikt om eenige Konst, Wetenschap, Gewoonten, Ziekten, Geneesmiddel, Plant, Bloem, Vrugt, Gereedschap, Werktuig enz. te benoemen.* 2 vols. Utrecht.
– 1769–78. *Nieuw en Volkomen Woordenboek van Konsten en Weetenschappen: Bevattende alle de Takken der Nuttige Kennis* [...] 10 vols. Amsterdam: n.p.
Chomel, Noël. 1743. *Huishoudelyk woordboek, vervattende vele middelen om zyn goed te vermeerderen, en zyne gezondheid te behouden* [...], *door M. Noel Chomel, Priester en Pastoor der Parochie van St. Vincent te Lyon. In 't Nederduits vertaald, in orde geschikt, en vermeerderd met nuttige Artikelen, door de Heeren Jan Lodewyk Schuer, Uitgever van 't Groot Algemeen Woordboek, A. H. Westerhof, V.D.M. en Rector der Latynse Scholen te GOUDA, en zeker Liefhebber, En met Kunstplaten verrykt,* 2 vols. Leiden/Amsterdam: Luchtmans, Uytwerf.
Corneille, Thomas. 1708. *Dictionnaire Universel, Géographique et Historique* ... 3 vols. Paris: n.p.
Croker, Temple Henry, Thomas Williams, and Samuel Clark. 1764–6. *The Complete Dictionary of Arts and Sciences.* 3 vols. London, Cambridge, Dublin: J. Wilson and others.
Furetière, Antoine. [1619–88]. 1690. *Dictionnaire universel, contenant généralement tous les mots françois.* The Hague, Rotterdam: Leers; and 1727.
– 1727. *Dictionnaire universel ..., Corr. et augm. par Henri Basnage de Beauval. Nouvelle éd. revû, corr. et considérablement augm. par Jean Baptiste Brutel de la Rivière.* 4 vols. The Hague: n.p.
Halma, Frans. 1725. *Tooneel der Vereenigde Nederlanden, En Onderhorige Landschappen, ..., Algemeen, Historisch, Genealogisch, en Staatkundig Woordenboek, Vervolgt door M. Brouërius van Nidek.* Amsterdam: n.p.
Herbelot de Molainville, Barthélemy d'. 1697. *Bibliothèque Orientale, Ov Dictionaire Universel* [...] Paris: n.p.
Historisches Journal von Mitgliedern des Königlichen Historischen Instituts zu Göttingen 1776 (7): 700. Accessed 27 July 2020. https://reader.digitale-sammlungen .de/de/fs1/object/display/bsb10738204_00005.html.
Hoogstraten, David van, Matthæus Brouërius van Nidek and Jan Lodewyk Schuër. 1725–33. *Groot Algemeen Historisch, Geographisch, Genealogisch, en Oordeelkundig Woordenboek* ... 10 vols. Amsterdam: n.p.
– 1743. *Huishoudelyk woordboek, vervattende vele middelen om zyn goed te vermeerderen, en zyne gezondheid te behouden ..., door M. Noel Chomel, Priester en Pastoor der Parochie van St. Vincent te Lyon. In 't Nederduits vertaald, in orde*

geschikt, en vermeerderd met nuttige Artikelen, door de Heeren Jan Lodewyk Schuer,
Uitgever van 't Groot Algemeen Woordboek, A. H. Westerhof, V.D.M. en Rector der
Latynse Scholen te GOUDA, en zeker Liefhebber, En met Kunstplaten verrykt. 2 vols.
Leiden, Amsterdam: n.p. Accessed 27 July 2020. www.dbnl.org/tekst
/chom003huis01_01/chom003huis01_01_0001.php.

Hübner, Johann. 1727. *Lexicon Genealogicum Portatile: Das ist: Ein Verzeichnis aller*
itzt-lebenden Hohen Häupter in der gantzen Welt, Welches man allezeit bey sich tragen
kann. 1st ed. Hamburg, Frankfurt, Leipzig: Felginer.

Iselin, Jacob Christoph. 1726–27. *Neu-vermehrtes historisch und geographisches*
allgemeines Lexicon […] 6 vols.; 3rd vol. [1726], 37 cm. Basel: Johann
Brandmüller.

Köster, Heinrich Martin Gottfried, and Ludwig Julius Friedrich Höpfner (and
Johann Friedrich Roos, starting with vol. 18). 1778–1804. *Deutsche Encyclopädie*
oder allgemeines Real-Wörterbuch aller Künste und Wissenschaften. 23 vols. (A–Ky).
Frankfurt am Main: n.p.

Luïscius, Abraham George. 1724–37. *Het Algemeen Historisch, Geographisch, en*
Genealogisch Woordenboek … 8 vols. The Hague: Delft.

Pivati, Gianfrancesco. 1749. *Nuovo dizionario, scientifico e curioso* […]. Vol. 7.
[Venice 1746/51].

Review article on Buys, Egbert, *Nieuw en Volkomen Woordenboek: Historisches*
Journal von Mitgliedern des Königlichen Historischen Instituts zu Göttingen 1776
(vol. 7), 87–8. Accessed 27 July 2020. https://books.google.de/books?id
=5OpLAAAAcAAJ&printsec=frontcover&hl=de&source=gbs_ge_summary
_r&cad=0#v=onepage&q&f=false.

Schuër, Jan Lodewijk, trans. 1727. *Johan Hubner de Jonge, Beknopt genealogisch*
woordenboek, behelzende alle thans in leven zynde keizere, koningen, keur- en
andere vorsten … van de gehele wereldt, … Uit het Hoogduitsch overgezet, en uit de
overgezondene berechten van … Johan Hubner … en eigene aantekeningen tot dezen
tydt vervolgt. Amsterdam: Bos.

– 1735. *Beknopte beschrijving van Dantzig.* Amsterdam: n.p.

– 1742. *Algemeene Nederlandsche geschiedenissen, zedert het Twaalfjarige*
bestandt van het jaar 1621 tot de Uitrechtse Vreede in 't jaar 1713 gesloten. 3
vols. Amsterdam: n.p.

– 1752. *Nederlands merkwaardigste gebeurtenissen sedert bijna twee eeuwen,*
beginnende in 1555 en eindigende met den dood van Willem IV van Oranjen. 3 vols.
Amsterdam: n.p. [2nd. ed. Utrecht: n.p., 1767].

Westerhovius, A.J. 1732. *De Staats- en Koeranten-Tolk of Woordenboek der Geleerden*
en Ongeleerden … in het Hoogduitsch uytgegeven en met een Voorede verzelt door
den Heer Johan Hubner … En nu volgens den twaalfden druk vertaalt. 2 vols.
Leiden: n.p.

Secondary Sources

Aa, Abraham Jacob van der. 1865. *Biographisch Woordenboek der Nederlanden.*
  Vol. 11. Harlem: n.p. Accessed 21 April 2020. www.dbnl.org/tekst
  /aa__001biog13_01/aa__001biog13_01_1512.php#11496.
Bunge, Wiep van. 2003. "Introduction: The Early Enlightenment in the
  Dutch Republic, 1650–1750." In *The Early Enlightenment in the Dutch Republic,
  1650–1750,* 1–16. Leiden: Brill.
– 2003. "Netherlands: An Overview." In *Encyclopedia of the Enlightenment,* edited
  by Alan Charles Kors, 3:163–9. Oxford: n.p.
Hunt, Lynn, Margaret Jacob, and Wijnand Mijnhardt, eds. 2009. *Bernard Picart
  and the First Global Vision of Religion.* Los Angeles: n.p.
Logemann, Cornelia, and Ulrich Pfisterer. 2012. "Götterbilder und Götzendiener
  in der Frühen Neuzeit. Bernard Picarts 'Cérémonies et coutumes religieuses
  de tous les peuples du monde' und das Konzept der Ausstellung." In
  *Götterbilder und Götzendiener in der Frühen Neuzeit. Europas Blick auf fremde
  Religionen,* exhibition catalogue, University of Heidelberg, edited by Maria
  Effinger, Cornelia Logemann, and Ulrich Pfister in cooperation with Margit
  Krenn, 9–21. Heidelberg: n.p.
Loveland, Jeff. 2010. "Varieties of Authorship in Eighteenth-Century
  Encyclopedias." *Das Achtzehnte Jahrhundert* 34, no. 1: 81–102.
Michel, Paul, and Ruth Affolter-Nydegger, "Frontispizien von Enzyklopädien."
  Accessed 1 February 2014. www.enzyklopaedie.ch/fronti/frontispizien
  _hauptseite.html.
Mulier, Haitsma, and G.A.C. van der Lem. 1990. *Repertorium van geschiedschrijvers
  in Nederland 1500–1800.* The Haag: Nederlands Historisch Genootschap.
  Accessed 26 July 2014. www.dbnl.org/tekst/hait001repe01_01/hait001repe01
  _01_0688.php.
Okel, Hugo Sebastiaan. 2004. *Der Bürger, die Tugend und die Republik. "Bürgerliche
  Leitkultur" in den Niederlanden im 18. Jahrhundert im Spiegel der Moralischen
  Wochenschriften.* PhD diss., University of Bonn.
Paul, Ina Ulrike. 2007. "Niemals ohne Gewähr. Über die Quellen
  nationaler Eigen- und Fremdbilder in europäischen Enzyklopädien und
  Universallexika." In *Allgemeinwissen und Gesellschaft,* edited by Paul Michel,
  Madeleine Herren, and Martin Rüesch, 195–225. Aachen: Shaker Verlag.
  E-book. Accessed 21 April 2020. www.enzyklopaedie.ch/kongress
  /publikation.htm.
– 2013. "'Dieses Universallexicon hat seines Gleichen nicht' – oder doch?
  Zedlers enzyklopädische Vorläufer in Europa." In *Die gesammelte Welt.
  Wissensformen und Wissenswandel in Zedlers Universal-Lexicon,* vol. 19 of *Schriften*

und Zeugnisse zur Buchgeschichte, edited by Kai Lohsträter and Flemming
    Schock, 9–16. Wiesbaden: n.p.
Proust, Jacques. 2005. "Sur la route des encyclopédies: Paris, Yverdon,
    Leeuwarden, Edo (1751–1781)." In *L'Encyclopédie d'Yverdon et sa résonance
    européenne: Contextes, contenues, continuités,* vol. 7 of *Travaux sur la Suisse des
    Lumières,* edited by Jean Daniel Candaux, Alain Cernuschi, Clorinda Donato,
    and Jens Häseler, 443–68. Geneva: n.p.
Rutten, Gijsbert (in collaboration with van Michiel Roscam Abbing). 2005. "De
    biograaf gebiografeerd. De vele levens van David van Hoogstraten (1658–
    1724)." *Voortgang: Jaarboek voor de neerlandistik* 23: 145–76. Accessed 27 July
    2020. www.dbnl.org/tekst/_voo004200501_01/_voo004200501_01_0006.php.
Sigelen, Alexander. 2002. "Freunde und Mäzene, Vermittler und Rezipienten
    – Subskribenten- und Pränumerantenverzeichnisse als Quellen zur
    Sozial- und Rezeptionsgeschichte der Volksaufklärung." *Jahrbuch für
    Kommunikationsforschung* 4: 52–103.
Strien-Chardonneau, Madeleine Van. 1997. "Hollande." In *Dictionnaire européen
    des lumières,* edited by Michel Delon, 547–50. Paris: n.p.
Waardt, Hans de. n.d. "Academic Careers and Scholarly Networks." In *The Early
    Enlightenment in the Dutch Republic, 1650–1750,* edited by Wiep van Bunge,
    19–38. Leiden, 2003.
Wittmann, Reinhard.1768. *Volkomen Konstwoordenboek, bevattende eene genoegzame
    verklaring van alle woorden, ontleend van de Grieksche, Spaansche, Fransche,
    Hoogduitsche en Nederduitsche Talen, die men gebruikt om eenige Konst, Wetenschap,
    Gewoonten, Ziekten, Geneesmiddel, Plant, Bloem, Vrugt, Gereedschap, Werktuig enz. te
    benoemen.* 2 vols. Utrecht: n.p.
– 1977. "Subskribenten- und Pränumerantenverzeichnisse als lesersoziologische
    Quelle." In *Buch und Leser. Vorträge des ersten Jahrestreffens des Wolfenbütteler
    Arbeitskreises für Geschichte des Buchwesens, 13./14. Mai 1976,* vol. 1 of *Schriften
    des Wolfenbütteler Arbeitskreises für Geschichte des Buchwesens,* edited by Herbert
    Göpfert, 125–59. Hamburg: n.p.

chapter four

Long Haul: Blussé's *Complete Description of Trades and Occupations*

ARIANNE BAGGERMAN

In the year 1822 the Dutch publisher and bookseller Pieter Blussé (figure 4.1) decided to write his autobiography. Presumably surrounded by a bulwark of collected family papers, he started with an outline of the important events and circumstances that had made him a successful and wealthy "self-made man" with nine children of whom several were participating in his ever-expanding enterprise. He planned to write about his personal life, his parents, his youth, his apprenticeship in the book trade, his engagement and marriage, and his political career. He reserved a central place for his publishing activities. First he had to decide which of the 1,400 book titles that he and his father had published since 1745 deserved a special mention in his autobiography. He compiled a short list of book titles for which he wanted to be remembered as a publisher after his death. That moment obviously arrived too soon, because he died, age seventy-four, without having developed his outline of twenty pages into a full autobiography.

In the short list of his five most memorable books, one was indicated with only one word: "De ambachten" or "The trades." In my study of this Dutch publishing house, recently published in English, this one word required an analysis of more than forty pages.[1] In this article I will limit myself to the completion of this work. However, it is difficult to be succinct when dealing with a publication that consisted of twenty-four volumes and one very long title: *Volledige beschrijving van alle konsten, ambachten, handwerken, fabrieken, trafieken, derzelver werkhuizen, gereedschappen, enz. Ten deele overgenomen uit de beroemdste buitenlandsche werken; en vermeerderd met de theorie en praktijk der beste inlandsche konstenaaren en handwerkslieden* (Complete description of all the arts, trades, crafts, factories, markets and their workplaces, tools, etc. Taken in part from the most

4.1. Portrait painted by G.A. Schmidt of Pieter Blussé Sr. (1748–1823), with
a book, writing implements, and a bust of Laurens Janszoon Coster in the
background, oil on canvas. Museum Mr. Simon van Gijn Dordrecht.

renowned foreign works: with a supplement on the theory and practice
of the finest domestic artists and artisans),[2] published over a period of
thirty-two years. It is not surprising that Blussé chose this series as the
crown jewel of his list. It was one of his most expensive undertakings,
and it is still unique in the annals of Dutch publishing. The production
of this work is also of interest from an international perspective. His work
belongs to a body of eighteenth-century encyclopedias that until now has
received very little consideration, although it was no less revolutionary

than Diderot's famous *Encyclopédie* published in twenty-eight volumes between 1751 and 1772.

Blussé's "Complete description" was partly inspired by a particular section in the *Encyclopédie*: the description of arts, crafts, and manufacturing. His enterprise, however, was much more elaborate. A greater source of inspiration – and as it turned out, also of information – was another encyclopedic book series published around the same time as the *Encyclopédie*, titled *Descriptions des arts et métiers* by de Réaumur and Du Monceau.[3]

When Diderot first began publishing his *Encyclopédie*, members of the French Académie Royale des Sciences, among them the physicist de Réaumur and the agriculturalist Du Monceau, had already been engaged in generating information about contemporary production methods used in France for more than half a century. This project was originally initiated by Louis XIV's minister Colbert, who wanted to encourage technological innovation in France. In fact, the results were not published until the second half of the eighteenth century. Under pressure from Diderot's rival project, it was decided to abandon the concept of a thematic encyclopaedic work, due in part to the delay. In 1761, four years after the author's death and ten years after the publication of Diderot's first volume, came the publication of de Réaumur's *Art du charbonnier* (The charcoal-burner's craft), the first part of the series *Description des arts et métiers* (Descriptions of arts and crafts). After the Académie's "repositories" had been emptied and a great many scholars had been commissioned to prepare de Réaumur's manuscripts for the press and write supplementary parts, things moved fast. By the time Blussé announced a similar series in Dutch adapted to the situation in the Netherlands in his prospectus of 1786, the series of monographs published by the Académie already consisted of ninety-nine volumes, dealing with subjects as diverse as the production of pins, knives, hats, wigs, pipes, rubber balls, Turkish baths, and locks, the operation of coal mines, shipbuilding, sugar refining, and textile manufacture.

In his prospectus, Blussé declared his admiration for the inspired nature of the French work – for its vitality, its thoroughness, and in particular for the way in which the French academics had not hesitated to descend from their ivory towers into the everyday realities of artisans and labourers. They did not consider it beneath their dignity to visit the workshops in the factories, the benches of the craftsmen, carrying out their investigations, consulting the artisans themselves, enquiring of them the different names and technical terms that they used, observing closely, comparing the way the work was performed, and applying their

own informed knowledge and mature insights in order to make improvements to what they had seen.[4]

Blussé's admiration was not without criticism, however. He thought the
French series was too expensive, and therefore its goal to disseminate
useful information as widely as possible could not be reached. Blussé
promised that his publication would be much more affordable. He
ensured that "den konstenaar of ambachtsman" (craftsmen or artisans
of limited means) would also be able to afford the separate volumes.[5] To
this end he decided to use the much cheaper octavo size rather than the
expensive folio format used by the French book. He would also avoid
redundancy, reduce the number of volumes by three quarters, make the
printing type smaller, and make the type page more economical by printing in columns. The French Academy, Blussé emphasized, had realized
too late the mistake it had made in this respect. At the last moment, when
most of the volumes in the French series had already been printed, they
had tried to economize, but it was too late to alter a number of design
aspects, such as the format. Blussé decided to set up his series on a much
sounder basis: "Daar wij nu in staat zijn om […] dit voetspoor te volgen
[…] is ons oogmerk ook, om hier […] regt oeconomisch te werk te gaan,
dat is, goede waar, maar tot den minsten prijs, te leveren" (Since we are
now able to follow in their footsteps […] our intention now is […] to
deliver good merchandise but at the lowest possible price."[6] Blussé did
not intend simply to translate the work from the French but rather "met
afsnijding van het overtollige, van verre na te volgen" (to prune away what
is superfluous and follow the main outline) while making use of similar
works that had meanwhile been published in England, Germany, and
Switzerland.[7] In addition, he would consult manufacturers and tradesmen in the Netherlands and use their knowledge to strengthen his series.

The typical Dutch character of this series, as envisaged by Blussé in
his prospectus, was in line with the ideals of the Oeconomische Tak (or:
Economic Branch of the Dutch Society of Sciences), a Dutch society for
economic revival of which he was a prominent member. Founded in
1777, the Oeconomische Tak urged the implementation of economic
reforms to counteract the huge rise in unemployment and poverty in
the Dutch Republic. Increased competition from neighbouring countries had caused the labour-intensive sectors of fishing and industry to
decline. The answer was a call for mercantilist policies: buy Dutch products! Numerous proposals to create employment were published.

Against this background Blussé planned to select from the French
series economic sectors that were relevant to the Netherlands. He would

not, however, confine himself solely to trades and occupations already found in the Dutch Republic. One of the economic remedies proposed by Oeconomische Tak was to stimulate new industries; Blussé therefore wrote that activities that "in ons Vaderland het naaste thuis hooren, of daarin met eenig vooruitzigt ondernomen kunnen worden" (can be undertaken in the Dutch Republic with some prospects for the future) were included in his series. He declared in his prospectus that this series was his way of contributing to the economic recovery of the Netherlands.[8]

The reader, Blussé suggested, would gain a lot by subscribing to the series. Artisans would benefit from the separate sections that covered their craft or trade. Public servants would acquire a universal knowledge that would be very helpful to them. And finally, by subscribing, the reader would contribute to the prosperity of his country. All these benefits were to be had at a bargain price, while Blussé offered his "reeds verworven goeden naam en bekende trouw" (already established good name and reliability) as an additional reassurance.[9]

Nevertheless, there was no great rush to subscribe. The list published in 1788 contains only 221 names. If we compare this figure to the 3,000 subscribers of the third edition of Wagenaar's twenty-one-volume *Vaderlandsche Historie* (Dutch history), which came out two years later, Blussé's harvest was a meagre one.[10]

If we compare the two lists of subscribers, we find that the readership was much the same in both cases. Aside from the large number of subscribers whose professions were not given, one finds tradesmen, teachers, doctors, surgeons, magistrates, soldiers, clergymen, lawyers, students, surveyors, and merchants.[11] However, in the case of Blussé's series we have an additional and quite unique source in the account books of his printing house. It then becomes clear that these 221 subscribers are only a fraction of the total number of readers and buyers. The print run of the volume on silkworm breeding that came out in 1798 was 880 copies – four times the number of subscribers ten years earlier. Fully 1,550 copies of the volume on the cultivation of madder were printed in 1801, and *The Vinegar Maker* (*De azijnmaker*) appeared in 1803 and ran 1,600 copies. These were realistic print runs, because these volumes were published at a time when Blussé already had a good idea of the market.

Because the records of the print runs of the latter two volumes were split up in the ledgers according to paper quality, it is also possible to get an idea of readers' preferences when it came to design. Interestingly enough, volumes that used more expensive paper sold the most. It would seem that most readers could afford a more expensive copy or at any rate were prepared to make a certain financial sacrifice. Of course, it makes sense that people would choose stronger paper when buying what was literally a handbook. Such books were not left on the shelf but frequently consulted, and therefore had to be more durable.[12]

Recruiting Authors and Illustrators

The series appeared over a period of thirty-two years. I doubt whether such a long publication period was envisioned at the outset. We know this delay was not caused by the illustrators and illustrations, for on closer inspection most of the engravings in the "Complete description" prove to be copies of plates in the corresponding volumes of the French publication *Description des arts et métiers*, not originals – and a limited selection at that. The plates had not been legitimately acquired, with copyright, from the French publishers. They were – as various discrepancies reveal – copied or even traced from the originals. The plates that have been copied may be detected because of the difference in size. The Dutch illustrations were smaller prints than the originals and so they could not be traced. The size of other plates corresponds to that of the original, but not to the page size of Blussé's series, which was far smaller. This problem was solved by folding the engravings so that they could fit in the book and then pasting them in. Evidently the publisher was trying to make a virtue of necessity. The engravings were printed with a wide margin on the left so that they acted as foldout sheets, allowing the reader to study the text and the relevant illustration at the same time.

In the eighteenth century copying someone else's engravings was not regarded as a criminal form of plagiarism (although Diderot was roundly criticized for this practice at the time), particularly if these engravings belonged to a foreign publisher, but it was certainly not good form.[13] Consequently Blussé did not refer to the illustrations or their makers in his advertisements, prospectuses, and forewords, except in those rare cases when original engravings were included. In the text of one of the volumes in the series, however, we are given some interesting information about the technique of tracing engravings (hinting at the fact that Blussé was indeed guilty of plagiarism). In the volume dealing with his own occupation, the engraver Arend Fokke provided an enthusiastic description of an "'gemakkelijke wijze [... om] de tekening, of prent die men in het koper nabootsen wil, op hetzelve over te drukken" (easy method of copying the drawing or print that you wish to imitate on the copper plate).[14]

Recruiting authors seems to have been a problem for Blussé. A large number of books in the series – eight of the first ten volumes – are compilations by a single author. The Amsterdam apothecary P.J. Kasteleijn had to learn all about paint-making, distilling, pottery-making, silk-dyeing, paper-making, soap-boiling, tanning, and more for his volumes in Blussé's series. This poverty-stricken author once declared to some friends that he expected to have an early death because he had already "te veel geschreven, te veel gezeten" (written too much and sat too much).[15] He did indeed die while working in 1794; otherwise, he probably would have contributed more volumes to the series.

After Kasteleijn's death, his work was given to the equally penniless and prolific writer Gerrit Paape.[16] Paape wrote a 1794 account on pottery making, an anonymously published volume dated 1797 on beekeeping, as well as another anonymous volume on silk production and the cultivation of mulberries dated 1798. In his autobiography, Paape later wrote that his volume on pottery was in fact a translation.[17] In Blussé's ledgers, however, this volume was credited to Kasteleijn. It is possible that Blussé preferred to publish the work under the name of a writer who was far less controversial and evidently more of an expert on this particular subject.

Two volumes by Paape were published years after Kasteleijn's death. Blussé therefore settled on a different solution. The works were to be published anonymously. We only know of Paape's involvement because he recommended the works (with a measure of pride) to the Department for National Education, adding that they "door gemelden auteur vry zyn gevolgd uit het hoogduitsch" (have been freely translated from the German by said author.)[18] In his autobiography, Paape comically describes how he was hired as a translator before he knew a word of German.[19]

Paape stopped working for Blussé in 1798. After this Blussé failed to find authors willing to write about more than one trade, and the production of the series grew ever more sluggish. The publication of the first fifteen volumes spanned ten years – from 1788 to 1798 – whereas twenty-two more years would pass before the other nine volumes saw the light of day. Unlike the publishers of the French series *Description des arts et métiers*, Blussé was unable to find original copy, and had no financial support from the king. Again unlike the French, Blussé was limited in that he did not have a group of scholars working collaboratively and under the auspices of an institution like the Académie Royale. After Kasteleijn's death and Paape's withdrawal Blussé had to rely on a few rare birds: people with sufficient knowledge of a foreign language to translate information from foreign manuals, who could write in a clear uncomplicated style, and who also knew what they were writing about when describing various crafts and occupations – knowledge they had preferably already acquired in their daily lives. We can deduce from the significant differences in the quality and scope of the volumes and the confusion of authors just how hard it must have been for Blussé to find a suitable number of authors to complete his series. His contributors wrote about their own professions. Some were skilled craftsmen like the aforementioned engraver Fokke, and others were bookbinders, brewers, and draftsmen. But Blussé also succeeded in recruiting enthusiastic dilettantes like Jan van Heurn (a professor of law and an organ enthusiast), who wrote a five-hundred-page volume on organ building.[20]

Before the first volume was even published, Blussé had to change his editorial policy. In his foreword to the first volume Blussé felt obliged to apologize in advance for the concessions he had been forced to make in respect to the original plan announced in the prospectus: "'Dus vergistten wij ons ook in het gezegde bericht, door te bepaalen, dat elk boekdeel ten minsten 30 bladen druks beslaan zoude. Ons hier naar te gedraagen, ware niet alleen thans, maar ook meermaalen, het publiek optehouden in zijne billijke verlangen, naar stukken, die gereed zijn om te verschijnen" (We made a miscalculation in the aforesaid announcement when we stated that each volume would contain at least 480 printed pages. Were we to comply with this promise, it would not only on this occasion, but on many more, thwart the public in its reasonable desire for works that are ready to appear).[21] In the choice of subject as well, pragmatism was decisive. A striking example of this is the volume "The architect," a highly theoretical work that replaced the proposed volume "The carpenter," which was to be a practical handbook for artisans (though no author was ever found to write it, or perhaps it did not have sufficient sale potential).

In 1786, Blussé promised subscribers that the series would consist of twenty-four volumes. Although he would keep his word, he never mentioned that subscribers would have to wait thirty-four years before the work was completed. The last and twenty-fourth volume of the series was published in 1820, and despite all the other compromises that Blussé made, he did manage to retain his original concept. There are three elements that recur to a greater or lesser degree in all the volumes: raw materials, tools, and the preparation or manufacturing of the product. The structure of the Dutch "Complete description" was clearly based on a deliberate decision to subordinate theory to the practice of the professional activities in question. And the message in almost every volume was the same: the domestic economy of the Netherlands would revive if rich citizens had the courage to invest in Dutch industries, if businessmen improved their methods of production, and if private individuals bought domestic products rather than imported goods. This message was constantly stressed in the publishers' forewords, while the authors missed no opportunity to hammer the point home to the readers. Some volumes of the series also make the case for small-scale production methods that are easily learnt and industries that require only a small start-up capital: "'Ieder die kaarsen weet te maaken, en wiens omstandigheden het toe-laaten, kan kaarsenmaaker worden, zonder dat hij eenigen omslag meer nodig hebbe, dan de daar toe dienende gereedschappen" (Anyone who knows how to make candles and whose circumstances permit can become a candle maker without needing any more than the tools for the job).[22]

With only one exception, the authors in this series have nothing to say about the workers themselves. Here too we may detect a consistent approach, but does this reflect a conscious choice on the part of the publisher? This almost unanimously impersonal approach does reflect Enlightenment ideology. As Diderot had declared in his *Encyclopédie*, his writers described the production process as a single static entity, stripped of the human factor, and never took into account possible complications, such as equipment breakdowns, accidents caused by misunderstandings, and so forth.[23] In this mechanistic vision the workers are mere cogs in a well-lubricated, perfectly functioning machine. Improvement can primarily be achieved by bringing in new equipment and machinery or by using other production methods, not by better schooling. It is only in the accompanying engravings that we see the workers or apprentices, though they appear just occasionally, chiefly to add a touch of local colour.

Another similarity between the volumes (which also reflects this mechanistic attitude) is the lack of interest in working conditions. Here again, though, Blussé and his authors were not unusual. Diderot paid just as little heed to the health and safety of tradesmen and factory workers. Even when he was obliged to deal with the subject, he trivialized it. For instance, printers had already recognized the danger of breathing in toxic fumes emitted by some of the substances used in printing. Diderot, however, dismissed inhaling the fumes as quite harmless (figure 4.2).[24]

There was more knowledge about and concern for safety in the Dutch Republic than one might suspect from reading the "Complete description." As early as 1700 the Italian scholar Bernardino Ramazzini published a standard work on occupational diseases, *De Morbis Artificum Diatriba*, subsequently translated into English as *Diseases of Workers*. The Dutch

4.2. Engraving in P.J. Kasteleijn's *De sterkwaterstooker, zoutzuur- en vitrioolöliebereider* (Dordrecht 1788). The plate was traced from or drawn after plate 2 of J.F. Demachy's *L'art de distillateur*, vol. 12 of *Description des arts et métiers* (Paris, 1773). National Library, The Hague.

translation of this work went into no less than three editions.[25] Blussé's authors could have found out everything they needed to know about the health hazards of the trade they were describing from Ramazzini's six-page treatise on the "diseases of potters": "first, trembling hands, then they become paralysed, melancholy, lethargic, a bad colour, toothless."[26] In Paape´s book on pottery we do not read one word on the occupational diseases of potters. Similarly, in his volume on silkworm breeding he made no mention of the stench associated with clearing dead and half-rotting silkworms: "'die derhalven desen koeken kammen, plegen met een scherpen hoest, en te gelijk met bezwaard ademhalen gekwelt te worden, en weinige van dese werklieden werden oud" (the workers who do this job are frequently plagued by a harsh cough accompanied by very painful breathing, and few of them live to be old).[27] Presumably, the owner of a Delft pottery and the important silk manufacturer in Dordrecht to whom these volumes were dedicated would not have been overjoyed to read a vivid description of the malodorousness of their factories: "'Het is aanmerkenswaardig, dat den dreck van so een klein ongedierte, als het leeft, en met moerbei bladeren werd gevoed, indien dat deselve op hoopjens gesmeten daar blijft leggen tot dat se rot, zo zwaren stank daar na, als se geroert werd, van sig geeft, datse een gantse buurt besmetten" (It is quite remarkable that the droppings of so tiny a creature, when it is alive and fed on mulberry leaves, if left to lie and piled in heaps until they rot, thereafter give off such an unbearable stench when they are touched that they contaminate an entire neighbourhood).[28]

This brings me to a final aspect of Pieter Blussé's series: the question of how this series was financed. The prospectus announcing the series in 1786 is optimistic about additional subsidies. Blussé hoped that the previously mentioned society Oeconomische Tak, with its more than three thousand members, would give financial assistance. It is no coincidence that the first volume in the series was dedicated to this society. I learned from research in the society's archive, however, that the only support given was a gold medal for the poor author, and a subscription for only one copy of the series.[29] Blussé's disappointment is clear from the introduction to the next volume (published in 1788), in which he wrote that he had nearly stopped its publication "daar alle onze moeiten, kosten, en poogingen met die van eenige weinige vrienden, ter voordzetting [... van deze] onderneeming [...] naauwlijks de oplettenheid onzer natie scheenen tot zich te trekken" (because all our efforts, expense, and attempts, together with those of a small number of friends, to continue with this project seemed scarcely to attract the notice of our country).[30]

With the mention of "eenige weinige vrienden" (a small number of friends) whose encouragement was not confined to words, Blussé was probably referring to the persons to whom, over the years, the various volumes of his series were dedicated. Many of the individual volumes in the "Complete description" are dedicated to entrepreneurs operating in the sector concerned or one allied to it. I assume that we are looking here at an early form of sponsorship. The volume on soap-boiling, for instance, was dedicated to "Den weledelen heere Willem Noodt, zeep-sieder te Delft" (Willem Noodt Esq., soap-boiler of Delft).[31] The volume on paper manufacture was addressed to the greater glory of "'de heeren Blauw en Briel, beroemde papierfabrikeurs te Wormerveer" (Messrs Blauw and Briel, renowned paper manufacturers of Wormerveer) and, incidentally, regular suppliers to the firm of Blussé. The volume on Delft-ware was proffered "met hartelijke toebede van alles goeds" (with warm wishes for all that is good) to, among others, Lambert Sanderus, owner of the Delft pottery De Porceleyne Claeuw. The volume on silkworm breed-ing was dedicated to the silk manufacturer Anthonij Balthasar van den Brandeler in Dordrecht; while Hendrik van Beek, owner of Rotterdam's vinegar factory De Eendracht, was saluted in the book on vinegar mak-ing. Their support may have been financial, but could have also been in the form of contributions to the books themselves: information about the production methods used in their business, or even the disclosure of trade secrets.

However, we have not examined all the possible motives that shaped Blussé's dedications in the "Complete description." If we explore the backgrounds of the individuals who are praised in these forewords, we will find that Blussé took every opportunity to settle accounts that were still open, secure political support, establish a political profile for himself as a publisher, and sometimes a combination of all of these motives.

Blussé's dedication in the 1798 book on silkworm breeding, to the Dordrecht silk manufacturer Anthony Balthasar van den Brandeler, is a good example of his mixed motives. What first comes to mind is that he had a financial objective. It would not seem too far-fetched to suppose that a wealthy manufacturer would be willing to provide funds for pro-duction costs in exchange for a flattering mention in the dedication of a standard work in his own field. All the more so considering that the book supported administrative measures that favoured the silkworm breeding industry – something Van den Brandeler had advocated in the past with-out success. Gerrit Paape's suggestion that silk manufacturing promoted employment, since even children could be put to work, must have been music to Van den Brandeler's ears. He belonged to a group of entre-preneurs who in 1793 put pressure on the governors of the Dordrecht Reformed Church Poor School to allow as many children as possible to leave school prematurely to work in silk manufacturing, an industry in need of "young hands to carry out the work there."[32] If we dig a little deeper, we find that Blussé had reason enough to be grateful to Van den Brandeler. For generations the Blussé family had been awarded the position of clerk in the post office controlled by the Van den Brandeler family, which proved to be crucial to the expansion of their book trade. By dedicating a book to this benefactor, Blussé managed to successfully kill a number of birds with one stone.[33]

Eventually, the delays in the series were skilfully turned into advantages by Blussé. In fact, delays meant that the costs could be spread over a longer period of time and that the series, should it not make a profit or cover its costs, could at least earn its keep as a calling card for the firm. Every time a new volume in the series was published the reading public was reminded yet again of the perseverance, the idealism, and the dependability of the firm that did not want to disappoint its subscribers and that was determined to contribute to the economic revival of the Dutch Republic.

NOTES

1 Arianne Baggerman, 2013, *Publishing Policies and Family Strategies: The Fortunes of a Dutch Publishing House in the 18th and Early 19th Centuries*, vol. 32 of *Library of the Written World – The Handpress World*, ed. by Andrew Pettegree (Leiden: Brill).

2 All book title translations are mine.

3 On the original intentions and history of *Description des arts et métiers*, see Arthur H. Cole and George B. Watts, 1952, *The Handicrafts of France as Recorded in the Description des Arts et Métiers 1761–1788* (Cambridge: Baker Library), and James Mosley, 1991, "Illustrations of Typefounding Engraved for the Description des Arts et Métiers of the Académie Royale des Sciences, Paris, 1694 to c. 1700," *Matrix* 11: 61–80.

4 *Algemeene genees- natuur-, en huishoudkundige jaarboeken* IV, pt. 2 (1786): 70.

5 *Algemeene genees- natuur-, en huishoudkundige jaarboeken* IV, 77.

6 *Algemeene genees- natuur-, en huishoudkundige jaarboeken* IV, 78.

7 *Algemeene genees- natuur-, en huishoudkundige jaarboeken* IV, 78.

8 *Algemeene genees- natuur-, en huishoudkundige jaarboeken* IV, 79. If we compare the sixty-eight topics that Blussé selected from the French version with the books that he finally published, it is clear that he really did produce a more compact work. Where the French series has separate entries for "wax maker" and "candle maker," these are combined under one heading in the Dutch version. The same is true in other instances – in the "Complete description" the French leather gilder, chamois leather maker, tanner, "Spanish leather" maker, and "Hungarian leather" maker are all lumped together under the

heading "the leather tanner." Blussé's selection of industrial branches could be interesting to economic historians. Among the trades he did not include in his series, for instance, were the charcoal burner, the anchor smith, the pin maker, the blacksmith, the slater, the wig maker, the Turkish bath owner, and the saddler, coal miner, and shipbuilder.

9 *Algemeene genees- natuur-, en huishoudkundige jaarboeken* IV, 81.

10 Jan Wagenaar, 1790–1803, *Vaderlandsche Historie*, 2 vols. (Amsterdam: Johannes Allart), list of names of subscribers.

11 For a breakdown of the type of people who subscribed to Wagenaar's history, see J.J. Kloek, 1984, "Lezen als levensbehoefte. Roman en romanpubliek in de tweede helft van de 18e eeuw," *Literatuur*, 1: 136–42. I have only counted the professions on Blussé's list of subscribers: fifty-one gave no profession, twenty-four are tradesmen, three teachers, eight doctors and surgeons; thirty-seven members of the magistracy and other city officials, nine soldiers, six clergymen, two lawyers, two students, three surveyors, and four merchants.

12 People could choose between a cheaper or more expensive quality of paper. The book on the cultivation of madder had 650 copies printed on the cheaper dessendiaan paper and 900 on best paper; for *The Vinegar Maker* there were 700 copies on dessendiaan and again 900 on best paper.

13 See Cole and Watts, *The Handicrafts of France*, 41, for an example of plagiarism in Diderot's *Encyclopédie*.

14 Fokke, *De graveur*, 292ff.

15 On this author see G. Brender à Brandis, 1801, "Levensschets van Petrus Johannes Kasteleyn," in *Proeven van geschied- en letterkundige oefeningen, zoowel den koophandel en de scheepvaart als de dicht- en letterkunde betreffende* (Haarlem: n.p.), 248–70.

16 See for instance Gerrit Paape, 1996, *Mijne vrolijke wijsgeerte in mijne ballingschap*, ed. Peter Altena, 7–68 (Hilversum: Verloren) [= *Egodocumenten* 11]; Gerrit Paape, 1998, *De Bataafsche Republiek*, ed. Peter Altena, 99–117 (Nijmegen: Van Tilt).

17 Paape, *Mijne vrolijke wijsgeerte*, 114; see also the commentary by Peter Altena on p. 157.

18 Nationaal Archief, The Hague, Archive of the Department of Home Affairs, inv. 284, dated 29 March 1800.

19 Quoted in A. Nieuweboer, 1997, "De 'Vrolijke reis van Gerrit Paape': Een uitstapje naar de achttiende-eeuwse vertaalpraktijk," in *Mededelingen van de Stichting Jacob Campo Weijerman*, 20: 57.

20 See the file of members of societies compiled by Gerard Schulte Nordholt, Van der Aa, University Library Leiden: Heynemeyer Ltk 1001 HE-HU: 77, 211–12.

21 Foreword of the publisher in P.J. Kasteleijn, *De Indigobereider en Blaauwverwer* (= *Volledige beschrijving van alle konsten* I) (Dordrecht: A. Blussé en Zoon, 1788).

22 P.J. Kasteleijn, 1792, *De waschbleeker en waschkaarsenmaaker* (The wax bleacher and candle maker) (Dordrecht: A. Blussé en Zoon), foreword.

23 Concerning these omissions in Diderot's work, see John R. Pannabecker, 1998, "Representing Mechanical Arts in Diderot's Encyclopédie," *Technology and Culture* 39, no. 1: 33–73, esp. 42–61.

24 Pannabecker, "Representing Mechanical Arts in Diderot's Encyclopédie," 61 ff.

25 [Bernardino Ramazzini]. *Historische, natuur- en geneeskundige verhandeling van de ziekten der konstenaars, ambagts-lieden en handwerkers,* 3rd ed. (Leiden: Jan Arnold Langerak).

26 [Ramazzini]. *Historische, natuur- en geneeskundige verhandeling,* 34–9.

27 [Ramazzini]. *Historische, natuur- en geneeskundige verhandeling,* 211.

28 [Ramazzini]. *Historische, natuur- en geneeskundige verhandeling,* 211.

29 He was given the gold medal "for his translation into Dutch of a work on marketing, of great importance to Netherlands manufacturers ... whereby he had greatly assisted the attempts of the Oeconomischen Tak ... and also to encourage him in his praiseworthy work of chemical experiment, from which flowed forth so many useful products" (Noord-Hollands Archief, Haarlem, Oeconomische Tak, *Resolutiën* 1787 [Haarlem, *s.a.*], 822–3).

30 P.J. Kasteleijn, 1791, *De zijdeverwer* (Dordrecht: A. Blussé en Zoon), foreword.

31 P.J. Kasteleijn, 1791, *De zeepsieder* (Dordrecht: A. Blussé en Zoon).

32 C. Esseboom, 1995, *Onderwysinghe der jeught. Onderwijs en onderwijstoezicht in de 18ᵉ eeuw op het Eiland van Dordrecht* (Rotterdam: Faculteit der economische wetenschappen, Erasmus universiteit), 117, 119–20. On 19 March 1794 some young workers from the silk manufacturers Van den Brandeler & Compagnie were presented with prizes for exemplary conduct by the Oeconomische Tak. In the words of the chairman's address: "'de mensch, aan wien verstand is gegeven boven de dieren, die armen en benen heeft, altijd iet(s) moet doen, doet hij nu geen goed, dan moet hij noodzakelijk kwaad doen" (human beings are given understanding above that of the beasts; they have arms and legs and these must be kept busy, for if a person is not doing good, then he is necessarily doing evil) (Gemeente Archief Dordrecht, Family Archive Repelaer van Puttershoek, inv. 36). I thank Cees Esseboom for allowing me to consult his notes.

33 In 1770 and 1771 Blussé had published *Kabinet van Nederlandsche en Kleefsche oudheden* (A cabinet of antiquities from the Netherlands and Cleves), which was dedicated to this same regent, entrepreneur, and son of the

postmaster François van den Brandeler "as a token of the highest esteem, in recognition of the many acts of favour and as a mark of our enduring commitment": A. Rademaker, 1770–1, *Kabinet van Nederlandsche en Kleefsche oudheden*, 6 vols. (Dordrecht: A. Blussé en Zoon).

Bibliography

Primary Sources

ARCHIVAL SOURCES

Municipal Archive, Dordrecht, Family Archive Repelaer van Puttershoek, inv. 36
National Archive, The Hague, Archive of the Department of Home Affairs, inv. 284, dated 29 March 1800.
Noord-Hollands Archive, Haarlem, Oeconomische Tak, *Resolutiën* 1787 (Haarlem, *s.a.*) 822–3.

PRINTED SOURCES

Blussé, Pieter. 1786. *Algemeene genees- natuur-, en huishoudkundige jaarboeken.*
Kasteleijn, P.J. 1791. *De zijdeverwer.* Dordrecht: A. Blussé en Zoon.
– 1792. *De waschbleeker en waschkaarsenmaaker* (The Wax Bleacher and Candle Maker). Dordrecht: A. Blussé en Zoon.
Rademaker, A. 1770–1. *Kabinet van Nederlandsche en Kleefsche oudheden.* 6 vols. Dordrecht: A. Blussé en Zoon.
[Ramazzini, B.]. 1744. *Historische, natuur- en geneeskundige verhandeling van de ziekten der konstenaars, ambagts-lieden en handwerkers.* 3rd ed. Leiden: Jan Arnold Langerak.
University Library Leiden: Heynemeyer Ltk 1001 HE-HU: 77, 211–12.
Wagenaar, Jan. 1790–1803. *Vaderlandsche Historie.* 2 vols. Amsterdam: Johannes Allart.

Secondary Sources

Baggerman, Arianne. 2013. *Publishing Policies and Family Strategies: The Fortunes of a Dutch Publishing House in the 18th and Early 19th Centuries.* Vol. 32 of *Library of the Written World – The Handpress World*, edited by Andrew Pettegree. Leiden: Brill.
Brender à Brandis, G. 1801. "Levensschets van Petrus Johannes Kasteleyn." In *Proeven van geschied- en letterkundige oefeningen, zoowel den koophandel en de scheepvaart als de dicht- en letterkunde betreffende*, 248–70. Haarlem: n.p.

Cole, Arthur H., and George B. Watts. 1952. *The Handicrafts of France as Recorded in the Description des Arts et Métiers 1761–1788.* Cambridge: Baker Library.

Esseboom, C. 1995. *Onderwysinghe der jeught. Onderwijs en onderwijstoezicht in de 18e eeuw op het Eiland van Dordrecht,* Rotterdam: Faculteit der economische wetenschappen, Erasmus universiteit.

Kloek, J.J. 1984. "Lezen als levensbehoefte. Roman en romanpubliek in de tweede helft van de 18e eeuw." *Literatuur,* 1: 136–42.

Mosley, James. 1991. "Illustrations of Typefounding Engraved for the Description des Arts et Métiers of the Académie Royale des Sciences, Paris, 1694 to c. 1700." *Matrix* 11: 61–80.

Nieuweboer, A. 1997. "De 'Vrolijke reis van Gerrit Paape.' Een uitstapje naar de achttiende-eeuwse vertaalpraktijk." In *Mededelingen van de Stichting Jacob Campo Weijerman,* 20: 51–60.

Paape, Gerrit. 1996. *Mijne vrolijke wijsgeerte in mijne ballingschap,* edited by Peter Altena, 7–68. Hilversum: n.p. [= *Egodocumenten* 11].

– 1998. *De Bataafsche Republiek,* edited by Peter Altena, 99–117. Nijmegen: Van Tilt.

Pannabecker, John R. 1998. "Representing Mechanical Arts in Diderot's Encyclopédie." *Technology and Culture* 39, no. 1: 33–73.

chapter five

Translation and Transfer of Knowledge in the *Encyclopédie méthodique*

KATHLEEN HARDESTY DOIG

Recent decades have seen many rediscoveries of works that were popular in their own time, or highly regarded, or sometimes both, but that fell by the wayside at some point and had been largely forgotten. Novels such as *Lettres d'une Péruvienne* by Françoise de Graffigny and *Ourika* by Claire de Duras are outstanding examples in the category of fiction. In a very different genre, but sharing the characteristic of renown followed by eclipse followed by rediscovery, is the *Encyclopédie méthodique*. This encyclopedia was an important feature of the intellectual landscape of Europe for many years, was superseded and lost from sight soon after its completion in 1832, and has gradually re-emerged on the scholarly scene in recent years. Numerous articles on various components of the *Méthodique* have been published, including the extensive collection edited by Claude Blanckaert and Michel Porret, *L'Encyclopédie méthodique* (2006). In her *Savoir et Matières* (2011), Martine Groult has examined the differences between the conceptual bases of the *Encyclopédie* project and the later *Méthodique*. Briefly, the *Encyclopédie* collected knowledge and organized it around the functions of the human mind; the *Méthodique* focused on individual sciences and their particular vocabularies, and was aimed at instructing a wide public and promoting advances in all disciplines.[1] A research group, the Atelier Panckoucke *Encyclopédie méthodique* (APEM), directed by Groult and Luigi Delia, has been organized under the auspices of the CNRS (Centre Jean Pépin) to study this massive encyclopedia. Two collections of selected articles from two dictionaries of the *Méthodique* have been published, with more planned.[2]

The history of the publication of the *Méthodique* is linked to the series of reprints, supplements, and revisions of the *Encyclopédie* undertaken in the 1770s. They included a folio reprint, two Tuscan editions, an extensive revision and a supplement published in Yverdon, as well as a slightly revised quarto edition that was also published in octavo size and a separate five-volume *Supplément*.[3] The publishing magnate Charles Joseph Panckoucke was involved in several of these ventures (the folio reprint, the quarto revision, and the *Supplément*). As a publisher, he appreciated the profits that could be turned in the encyclopedia industry. But Panckoucke's ambitions extended well beyond the commercial sphere. The intelligence, imagination, and organizational ability that he deployed in business were also used for serious study; he read widely and wrote several essays on mathematical, moral, and philosophical subjects.[4]

Panckoucke had already put a group to work on a revision of the *Encyclopédie* when he heard about a new proposal being floated by the Liège publisher Devéria. This one boasted an innovation, a methodical format consisting of separate dictionaries rather than a single whole where subjects were arbitrarily and confusedly mingled by the alphabet. At some point, Panckoucke took over this project and changed his own revision into this methodical format. It was to be made a real encyclopedia, an integrated circle of knowledge, through overviews of the subject in each dictionary, but more importantly, through a "Vocabulaire universel" that would include all the terms in every dictionary. One could therefore look up a term, for example "Commerce des grains," and see how it figured in various contexts.[5]

Such an enterprise involved at least two major challenges. With forty-six volumes of text and seven volumes of plates projected to be completed in seven years, considerable start-up financing was required, and a sizeable team of expert subject editors, most of whom would need collaborators, had to be recruited. Panckoucke could supply the initial funding on his own; there is no evidence that he had to form a consortium of backers, as was often the case with encyclopedic projects. As for the team, Panckoucke identified potential editors through his many contacts (and with the help of his brother-in-law, Jean Baptiste Antoine Suard, who had been working with him on the originally planned revision). Most of those approached agreed to join in the new venture. They were on the whole paid generously and had substantial leeway in choosing their collaborators.

The prospectus was published in Panckoucke's *Mercure de France* on 8 December 1781. After a few changes to the format of the encyclopedia (the page layout of three columns, for example, was roundly rejected), approximately five thousand subscribers signed on.[6] The first sections of the *Méthodique* were published on 18 November 1782, and instalments appeared regularly through the 1780s.[7] During this period the main challenge was the expansion of many dictionaries of the *Méthodique*. Editors found that it was not possible to treat their subject appropriately in the number of volumes they had projected, and certain areas had been overlooked. It was soon clear that the *Méthodique* would fill many more volumes than subscribers had agreed to purchase, and complaints and suits followed. Then came the Revolution, and problems snowballed: scarcity of paper and presses, increased labour costs, the loss of as many as two thousand subscribers, the withdrawal of editors and collaborators. The stress made Panckoucke ill, and in 1794 he sold the enterprise to his son-in-law, Henri Agasse. Agasse managed to keep producing instalments until his death in 1813. His widow, Panckoucke's daughter Pauline, took over and persevered for another nineteen years, finally publishing the last installment, the 102nd, on 29 September 1832. It should be stressed that she did not simply shut down the project at that point; she finished every dictionary that was underway.[8] There is some confusion about the exact number of volumes in the complete *Méthodique*, because subscribers bound the small dictionaries differently and because of size variations among the plates. The most reliable listing shows forty-three separate dictionaries in 177 volumes of text; the 6,439 plates fill twenty-six volumes more, for a total of 203 volumes.[9]

An analysis of the transfer and translation of knowledge in an encyclopedia of the dimensions of the *Méthodique* could be organized in various ways. It could, for example, concentrate on one or a cluster of sources as they are used in a single dictionary or in several related dictionaries. I have chosen a more global approach. I will examine a wide range of individual dictionaries of the *Méthodique*, identifying non-French sources in them. Special attention will be paid to the use – possible, probable, or certain – of the French translations of these texts. I cannot therefore offer an exhaustive examination of any one source, any language group, or any subject, but this limited sampling can convey a good sense of the breadth of learning that the *Méthodique* offered its readers.

Extensive citation of sources, both French and non-French, was integral to the *Méthodique*'s updating of the base texts, to its more extensive treatment of most subjects, and especially to its vastly increased nomenclatures. The rich documentation has additional bearing on the encyclopedic enterprise in at least two ways. In support of the *Méthodique*'s mission to distil the essential and most reliable overviews of every subject from the multiplicity of extant sources, the summaries and extracts of scholarly works that it provides facilitate the search for basic knowledge.

They also serve as a bibliographical guide for the reader desiring to go beyond the confines of an encyclopedia article. By including numerous works originally written in foreign languages among their sources, *Méthodique* collaborators enhanced both aspects of their coverage, assembling pertinent information from experts beyond France's linguistic borders and pointing the interested reader to a much wider range of additional reading.

Several of the dictionaries, such as *Encyclopédiana* and *Marine*, in which there appears to be little or no direct reference to non-French sources, will not be considered here. Two caveats to these exclusions must be noted. First, some contributors simply did not mention their sources very often, although transfers of knowledge are indeed being made. Second, many of the French sources are themselves cases of such transfers, but it is beyond the scope of this study to unravel such genealogies. As regards documentation, I will normally mention only one of the often numerous examples of articles where a source is mentioned. Special attention is paid to any comments about translations used. Where possible, full titles of works and full, corrected names of authors, which are often stated in the *Méthodique* in the casual style of the eighteenth century, have been restored. Sources mentioned are in articles new to the *Méthodique* unless otherwise noted; transfers involving articles carried over from the *Encyclopédie* and the *Supplément* are not included unless otherwise noted. They are numerous in certain dictionaries and often themselves involve translations, in that long line of knowledge transfer characteristic of encyclopedias.

The first language to be considered is Latin. Familiarity with this classical language was so widespread that in one sense it might not be regarded as a foreign tongue, and many *Méthodique* contributors had mastered it sufficiently to be able to write in it.[10] The dictionaries of anatomy, medicine, botany, natural history, antiquities, and ancient history show the prevalence of Latin terminology – as is still the case in some of these disciplines. One whole dictionary of the *Méthodique*, *Géographie ancienne*, presents its nomenclature mostly in Latin, on the grounds that persons interested in the subject are dealing with texts in Latin.

A listing of modern sources written in Latin that are mentioned by *Méthodique* contributors as sources would number at least in the hundreds. It would include publications by renowned European scientists and physicians such as Carl von Linnaeus in Sweden, Herman Boerhaave in the Dutch Republic, and Albrecht von Haller in Switzerland. The *Tabulæ sceleti et musculorum corporis humani* of the German-born

Dutch anatomist Bernhard Siegfried Albinus is an important reference, especially in *Système anatomique*. In philosophy, the German historian Johann Jakob Brucker's *Historia critica philosophiæ* is a significant source, through its use in the articles by Diderot that are carried over by his disciple Jacques-André Naigeon, the editor of *Philosophie ancienne et moderne* in the *Méthodique*. Naigeon, who had reservations about Brucker's work, scrupulously retains these articles.[11] In *Antiquités*, Antoine Mongez acknowledges major sources in the preface that include Latin works by two Germans, Johann Georg Grævius's *Thesaurus antiquitatum Romanarum*[12] and *Pantheon Ægyptiorum* by the theologian and Orientalist Paul Ernst Jablonski, as well as another reference work by a Dutch scholar, Jakob Gronovius, editor of *Thesaurus antiquitatum Græcarum*. In addition to these often-quoted sources, other modern works written in Latin, some translated and some not, are mentioned in series across the *Méthodique*. A single example of an apparently untranslated work: the entry on Pope Adrian VI in *Histoire* is based on the information in Gaspard Burman's biography *Hadrianus VI, sive Analecta Historica de Hadriano Sexto Trajectino Papa Romano*.

But many other modern works written in Latin were subsequently translated. It is seldom possible to tell whether references in the *Méthodique* are to the original Latin or a translation, since contributors tend to paraphrase content rather than quote it directly. This is particularly true when one turns to the ancient writers, many of whom had long been translated into French. Direct quotations are almost always in French but generally without any indication of the translation being used, nor are there many statements suggesting that writers are aware of the unavoidable disjunction between the original and the translation, not to mention the errors that might be transmitted in a poorly rendered version. But at least one editor, Antoine Chrysostôme Quatremère de Quincy, was aware of this pitfall. By far the most often cited source in his series on architecture is Vitruvius, author of the seminal study of the aesthetic and construction principles of Roman architecture *De architectura*, written during the first century BC and translated by Claude Perrault under a commission from the Académie française. Quatremère de Quincy notes that Perrault had laboured under the major impediment of never visiting Rome or seeing the monuments discussed. The translator of Vitruvius, he says, must possess the rare combination of artistic talent and erudition. He gives Perrault credit for the artistic ability, as evidenced by his attempt to illustrate the principles of Vitruvius in a set of plates; but overall, "Sans aucun doute la traduction de Perrault a été surpassée en bien des points"

(There is no doubt that Perrault's translation has been surpassed in many respects) (*Architecture*, 3:93).[13] The imperfections of this translation may explain why the collaborator who covered most of the practical aspects of construction in *Architecture*, Antoine Jean Baptiste Rondelet, chose to translate Vitruvius himself.[14]

That various dictionaries of the *Méthodique* transmit the learning and thought of the ancients to contemporary readers is hardly surprising, since the half-century of its publication continued to be characterized in the humanities, as well as in some of the sciences, by classical and neo-classical influences. In addition to *Architecture*, the dictionaries that are most reflective of the continuing presence of ancient writings include *Géographie ancienne*, *Grammaire et littérature*, *Médecine*, *Philosophie ancienne et moderne*, and *Logique, métaphysique et morale*. *Antiquités*, in spite of its apparent relevance in this respect, does not figure in this group because it is more concerned with reporting the discoveries and scholarship of modern authors, several of whom were noted above.

In dozens of articles, Edme Mentelle, the editor of *Géographie ancienne*, makes the expected use of Pliny and of the historians Strabo and Herodotus. Pliny, for example, is a source for "Scandia Insula," and Strabo for "Irlande." In the case of Herodotus, Mentelle refers to the recent annotated translation by Pierre Henri Larcher, *Histoire ... avec des remarques historiques et critiques* ("Ichthyopage"). In *Grammaire et littérature*, Jean-François Marmontel uses numerous examples from classical authors, especially Cicero, to illustrate points of style ("Division"). *Médecine* often gives the same weight to the diagnoses and treatments of Greek physicians from antiquity as to more modern medical authorities. Predominating among these Ancients is Hippocrates, whose humoralism was still widely accepted by many of the physicians who contributed to the earlier volumes of the *Méthodique* dictionary.[15] Many other ancient physicians, the more obscure as well as the famous, are quoted as well. Two random examples chosen from the letter "H" include Paul of Ægina ("Hydatide") and Galen ("Hyalode"). The *Méthodique* physicians may well have read some of these authors in the original Greek, although French translations of most were available. Hippocrates, for example, had been translated as early as the sixteenth century.[16]

The two series *Logique, métaphysique et morale* and *Philosophie ancienne et moderne* are particularly rich sources of classical thought. The first is largely a compilation of entries taken from published works. French versions of the classics compiled in this dictionary had long been available, in volumes such as *Traité des bienfaits de Sénèque*, translated in 1641 by

François Malherbe, and Cicero's *De Oficiis* (*Traité des devoirs*), translated as early as 1500. Cicero's treatise is the source of many articles, including the twenty-eight-page essay "Devoir." A specific translation is referenced in the case of Plutarch, Jacques Amyot's 1572 *Œuvres morales de Plutarque* ("Curiosité").

Philosophie ancienne et moderne is, as the title indicates, chronologically comprehensive.[17] Of the thirteen articles in the 289 pages of volume 1 comprising "A," eight pertain to ancient philosophy: "Académiciens," three entries, including forty-five pages on Cicero's philosophy; "Académie"; "Antédiluvienne" (Diderot's unsigned article from the *Encyclopédie*); "Artistotélisme"; "Athées anciens"; and "Atomisme." Naigeon quotes liberally from works written in Latin, often giving the text in French in the body of the article and the original language in a note. The first example of this practice appears on the very first page of the "Discours préliminaire" of the series, in a quotation from Francis Bacon about the need for a solid history of ancient philosophy. It is by coincidence that Naigeon enunciated his editorial principle for the use of Latin quotations in the article on Bacon ("Baconisme"). He explains that he chose not to multiply Latin quotations "dans un ouvrage destiné indistinctement à toutes les classes de la société, & dans lequel il faut autant qu'il est possible, se mettre à la portée du plus grand nombre des lecteurs" (in a work intended for every class of society, with no distinctions, and which must be geared as far as possible to the greater number of readers) (*Philosophie*, 1:440). But in fact he includes numerous untranslated quotations. Some, it is true, seem to be so canonical that the "plus grand nombre des lecteurs" would indeed recognize them. In other cases, there is perhaps an additional layer of meaning. In an intriguing example, Naigeon adds a note consisting of a few untranslated lines from Horace to Diderot's short entry "Résurrection." The quotation reinforces Diderot's skepticism about the possibility of the resurrection of a human.[18] This article was in an installment of *Philosophie* published in 1797, long after the censorship apparatus of the Ancien régime had crumbled, but we do not know when Naigeon prepared the copy (he was among the more dilatory of Panckoucke's editors). The untranslated Latin can therefore be viewed as either an expression of confidence in the literacy of his readers, or a disguise for a daring allusion.

The practice of limiting the use of quotations in the original Latin or Greek seems to have been shared by fellow editors of the *Méthodique* and may have been among Panckoucke's recommendations to editors. It suggests that the projected audience for this new encyclopedia was somewhat less familiar with Latin than the public of encyclopedia subscribers earlier in the century. One subtle indication of this evolution is that quotations given in Latin in the *Encyclopédie* entry are sometimes deleted when the article is carried over to the *Méthodique*. One example is "Ochlocratie" in *Economie politique,* for example, which deletes both the etymology of the term with its words in Greek and a short quotation in Latin from Cicero.

Among the modern languages, works originally written in English appear to be cited the most frequently. American English is not particularly well represented, although *Logique, métaphysique et morale* contains several extracts from Benjamin Franklin's *Poor Richard's Almanac,* which had been translated by Pierre Samuel Dupont de Nemours in 1777 ("Industrie"), and in the same series Thomas Jefferson supplied notes and advice for "États-Unis" and "Virginie." But for the most part, *Méthodique* editors concentrate on British works.

In the sciences, *Mathématiques* and *Physique* are particularly aware of research carried out across the Channel. Isaac Newton's work is cited often in *Mathématiques,* particularly on astronomical topics ("Aphélie"). John Flamsteed's *Atlas cœlestis* is another important source in astronomy. The article "Cartes célestes" describes this atlas as "Le plus bel ouvrage que l'on ait en ce genre" (the most beautiful work that we have in this genre), a sumptuous volume said to cost two guineas; the author gives information on two recent revisions and translations, a more affordable quarto edition in French published in 1776 (it went through several later editions), and a German edition published in 1782. While few contributors provide such information about cost, virtually all of them share the goal implied in this detail: the *Méthodique* was to serve as a vehicle for transmitting knowledge and information to both specialists and a wider audience.

In *Physique,* Newton's *Traité d'optique* is cited at length in "Halo," along with speculations by other scientists (Descartes, Gassendi, Huyghens) about the formation of haloes, a phenomenon that remained mysterious. Flamsteed is also a source for several articles in *Physique* ("Propagation du son"). Humphry Davy and Count Rumford ("Chauffage") are among other British researchers mentioned in this dictionary.[19]

Chymie includes ground-breaking material on the new Lavoisian chemistry, and internal references indicate that the main author, Louis Bernard Guyton de Morveau, was in contact with British colleagues who shared information about similar research taking place in Great Britain. In "Acier," for example, he notes that Richard Kirwan had sent him Joseph

Priestley's *Experiements and Observations on Different Kinds of Air*, which corroborated his own research. In another area of contemporary chemistry, pharmaceutical preparations, *Chymie* acknowledges John Quincy's *Pharmacopée universelle raisonnée* ("Calotte ou Bonnet céphalique").

The *Méthodique* dictionaries concerned with medicine and physiology show ample evidence of wide reading in English sources. *Système anatomique* is a research-intensive dictionary begun by the noted physician and anatomist Félix Vicq d'Azyr and continued by Hippolyte Cloquet after Vicq d'Azyr's death in 1794. Among the many sources cited are the accounts of explorers such as the Scot Mungo Park ("Girafe").[20] Contributors to *Médecine* were well aware of the advanced medical training available in Edinburgh and refer to contemporary Scottish physicians, among others the obstetrician William Smellie ("Ecartement des Os pubiques") and another eminent figure of the Scottish Enlightenment, the physician and chemist William Cullen ("Quassia"). The third dictionary in the medical cluster of the *Méthodique*, *Chirurgie*, reproduces an extensive tableau of illnesses that can be treated with surgery (*Chirurgie*, 1:15–33). The listing, in French, is attributed to a work whose title is given in English, John Aitken's *Elements of the Theory and Practice of Physic and Surgery*.[21] Since no French edition seems to have been published, the editor of *Chirurgie*, the Swiss military physician Daniel de La Roche, must have acquired a translation or supplied his own.

Various industrial and practical improvements conceived by the British are covered in the *Méthodique*. Jethro Tull's innovations in ploughing are explained in *Art aratoire* ("Défricher"), and *Artillerie* refers to Benjamin Robins's *Nouveaux principes d'artillerie* ("Pendule"). This latter reference is an example of the many time-tested sources cited by scientific contributors to the *Méthodique*, in addition to the more numerous recent publications that predominate in their articles. Robins's book was published in English in 1742 as *New Principles of Gunnery* and was translated into German with additional commentary by the great Swiss mathematician Leonhard Euler in 1745. A French translation was made from the German by a certain Lombard in 1783. Robins's original publication had therefore been available in English for eighty years, and in French for about half that time, when *Artillerie* appeared in 1822 – a remarkable illustration of the tortuous path sometimes required to transfer knowledge from one linguistic group to another.

Arts et métiers updates and expands the already exceptional coverage of industrial processes in the *Encyclopédie*. The additions include reports on various technological advances made in Great Britain, usually with somewhat vague references to a source. In one case, the contributor seems to have relied on an unpublished translation, although a formal title is cited. The 142-page manual "Imprimerie-librairie" includes an extract attributed to the Scottish printer William Ged's *Nouveaux essais d'imprimerie* (*Arts et métiers*, 2: 519–21). I have not been able to find evidence of a French work under this title, which appears to refer to Ged's *Biographical Memoirs ... Including a Particular Account of His Progress in the Art of Block-Printing.* If the French title was not in fact a published translation, the extract represents a kind of intermediate transfer of a foreign-language text: more than a paraphrase or summary, but less than a full published work to which readers might be referred. The book is said to have been communicated to the author by "un Anglois amateur" (an English person interested in the subject), an acknowledgment suggesting the informal exchange of books between Great Britain and France beyond the milieu of book importers and exporters.[22]

The companion series to *Arts et métiers* was *Manufactures*, written by the industrial inspector Jean Marie Roland de la Platière (assisted by his wife, Marie Philipon Roland, the famous Mme Roland). Among examples of British involvement in this area is a memoir on wool production, part of which is extracted in "Moutons." Roland had received the memoir from Pierre Collinson, a wealthy British amateur who studied natural history and corresponded with many luminaries, including Benjamin Franklin. Collinson in turn had received the treatise from an unnamed Spanish gentleman. Of interest here are two points. The memoir took a circuitous route on its way to Roland's desk, necessitated perhaps by the relatively limited intellectual exchanges between Spain and France. And Collinson's willingness to share access to commercially valuable knowledge is further evidence that the European republic of letters embraced exchanges in multiple areas of human thought.

Two British sources were used widely in *Logique, métaphysique and morale.* They are Joseph Addison's *Spectator* ("Singularité"), frequently translated since 1714, and the works of Locke ("Infinité"). Locke is also cited in other dictionaries on such varied subjects as military education in (*Art militaire*, "Éducation militaire") and a rhetorical term (*Grammaire et littérature*, "Catachrèse"). Joshua Reynolds's *Discourses on Art*, published as *Seven Discourses Delivered in the Royal Academy by the President* in 1778 and translated in 1782, is a major reference work in *Beaux-arts* ("Pensée"). The same series attributes "Gravure" to Joseph Strutt's *A Biographical Dictionary of All the Engravers*, which does not appear to have been published in French. Finally, *Musique* cites Charles Avison's *An Essay on Musical Expression*, translated into German in 1775 but apparently not into French ("Expression"). Certain articles also refer to or quote directly from unidentified works of Charles Burney, probably his *The Present State of Music in France and Italy*. A French translation was published in 1809–10, in time, for example, for the references and direct quotations in "France."[23]

In addition to the physicians mentioned above, several seminal figures of the Scottish Enlightenment are prominent in certain dictionaries of the *Méthodique*. The reputation of these writers had insured that their major works would be translated into French, although few *Méthodique* contributors or compilers name specific translations. The historian-philosopher-moralist Adam Ferguson's *Essay on the History of Civil Society* is identified as a source in *Economie politique* ("Sauvages"), *Théologie* ("Indifférence de religion"), and *Logique, métaphysique et morale* ("Bienveillance"); collaborators would have been able to use a French translation published in 1783. David Hume's *History of England* is quoted in *Grammaire et littérature* on Edward I's mass execution of the Welsh bards ("Barde"). The French translation of this history had been produced quickly and by a professional, Octavie Belot, and appeared in 1763. Hume's *Philosophical Essays concerning Human Understanding* are cited in *Logique, métaphysique et morale* ("Infinité"). One of the few non-French sources identified in *Commerce* consists of several pages of "Balance du commerce," attributed simply to "Hume." Hume is also among a small number of British philosophers whose thought is analysed in *Philosophie ancienne et moderne*.[24] Adam Smith's *The Theory of Moral Sentiments*, translated three times between 1759 and 1798, is extracted in several articles in *Logique, métaphysique et morale* ("Approbation"). Smith's *Wealth of Nations* is omnipresent in *Economie politique*: on taxes, colonies, the poor, cities, the clergy, public debt ("Impôts," "Colonies," "Pauvres," "Villes," "Clergé," "Dette publique"). The first translation of *Wealth of Nations* by Jean Antoine Roucher appeared in 1778–9, easily in time to be used in *Economie politique*, of which volume 1 was published in 1786.

Germanophone specialists, who could have been read in Latin (as we saw above with Haller), in French translation, or in their native language, constitute a significant group of sources for *Méthodique* contributors. This is particularly true in the sciences. The editor of *Chymie*, Guyton de Morveau, explicitly acknowledges this debt in the preface to his dictionary. While pointing out one of the main strengths of *Chymie*, that it refers to many sources written in foreign languages, he singles out German for special note, claiming that it will soon be the international language of science.[25] His statement is corroborated by the number of contemporary Germanophone researchers named in various science dictionaries. The six-page entry "Chrysolite" in *Chymie* is a vivid example. Although chemists and geologists from other linguistic groups are mentioned (Pliny, John Hawkins), the majority are German and all but one were contemporaries still active in research. A note states that the main part of the article was translated from Martin Heinrich Klaproth's analysis of chrysolite and published in the *Journal des mines*. The German scientists referenced in it are Abraham Gottlob Werner, (Louis?) Hecht, Johann Ehrenreich von Fichtel (a note refers to his *Mineralogische Bemerkungen von den Karparten*), and Johann Thaddeus Landacker, with a reference to the collection *Sammlung physicalischer Aufsœtze* (these two German titles are translated for the *Méthodique* reader).

The German presence is also strong in other scientific dictionaries. As in the article "Chrysolite," most are contemporary or nearly so, but older authorities are not excluded. The editor of *Géographie-physique*, Nicolas Desmarest, opens his series with 672 pages of extracts from and summaries of the works of thirty-seven authors. They include three Germans who had written on earth science, Johann Friederich Henckel (1:234–46), Johann Gottlob Lehmann (1:271–301), and the philosopher Gottfried Wilhelm Leibniz, who also published scientific writings and who represents a slightly earlier authority, since he died in 1716 (1:301–4). Two Germanophone Swiss are also included, Johann Jakob Scheuchzer (1:432–6) and Gottlieb Sigmund Gr[o]uner (1:188–201). In *Médecine*, the treatise "Médecine morale" refers to several Germanophone physicians and scientists: the Swiss naturalist and physician Johann Georg Zimmermann; the vitalist and chemist Georg Ernest Stahl; and two physicians of Austrian-Dutch background, Gerard van Swieten and Anton de Haen. In *Système anatomique*, in addition to Albinus, the works of Johann Christian Polycarp Erxleben are often cited ("Girafe"), as is the Prussian natural historian Jacob Theodor Klein in the section of *Histoire naturelle* on invertebrates (*Vers*, "Anatises"). In *Physique*, Christian Ernst Wünsch is among the authorities named in the above-mentioned "Propagation du son."

The renown of Prussian military tactics meant that the subject was thoroughly covered in several important articles in *Art militaire*. They include "Tactique," with a translation attributed to baron Georg Ernst Freiherr von Holtzendorff, author of works published in French as *Campagne du roi de Prusse, de 1778 à 1779* and *Elémens de tactique, demonstrés géométriquement.*[26] On a more theoretical question, Samuel von Pufendorf is a source for "Arbitre" in the same dictionary.

The erudition of Jablonski and Grævius, as we saw, was marshalled to support articles in *Antiquités.* In the arts, Johann Joachim Winckelmann's ground-breaking 1764 *Geschichte der Kunst des Alterthums* was quickly translated, appearing in French in 1766. Several *Méthodique* editors relied heavily on this work: Quatremère de Quincy in *Architecture* treats it as a standard work known by all ("Aigle"), *Antiquités* names Winckelmann in the preface as a major source, and *Beaux-arts* refers to it liberally ("Mythologie"). The latter dictionary also quotes extensively from a translation of the critical works of Anton Raphael Mengs, who propounded early neoclassical theories ("Équilibre").[27] An example of an occassional German source in *Beaux-arts* is Johann Jakob Engel's *Ideen zu einer Mimik,* which is extracted in "Pantomime." Like the compiler of "Chrysolite," the contributor of "Pantomime" was aware of the reader's possible need for a French translation: there is a precise reference to volumes 3 and 4 of Hendrik Jansen's *Recueil de pièces intéressantes* for the relevant text, entitled *Idées sur le geste.* Another author who wrote in German appears in both *Musique* and *Grammaire et littérature,* the Swiss Johann Georg Sulzer, whose *Allgemeine Theorie der Schönen Künste* had furnished more than sixty articles to the *Supplément.*[28] The editors of both *Musique* and *Grammaire et littérature* transfer a number of these articles to the *Méthodique* (*Grammaire et littérature,* "Caractère"; *Musique,* "Accord").

The German church historian Johann Lorenz (von) Mosheim appears hundreds of times in *Théologie,* but not as a source of knowledge to be transferred. Rather, the editor of *Théologie,* the well-known apologist Nicolas Sylvestre Bergier, responds critically to Mosheim on major points of church history, from the role of the Fathers of the Church to monasticism in the sixteenth century ("Pères de l'Eglise," "Moine, Monastère, Etat monastique"). Bergier usually refers to Mosheim only by name, but he occasionally includes the Latin title of one of the dozens of works Mosheim wrote in Latin. More often, he mentions the French title of the Mosheim work that he seems to have consulted most frequently, *Histoire ecclésiastique ancienne et moderne.* This was the translation of Mosheim's *Institutiones historiæ ecclesiasticæ,* first published in 1726 and translated into French in 1776 by Marc Antoine Eidous.[29] One can surmise that Bergier, who read Latin fluently, guides his readers to the French translation as a more accessible source for the majority of them; it seems likely that he himself had studied the work much earlier in its original Latin edition.

The Netherlands continued in the eighteenth century to produce scientists and scholars who achieved a European reputation. Then as now, many published their work in a language other than Dutch in order to reach a wider audience. Failure to do so meant that valuable contributions risked remaining obscure, as Nicolas Desmarest points out in the case of the Leiden professor and hydrologist Johan Lulofs (*Géog.-physique*, 1:307). Desmarest, like fellow *Méthodique* writers in similar circumstances, summarizes Lulofs in French.[30]

Thanks to the fact that most Dutch scholars and scientists used more widely read languages and thanks to translations, the number of Dutch figures whose ideas are transferred in the *Méthodique* is significant. They include certain luminaries from the seventeenth century. Several examples from articles already mentioned include the jurisconsult and polymath Hugo Grotius (*Art militaire*, "Arbitre"), Jan Baptist van Helmont and Boerhaave (*Médecine*, "Médecine morale"), and Christiaan Huyghens (*Physique*, "Halo"). As we saw, *Antiquités* includes among its major sources Gronovius's *Thesaurus antiquitatum Græcarum*. The anthropologist Cornelius de Pauw, author of the controversial *Recherches philosophiques sur les Américains* and the *Recherches philosophiques sur les Égyptiens et les Chinois*, is credited as another major source in *Antiquités* and is also quoted in *Architecture* on the Chinese style ("Architecture").[31]

A final group of sources with considerable weight in the *Méthodique* includes works written by Italians. Contributors across a variety of disciplines refer to the major (and occasionally more minor) Italian authors in their discipline whose publications were generally fairly accessible in France, if not always in translation. Few of the works of Lodovico Antonio Muratori, the prolific historian and man of letters, for example, were translated into French from their original Latin or Italian during the eighteenth century, but this was no impediment for Mongez, the editor of *Antiquités*, who refers often to Muratori ("Colosse de Rhodes"). In other areas, Cesare Bonesana, marquis de Beccaria, had seen two of his works translated and adapted by André Morellet: *Ricerche intorno alla natura dello stile*, translated as *Recherches sur le style*; and *Dei delitti e delle pene*, translated as *Traité des délits et des peines*. *Grammaire et littérature* extracts a section from the first work ("Enthousiasme," in the supplement, vol. 3), and there are references to the latter in *Jurisprudence* ("Peine de mort") and its last two volumes, *Police et municipalités* ("Abandon"), as well as a few in *Economie politique* ("Crime"). Although the mentions of his name or his works are relatively sparse in the *Méthodique*, Beccaria's ideas inform many articles in relevant series.[32]

In the sciences, the sixteenth-century naturalist Ulisse Aldrovandi remains a reference (*Système anatomique*, "Crustacés"), read in Latin since there were no French translations of his works. Authors tend, however, to show a higher regard for more recent research. Experiments of the contemporary biologist Lazzaro Spallanzani are described in "Fécondation," covered in both *Agriculture* and *Forêts et bois*. A nearly three-hundred-page section of the latter was a treatise on plant physiology by the Genevan botanist Jean Senebier. He was also the major translator of Spallanzani's works.[33] And Giovanni Battista Morgagni, whose ground-breaking work on pathology, *De Sedibus et causis morborum per anatomem indagates*, was published when its author was eighty, is a frequently named source in *Médecine* ("Fausse grossesse"). There appears not to have been a translation made before 1820–4, but as noted, most *Médecine* physicians could read Latin.

Quick reference should be made to a relatively new encyclopedic category through which transfers of knowledge can be said to have been at least initiated, if not developed to any extent. Biographical entries are provided in various dictionaries and constitute the bulk of the six volumes of *Histoire*. These entries are admittedly often sketchy about the subject's writings (notably in *Histoire*), but other dictionaries give more detail about the person's discoveries and publications (particularly in *Médecine* and *Chirurgie*). Brief as they are, these entries served to introduce many non-French figures to *Méthodique* readers.[34]

This brief overview can suggest several features of the use that *Méthodique* editors and contributors made of sources not published originally in French. First, in Panckoucke's conception of the *Méthodique*, specialists were to be put in charge of each series, so readers could expect that articles would give evidence of mastery of the entire literature of a given subject. This is generally the case. Older authorities are recognized and sometimes corrected as their contributions are transmitted to a modern readership. But it is up-to-date researchers and scholars who predominate. The *Méthodique* team members were generally attuned to, and in many cases active members of, the European intellectual scene during the decades that the encyclopedia was in production. They knew the work of those who were already eminent and who would remain so – thinkers like Haller, Adam Smith, Beccaria – as well as other important scholars whose names are less familiar today.

Language barriers were not as significant as might be expected among a group representing at least five languages, Dutch, English, French, German, and Italian. For many, Latin functioned as a common language.

Mobility was an accepted feature of the intellectual landscape of Europe, and with it went learning additional languages. Translations of major scholarly works had a market, and many were published rapidly.

The *Méthodique* thus incorporated a wide variety of non-French sources, written originally in several different languages. If similar acknowledgments of sources named in the *Encyclopédie* and the *Supplément* in articles that are carried over in various *Méthodique* dictionaries were included, the breadth of non-French coverage would be even more extensive. But certain qualifications need to be made to this overview of knowledge transfers from non-French sources in the *Méthodique*. It bears repeating that many of the references to ancient authors do not really constitute a transfer from a foreign body of knowledge, given the classical education received by most contributors. In addition, the genealogy of certain seminal ideas cannot be as neatly delineated as a survey of the present kind suggests. As I suggested in the case of Beccaria, many ideas, from antiquity on, were assimilated and retransmitted over and over, to the point that their actual provenance is no longer mentioned or perhaps even remembered. The number of language groups or geographical areas that are *not* represented to any extent in the *Méthodique* is also worth mentioning. Almost nothing is attributed to works emanating from Russia, the Orient, the Middle East, or Africa; and in Europe itself, the Iberian peninsula is largely silent except as the subject of travel writers. Finally, while the number of non-French sources is remarkable, they are greatly outnumbered by French sources. I shall call on the useful camel to illustrate this point. The camel and the dromedary are members of the first genus of the family of ruminants and are covered together in Félix Vicq d'Azyr's "Ruminans" (*Système Anatomique*, 3:249–57). There are seventy-nine scientific citations in this section. Nine are to Buffon; forty-three are to Louis Jean Marie Daubenton, who collaborated with Buffon, also published articles in the *Encyclopédie*, and was an editor of the section on natural history in the *Méthodique*. Cuvier is referenced for ten more, Claude Perrault for six (*Mémoires pour servir à l'histoire naturelle des animaux*), and Louis Daniel Arnault de Nobleville and François Salerne for one.[35] Only the remaining ten sources are non-French: one reference to Aristotle,[36] five to Linnaeus, two to Erxleben's *Systema regni animalis*, and three to French translations of travel writers, the German Adam Olearius (*Relation du voyage de Moscovie, Tartarie et de Perse*), the English clergyman David Shaw (*Voyage dans la régence d'Alger*), and a Dane, Carsten Niebuhr (*Description de l'Arabie*).

This contingent of non-French sources is repeated in different proportions throughout the *Méthodique*. Minority though it may be, it clearly enriches the *Méthodique* and contributes to making it the superlative vehicle for the transfer of knowledge that Panckoucke had described in the prospectus: "Elle [la nouvelle encyclopédie] formera le recueil le plus riche, le plus vaste, le plus intéressant, le plus exact, le plus complet & le mieux suivi qu'on puisse désirer, puisqu'elle réunira avec ordre ce que renferment de connoissances réelles plusieurs milliers de volumes, sans en copier aucun, dont la recherche seroit pénible & souvent infructueuse, la lecture impossible & le prix énorme." ([The new encyclopedia] will be the richest collection, the most comprehensive, the most exact, the most complete, and the most consistent that one could hope for, since it will assemble in an orderly way the real knowledge contained in several thousand volumes, without copying any of them. Trying to obtain all those volumes would entail a tedious and often fruitless search, reading them all would be impossible, and the price would be enormous; *Beaux-arts*, 1:iv). Among these thousands of inaccessible, difficult-to-read, expensive source works were a large number written in languages other than French, including many that had not been translated. The *Méthodique* serves as a conduit of this European store of knowledge to at least two significant readerships: subscribers in the late eighteenth and early nineteenth centuries; and since then and especially as of the last few decades, historians of that seminal period.

Schematic List of Component Dictionaries of the Encyclopédie Méthodique

Agriculture. 6 vols., 1787–1816. Editors: Alexandre Henri Tessier, André Thouin, Auguste Denis Fougeroux de Bondaroy, Louis Augustin Guillaume Bosc. *Dictionnaire de la culture des arbres et de l'aménagement des forêts* (vol. 7 of *Agriculture*), 1821–[3].[37] Editors: Bosc, Jacques Joseph Baudrillard.

Antiquités, mythologie, diplomatique des chartres, et chronologie. 5 vols., 1786–[95]. Editor: Antoine Mongez. 380 plates, 1804–[11]. Editor: Antoine Mongez; plates drawn by Angélique Mongez.

Architecture. 3 vols., 1788–[1828]. Editor: Antoine Chrysostome Quatremère de Quincy.

Art aratoire et du jardinage. 1 vol., 1797. Editor: Jacques Lacombe. 54 plates, 1802.

Artillerie. 1 vol., 1822. Editor: Gaspard Hermann Cotty.

Art militaire. 4 vols., 1784–[1802]. Editor: Louis Félix Guinement de Kéralio, Jean Gérard Lacuée de Cessac, Joseph Servan. 60 plates.

Arts académiques, équitation, escrime, danse, et art de nager. 1 vol., 1786. 16 plates.

Arts et métiers mécaniques. 8 vols., 1782–[92]. Editor: attributed to Jacques
Lacombe. Plates, *Recueil de planches,* covering *Arts et métiers mécaniques,
Manufactures,* and other areas, 8 vols., 1783–90.[38]

Assemblée nationale constituante. 1 vol. (marked vol. 2), 1792. Editor: Jacques
Peuchet.

Beaux-arts. 2 vols., 1788–[93]. Editor: Pierre Charles Levesque. 115 plates, 1805.

Botanique. 8 vols. + *Supplément,* 5 vols., 1783–1817. Editors: Jean Baptiste de
Lamarck, Jean Louis Marie Poiret. 1,000 plates, 1823; editor, Lamarck.
Explanatory volumes of plates: *Tableau encyclopédique et méthodique des trois
règnes de la nature. Botanique.* 3 vols., 1791–1823.

Chasses. 1 vol., 1795. Editor: attributed to Jacques Lacombe. 32 plates, 1811.

Chirurgie. 2 vols., 1790–[98]. Editors: Daniel de La Roche, Philippe Petit-Radel.
113 plates, 1798.

Chymie, pharmacie et métallurgie. 6 vols., 1786–1815. Editors: Louis Bernard
Guyton de Morveau, Hugues Maret, Jean Pierre François Duhamel, François
Chaussier, Louis Nicolas Vauquelin. 62 plates, 1813–14.

Commerce. 3 vols., 1783–[7]. Editor: Nicolas Baudeau.

Dictionnaire des jeux familiers, ou des amusemens de société. (In vol. 4 of
Mathématiques, 1797.) Editor: Jacques Lacombe. *Jeux mathématiques.* 1 vol.,
1799. Editor: Jacques Lacombe.

Dictionnaire encyclopédique des Amusemens des sciences, mathématiques et physiques. 1
vol., 1792. Editor: Jacques Lacombe. 86 plates.

Economie politique et diplomatique. 4 vols., 1784–[90]. Editor: Jean Nicolas
Démeunier.

Encyclopédiana. 1 vol., 1791; attributed to Jacques Lacombe.

Finances. 3 vols., 1784–7. Editor: Jacques Philibert Rousselot de Surgy.

Forêts et bois. 1 vol., 1791–1815. Editors: Louis Marie Blanquart de Septfontaines,
Gaspard Clair François Marie Riche de Prony.

Géographie ancienne. 3 vols., 1787–[96]. Editor: Edme Mentelle.

Géographie moderne. 3 vols., 1782–8. Editors: Nicolas Masson de Morvilliers,
François Robert.

Atlas, géographie ancienne et géographie moderne. 2 vols., 77 maps and 63 maps,
1787–88.

Géographie-physique. 5 vols., 1795–[1832]. Editors: Nicolas Desmarest, Jean
Baptiste Bory de Saint-Vincent, Guillaume Tell Doin, Claude Joseph Ferry,
Jean Jaqcques Nicolas Huot. *Atlas, Géographie-physique.* 48 plates, 1827.
Editors: Desmarest, Bory de Saint-Vincent.

Grammaire et littérature. 3 vols., 1782–[8]. Editor: Panckoucke (?). Main
contributors: Nicolas Beauzée, Jean-François Marmontel.

Histoire. 6 vols., 1784–1804. Editor: Gabriel Henri Gaillard. 33 plates.

Histoire naturelle des animaux. 10 vols., 1782–[1828]. Editors: Louis Jean Marie Daubenton, Pierre Jean Claude Mauduyt de la Varenne, Guillaume Antoine Olivier, Pierre André Latreille, Jean Baptiste Godart, Amédée Louis Michel Lepeletier de Saint Fargeau, Jean Guillaume Audinet-Serville, Félix Edouard Guérin Méneville.

Histoire naturelle des vers. 4 vols., 1792–[1827]. Editors: Jean Guillaume Bruguière, Gérard Deshayes, Jean Baptiste Lamouroux, Bory de Saint-Vincent, Jacques Amand Eudes Deslongchamps. Plates for *Histoire naturelle*: 1,447, 1788–1828.

Jurisprudence [vols. 9 and 10: *Police et municipalités*], 10 vols., 1782–[92]. Editors: Lerasle, Jacques Peuchet.

Logique et Métaphysique [*Morale* added to title in vol. 2]. 4 vols., 1786. Editor: Pierre Louis Lacretelle.

Manufactures, arts et métiers. 4 vols., 1785–1828. Editors: Jean Marie Roland de La Platière, Guillaume Tell Doin, Poutet. 580 plates.

Marine. 3 vols., 1783–[9]. Editors: Honoré Sébastien Vial de Clairbois, Etienne Nicolas Blondeau. 173 plates.

Mathématiques. 4 vols., 1784–89. Editors: Charles Bossut; Jean le Rond d'Alembert; Jérôme de Lalande; Antoine Caritat, marquis de Condorcet; Jacques Charles. 108 plates. *Dictionnaire des jeux.* (In vol. 3 of *Mathématiques*, 1792.) 16 plates.

Médecine. 13 vols., 1787–[1832]. Editors: Félix Vicq d'Azyr, Louis Jacques Moreau de La Sarthe, Auguste Thillaye.

Musique. 2 vols., 1791–[1821]. Editors: Nicolas Etienne Framery, Pierre Louis Ginguené, Jérôme de Momigny. 188 plates at end of vol. 2.

Pêches. 1 vol., 1796. Editor: attributed to Jacques Lacombe. 114 plates, 1793.

Philosophie ancienne et moderne. 3 vols., 1791–[7]. Editor: Jacques-André Naigeon.

Physique. 4 vols., 1793–[1824]. Editors: Gaspard Monge, Jacques Dominique Cassini, Pierre Nicolas Bertholon, Jean Henri Hassenfratz. 133 plates, 1816–24.

Système anatomique. 4 vols., 1792–1830. Editors: Vicq d'Azyr, Hippolyte Cloquet. 96 plates, 1825.

Théologie. 3 vols., 1788–[91]. Editor: Nicolas Sylvestre Bergier.

NOTES

1 See also Groult's *Charles-Joseph Panckoucke, Prospectus et mémoires*, 2011; a second volume containing additional communications with subscribers is forthcoming.

2 Delia and Groffier 2012, and Boulad-Ayoub 2013.

3 See Morris 1994; and Doig 1994, "The Quarto" and "Yverdon Encyclopédie."
   On the *Supplément,* see Hardesty 1977.

4 His essays were included in the *Méthodique.* In all cases Panckoucke's
   contribution was one of several articles under a given term. His
   "Quadrature" is in *Mathematiques* and three additional articles are in *Logique,
   métaphysique et morale.* "Discours sur l'existence de Dieu" (under "Dieu"),
   "Plaisir," and "Discours sur le beau, le juste, & la liberté" (under "Beau").

5 The "Vocabulaire" was never published. On its role in Panckoucke's
   conception of the *Méthodique,* see Groult 2011, 299–305 and passim.

6 For more detailed accounts of the publication of the *Méthodique,* see Tucoo-
   Chala 1977, 323–44, 396–403, 491–5, and *L'Encyclopédie méthodique* 2006, 21–53.

7 For the exact dates of the 102 instalments, see Evanhuis 2003, 39–48.

8 A new series, *Histoire de la Révolution,* three volumes to cover events and
   decisions of the Revolutionary period, had been abandoned. Only vol.
   2, *Assemblée Constituante* (1792), was published, and it covered only terms
   under the letter "A." See Boulad-Ayoub 2013, 25–42.

9 This list is in Groult 2011, *Savoir et Matières,* 331–50; it is based on the
   inventory of the sets at the Bibliothèque Sainte-Geneviève (Paris) and the
   Bibliothèque Interuniversitaire Lettres et Sciences Humaines (Lyon). See
   above, pp. 130–2, for a schematic listing of the *Méthodique.*

10 For example, the physician Nicolas Chambon de Montaux published
   a collection of clinical observations (*Observationes clinicæ, curationes
   morborum*) and a treatise on noxious airs (*An aer corruptus expurgari possit*).

11 Naigeon judges both Brucker and Diderot's other basic source, Thomas
   Stanley's *The History of Philosophy,* as prolix and excessively erudite and
   thereby missing the essential points of the philosophies they treat (preface
   of *Philosophie ancienne et moderne,* 1:viii–xiii). Brucker is also referred to in
   the *Méthodique*'s series on theology.

12 Grævius also began *Thesaurus antiquitatum et historiarum Italiæ,* published
   posthumously and completed by others.

13 Perhaps Quatremère de Quincy was thinking of Moreau de Brioul's recent
   translation, the 1816 *L'Architecture de Vitruve* (this volume of *Architecture*
   appeared in 1825).

14 In the context of a quotation from Vitruvius in "Maçonnerie," Rondelet
   states that he had translated the material for his own *Traité théorique et
   pratique de l'Art de bâtir.*

15 On humoralism, see Williams 1994, 57–62. In *Médecine,* see for example
   Chambon's "Constitution des femmes" and Louis Charles Henri Macquart's
   "Liqueur."

16 *Médecine* gives direct quotations, in French, in certain articles. See, for
   example, "Descente de matrice," 5:399.

17 If not philosophically. Naigeon is openly favourable towards philosophers
   opposed to religion ("Fréret") and critical of philosophers with a spiritual
   or metaphysical bent ("Berkeleisme").

18 The text is from Horace's *Satire 10*, book 1, verses 14–15: "Ridiculum acri //
   Fortius & melius magnas plerumque secat res."

19 Rumford is an example of the fluid national borders of many scientists of
   the period. Born Benjamin Thompson in Massachusetts, he was a Loyalist
   during the Revolutionary War and moved to Great Britain afterwards. He
   eventually became an employee of the Bavarian government, which granted
   his title.

20 Another traveller, James Bruce, provides information for articles in
   Géographie ancienne. "Troglodytæ," for example, refers to his *Travels to
   Discover the Source of the Nile*.

21 An earlier one-volume edition was published in 1779 under the title
   Systematic Elements of the Theory and Practice of Physic and Surgery.

22 In a similar example in the same series, "Fer (Art du)" refers to a French
   title, "Traité de M. Horne," that does not seem to have existed, although the
   work in question is clearly Henry Horne's *Essays Concerning Iron and Steel*.

23 This article appears in the second half of volume 1 of *Musique*, delivered to
   subscribers in 1813. Charles Brack's translation appeared in 1809–10.

24 Others include Francis Bacon ("Baconisme"); Nehemiah Grew, better
   known for his *Anatomy of Plants* than for the *Cosmologia sacra* that is the focus
   of Naigeon's article; and John Locke.

25 He notes, without further explanation, that French could have retained this
   position (preface, *Chymie*, 1:ii).

26 I have not been able to identify German titles for these works, although the long
   title of *Elémens de tactique* indicates that it was translated from a German work.

27 Like many scholars of the period whose national identity was mixed, Mengs
   can be associated with another language group. Born in Bohemia, he lived
   mainly in Rome for many years and also spent time in Madrid. The Spanish
   ambassador to the Papal States, Jose Nicolas de Azara, published Mengs's
   theoretical writing in Italian as *Opere di Antonio Raffaello Mengs*; it was
   translated into French by Hendrik Jansen.

28 Translated by Jean Henri Samuel Formey. See Cernuschi 2000, 652.

29 Whose base text was the second edition of a 1765 English translation by
   Archibald Maclaine.

30 Desmarest says that he had received Lulofs's memoir (thirty-eight pages)
   but gives no information about any translation, and there does not appear

to have been one. It is not known if he read Dutch. His summary of Lulofs (Lolofs) (*Géog.-physique*, 1:307–18) is entitled "Remarques sur l'élévation de la mer & sur l'abaissement des terres le long des côtes de la Hollande", the exact translation of the title of Lulofs's memoir. I am grateful to Kenneth L. Taylor and Wilfried Van Steen for providing information about Lulofs.

31 I have classified De Pauw with Dutch figures because he was born in Amsterdam. He was educated in Gottingen and spent most of his life in Germany. His major works were published in Berlin in French.

32 For an overview of the penetration of Beccaria's ideas among the encyclopedists, see Delia and Groffier 2012, 72–120; and Delia's contribution to the present volume.

33 Their French titles: *Expériences sur la digestion; Opuscules de physique animale et végétale; Expériences pour servir à l'histoire de la génération des animaux et des plantes; Mémoires sur la respiration.*

34 These biographical notices are not to be confused with the analytical accounts in such dictionaries as *Philosophie* and *Géographie-physique*, which include, as we saw, extracts from or summaries of the works of a major figure.

35 The latter source can be identified as *Histoire naturelle des animaux.*

36 And "la plupart des Anciens," on the age when camels can reproduce; their view is said to be corrected in de Nobleville and Salerne (*Syst. Anat.*, 3:256).

37 The *Méthodique* was published in half-volumes. In cases where the last section was delivered in a year other than that printed on the title page, the date is given in brackets.

38 In this list, when no date is given for plates, they are found in the *Recueil.*

Bibliography

Aitken, John. 1779. *Systematic Elements of the Theory and Practice of Physic and Surgery.* Edinburgh: W. Gordon and W. Creech; London: J. Murray.

– 1782. *Elements of the Theory and Practice of Physic and Surgery.* 2 vols. London: n.p.

Arnault de Nobleville, Louis Daniel, and François Salerne. 1756. *Histoire naturelle des animaux.* Paris: Desaint et Saillant.

Avison, Charles. 1752. *An Essay on Musical Expression.* London: C. Davis.

Beccaria, Cesare Bonesana, marquis de. 1761. *Recherches sur le style* … Translated by André Morellet. Paris: Molini.

– 1764. *Dei delitti e delle pene.* Monaco: n.p.

– 1770. *Ricerche intorno alla natura dello stile.* Milan: Galeazzi.

– 1766. *Traité des délits et des peines* … Translated by André Morellet. Lausanne [Paris]: n.p.

Blanckaert, Claude, Michel Porret, and Fabrice Brandli. 2006. *L'Encyclopédie méthodique (1782–1832): Des Lumières au positivisme.* Geneva: Droz.

Boulad-Ayoub, Josiane. 2013. *La Vision nouvelle de la société dans l'Encyclopédie méthodique,* vol. 2: *Assemblée constituante.* Quebec City: Les Presses de l'Université Laval.

Bruce, James. 1790. *Travels to Discover the Source of the Nile …* 5 vols. London: G.G.J. and J. Robinson.

Brucker, Johann Jakob. 1742–4. *Historia critica philosophiæ …* 5 vols. Leipzig: B.C. Breitkopf.

Bruman, Gaspard. 1727. *Hadrianus VI, Sive Analecta Historica de Hadriano Sexto Trajectino Papa Romano.* Utrecht: n.p.

Burney, Charles. 1771. *The Present State of Music in France and Italy …* London: T. Becket.

— 1809–10. *De l'état présent de la musique en France et en Italie, dans les Pays-Bas, en Hollande et en Allemagne …* 3 vols. Translated by Ch. Brack. Genoa: J. Giossi.

Cernuschi, Alain. 2000. *Penser la musique dans l'Encyclopédie. Étude sur les enjeux de la musicographie des Lumières et sur ses liens avec l'encyclopédisme.* Paris: Honoré Champion.

Chambon de Montaux, Nicolas. 1778. *An aer corruptus expurgari possit …* Paris: Quillau.

— 1789. *Observationes clinicæ, curationes morborum.* Paris: A. Croulleboix.

Cicero. 1569. *Les offices de M. Tulle Cicéron …* Chambéry: n.p.

Delia, Luigi, and Éthel Groffier, eds. 2012. *La Vision nouvelle de la société dans l'Encyclopédie méthodique,* vol. 1: *Jurisprudence.* Quebec City: Les Presses de l'Université de Laval.

Doig, Kathleen Hardesty. 1994. "The Quarto and Octavo Editions of the *Encyclopédie.*" In *SVEC* 315, *Notable Encyclopedias of the Late Eighteenth Century: Eleven Successors of the Encyclopédie,* edited by Frank A. Kafker, 117–42. Oxford: Voltaire Foundation.

— 1994. "The Yverdon *Encyclopédie.*" In *SVEC* 315, *Notable Encyclopedias of the Late Eighteenth Century: Eleven Successors of the* Encyclopédie, edited by Frank A. Kafker, 85–116. Oxford: Voltaire Foundation.

Engel, Johann Jakob. 1785–6. *Ideen zu einer Mimik.* 2 vols. Berlin: A. Mylius.

Erxleben, Johann Christian Polycarp. 1777. *Systema regni animalis …* Leipzig: Weygandianis.

Evanhuis, L. 2003. "Dating and Publication of the *Encyclopédie Méthodique* (1782–1832), with Special Reference to the Parts of the *Histoire Naturelle* and Details on the *Histoire Naturelle des Insectes,*" *Zootaxa* 166, no. 1: 1–48.

Ferguson, Adam. 1767. *Essay on the History of Civil Society.* London: A. Millar and T. Cadell.

Fichtel, Johann Ehrenreich von. 1791. *Mineralogische bermerkungen von der Karpaten.* Vienna: Edlen von Kurzbeck.

Flamsteed, John. 1729. *Atlas cœlestis.* London: n.p.

– 1776. *Atlas céleste de John Flamsteed.* Translated by Jean Nicolas Fortin. Paris: F.G. Deschamps.

[Flamsteed, John.] Johann Elert Bode. 1782. *Vorstellung der Gestirne …* Berlin, Stralsund: August Lange.

Franklin, Benjamin. 1777. *La science du bonhomme Richard …* Translated by Pierre Samuel Dupont de Nemours. Paris: Ruault.

Ged, Wiliam. 1781. *Biographical Memoirs … Including a Particular Account of His Progress in the Art of Block-Printing.* London: J. Nichols.

Grævius, Johann Georg. 1694–9. *Thesaurus antiquitatum Romanarum.* 12 vols. Leiden: Pieter Van der Aa; Utrecht: F. Halman.

Grævius, Johann Georg, et al. 1704–23. *Thesaurus antiquitatum et historiarum Italiæ.* 30 vols. Leiden: Pieter Van der Aa.

Grew, Nehemiah. 1682. *The Anatomy of Plants …* [London]: W. Rawlins.

– 1701. *Cosmologia sacra: or a discourse of the universe …* London: W. Rogers, S. Smith, and B. Walford.

Gronovius, Jakob. 1697–1702. *Thesaurus antiquitatum Græcarum.* 13 vols. Leiden: Pieter Van der Aa.

Groult, Martine. 2011. *Charles-Joseph Panckoucke, Prospectus et mémoires de l'Encyclopédie méthodique. Volume I: Prospectus général précédé de la Préface au Grand Vocabulaire François.* Saint-Étienne: Publications de l'Université de Saint-Étienne.

– 2011. *Savoir et Matières: Pensée scientifique et théorie de la connaissance de l'Encyclopédie à l'Encyclopédie méthodique.* Paris: CNRS Éditions.

Hardesty, Kathleen. 1977. *The Supplément to the Encyclopédie.* The Hague: Nijhoff.

Herodotus. 1786. *Histoire … avec des remarques historiques …* 7 vols. Translated by Pierre Henri Larcher. Paris: Musier.

Holtzendorff, Georg Ernst Freiherr von. 1777. *Élémens de tactique demonstrés géométriquement …* Paris: Nyon aîné.

Horne, Henry. 1773. *Essays Concerning Iron and Steel.* London: T. Cadell.

Hume, David. 1753–6. *Essays and Treatises on Several Subjects.* 4 vols. London: A. Millar.

– 1754–61. *History of England …* 6 vols. Edinburgh: Hamilton, Balfour, Neill.

– 1758. *Essais philosophiques sur l'entendement humain.* 2 vols. Amsterdam: n.p.

– 1763. *Histoire d'Angleterre …* Translated by Octavie Belot. Amsterdam: n.p.

Jablonski, Paul Ernst. 1750–2. *Pantheon Ægyptiorum.* 3 vols. Frankfurt: J.C. Kleyb.

Landacker, Johann Thaddeus. 1592. "Collection de Mémoires concernant particuliérement l'Histoire naturelle de Bohême," Dresden, 2 vols. In Johann Mayer et al., 1793, *Sammlung physicalischer Aufsœtze …* Dresden: Walther.

Lulofs, Johan. 1754. *Aanmerkingen over het ryjzen der zee en het zinken der landen aan de Nederlandsche kusten*. Haarlem: n.p.

Mengs, Anton Raphael. 1780. *Opere di Antonio Raffaello Mengs* ... 2 vols. Translated by Jose Nicolas de Azara. Parma: Stamperia reale.

– 1786. *Œuvres complètes d'Antoine Raphaël Mengs*. 2 vols. Translated by Hendrik Jansen. Paris: Hôtel de Thou.

Morgagni, Giovanni Battista. 1820–34. *Recherches anatomiques sur le siège et la cause des maladies*. 10 vols. Translated by Marie-Alexandre Désormeaux and J.P. Destouet. Paris: Caille et Rabier.

Morris, Madeleine F. 1994. "The Tuscan Editions of the *Encyclopédie*." In *SVEC* 315, *Notable Encyclopedias of the Late Eighteenth Century: Eleven Successors of the Encyclopédie*, edited by Frank A. Kafker, 51–84. Oxford: Voltaire Foundation.

Mosheim, Johann Lorenz (von). 1726. *Institutionum historiæ ecclesiasticæ* ... Frankfurt and Leipzig: J. Meyer.

– 1765. *An Ecclesiastical History* ... 2 vols. Translated by Archibald Maclaine. London: A. Millar.

– 1776. *Histoire ecclésiastique* ... Translated by Marc Antoine Eidous. Yverdon: de Felice.

Newton, Isaac. 1720. *Traité d'optique* ... 2 vols. Translated by Pierre Coste. Amsterdam: P. Humbert.

Niebuhr, Carsten. 1773. *Description de l'Arabie* ... Copenhagen: N. Möller.

Olearius, Adam. 1656. *Relation du voyage de Moscovie, Tartarie et de Perse* ... Translated by Abraham de Wicquefort. Paris: G. Clouzier.

Pauw, Cornelius de. 1768–9. *Recherches philosophiques sur les Américains* ... 2 vols. Berlin.

– 1773. *Recherches philosophiques sur les Égyptiens et les Chinois*. 2 vols. Paris: Decker.

Plutarch. 1572. *Les œuvres morales et meslées de Plutarque* ... Translated by Jacques Amyot. Paris: Michel de Vascosan.

Priestley, Joseph. 1774–7. *Experiments and Observations on Different Kinds of Air*. 3 vols. London: J. Johnson.

Quincy, John. 1749. *Pharmacopée universelle raisonnée* ... Translated by Clausier. Paris: Houry père.

Reynolds, Joshua. 1778. *Seven Discourses Delivered in the Royal Academy by the President*. London: T. Cadell.

Robins, Benjamin. 1742. *New Principles of Gunnery*. London: J. Nourse.

– 1745. *Neue Grundsätze der Artillerie* ... Berlin: A. Haude.

– 1783. *Nouveaux principes d'artillerie* ... Dijon and Paris: Jombert.

Rondelet, Antoine Jean Baptiste. 1802–17. *Traité théorique et pratique de l'Art de bâtir*. 4 vols. Paris: chez l'auteur.

Seneca. 1641. *Traité des bienfaits*, in *Les œuvres de Messire François de Malherbe* …
Troyes: Nicolas Oudot.

Shaw, David. 1743. *Voyages de Mr. Shaw* … The Hague: Jean Naulme.

Smith, Adam. 1759. *The Theory of Moral Sentiments*. London: A. Millar; Edinburgh:
A. Kincaid and J. Bell.

– 1764. *Théorie des sentiments moraux* … 2 vols. Translated by Marc-Antoine
Eidous. Paris: Briasson.

– 1774. *Théorie des sentiments moraux* … Translated by Jean-Louis Blavet. Paris: n.p.

– 1776. *An Inquiry into the Nature and Causes of the Wealth of Nations*. London: W.
Strahan and T. Cadell.

– 1778–9. *Recherches … richesse des nations*. 4 vols. Translated by Jean Antoine
Roucher. The Hague: n.p.

– 1798. *Théorie des sentiments moraux* … 2 vols. Translated by Sophie de Grouchy,
marquise de Condorcet. Paris: F. Buisson.

Spallanzani, Lazzaro. 1783. *Expériences sur la digestion* … Translated by Jean
Senebier. Geneva: B. Chirol.

– 1785. *Expériences pour servir à l'histoire de la génération des animaux et des plantes*.
Translated by Jean Senebier. Geneva: B. Chirol.

– 1787. *Opuscules de physique animale et végétale*. 2 vols. Translated by Jean Senebier.
Pavia and Paris: P.-J. Duplain.

– 1803. *Mémoires sur la respiration* … Translated by Jean Senebier. Geneva: J.J.
Paschoud.

Stanley, Thomas. 1655–62. *The History of Philosophy*. 4 vols. London: Humphrey
Moseley and Thomas Dring.

Strutt, Joseph. 1785–6. *A Biographical Dictionary of All the Engravers* … 2 vols.
London: R. Faulder.

Sulzer, Johann Georg. 1771–4. *Allgemeine Theorie der Schönen Künste* … 2 vols.
Leipzig: M.G. Eidermanns Erben und Reich.

Tucoo-chala, Suzanne. 1977. *Charles-Joseph Panckoucke & la librairie française
1736–1798*. Pau and Paris: Marrimpouey Jeune and Jean Touzot.

Vitruvius. 1673. *Les Dix Livres d'architecture*. Translated by Claude Perrault. Paris:
J.-B. Coignard.

– 1816. *L'Architecture de Vitruve*. Translated by Moreau de Brioul. Brussels: A. Stapleaux.

Williams, Elizabeth A. 1994. *The Physical and the Moral: Anthropology, Physiology,
and Philosophical Medicine in France, 1750–1850*. Cambridge: Cambridge
University Press.

Winckelmann, Johann Joachim. 1764. *Geschichte der Kunst des Alterthums*. Dresden:
Walther.

– 1766. *Histoire de l'art chez les anciens*. 3 vols. Translated by Hendrik Jansen.
Paris: n.p.

chapter six

Branding Knowledge through Translation in Late Eighteenth-Century Encyclopedias: Italy, Spain, and Switzerland

CLORINDA DONATO

So knowledge has to be organized; it has to be accessible. If you can't access it, if knowledge exists somewhere and you need it but you can't find it, then it's no good to you. And so, a lot of progress depends on the emergence of search engines. And in fact it is not perhaps an accident that the Industrial Revolution occurred at the same time as the emergence of the first search engine, which is the encyclopedia. So, the encyclopedia organized things in a certain way and it allowed you to search for something rather quickly, because it is arranged alphabetically.

Joel Mokyr, 2017

The evolution of compiled and encyclopedic knowledge from 1650 to 1850 offers significant documentary evidence of the ways in which a nation's media footprint and reach might be equated with its real power, impact, and future. In the two-hundred-year period under examination in this volume, power, impact, and future were increasingly tied to economic prowess and the ability to grow in global markets through encyclopedias – print-culture phenomena that were transnational in scope, practice, and sentiment. Translation, both cultural and linguistic, set in motion the transnational scale of encyclopedias and encyclopedism. For any number of nation states, including geopolitical areas that functioned culturally as nations, the compiling of knowledge in one, accessible location – that is, encyclopedias – and organized in accordance with national cultural and linguistic parameters constituted one of the driving goals of intellectual elites throughout Europe and beyond.[1] This study will investigate those parameters and the combination of political will, local and transnational talent, and cultural/linguistic competition that played themselves out in three specific encyclopedias published by national elites that moved purposefully to produce encyclopedic compilations in order to promote and showcase the quality of their minds and products. These three are: the Padua edition of the *Encyclopédie méthodique*, that is, the *Encyclopédie méthodique* de Padoue; the Spanish translation of the *Encyclopédie méthodique*, that is, the *Encyclopedia metódica*; and the Swiss *Encyclopédie* d'Yverdon.

As economic historian Joel Mokyr has noted in his 2017 monograph *A Culture of Growth: The Origins of the Modern Economy*, the accessibility to knowledge that encyclopedic compilations afforded nations proved a dynamic feature of economic growth. And while Mokyr certainly recognizes the importance of the encyclopedic product, credit is shared equally with the intellectual elites in each nation that organized and nurtured encyclopedic enterprises at every level, shepherding them to fruition. To be sure, Diderot and d'Alembert's *Encyclopédie* revolutionized access to knowledge through its status as "search engine" referred to in the quote above, though cultural and literary historians have tended to focus solely on its role as the quintessential symbol of *philosophie* and critical reason. The establishment of locally produced and sourced encyclopedic search engines throughout Europe and, to some extent, the world would fuel economic growth and competition from 1770 to 1800. I investigate how this occurred in a discrete set of national contexts in order, first, to demonstrate the most salient, and heretofore overlooked, role of encyclopedias as indicators of economic health and the desire to grow and expand a nation's visibility; and second, to chart the prosopographic features of the creators of such compilations and their national motivation to promote their own brand of knowledge.

This study examines how three national contexts, the Italian, the Spanish, and the Swiss, fully entered the encyclopedic fray during the last three decades of the eighteenth century and how they sought to reach a reading public that had been fed almost exclusively French-based ideas and ideals about the content, design, shape, and mode of knowledge and its transfer. This meant that Italy, Spain, and Switzerland recognized the danger to individuality and diversity in the commodification of knowledge from a single perspective, that is, the perspective of the *philosophes*, in the ways that have been analysed in Adorno and Horkheimer's *Dialectic of Enlightenment*. The importance of the encyclopedic compilation in the intent of the *philosophes* cannot be underestimated in this regard. And while Robert Darnton has rightly identified the success of the compilation as a knowledge dissemination model and, from his perspective, its successful role in establishing French as the motor for the knowledge debate, there are many new chapters of the knowledge debate that are being written as we acquire a better understanding of the role of translation as an intercultural and domesticating process that responds to and transforms knowledge for new audiences and purposes.

Moving beyond the *Encyclopédie*: Three Examples

The economic role of encyclopedias has only been given serious consideration in the last fifteen years as economic historians have realized their enormous potential as predictors and harbingers of economic growth in pre-industrial and industrial Europe. We mention the work of Joel Mokyr once again, this time to note his prize-winning monograph *The Gifts of Athena: Historical Origins of the Knowledge Economy* (2002), where he traces the emergence of the knowledge industry and the institutions that spawned it in early modern Europe. Among them we may count extensive social networks that included publishers, academies, masonic lodges, and universities, all of which began to operate transnationally as integral pieces of the Republic of Letters. Loosely constituted membership in the Republic of Letters was predicated upon published scholarship that circulated through the periodical press, correspondence, or encyclopedias. The study of the transnational nature of periodicals in early modern Europe has received extensive attention from an international network of scholars spearheaded by Jean-Pierre Vittu and Jeanne Pfeiffer in multiple publications resulting from their seminars "Les périodiques savants dans l'Europe des XVIIe et XVIIIe siècles."[2] Correspondence has also been treated seriously on a European scale by scholars who have published an exemplary volume on correspondence networks,[3] as well as by the group of scholars that continues to plumb the depths of correspondence networks and their influence led by Corrado Viola at the Research Center for Eighteenth-Century Correspondences (Centro Studi sugli epistolari del Settecento). By contrast, the transnational dimension of encyclopedic compilations has receive short shrift.

The standoff between reason and religion that the French enlightenment brandished as the most pivotal issue faced by humanity would be laid out in the distinctive subset of "philosophical articles" that would define both the *Encyclopédie* and, ultimately, the French enlightenment. However, from the perspective of economic history, the *philosophie* of the *Encyclopédie* may ultimately prove to be far less consequential than the accumulation of so much knowledge in a central location and the search engine of alphabetical order that facilitated its access. Of paramount importance as well was the intellectual elite of scientists and scholars of every stripe who presented themselves as the Republic of Letters to produce and disseminate knowledge. However, the national contours of knowledge and the knowledge-producing industry increasingly became identifiable with the translation of enyclopedias, and the periodical that most embodied encyclopedism, the *Journal encyclopédique*, began to transform knowledge in new places, as Charles Withers has described in his work on the geography of enlightenment.

Just as we speak of "enlightenments," so too must we speak of "encyclopedisms," for the responses to the French Enlightenment and the spawning of new enlightenments may best be charted in the extensive responses to the French *Encyclopédie* and *Encyclopédie méthodique* in the form of new compilations that translated, either linguistically, culturally, or both, the content of these compilations. Encyclopedism and the philosophical, French branding of the *Encyclopédie* spawned an "encyclopedia moment" that propelled encyclopedias as vehicles of information branding in a national context. Indeed, issues of language and translation lie at the heart of nationalizing questions when one discusses eighteenth-century encyclopedias. These issues are directly tied to economic considerations and the ways in which encyclopedic compilations allowed publishers to promote national interests while aiming for "bestseller" status, to adopt Robert Darnton's concept in the volume that launched encyclopedia studies in the English-speaking world and beyond, *Business in the Enlightenment: A Publishing History of the Encyclopédie* (1979).

But how did this occur? Encyclopedias required multiple authors, the famous "Société de gens de lettres" touted as visionary authors by Diderot and d'Alembert on the frontispiece as well as in d'Alembert's "Discours préliminaire" to the *Encyclopédie*. To be sure, this was the most substantial aspect distinguishing the *Encyclopédie* from Bayle's *Historical and Critical Dictionary* (1695–7). Indeed, Diderot and d'Alembert assembled the most innovative thinkers in multiple disciplines that they could find, at first to translate the articles in Ephraim Chambers's *Cyclopædia*, but within a matter of months to also, and then primarily, write new articles addressing the explosion of knowledge that had taken place over the thirty years separating the two enterprises. In the case of the evolution and translation from English to French, a number of new content areas were added to the mix. These included political content and revealed France's growing (and exaggerated) sense of itself as a nation that could offer intellectual leadership, based on rhetorical strategies and linguistic policies that promoted their brand. Voltaire's *Siècle de Louis XIV*, published in 1751, the same year as the first volume of the *Encyclopédie*, may be read as a manifesto of French cosmopolitan goals. And while the *philosophes* and their British counterparts saw themselves as "citizens of the world," that world was quintessentially French, through the looking glass of admiration for Britain. However, these world citizens held a very narrow view of what the rest of the world might be like. Ironically, their understanding of nations or political configurations beyond those of Europe would prove to be superficial, condescending, and, ultimately, wrong. For all of their interest in being citizens of the world, that world was a nebulous construct that had not even warranted a real category in the *Encyclopédie*.

Producing an encyclopedia meant mobilizing the nation's "brain trust" to brand knowledge as French or British, or to rebrand knowledge as distinctly Italian, Spanish, or Swiss, and to position the nation in the best of all possible lights, through the paratextual material that presented its producers and their enterprise to the world. I will therefore discuss the strategic aspects of this rebranding as revealed in the correspondences, announcements, and declarations about encyclopedic compilation projects made by three publishing houses, the Société Typographique d'Yverdon, the Seminario di Padova in the Republic of Venice, and Antonio de Sancha's pubishing house in Madrid. I will also explore how translation (cultural and linguistic) and rewriting created identifiable Italian, Spanish, or Swiss content that ultimately galvanized the scholarly communities of all three nations, in an attempt to create new knowledge that would effectively accompany the brand. In other words, the three sought an alignment of form and content. Finally, in all three cases, I will look at intersecting circles of knowledge to demonstrate how the encyclopedic enterprises tapped into successful compilation ventures that were already recognized as Italian, Spanish, or Swiss in an effort to "brand transfer" one success to the other.

Switzerland

When Diderot and d'Alembert realized the need to document the world in some capacity, they charged Jaucourt with the task. Imbued with the cavalier spirit of *philosophie* as he approached the writing of geographical articles, Jaucourt relied on limited sources, often penned by his fellow *philosophes*. The articles on Italy and Spain, for example, borrowed heavily from Voltaire's *Le Siècle de Louis XIV*, resulting in short, derisive articles that portrayed nothing of the countries in question, only blatant, derogatory stereotypes. Switzerland fared a bit better: the Swiss encyclopedists gathered by Fortunato Bartolomeo De Felice for the writing of the Yverdon *Encyclopédie* were motivated by a desire to bring recognition not only to the natural wonders of Switzerland that attracted grand tourists in droves during the second half of the eighteenth century, but also to Swiss thinkers, political culture, and religion.[4] This plan was foremost in the mind of Bernard Vincenz von Tscharner, a member of the governing body of Berne, *Leurs Excellences de Berne*, when he personally sought someone with broad-based encyclopedic knowledge of French *lumières*, to be sure, but also of different enlightened positions that would be far more inclusive of varied knowledge perspectives. That person was Neapolitan Fortunato Bartolomeo De Felice, who taught natural philosophy at the University of Naples, and who had translated works ranging from air quality to anatomy and philosophy, to name only a few.[5] Tscharner was looking for someone to launch a literary cafe and to populate a new publishing house in Yverdon-les-Bains, under Bernese control, as was the entire Pays de Vaud, with a list of enlightened volumes that might serve as alternate readings to *philosophie*. But most important of all, Tscharner sought someone who could spearhead a Swiss encyclopedic endeavour that would engage the Swiss intellectual class as its authors, with the intention of offering a Protestant-based epistemology. This plan is quite remarkable if one considers Switzerland's unique role in encyclopedia endeavours, which by and large was that of publishing the remaining eight volumes of the *Encyclopédie* once publication was resumed by the Société Typographique de Neuchâtel, as well as the publishing of the quarto edition and the octavo editions.[6] However, Tscharner, a political and intellectual leader, wanted Swiss erudition to connect with the world through its own brand, for he fully understood the economic importance of such a move and wanted to distinguish Swiss erudition and scientific prowess from that associated with French and German names. This was difficult, as two of the most famous contributors were Genevan Charles Bonnet and Bernese Albrecht von Haller: the former wrote in French and the latter was often identified with Gottingen, where he taught for many years and edited the *Göttingische gelehrte Anzeigen*. But Bonnet had never left Geneva, and Haller was newly returned to Berne, homesick for his native Switzerland, an experience he would immortalize in the article "Nostalgie, mal du pays, Heimweh." Not only did this article articulate the emotional ties one might feel toward one's place of birth and upbringing, but it also came to characterize the all-encompassing view of national culture and science that the Swiss encyclopedists embraced as they planned and created the Swiss content of the Yverdon *Encyclopédie*, with several new articles (with respect to the Paris *Encyclopédie*) on emotion, sensibility, and aesthetics, hallmarks of Swiss pre-Romanticism as identified with Jean-Jacques Rousseau.[7] Newly ensconced in Berne following many years in Göttingen, Haller found that the idea of writing for a Swiss encyclopedia appealed to him, as a way of re-establishing his identity as a Swiss scientist and writer, yet one with a European reputation and scope, as his extensive correspondence network indicates.[8] Indeed, the interplay between Switzerland's role as European mediator and as purveyor of global knowledge became one of the primary marketing strategies deployed by De Felice, while at the same time he tried to fill in all of the gaps of Swiss material in the *Encyclopédie.*

It was also clear that the French very much saw De Felice's enterprise as a Swiss endeavour and a threat, as opposed to the pirated editions of Lucca and Livorno. Voltaire recognized the challenge posed by Swiss erudition that was gaining momentum, and the potential for an edition that appealed to *Lumières protestantes* spearheaded by the Italian, De Felice, whom he pretended was unknown to him: "Quant à l'Italien qui veut, dit-on, refondre, avec quelques Suisses, l'Encyclopédie faite par des Français, je n'ai jamais entendu parler de lui dans ma retraite." (As far as the Italian who, it is said, wants to recast, with a few Swiss, the Encyclopédie made by the French, I have never heard of him here in my abode.)[9] Gosse and Pinet, the Dutch book dealers who purchased three-quarters of the Yverdon *Encyclopédie*, based their marketing strategy on the Swiss men of letters whom they assumed would be contributing. They were confident in marketing a Protestant-leaning encyclopedia in Holland by announcing in the *Gazette de Leyde* on 14 February 1769 that Haller, Tissot, Bernouilli, Ostervald, Bertrand, Gesner, Bonnet, and Felice himself (here considered Swiss!), were among the principal contributors.[10] Another reason for interest in the work was Holland's economic dynamism. As Arianne Baggerman and I note in our contribution to this collection, encyclopedism and commercial enterprise went hand and hand in Holland. Though Bonnet, Haller, and Tissot all denounced the announcement in the *Gazette de Leyde* as untrue, it still served its purpose of promoting the work and causing readers throughout the French-speaking Republic of Letters to take notice. Ultimately, both Haller and Bonnet would end up in favour of the enterprise, with Haller contributing thousands of articles and Bonnet conducting an article-by-article comparison for twenty-five articles, noting the superiority of the Yverdon edition over the French, and remarking with pleasure on the number of times he was cited in the Swiss edition.[11] Indeed, Bertrand and Bernouilli would contribute, not to mention a host of other noteworthy Swiss contributors including Gabriel Mingard, whose intellectual and philosophical prowess De Felice boasted about in both his correspondence and the paratextual material he penned for the Yverdon edition when he extolled its virtues with regard to the French one.[12]

De Felice fully embraced his new Helvetic identity, all the while maintaining pride in his Italian origins. He was fully cognizant of what Switzerland's political structure had afforded him, and he wished to showcase it. Thus he spoke affectionately about wanting to describe "la patrie," referring to Switzerland, his new home, to which he properly belonged thanks to his marriage and the granting of his bourgeois status. Yet a number of letters written to Albrecht von Haller's son, Gottlieb, who was contributing articles on Switzerland, dissuade Gottlieb from writing about local customs and national minutiae that are of no interest to the rest of Europe and are not encyclopedia worthy. De Felice emphasizes the importance of addressing Swiss politics and the functioning of the confederation for their exemplary status, sure of the interest such articles would engender both at home and abroad. He wants to showcase Switzerland's "geographical and political systems," seeing the two as intrinsically linked and as having the capacity to serve as a model to others. Therefore, he discusses the way in which geography and politics should be enmeshed in his communication with Gottlieb von Haller:

> Je crois qu'il faudroit commencer le Systeme Geographique par l'Art[icle] Canton, que M. Tscharner a proposé de faire; et la Politique par Corps Helvetique, ou Confederation Helvetique. Lorsqu'on auroit fait ces deux Systemes, vous pourriez convenir avec M. Tscharner du partage des Articles, et de la maniere de les traiter. Si vous aviez un moment de tems, pour le faire, je crois que ce preliminaire vous epargneroit bien de la peine, et il vous meneroit à travailler avec plus d'assurance.[13]

> (I think the geographical system should begin with the article Canton, which Mr. Tscharner has proposed doing, and the political system with the article Helvetic Corps, or the Helvetique Confederation. Once these two systems are in place, you could arrange the dividing up of the articles and the best approach for writing them. If you have the time to do it, I believe that this preliminary measure will save you a great deal of effort and will guide you in working with greater confidence.)

He was most concerned about being accused of committing the same error that plagued the *Encyclopédie* of Diderot and d'Alembert, with its abundance of partisan, localized information, which he clearly explains in his instructions to Gottlieb, referenced above. Gottlieb was writing the articles on Switzerland in collaboration with Vincenz Bernard von Tscharner, a member of the Bernese government who had written a multivolume work on Switzerland, the *Dictionnaire géographique, historique, et politique.*[14] De Felice was frustrated by Gottlieb's tendency to focus on minutiae in his geographical entries on Switzerland and, in the following excerpt from a letter written some seven months after the previous letter cited, felt the need to establish the criteria for geographical articles of quality:

> Nous faisons un ouvrage qui doit interesser toutes les nations egalement. Les Parisiens en ont fait un dont la moitié au moins n'interessait que la France; je fais main basse sur toutes ces miseres nationales; or je ne voudrois pas qu'on nous reprochat qu'à la place des articles François nous y en avons substitué des Suisses. L'ouvrage sera deja immense sans l'augmenter par des articles peu importans.

> (We are creating a work that should be of equal interest to all nations. The Parisians created one in which half of the articles are only of interest to France; I denounce in no uncertain terms all of these worthless national articles; now, I wouldn't want to have our work reproached for having substituted French articles with Swiss. The work will be immense enough without making it even bigger by adding articles of little importance.)[15]

De Felice's strategy was ultimately a winning one, with his branding of knowledge as both Swiss and European. The lines were definitely drawn, and there was no doubt that Yverdon and its Swiss encyclopedists would square off against the next generation of quintessentially French encyclopedists, those who wrote for Charles-Joseph Panckoucke's *Encyclopédie méthodique,* which is certainly a French response to the Swiss Yverdon *Encyclopédie,* and in its turn would become the platform against which the Venetian Republic and the Spanish crown responded with national versions of their own.

Panckoucke's *Encyclopédie méthodique*

Charles-Joseph Panckoucke was a publisher from Lille who learned the trade from his father and his mother, who bequeathed his father's publishing enterprise to him. In 1762 he moved to Paris, where he became a sort of "libraire-philosophe" who embraced encyclopedism, the lucrative potential of which he attempted to capitalize upon in 1769 by trying to convince Diderot that a supplement to the *Encyclopédie* would add value to the enterprise by updating it. He was already a contributor to Pierre Rousseau's Bouillon-based *Journal encyclopédique* and envisioned a leading role for himself in the burgeoning encyclopedia enterprises, although the initial plan for a supplement would not come to fruition in 1769. Nonetheless, Panckoucke was keenly aware of the looming competition from the Yverdon *Encyclopédie*. As book historian Jean-Pierre Perret has noted, De Felice found himself between two keen adversaries as he was poised to publish the first volume of the Yverdon *Encyclopédie* in 1770:

> l'un composé de Voltaire, de d'Alembert, de Diderot et de Grimm, l'autre composé du libraire Panckoucke et des journalists de Bouillon. Les griefs que les uns et les autres formulent contre Félice et ses collaborateurs sont différents. Les premiers se meuvent sur le plan des idées et s'attaquent aux doctrines, les seconds n'avisagent que le côté materiel et financier de l'affair, craignant la concurrence d'Yverdon.

> (the first made up of Voltaire, d'Alembert, Diderot, and Grimm, the other made up of the publisher Panckoucke and the journalists of Bouillon. The grievances each group held against De Felice were different: the first group was animated by ideological issues and attacked De Felice's doctrines, while the second was solely motivated by the threat to material gain from their own future encyclopedic works, fearing the competition.)[16]

Panckoucke, ever the entrepreneur, would turn the competition to his advantage when he eventually produced the *Supplément* (1775–6), pirating vast amounts of the Yverdon content.[17] From the *Supplément* he would taste the material success of encyclopedism, and be poised to take on the biggest venture of his career and, as many have argued recently, what is perhaps the most important of all encyclopedic endeavours, the *Encyclopédie méthodique*. From the latter a new round of national encyclopedic competitions would emerge, of which I will examine two, the Padua and Madrid editions.[18]

Panckoucke's *Encyclopédie méthodique* constituted the new "generation" of encyclopedic compilations that divided knowledge by discipline rather than linking knowledge through the metaphor of the circle or the tree of life, although in each series of discipline-specific volumes, knowledge was arranged in alphabetical order, albeit within a discrete discipline. As far as branding and the phenomenon I am referring to as "brand transfer" are concerned, Panckoucke continues to utilize the word "encyclopédie" in his title, to evoke the genealogy of Chambers, Diderot/d'Alembert, and De Felice. While he has dropped the work "dictionnaire" from the title of the work, it is used for certain select series of discrete volumes, i.e., the *Dictionnaire de Théologie* in three volumes. Perhaps the greatest success of the enterprise may be documented in the two derivative compilations we will now study, the *Encyclopédie méthodique* de Padoue and the Spanish translation of the *Methodique*, the *Enciclopedia metódica*.

The *Encyclopédie méthodique* de Padoue

While Venice is certainly not the Italian nation, the Venetian case does in some ways represent the situation for the many Italian regions that had an encyclopedic presence, of which the most famous is certainly Peter Leopold's Tuscany, with the editions of Lucca (1758–76) and Livorno (1770–9), the Tuscan encyclopedias that were, to a large extent, pirated editions of the *Encyclopédie*. What is most important about them, however, is the desire to recast the *Encyclopédie* as Italian, with the sentiment of rebranding knowledge as Italian as a way of regaining status for Italy's intellectual traditions, a value that we will find in the expressed intent of the encyclopedists of the *Encyclopédie méthodique* of Padua. We also note that local elites raised money for these ventures and took pride in them as Italian. Ottaviano Diodati, editor of the Lucca edition, added notes and rewrote some of the entries, especially when the information provided by the *philosophes* was deemed to be inadequate or incorrect from an Italian perspective. Also in the interest of appealing to an Italian readership, Giuseppe Aubert, editor of the Livorno edition, reproduced Diodati's notes while at the same time adding some of his own. He dedicated the work to Peter Leopold, archduke of Tuscany. These publications, with their Tuscan- and Italian-oriented branding, were viewed as a means of representing a new configuration of political prowess to both the peninsula and Europe. With the advent of the *Encyclopédie méthodique* in the early eighties, the Padua enterprise would mount a similar effort, with the intent of promoting Venetian/Italian intellectual prowess. Indeed, from the beginning, the editors of the Venetian Republic edition conceived of an Italian "société des gens de lettres." It is here that the enterprise becomes Italian and more representative of the knowledge of the nation. Giovanni Coi, managing editor of the *Méthodique* de Padoue, writes to none other than two of the most famous Italian men of letters and science in Europe, Girolamo Tiraboschi and Lazzaro Spallanzani, to lend their names to the enterprise. While Spallanzani's involvement is minimal, Tiraboschi's is significant and his becomes the name associated with the intellectual agenda of the enterprise. Tiraboschi was an ex-Jesuit who was nominated successor to renowned historian Ludovico Muratori as librarian to Francis III, duke of Modena. From the sources of this library he composed the *Storia della letteratura italiana*, the first comprehensive reflection on the legacy of Italian literature, culture, and science, for the term *letteratura* was broadly conceived. It traced Italian literature from the time of the Etruscans to the end of the seventeenth century, and was published in 1782. A second enlarged edition in sixteen volumes was published in 1794. Abridged versions of the work appeared in German and French, evidence of his European reputation.

Girolamo Tiraboschi was Italy's encyclopedist, and though he had never been affiliated with encyclopedic productions involving multiple authors before his involvement with the Padua effort, he understood the importance and impact of compilations as status symbols for a nation, a phenomenon he had witnessed through international feedback to his compilation. Giovanni Coi fully understood the value of having Tiraboschi's name lead the list of Italian savants whose intellectual energy had guided the new edition. Numerous letters exchanged between Coi and Tiraboschi inform us about how they collaborated, but even more important for our purposes, how they decided to use the Tiraboschi name as a means of branding the *Encyclopédie méthodique* de Padoue. Coi counts on Tiraboschi's name recognition in the fields of history, geography, and literature to immediately brand the new *Méthodique* as Italian. "Things related to Italy have been omitted or badly treated, and this must be corrected and the additions more pleasing to our people as well as to foreigners. For this reason, I have decided to begin with the volumes on Geography and Belles Lettres at the same time."[19] Tiraboschi answered that the extent of the errors in the geographical entries for Italy surprised him and that the others were flawed as well. He vowed to fix the geographical articles for as many nations as he could.[20] This use of Tiraboschi brings up an issue that is hotly debated at the Seminary of Padua, the publishing house that will produce the work – whether to publish in French or Italian. Ultimately, they decide for French, intending to standardize the uneven French orthography by having all of the volumes printed at their presses with the same person correcting, as opposed to Panckoucke's use

of forty-five different presses in different cities to produce his *Méthodique*.
Tiraboschi asks Coi several times to make sure his French is correct as he
was translating many of his own texts from Italian into French. The operation of self-translating from Italian into French for an Italian compilation written in French constitutes yet another form of transfer through
translation in encyclopedic compilations. Coi would send Tiraboschi the
volumes to be corrected and Tiraboschi would send his additions and
rewritings, often commenting in the letters that accompanied his transmission about how much he had to correct and how shocking the level of
misinformation was in Panckoucke's *Encyclopédie méthodique*, in relation
to Italy and Spain in particular. So extensive are his corrections that he
tells Coi he should just explain in the prefatory material that Tiraboschi
has collaborated heavily, in lieu of mentioning his every intervention
separately.[21]

While the *Encyclopédie méthodique* de Padoue, published in Padua from
1783 to 1817, would precede the publication of the first volume of the
Spanish *Encyclopedia metódica*, 1788–94, by some five years, both enterprises shared a common motivation: to reject the disparaging French
geographical articles in Panckoucke's *Encyclopédie méthodique* through
a thorough revamping of the three volumes comprising modern geography, published 1782–8. The first volume of Panckoucke's enterprise
would send shock waves throughout Europe due to the article "Espagne,"
which levelled an onslaught of criticism against Spain and the entire
Spanish empire in a fourteen-page rant. The author, Masson de Morvilliers, an armchair geographer who combined an oversized Franco-
centric ego with little travel experience save a very selective set of *voyages*,
discredited the geographical volumes in one fell swoop. The Spaniards
halted their importing of the encyclopedias, and intellectuals throughout Europe contested Panckoucke's high-handed abuse, which brought
back the negative memories of unfair representation that constituted
the major critique of Diderot and d'Alembert's *Encyclopédie* some twenty
years before. The *Encyclopédie* de Padoue capitalized on this new round of
European disappointment with French geography and history by elect-
ing to write a special "Avertissement" to the volumes on modern geography. The editors address three concerns in this piece. In a subtle opening
paragraph, they discuss the reasons for which geographical writing must
be constantly updated: "La Géographie est une partie des plus utiles,
des plus agréables, des plus intéressantes de l'Encyclopédie Méthodique;
mais elle est aussi plus que toute autre sujete à des variations continueles"
(Avertissement, v) (Geography is one of the most useful, enjoyable, and

interesting parts of the *Encyclopédie méthodique*, however, it is also the part that is subject to the most continual variation.)

A list of natural and political events is then provided to prove this point, evidence of the need to constantly update geography in encyclopedic compilations. In particular, the editors remind readers of the dramatic changes in Great Britain that had diminished the British empire:

> Que de colonies, que de comptoirs, que de branches de commerce a coûté à la Grande-Bretagne la ruineuse guerre terminée par le traité de Versailles de 1783! Il faut que le Géographe les retranche de la liste des possessions de ce royaume; qu'il démontre une nouvele République fondée sur les côtes orientales de l'Amérique Septentrionale, qu'il donne aux François & aux Espagnols les îsles, les forts, les villes qu'ils ont acquis. Nous avons dû remarquer tout cela dans ce premier volume que nous offrons au public, & nous ferons de même dans ceux qui viendront ensuite. (Avertissement, v)

> (How many colonies, how many trading companies, how many branches of trade has the ruinous war ended by the Treaty of Versailles of 1783 cost Great Britain! The geographer must reduce the list of possessions of this kingdom; he must mark a new republic established on the eastern shores of North America, giving to the French and the Spanish the islands, forests, and cities that they have acquired. We have duly remarked on all of that in this first volume that we offer to the public, and we will do the same in those that follow.)

The astute reader will note that the editors have used Great Britain as the example of a weakened nation, not Spain, which was usually the case in French compilations.

The next paragraph broaches the second reason for rewriting the articles for the volumes treating geography:

> Un autre objet non moins intéressant & plus proche de nous, est tout ce qui a raport à l'Italie. Les François en general, soit faute de lumieres, soit genie nationale, ne se soucient point de ce qui n'apartient pas à la France; ainsi ils ont omis bien des choses à l'égard de cette belle partie de l'Europe, qui a tant de droits à l'admiration universele. Nous tâcherons de mettre en vue tout ce qu'il y a de plus considerable, & de rendre son lustre naturel à ce charmant pays *Ch' Apennin parte, e'l Mar circonda e l'Alpe.* (Avertissement, v)

> (Another object no less interesting and closer to us is everything that is related to Italy. The French, in general, due either to a lack of enlightenment

or national bias, never worry much about what does not belong to France; thus, they have omitted a great deal about this beautiful part of Europe, which has strong claims to universal admiration. We will seek to expose that which is most noteworthy and to restore to this charming country "Which the Appenines divide, and the sea and Alps surround" its natural brilliance.)

However, the Padua editors save the best for the last: "Que dirons-nous des Espagnols?" (What can we say about the Spaniards?), editing Masson's infamous "Que doit-on a l'Espagne?" (What can we say about Spain?), the phrase in the article "Espagne" that most outraged the Spaniards, not to mention the editors of the Padua edition of the *Encyclopédie méthodique*.

Que dirons-nous des Espagnols? Peut-on lire sans être rebuté les injustes imputations de M. Masson, qui lui ont attiré les reproches de ses concytoiens les ressentimens des Espagnols, & l'indignation de toute l'Europe? C'est un juste tribute que nous devons à la vérité que de dévoiler des mensonges si insultans, de rabatre des injures si grôssiers, de produire des témoignages si Glorieux, qui honorent cette nation. Quoi! Elle est oisive, elle est pauvre, elle n'a rien fait *pour l'Europe depuis deux siecles, depuis mille ans?* Elle nous a donné un nouveau monde: elle verse, avec une prodigalité aussi surprenant que continuele, son or & son argent dans le sein de l'Europe: elle est d'un grand poids dans la balance politique des deux Hémispheres. En revendiquant l'honeur de l'Espagne, en mettant au plus grand jour les prerogatives éclatantes qui la caractérisent, nous nous ferons un devoir de suivre les renseignemens de M. l'Abbé Cavanilles, qui a donné des observations admirables sur l'article *Espagne* dans lequel M. Masson a étalé toute l'amertume de son style mordant & de son haine contre les Espagnols. (Avertissement, v–vi)

(What can we say about the Spaniards? Can we read without being outraged the unfair imputations of M. Masson, which have drawn the reproach of his own countrymen, the resentment of the Spaniards, and the indignation of all of Europe? It is our duty to pay truth its proper due by unmasking such insulting lies and countering such outlandish injuries by offering the glorious testimonials that honour this nation. What! Spain is lazy, Spain is poor, Spain has done nothing *for Europe for the last two centuries, for the last thousand years?* Spain gave us a new world: Spain pours her gold and her silver into the heart of Europe with a generosity that is as surprising as it is continuous. Spain is the great weight in the political equilibrium of the two hemispheres. By reclaiming Spain's honour, by placing greater emphasis on the amazing characteristics that define it, we have taken it upon ourselves to follow the indications of M. l'Abbé Cavanilles, who has given some admirable observations about the article *Espagne* in which M. Masson has displayed all of the bitterness of his trenchant style and his hatred against the Spaniards.)

The article itself has been thoroughly edited and restructured in the *Encyclopédie méthodique* de Padoue. The factual portions of Masson's article have been salvaged and corrected. They have also been thoroughly edited to remove all traces of Masson's biting style. To preserve the reader's indignation towards Masson, the most offensive passages have been left intact, followed directly by the counterarguments taken from one of the essays of rebuttal by Cavanilles. Among the issues addressed and rebutted are the Inquisition, with Masson denouncing it as the most egregious expression of institutionalized oppression and fanaticism that Europe has ever seen, while Cavanilles praises the Inquisition for keeping Protestants out of Spain and Italy, thus protecting both countries from the destructive wars of religion that tore apart France, Germany, and England. Equally interesting observations are made about the expulsion of the Moors from Spain. Masson emphasized the loss of a population that would have brought prosperity to Spain had they stayed, while Cavanilles remarks on the advantages of having routed out a culturally and religiously diverse population.

The *Encyclopédie méthodique de Padoue* emerged during the final years of the Venetian Republic and became an important symbol to the Veneto of the empire's future viability. But the Venetian was not the only empire that waned – Spain also needed to reaffirm itself in an increasingly hostile print world.

The *Encyclopedia metódica*: The Spanish Translation of the *Encyclopédie méthodique*

In the late enlightenment period, controversy over the present, past, and future role of Spain and its colonies filled encyclopedic compilations and the periodical press. However, it was the compilation, the encyclopedic work, that had become a real cause for concern, for the compilation was proving to be far more powerful than the periodical. Spain, as I have mentioned above, discovered this the hard way, when French geographer Masson de Mortvillier's article "Espagne" was published in the first volume of the three-volume series *Géographie moderne*. In Internet parlance, we might say that the text went viral. Never had bad encyclopedia press travelled faster. Indeed, Mortvillier's article "Espagne" ranks with the likes of the articles "Genève" and "Autorité politique" in the *Encyclopédie* for the amount of attention it attracted. However, no single text provoked more debate and soul-searching than the article "Espagne" that appeared in the most famous of late eighteenth-century encyclopedias, the *Encyclopédie méthodique* (1782–1832). While Hispanists and French and francophone scholars alike are somewhat familiar with the controversy surrounding Masson de Mortvilliers's 1785 article "Espagne" and cite it in their work, few have ever read the article in its entirety, quoting only the provocative question posed by the author halfway through his article. Let us cite the most salient paragraph of the infamous article:

> Mais que doit-on à l'Espagne? Et depuis deux siècles, depuis quatre, depuis dix, qu'a-t-elle fait pour l'Europe? Elle ressemble aujourd'hui à ces colonies foibles & malheureuses, qui ont besoin sans cesse du bras protecteur de la métropole: il nous faut l'aider de nos arts, de nos découvertes; encore ressemble-t-elle à ces malades désespérés qui, ne sentant point leur mal, repoussent le bras qui leur apporte la vie! Cependant, s'il faut une crise politique pour la sortir de cette honteuse léthargie, qu'attend-elle encore? Les arts sont éteints chez elle; les sciences, le commerce! Elle a besoin de nos artistes dans ses manufactures! ("Espagne," 565)

> (But what do we owe Spain? After two centuries, after four, after ten, what has she done for Europe? Today she resembles those weak and unfortunate colonies that always need the protective embrace of the metropolis. It is thus necessary to aid her with our arts, our discoveries. What is more, she resembles those sick, desperate people who, unaware of their disease, reject the arm that brings them life! But if all she needs is a political crisis to bring her out of this shameful lethargy, then what is she still waiting for? The arts have faded in her land, so too have the sciences and trade! She needs our artisans in her manufactories!)

Spain woke up abruptly to the reality of how the empire was being portrayed in encyclopedic compilations circulating in the French-speaking world in the 1770s and 1780s. For years, Spain had only received French books through the clandestine book trade and had tended to ignore the empire of the word that had begun to rival the empire of land. Controlling one's image through the written word rapidly became imperative for Spain. A partial Spanish translation of the *Encyclopédie méthodique*, the *Encyclopedia metódica* (1788–94) was realized by Antonio de Sancha, publisher to the Spanish crown; it was the same press that had commissioned the Spanish translation and correction of Raynal's negative portrayal of Spain in the *Histoire des deux Indes*. As had been the case in the Spanish translation of Raynal, the Spanish translation of the *Encyclopédie méthodique* sought to Hispanicize encyclopedic knowledge, but first it had to rebut and rewrite the damaging portrayal of Spain and its entire colonial enterprise. In a rapidly shifting context of global knowledge transfer, encyclopedic compilations were highly sought-after sources of information, especially those published in French. Spaniards took the article as both a call to arms and an opportunity for self-reflection and examination at a moment when the interdependency of the colonial empires was increasingly evident, becoming the backdrop against which the French justified their critiques.

The "Advertencia del editor" that precedes the geographic articles in the Spanish edition of the *Encyclopedia metódica* explains:

La Geografía es por consiguiente una colecccion de hechos é investigaciones prácticas siempre esclavas de la observación y considerada baxo este aspecto no hay que admirar carezca de aquella exâctitud y verdad apetecibles en todas las ciencias. Con todo hemos procurado en la traduccion que se publica mejorar notablemente el original y se han añadido innumerables articulos de España y América en que la poca instrucción de los Autores franceses sobre nuestras cosas ó sea el poco caso que hacen de ellas ha dexado vacíos y errores de mucha consideración que hemos procurado enmendar del mejor modo possible. ("Advertencia," vol. 1, n.p.)

(Geography is therefore a collection of facts and practical forays always beholden to observation, and considered from this point of view, we do not have to accept the lack of that exactitude and truth that is appealing in all sciences. Thus, in the translation we are publishing, we have improved upon the original immensely, having added numerous articles about Spain and America, and in the best way possible, filling in the gaps and errors left by the French authors, due to the lack of information they possess about our matters, or the scant attention they actually pay to what we do.)

Indeed, the Spanish crown had selected two highly capable authors as translators and collaborators for the improvement of the geographical volumes: Juan de Arribas y Soria and Julián de Velasco. Soria had been named to the Council of Castile in 1784 as censor of the French edition for geography. He had declared that all of the geographical volumes were plagued with errors, and he advised that all articles of "Geografía" be immediately suspended and that a body of savants be formed, as had been done for history and other disciplines, so that the articles belonging to the geography of the empire could be properly treated. Don Julián de Velasco was an active journalist and scholar who articulated the ideals of the *Illustración* in his work and was thoroughly committed to improving education throughout Spain, especially for women. His career as a reformer and the breadth of his contributions can be charted through the many articles and reviews he wrote for the periodical *Diario de Madrid*, which he co-edited with Pedro Salanova in the aftermath of the French Revolution. Wary of the potentially subversive nature of the information coming from France during this period, the crown valued Julián de Velasco's knowledge of French language, literature, and culture. He was a valuable asset to the state for his ability to filter progressive information from what might be of potential harm. In general, the name of Julián de Velasco appears at the most critical junctures of French-Spanish knowledge transfer as translator and intercultural mediator. His interest and expertise in cultural, historical, and political geography and its comparative features earned him the difficult assignment of translating, correcting, and rewriting Masson de Morvillier's article "Espagne" for the *Encyclopédia metódica*. In his editor's preface to the volumes on modern geography, Antonio de Sancha announced the team of Julián de Velasco and Juan de Arribas as those appointed to the delicate task of translating the geographical articles. He cites Julián de Velasco in particular as "el que se ha encargado de mucha parte de la correcciones de lo que mira á nuestra nacion han hecho quanto ha estado de su parte para perfeccionar este trabajo verdaderamente util á nuestros compatriotas mayormente quando temenos tan pocas obras en castellano, que traten esta materia con la debida extension [...]" (the one who has taken on the majority of the corrections concerning our nation, has done as much as possible to perfect this work that is truly useful to our citizens, especially now, when we have so few works in Castilian that treat this material with the required care and depth [...]).[22] In 1792, the year in which the translated and corrected volumes of modern geography were published, the Conde de Aranda elicited a royal ordinance to the *Consejo* granting Julián de Velasco a licence to open an "aula pública de Geografía" in his home for the training and educating of future geographers. Julián de Velasco's knowledge of geography and French philosophical discourse and his ability to authoritatively counter, with an eloquent and informed response, the French characterization of Spain in his translated, rewritten articles launches a bold rebuttal with measured ire against France. Far from portraying Spain as victim, Velasco scripts the Spanish empire by taking the moral high ground, addressing critiques with historical insight and wisdom, while presenting a wealth of new content about the empire that is argued from an inclusive, morally conscious perspective with an eye towards the future in a confidence-generating rhetoric that reflects how Spain has found its encyclopedic voice in this new era of using compilations to market and promote the nation.

Conclusion: Minor Transnationalism Theory in Translated Encyclopedias

There was an urgent sense that the representation of Spain in geographical articles could have a profound effect on the empire. The crown and the intellectual class had finally woken up to the fact that they had been absent from the geographical discourse waged about Spain in encyclopedic compilations for nearly a hundred years, with devastating consequences. The permanence and potential of the encyclopedic format could not be denied. For while erudite journals might be useful for the quick transfer of new and partial knowledge, encyclopedic compilations had become instruments whose profound value for solidifying and immortalizing knowledge was far superior to that of the journal. A shift in perspective had taken place. The previously much maligned compilation now, in the second half of the eighteenth century, was seen as a medium of permanence, the fixing of scientific and cultural moments in time. Indeed, the role of encyclopedias in the transfer of knowledge cannot be underestimated. With their mounting of comparable and intentionally competitive compilations to Diderot and d'Alembert's *Encyclopédie* and Panckoucke's *Encyclopédie méthodique,* intellectual elites in Spain, Switzerland, and the Venetian Republic pushed back against the French version of the world, supplanting it with new encyclopedic instruments of information transfer that would affect both the economic and cultural viability of their nations in an increasingly competitive transatlantic market. As our understanding of the complex set of intercultural harmonies and tensions that drove compilers of encyclopedic works increases, we as scholars will have access to numerous untapped sources that have much to teach us about the global eighteenth century. There is no doubt that these compilations constitute overlooked sources for better understanding the intercultural dynamics of the global enlightenment. Seen through the prism of competing empires, the juxtaposition of the Venetian, Spanish, Swiss, and French perspectives in these compilations reflects the stress and competition for control of the world economy through the projection of an image of control in deed, but more importantly in word. Of all of the areas of encyclopedic knowledge transfer in which translation played a role, geography may be one of the most documentable, precisely because of its branding function, linked directly with the growing ability of media to shape identity. As one peered through the pages of an encyclopedia in the late eighteenth century, the representation of one's nation, city, state, region, or village had a profound effect on one's identity, and on the identity of one's nation. The Venetian Republic, Spain, and Switzerland were pushing back against France's cultural and philosophical interference in the perception of their own cultures from both without and within in ways that may be characterized as a form of colonial imposition. This chapter has focused on the lateral connections between the encyclopedic production of the Venetian Republic, Spain, and Switzerland in the second half of the eighteenth century. I note a form of "horizontal" solidarity among them, and though the national expressions being studied here are far from regional entities, a comparison may be made in their reaction to the "centre" in the way they define themselves vertically, but also with a nascent sense of the lateral connections they made in constructing their encyclopedias, similar enough to those made by regional cultures as noted by Françoise Lionnet and Shu-Mei Shin in their 2005 collection of essays *Minor Transnationalism* to warrant reflection through the minor transnationalisms prism. While they do identify and differentiate themselves vis-à-vis dominant French culture, they are fully aware of the transgressions levied against other cultures in the pages of French encyclopedias and the need to look at how other cultures besides their own have been treated in French encyclopedic compilations, a feature that figured prominently in the rationale for producing nationally sourced encyclopedias, particularly in the materials we have seen in this chapter. Their concerns are not unlike ours as we seek to fully understand transnationalism and its historic underpinnings, to which the vertically but also laterally empowering gesture of linguistic and cultural translation of the encyclopedic texts featured in this essay surely belongs. They find common ground in their related statuses, all of which possess a refusal of the French cultural codes that have sought to define them, despite their prominent statuses, as subaltern. They warrant our attention as harbingers of how the effects of globalization and transnationalization on identities, both personal and national, first emerged.

NOTES

1 Joel Mokyr makes this argument in two of his books. First, in *The Gifts of Athena: Historical Origins of the Knowledge Economy* (Princeton: Princeton University Press, 2002), he argues that access to knowledge is paramount for economic growth, and opines that encyclopedias, particularly Diderot and d'Alembert's *Encyclopédie*, with its marriage of natural philosophy with the manual arts, forged an ideal knowledge union. He picks up the argument again in *A Culture of Growth: The Origins of the Modern Economy* (Princeton: Princeton University Press, 2018) to discuss with even greater conviction how encyclopedias could serve as indicators of active national economies with insights into what has differentiated the economies of China and Europe. While China did produce encyclopedias, they were not widely circulated and access was limited to a very few scholars, as opposed to the burgeoning encyclopedic practices in Europe.

2 See "Les périodiques savants dans l'Europe des xviie et xviiie siècles. Instruments et vecteurs du travail savant," 2007, in *Action concertée "Histoire des savoirs," 2003–2007. Recueil de synthèses* (Paris), 115–20; and "Les journaux savants, formes de la communication et agents de la construction des savoirs (17e-18e siècles)," 2008, *Dix-huitième siècle* 40: 241–59.

3 See *Les grands intermédiaires culturels de la République des Lettres. Études de réseaux de correspondance du XVIe au XVIIIe siècle*, ed. Christiane Berkvens-Stevelinck, Hans Bots, and Jens Häseler (Paris: Honoré Champion, 2005).

4 Claude Reichler, 2013, *Les Alpes et leurs imagiers: Voyage et histoire du regard* (Lausanne: Presses polytechniques et universitaires romandes); and Claude Reichler and Roland Ruffieux, 1998, *Le voyage en Suisse: Anthologie des voyageurs français et européens de la renaissance au XXe siècle* (Paris: Robert Laffont).

5 For an in-depth look at De Felice and his encyclopedic vision see my "Reconceptualizing Enlightened Networks and Their Mediators: Fortunato Bartolomeo De Felice and the Transmission of Knowledge across Eighteenth-Century Europe," in *The Internationalization of Intellectual Exchange in a Globalizing Europe, 1636–1780*, ed. Robert Mankin (Lewisburg: Bucknell University Press, 2017), 163–95.

6 See Madeleine Pinault, 2002, "Encyclopedia," in *Encyclopedia of the Enlightenment*, ed. Michel Delon (Chicago: Fitzroy Dearborn), 1:439–44.

7 See *La Suisse sensible 1780–1830*, ed. Joël Aguet, Claire Jaquier, and Maud Dubois (Lausanne: Institut Benjamin Constant, 2001).

8 See Martin Stuber, 2005, *Hallers Netz: Ein europäischer Gelehrtenbriefwechsel zur Zeit der Aufklärung; [Forschungsprojekt Albrecht von Haller (Berner Haller-

Projekt; Gemeinschaftsprojekt des Instituts für Medizingeschichte der Universität Bern vormals: Medizinhistorisches Institut) und der Burgerbibliothek Bern] (Basel: Schwabe).

9 Jean-Pierre Perret, 1981 [1945], *Les Imprimeries d'Yverdon au XVIIe et au XVIIIe siècle* (Geneva: Slatkine), 211. All translations are mine unless otherwise indicated.

10 Perret, *Les Imprimeries d'Yverdon*, 213.

11 See my "Sur les traces de Charles Bonnet: Une comparaison electronique de ses Notices raisonnées de l'Encyclopédie et de l'Encyclopédie d'Yverdon," in *Recherches sur Diderot et sur l'Encyclopédie Actes du Colloque: 1751–2000. 'L'Encyclopédie' en ses nouveaux atours électroniques: Vices et vertus du virtuel*," special issue of *Recherches sur Diderot et sur l'Encyclopédie*, 31–2 (2002): 234–50; and "Charles Bonnet et L'*Encyclopédie*," 2002, in *Sciences, musiques, Lumières. Mélanges offerts à Anne-Marie Chouillet* (Ferney-Voltaire: Centre International d'étude du XVIIIe siècle), 11: 421–32.

12 De Felice wrote about Gabriel Mingard in the preface to the third volume of the *Encyclopédie* d'Yverdon: "Les talents de M. Mingard ayant ete admires, s'attirerent necessairement des envieux qui commencerent a repandre qu'on trouvoit dans les articles (G.M.) des endroits qui n'etoient pas conformes a l'orthodoxie de notre sainte religion." (Mr. Mingard's talents, having been duly admired, nonetheless attracted the attention of envious people who began to spread around the idea that the articles signed G.M. contained information in some places that was not in alignment with the orthodoxy of our holy religion.) De Felice goes on to say that Mingard was far more orthodox than many others, but that in order to protect him, he was given another set of initials with which he signed his articles.

13 Letter from F.-B. De Felice to Gottlieb Emanuel von Haller, 6 April 1771, ed. Léonard Bernand, www.unil.ch/defelice/files/live/sites/defelice/files /shared/DF_HALLER_GEv.pdf.

14 See my "La Géographie républicaine: Republicanism and Representation in Bernard Vincenz von Tscharner's Dictionnaire géographique, historique, et politique de la Suisse 1775," in *Republican Virtue: The Conception of a National Consciousness and the Education of a New Citizen* (Geneva: Slatkine, 2000).

15 Letter from F.-B. De Felice to Gottlieb Emanuel von Haller, 12 November 1771, accessed 21 April 2020, www.unil.ch/defelice/files/live/sites/defelice /files/shared/DF_HALLER_GEv.pdf

16 Perret, *Les Imprimeries d'Yverdon*, 210.

17 See Kathleen H. Doig, 1977, *The Supplément to the Encyclopédie.* The Hague: Nijhoff.

18 Martine Groult, 2011, *Savoir et matières: Pensée scientifique et théorie de la connaissance de l'Encyclopédie à l'Encyclopédie méthodique* (Paris: Editions du CNRS).

19 Coi to Tiraboschi, 4 June 1785, Biblioteca Estense Universitaria.
20 Tiraboschi to Coi, 18 August 1785, Biblioteca del Seminario di Padova.
21 Tiraboschi to Coi, 18 August 1785, Biblioteca del Seminario di Padova.
22 Antonio de Sancha, "Advertencia del editor," *Encyclopedia metódica, Geografia moderna* (Madrid: La Imprenta de Sancha 1792), 1:2.

Bibliography

Primary Sources

1785–91. "Avertissement des éditeurs de Padoue." In *Encyclopédie méthodique, Géographie moderne*, 1:v–vi. Padova: Seminario di Padova.

1792. "Advertencia." In *Encyclopedia metódica. Geografía moderna*, translated by Juan Arribas y Soria and Julián de Velasco, 1:n.p. Madrid: Sancha.

Büsching, Anton Friedrich. 1768–79. *Nouveau Traité de géographie*. 14 vols. The Hague: Gosse & Pinet.

Cavanilles, Antonio José. 1784. *Observaciones sobre el artículo 'España' de la Nueva Enciclopedia*. Translated by Mariano Rivera. Madrid: Imprenta Real.

– 1784. *Observations de M. l'abbé Cavanilles sur l'article "Espagne" de la Nouvelle Encyclopédie*. Paris: Alex. Jombert.

Coi, Giovanni, to Tiraboschi, Girolamo. Correspondence. Biblioteca Estense Universitaria.

– 1784–1817. *Encyclopédie méthodique, nouvelle édition enrichie de remarques dediée à la Sérénissime République de Venise*. Padoue: Tipografia del Seminario, 40 vols.

– 1791. "Espagne." In *Encyclopédie géographique, Géographie moderne*, 1:572–91. Padua: Tipografia del Seminario.

Denina, Carlo. 1761. *Discorso sopra le vicende della letteratura*. Turin: Stamperia Reale.

– "Réponse à la question: Que doit-on à l'Espagne? Discours lu à l'Académie de Berlin." In *L'Assemblée publique du 26 janvier l'an 1786 pour le jour anniversaire du Roi*. Berlin: Decker.

– 1786. *Réponse à la question: Que doit-on à l'Espagne?* In *Oración apologética por España y su mérito literario by Juan Pablo Forner*. Madrid: Imprenta Real.

– 1786. *Respuesta a la pregunta: ¿Qué se debe a España?* Translated by Manuel de Urqullu. Cádiz: Manuel Ximénez Carreño.

Diodati, Giovanni. 1751–80. *Encyclopédie, ou Dictionnaire raisonné des sciences, des arts et des métiers*, 2nd ed., 28 vols. Lucques: Giuntini, 1758–76 (text: vols. i–xvii, 1758–71; plates: vols. i–xi, 1765–76).

– 1756–9. *Il Giornale enciclopedico di Liegi*. Lucca: Vincenzo Giuntini.

Felice, Fortunato Bartolomeo de. 1770–80. *Encyclopédie, ou Dictionnaire universel raisonné des connaissances humaines*. Yverdon: n.p.

Forner, Juan Pablo. 1786. *Oración apologética por la España y su mérito literario: Para que sirva de exornación al discurso leído por el Abate Denina en la Academia de Ciencias de Berlín, respondiendo a la questión "Qué se debe a España?"* Madrid: Imprenta Real.

Jaucourt, Louis de. 1751–80. "Espagne." In *Encyclopédie, ou dictionnaire raisonnée des sciences, des arts et des métiers,* edited by Denis Diderot and Jean le Rond d'Alembert, 5:953. Paris, Neuchâtel: Briasson.

Masson de Morvilliers, Nicolas. 1782–8. "Espagne." In *Encyclopédie méthodique, Géographie moderne,* 2:554–68. Paris: Panckoucke.

Sancha, Antonio de. 1782. *Prospecto de "la Encyclopedia metódica."* Madrid: Casa de Sancha.

– , ed. 1788–94. *Encyclopedia metódica.* Madrid: Antonio de Sancha.

– 1792. "Advertencia del editor." In *Encyclopedia metódica, Geografía moderna,* translated by Juan de Arribas y Soria and Julián de Velasco, 1: n.p. Madrid: Sancha.

Tiraboschi, Girolamo. 1772–95. *Storia della letteratura italiana.* 11 vols. Modena: Società Tipografica.

Tiraboschi, Girolamo, to Coi, Giovanni. Biblioteca del Seminario di Padova, Cod. 721.

Velasco, Julián de. 1752. "Geografía moderna." In *Encyclopedia metódica,* vol. 2. Madrid: Antonio de Sancha.

– 1792. "España." In *Encyclopedia metódica, Geografía moderna,* translated by Juan de Arribas y Soria and Julián de Velasco, 2:79–105. Madrid: Sancha.

Voltaire. 1752. *Le Siècle de Louis XIV.* 2 vols. London: Dodsley.

Secondary Sources

Anes, Gonzalo. 1970. "L'Encyclopédie, ou Dictionnaire raisonné des sciences, des arts, et des métiers en España." In *Homenaje a Xavier Zubiri,* 123–30. Madrid: Moneda y Crédito.

– 1978. "La Encyclopédie méthodique en España." In *Ciencia social y análisis económico: Estudios en homenaje al profesor Valentín Andrés Alvarez,* 105–52. Madrid: Tecnos.

Darnton, Robert. 1979. *The Business of Enlightenment: A Publishing History of the "Encyclopédie," 1775–1800.* Cambridge, MA: Harvard University Press.

Doig, Kathleen Hardesty. 2013. "From 'Encyclopédie' to 'Encyclopédie méthodique': Revision and Expansion." In *SVEC,* 11.

Donato, Clorinda. 1992. "La Encyclopedia metódica: La traduction espagnole de l'Encyclopédie méthodique." *Recherches sur Diderot et sur l'Encyclopédie* 12: 155–64.

– 2000. "La géographie républicaine: Republic and Representation in Vincenz Bernhard von Tscharner's Dictionnaire géographique, historique, et politique de la Suisse, 1775." In *Republikanische Tugend: Ausbildung eines Schweizer Nationalbewusstseins und Erziehung eines neuen Bürgers: Contribution à une nouvelle approche des Lumières helvétiques*, edited by Michael Böhler, Etienne Hofmann, Peter H. Reill, and Simone Zurbuchen, 301–37. Geneva: Slatkine.

– 2002. "Charles Bonnet et L'*Encyclopédie*." In *Sciences, musiques, Lumières. Mélanges offerts à Anne-Marie Chouillet* (Ferney-Voltaire: Center international d'études du XVIIIe siècle), 11: 421–32.

– 2002. "Sur les traces de Charles Bonnet: Une comparaison électronique de ses Notices raisonnées de l'Encyclopédie et de l'Encyclopédie d'Yverdon." In *Recherches sur Diderot et sur l'Encyclopédie Actes du Colloque: 1751–2000. 'L'Encyclopédie' en ses nouveaux atours électroniques: Vices et vertus du virtuel*, special issue of *Recherches sur Diderot et sur l'Encyclopédie* 31–2: 233–50.

– 2006. "*La Encyclopedia metódica*: Transfer and Transformation of Knowledge about Spain and the New World in the Spanish Translation of the *Encyclopédie méthodique*." In *Das Europa der Aufklärung und die außereuropäische koloniale Welt*, edited by Hans-Jürgen Lüsebrink, 74–112. Göttingen: Wallstein.

– 2013. "Illustrious Connections: The Premises and Practices of Knowledge Transmission between Switzerland and the Italian Peninsula." In *The Practice of Knowledge and the Figure of the Savant in the Eighteenth Century*, edited by André Holenstein, Hubert Steinke, and Martin Stuber, with the collaboration of Philippe Roger, 2:535–67. Leiden: Brill.

– 2013. "Writing the Italian Nation in French: Cultural Politics in the *Encyclopédie méthodique de Padoue*." *New Perspectives on the Eighteenth Century* 10, no. 1: 12–27.

Gies, David T. 1999. "Dos preguntas regeneracionistas: ¿Qué se debe a España? y ¿Qué es España?: Identidad nacional en Forner, Moratín, Jovellanos y la generación de 1898." *Dieciocho* 22, no. 2: 307–30.

Gnan, Pietro. 2005. *Un affare di dinaro, di diligenza, di scienza': L'edizione padovana dell' Encyclopédie méthodique (1784–1817)*. Padua: Biblioteca Universitaria.

Groult, Martine. 2011. *Prospectus et mémoires de "l'Encyclopédie méthodique,"* vol. 1: *Prospectus général précédé de la "Préface" au "Grand vocabulaire françois."* Paris: Garnier.

– 2011. *Savoir et matières: Pensée scientifique et théorie de la connaissance de "l'Encyclopédie" à "l'Encyclopédie méthodique."* Paris: CNRS.

Lionnet, Françoise, and Shumei Shi, eds. 2005. *Minor Transnationalism.* Durham: Duke University Press.

Morris, Madeleine F. 1994. "The Tuscan Editions of the Encyclopédie." In *Notable Encyclopedias of the Late Eighteenth Century: Eleven Successors of the "Encyclopédie,"* edited by Frank A. Kafker, *SVEC* 315: 51–84.

Perret, Jean-Pierre. 1981 [1945]. *Les Imprimeries d'Yverdon au XVIIe et au XVIIIe siècle.* Geneva: Slatkine.

Pethothukis, James. 2017. "A Culture of Growth: A Long Read Q&A with
    Economic Historian Joel Mokyr" (15 September 2017). Accessed 21 April
    2020. www.aei.org/publication/a-culture-of-growth-a-long-read-qa-with
    -economic-historian-joel-mokyr/.
Sonntag, Otto, ed. 1983. *The Correspondence between Albrecht von Haller and Charles
    Bonnet.* Berne: Hans Huber.
Withers, Charles W.J. 2007. *Placing the Enlightenment: Thinking Geographically
    about the Age of Reason.* Chicago: University of Chicago Press.

chapter seven

The Migration of Beccaria's Penal Ideas in Encyclopedic Compilations (1770–1789)

LUIGI DELIA

This chapter addresses the place of penal law in the principal French-language encyclopedias published between 1770 and 1789. In particular, I focus on the reception in these encyclopedias of the ideas of an Italian enlightenment *philosophe*, the marquis Cesare Beccaria.[1] Beccaria still embodies today the emblematic figure of the enlightenment reformer who wished to humanize penal law in his time. A man of letters and attentive reader of Montesquieu, Rousseau, Helvétius, and Diderot and d'Alembert's *Encyclopédie*, he published his little treatise, *On Crimes and Punishments*, anonymously in Livorno in 1764. Written with passion, elegance, and a spirit of philanthropy, this work crowned its author as the champion of the abolition of capital punishment. Indeed, Beccaria's work on reform is vast and marked a watershed moment in the history of law in the years prior to the French Revolution. It encompassed the abolition of judiciary torture and the death penalty for crimes of common law, pleading for strengthening of the accused's right to defence, abandonment of corporal punishment in favour of prison and forced labour, depenalization of homosexuality and suicide, and codification and education. Indeed, Beccaria's penal philosophy establishes the foundations of the modern law state. His treatise, translated into many languages, spawned a number of related works.

The history of Beccaria's relationship with encyclopedism is hardly known. It begins prior to the publication of *On Crimes and Punishments*, in his correspondence, which is as precious a source of information about the Republic of Letters during the Age of Enlightenment as it is about the existing liaisons between French and Italian intellectuals. Beccaria mentions his readings of the "divina e immortale enciclopedia" (divine and immortal encyclopedia) as among those that he most treasured.[2] He is undoubtedly thinking about Diderot's texts, but also about the juridical articles written by Boucher d'Argis, as well as the natural law articles penned by the Chevalier de Jaucourt that are found in the first seven volumes of the *Encyclopédie*, published between 1751 and 1757. Beccaria also corresponded with d'Alembert and attended the encyclopedists' circle during a trip that he took to Paris at the end of 1766. Beccaria's proximity to the French culture of enlightenment explains how the treatise *On Crimes and Punishments* came to be known in France upon its publication and was rapidly translated and commented upon by two encyclopedists: Morellet and Voltaire. Morellet's French translation, published in January 1766, played a decisive role in the diffusion of Beccaria's ideas, as did Voltaire's *Commentaire*,[3] which appeared in September 1766 during the Chevalier de La Barre's judiciary scandal. Within six months seven editions of the French translation were published. The book met with immense success, but that success did not resonate in the pages of the Paris *Encyclopédie*, whose last ten volumes of articles, covering the letters "H" to "Z," had already been completed when Beccaria's work appeared.[4]

It is therefore not surprising that no mention of Beccaria or his work can be found in the *Encyclopédie* of Diderot and d'Alembert. However, the situation is different for the encyclopedias published between 1770 and 1780, which borrow heavily from *On Crimes and Punishments*. These compilations refer less and less to Montesquieu's *Esprit des lois*, and more and more to Beccaria, whose penal ideas are cited extensively and juxtaposed with those of other authors, jurists, or philosophers. Thus Beccaria's book has consequences for the encyclopedic process itself. The encyclopedias produced during the decade between 1770 and 1780 offer a unique vantage point from which the evolution of mentalities surrounding the looming and difficult issue of the death penalty may be analysed. Let us explore this question by examining a Swiss compilation, the l'*Encyclopédie* d'Yverdon, together with the *Dictionnaire de Jurisprudence* of the French *Encyclopédie méthodique*.[5]

The forty-two volumes of text that make up the *Encyclopédie* d'Yverdon constitute an original enterprise brought to fruition by the *philosophe* De Felice and his international collaborators.[6] The issue of the death penalty is emblematic of what is new in the field of penal justice in the Yverdon edition with respect to the Paris *Encyclopédie*. Two articles make it possible to detect the general orientation of the *Encyclopédie* d'Yverdon in this regard: the article "Carcan" (Collar shackle) by Paul-Joseph Vallet, a eminent employee of the police,[7] and the article "Peine" (Punishment), signed by De Felice himself. Located in volume 7, "Carcan" is the only place where Beccaria's name appears. The article consists of merely two short paragraphs, while "Peine" has been constructed by assembling excerpts of several passages from *On Crimes and Punishments*, without, however mentioning the name of Beccaria. In each case, not only is death as punishment reduced to an acquired notion, but the indictment of the death penalty is systematically accompanied by proposals for alternative punishments. "Carcan" (Collar shackle) opens with the same definition given by the jurist Toussaint in the article by the same name in the Paris *Encyclopédie*: the collar shackle "is a post planted in the ground, with an iron collar attached to it at a man's height, to which one attaches the necks of evildoers whom one does not deem deserving of death [...]. Most of those attached to the collar shackle, have previously been whipped by the executioner and branded with a hot iron. Later on, they are often banished or sent to jail."[8] Entirely new, however, the following text constitutes a radical opposition to the death penalty. Without entirely calling for its abolition, the author suggests, in line with Beccaria's ideas, that the death penalty be replaced by punishments that deprive one of one's liberty, with the addition of forced labour as being useful:

M. de Montesquieu, dans l'*Esprit des lois*; le marquis de Beccaria, dans le *Traité des délits et des peines*; Servant, avocat-général; William Mérédith, et Phileon, avocat à Besançon, ont démontré dans leurs discours sur l'administration et sur la réformation de la justice criminelle, que la peine de mort a toujours été pour l'ordinaire injuste, inutile et nuisible au bien public, et que le carcan, ou quelque peine semblable, peuvent suppléer avantageusement aux supplices de la corde, de la roue et du feu [...]. Si les condamnations étaient proportionnelles au délit, et si le plus grand des supplices se bornait au carcan ou aux galères de mer ou de terre; alors chacun se ferait un devoir de contribuer à rétablir l'ordre public, en dénonçant avec exactitude et en jugeant avec célérité tous les criminels. (V.A.L.)[9]

This text restores the ideology of reform by a justice professional, who lays claim to the great philosophical authorities, starting with Montesquieu and Beccaria. Throughout his article, of which only a short passage is cited above, Vallet considers the death penalty to be "useless and harmful to the public good," because it can in some cases result in impunity, as was the case for example with domestic robbery: subject to the death penalty, it was no longer being reported by its victims, due to the severity of the punishment.

In his capacity as encyclopedist, therefore, Vallet espouses Beccaria, nonetheless limiting himself to a few points. De Felice goes further in his sweeping article "Peine," publishing a precise and instructive summary of Beccaria's *On Crimes and Punishments*. As a synthetic presentation of the new foundations upon which penal law must rest, Beccaria's little book lends itself perfectly to being used in an encyclopedic text. Though of Neapolitan origin, De Felice used the French version of *On Crimes and Punishments*, precisely because he himself had published the French translation in 1766 at his Yverdon press.[10] Additionally, Beccaria was invited to join the Yverdon team of encyclopedists, but he chose not to sign on.[11] De Felice nonetheless borrows from Beccaria's work, more often than not without citing it as a source. He continues in the same manner in the *Suppléments à l'Encyclopédie*, published by Robinet, something Kathleen Hardesty Doig duly noted in her superb volume on the *Supplément*.[12] In 1776 De Felice composed the article "Accusation secrète" (Secret accusation), replicating the chapter by the same title in *On Crimes and Punishments*. The article "Peine" (Punishment) in the *Encyclopédie* d'Yverdon also relies heavily on borrowings from several different chapters of Beccaria's treatise.

Published in 1774 in volume 32 (pp. 620–9), "Peine" consists of nine pages and eighteen columns. It opens with a short definition that reproduces the one found in the article by the same name in the *Encyclopédie*. A long introduction establishing the moral and political points of reference required for rethinking penal law in the name of enlightenment follows. This introduction picks up the first two chapters of Beccaria's books *Origine des peines* (The origin of punishment) and *Droit de punir* (The right to punish), which Morellet had merged into one: *De l'origine des peines, et du fondement du droit de punir*. It prompts consideration of the general characteristics that penal laws must possess in enlightened legislation. The article is divided into sections whose titles and italicized texts echo the titles of the chapters of *On Crimes and Their Punishments*. They are enumerated in the following order by De Felice: (1) *Douceur des peines* (Of the mildness of punishments); (2) *Peine de mort* (Of the punishment of death); (3) *La punition doit être prompte, analogue au crime, et publique* (The punishment must be swift, analogous to the crime, and public); (4) *La punition doit être certaine et inévitable*[13] (The punishment must be certain and inevitable); (5) *Proportion entre les peines et les crimes* (Of the proportion between crimes and punishments).

In this way, l'*Encyclopédie* d'Yverdon may boast an important precedent: that of being the first work of its kind to reproduce Beccaria's chapter on the death penalty. By republishing this revolutionary text, De Felice fully assumes the role of director of an enlightenment encyclopedia. Aware that "good books belong not to book dealers but to humanity, which desires to be enlightened and educated in virtue" and that the "book dealers are merely the intermediaries in this salutary enterprise,"[14] he makes of his compilation a vehicle for the new penal philosophy.

De Felice leaves the last word to the champion of the abolition of capital punishment, without adding any supplementary commentary. He explains his editorial politics as being focused on the idea of the reader's essential liberty in a letter that says: "we will avoid all direct critiques and all disputes, but we will present the facts and their rationale, leaving to the reader the freedom to examine and the right to judge."[15] In the absence of other articles that might compromise the challenge to gallows ideology expressed by the director of the *Encyclopédie* d'Yverdon through his use of Beccaria, we can assign to this compilation the status of an abolitionist work with regard to the death penalty.[16]

It is worth noting that in 1777 and 1778, De Felice republished the article "Peine" (and therefore Beccaria's chapter on the death penalty) in a discrete compilation on law stemming from the *Encyclopédie* d'Yverdon: the *Dictionnaire universel raisonné de justice naturelle et civile*, better known under the provocative title *Code de l'Humanité, ou la Législation universelle, naturelle, civile et politique*, vol. 10 (1778), article "Peine" (*Peine de mort*), 450–4.[17] The thirteen volumes of the *Code de l'Humanité* were well received by the periodical press when they appeared,[18] and were described as being among "the most precious and useful of works" by the *Manuel du libraire et de l'amateur de livres*, founded by Jacques-Charles Brunet (Paris, chez l'auteur, 1820, vol. 4, no. 1537, 37). Additionally, the *Code de l'Humanité* crossed European borders, influencing the founding fathers of the United States. Thomas Jefferson sent a copy of this work to Edmund Randolph, with a letter dated from Paris, 20 September 1785:

Being in your debt for ten volumes of Buffon, I have endeavored to find something that would be agreeable to you to receive in return. I therefore send you by way of Havre a dictionary of law Natural & municipal in 13. vols 4to. called the *Code de l'humanité*. It is published by Felice, but written by him & several other authors of established reputation. It is an excellent work. I do not mean to say that it answers fully to its title. That would have required fifty times the volumes. It wants many articles which the title would induce us to seek in it. But the articles which it does treat are well written.

It is better than the voluminous *Dictionnaire diplomatique*, & better also that
the same branch of the *Encyclopédie méthodique*.[19]

Also within the English-language zone[20] (see Draper 2000), we can add
that *On Crimes and Punishments* is cited in a late edition of Chambers's
Cyclopaedia, published 1778–88 by Abraham Rees. Though less prolix
on the topic of penal law, this English compilation endorses Beccaria
without reservation in the article "Crime" (vol. 1): "There is an excellent book on the subject of crimes and punishments, published by the
marquis de Beccaria."[21]

In spite of Jefferson's negative assessment of Panckoucke's *Encyclopédie
méthodique*, it behooves us to call attention to the discussion that the *Dictionnaire de jurisprudence* of the l'*Encyclopédie méthodique* reserves for capital
punishment. Once again, Beccaria plays a central role. Directed by a
"société de jurisconsultes" (society of jurists), this specialized dictionary
is made up of eight volumes published in Paris between 1782 and 1789.
Borrowing from several contemporary sources, its authors offer a synthesis of the most relevant penal concepts, placing "within this text the
encounter and exchange between two juridical cultures."[22] The question
of the legitimacy and use of capital punishment is addressed in two stages,
first in the pair of articles "Assassin" (Murderer) (*Droit naturel et criminel*)
and "Assassinat" (Murder) (*Jurisprudence criminelle*), and a second time
under the heading "Peine de mort" (Death penalty). In both cases, a
privileged place is carved out for the position of the reformers, although
the reasoning of the conservative criminalist camp is not ignored. While
"Assassin" replicates philosopher John Locke's ideas according to which
the evildoer who violates the safety of the innocent places himself outside
of the behaviours that are consonant with human nature and therefore
exposes himself to being eliminated "like a ferocious beast,"[23] "Assassinat" states the opposite. Reproducing word for word the anonymous
article by the same title found in the *Suppléments à l'Encyclopédie* (vol. 1
[1776], 654a), the author advocates for the abolition of the death penalty. Here is the closing argument of that article:

[E]n dérobant l'assassin à la peine de mort, nous ne prétendons pas le
soustraire au supplice. Qu'on ne s'y trompe pas, la mort n'en est pas un;
et c'est précisément pour le livrer à la peine, à la douleur, à l'infamie, à un
travail dur et utile à la société, que nous voudrions l'arracher à la mort.
Un pendu, un roué ne sont bons à rien. Il serait pourtant à désirer que les
souffrances et les tourments de ceux qui ont nui à la société, fussent bons à

quelque chose. C'est la seule manière de dédommager cette société, dont ils ont troublé l'ordre, et trahi les intérêts. Or, voilà ce qu'on ne peut faire qu'en les laissant vivre. Leur supplice devenu utile, ne sera même que plus grand; l'impression journalière qu'il fera sur les âmes, n'en acquerra que plus de force; et les effets qui en résulteront ne seront que plus sûrs et plus durables.[24]

This discourse mirrors Beccaria's criminal reforms, which state that it is better to condemn those who are guilty of a serious crime to perpetual servitude rather than condemn them to death. There are two reasons for this: on the one hand, forced labour in perpetuity offers an ongoing spectacle, with the ensuing effect of intimidation among the public that witnesses it; on the other hand, these labours procure material benefits for society. We note that the encyclopedist writing the *Méthodique* article not only attributes these reflections directly to Beccaria but radicalizes Beccaria's thought: "such is the language that gentleness and humanity have inspired [...] in the marquis Beccaria, who, in a text full of fire and enthusiasm, maintained that no man has the power, not even the juridical power, to take away the life of another human being" (*Encyclopédie méthodique* [*Jurisprudence*], art. "Assassinat," 494a).

Now, this last declaration is far from obvious, and it requires commentary. On the one hand, Beccaria appears to acknowledge two deviations from the principle of abolishing the death penalty: about the first of them we read: "though deprived of liberty, [the condemned person] still has a certain network of relationships and a certain power, both of which are of interest to the security of the nation [...] his existence can provoke a dangerous revolution to the existing form of government"; and the second deviation is when "his death is the only true curb to be used to discourage others from committing crimes."[25] In reality, Beccaria's relative abolitionism raises a number of issues and remains a source of conflicting interpretation.[26] On the other hand, the author lends Beccaria's proposals a humanitarian air, while it is precisely over the issue of alternative measures to capital punishment that the Milanese *philosophe* appears to question the efficiency of humanistic principles. Diderot noted this discrepancy:

[J]'observe qu'il [Beccaria] renonce, et avec raison, à son principe de douceur et d'humanité envers le criminel. "Dans les chaînes, sous les coups, dans les barreaux de fer, le désespoir ne termine pas ses maux, mais il les commence." Ce tableau est plus effrayant que celui de la roue, et le supplice

> qu'il présente est en effet plus cruel que la plus cruelle mort. Mais parce
> qu'"il donne des exemples fréquents et durables," son efficacité le rend
> préférable au dernier supplice, qui ne dure qu'un instant, et sur lequel
> les criminels déterminés prennent trop souvent leur parti [...]. Un dur et
> cruel esclavage est donc préférable à la peine de mort, uniquement parce
> que la peine en est plus efficace.[27]

Whatever the case may be for allowing the death penalty in exceptional cases, along with the difficulty of reconciling humanitarianism and utilitarianism within Beccaria's approach, it is important to emphasize that the encyclopedist writing for the *Méthodique* associates Beccaria's name with the radical rejection of this punishment as the normal solution adopted in criminal politics. Besides, it is by laying claim to Beccaria that the editor of the article "Assassinat" rails against the harshness of the pre-Revolutionary French penal system and calls for a more moderate justice system: "Certainly, our penal code is excessively rigorous and there is a place reserved for Louis XVI to order the abolition of torture, the death penalty against deserters, the reform of injustice, and the barbarism of our criminal laws."[28]

The same need to lighten punishments and to rationalize the right to punish has also been proposed in the substantive article "Peine de mort (Death penalty). Appearing unsigned in 1786 in the sixth volume of the *Dictionnaire de Jurisprudence* of the *Méthodique*, this article constitutes a three-part essay on the subject of capital punishment. Early on in the piece, Beccaria takes centre stage, with his chapter on the death penalty once again reproduced in its entirety. A second part follows as an antithesis to the first with a summary of the reasons given by proponents of capital punishment. This apology for the justification of eliminating human life rests on the arguments made by the jurist Merlin in another dictionary of the period, the *Répertoire universel et raisonné de jurisprudence* de Guyot, as well as on the ideas expressed by the lawyer François-Michel Vermeil (1730–1810), author of the *Essai sur les réformes à faire dans la législation criminelle* (1781). We can synthesize Vermeil's views as follows:

> [C]'est la peine du talion, celle qui touche de plus près aux premiers princi-
> pes de l'équité naturelle. Si, à la perte d'un citoyen, elle ajoute la mort d'un
> autre, cette mort doit paraître utile; elle délivre la société d'un homme
> pervers qui ne doit plus lui appartenir, puisqu'il a rompu le lien des conven-
> tions sociales. Le supplice de cet assassin prévient d'ailleurs de nouveaux

crimes, qu'il aurait pu commettre, et son châtiment devient un exemple important pour la perversité.[29]

Thus "Peine de mort" outlines the reasons for and against the death penalty. This article does not, however, constitute a form of sceptical *isothenie*, where thesis and antithesis become a formal exercise. The argumentative strategy of this encyclopedist seeks to give credence to the idea that no one can concede to another the right to life or death. In order to do this, the author repeats the reasons for abolishing the death penalty contained in the contemporary work *De l'état naturel des peuples*.[30] The entire third and final section of "Peine de mort" was inspired by this work written by the author Jean-François Gavoty de Berthe (2, 2, §1–6).[31] Lacking the urgent eloquence that characterizes Beccaria's prose, the discourse that the encyclopedist borrows from Gavoty nonetheless develops a rich debate. I will limit myself here to discussing a few of the most important excerpts. I will look at six passages, some original while others merely reformulate Beccaria's ideas:

1. The first finds "an exact resemblance" between paternal authority and sovereign authority (*Encyclopédie méthodique*, vol. 6 [1786], 526a). Gavoty reasons that just as the father holds no power over the life or death of his children, neither should the king hold such power over the members of the society that he governs. In this way, the royal prerogative to assign the death penalty appears unfounded.
2. A second line of argumentation denounces the ineffectiveness of severe punishments in combatting crime and defending society. After suggesting that those peoples "still close to the state of nature paid a great deal of attention to human life and did not believe that they were allowed to purposely spill human blood," he questions punishment's efficacy with polemical flair: "What has been gained since the wheel, the gallows, and torture[?]: the prisons do not empty themselves and bloody executions are taking place on a daily basis. The condition of men united in political societies has not improved" (*Encyclopédie méthodique*, vol. 6 [1786]: 527ab).
3. Thirdly, Gavoty outlines the deleterious and criminal consequences resulting from the taking of men's lives as a form of justice, denouncing it as a true source of corruption that accustoms people to violence: "It seems that the more the blood of the guilty is spilled, the more we have taught them that human blood can be spilled" (*Encyclopédie méthodique*, vol. 6 [1786]: 527b).

4. The fourth argument sets forth theological considerations: the death
   penalty is "diametrically opposed to the spirit of the divine legislator, who [desires] the preservation of his creatures and their betterment." This point is linked to a utilitarian reflection: "To destroy the
   murderer is to doubly offend nature, for two men perish at the same
   time; and in order to preserve the members of society, one doubles
   society's loss" (*Encyclopédie méthodique*, vol. 6 [1786]: 527b).
5. The fifth example proposes that the death penalty be excluded from
   the right to punish, contrary as it is "to the three reasons for punish-
   ing the guilty": the "betterment of the guilty," "the benefit of he who
   has interest in preventing the crime," and "the general utility of all"
   (*Encyclopédie méthodique*, vol. VI [1786]: 528ab).
6. Last, Gavoty wonders if alternative punishments to the justice that
   kills might exist. His positive response reflects Beccaria's position.
   Gavoty guarantees that "there are a thousand ways of protecting
   against the recidivism of the murderer, without taking his life," for
   example, "by locking him in a prison," "sending him somewhere
   far away," or "finally teaching him to behave better through the
   experience of the pain that he will be made to suffer" (*Encyclopédie
   méthodique*, vol. 6 [1786]: 430a). Stated differently, nothing forces
   the legislator to condemn a murderer to death, because there are at
   least three other punishments that can replace capital punishment:
   prison, exile, and chains.

There is no doubt that behind Beccaria's and Gavoty's positions we
can hear the voice of the author of "Peine de mort" from the *Méthodique*:
"we cannot deny," he writes, "that [these reasons] have been borrowed
from the nature of the thing, from good sense and from the law of
nature" (*Encyclopédie méthodique*, vol. 6 [1786]: 430b). In the hope of
having an impact on contemporary political dynamics, the encyclopedist makes an appeal that the voice of *philosophie* might reach the
throne:

> Puissent les souverains, les législateurs et les magistrats, méditer des vérités
> aussi importantes pour le bonheur des peuples confiés à leur soins, et hâter
> une réforme des codes criminels, qui doivent être l'ouvrage d'un siècle
> aussi éclairé que le nôtre![32]

This appeal will not entirely fall on deaf ears: the first French
Code pénal of 1791 authorizes the death penalty, but "without the

exercising of torture of any kind on those condemned" (I,1,2). After some hesitation regarding the modality, the Assembly opts for decapitation: "Those condemned to death will have their heads cut off" (I,1,3). In this way, the road was paved for the arrival of the guillotine. A judiciary machine capable of killing without inflicting pain, the guillotine therefore marks juridical progress to the extent that it equalizes the final situation of the condemned, limiting as much as possible the duration of the fatal act (see Castronuovo, 2009; Delia, 2012; Gerould, 1992.)

This study has offered a brief view of the extensive influence that Beccaria's philosophy exercised over encyclopedias. Let us end with two general remarks about the transforming force of ideas and the importance of intellectual history for the understanding of our political and judicial reality. First, when Beccaria published his book, the death penalty was a blatant reality for the European consciousness: no one before Beccaria – neither legislators, jurists, nor *philosophes* – had systematically argued against this form of punishment. That is why Beccaria's work unquestionably changes our perception of the issue. By relaying his philosophical ideas, encyclopedias perform as cultural vectors that contribute to "changer la façon commune de penser" (changing the common way of thinking).[33] Second, we must never forget that before the death penalty became an object of study interfacing with a number of disciplines, it was an everyday judicial reality. Even today, we don't have to travel very far to find it. In California, punishment by death is in force through lethal injection, though its occurrence is rare and it is highly contested. Does society have the right to inflict the death penalty? Sparked some three centuries ago by a Milanese *philosophe*, the great debate over the legitimacy of the death penalty, its utility as a disincentive to crime, and its compatibility with human rights never ceases to trouble the contemporary public space of certain democratic countries that nevertheless claim for themselves the enlightenment tradition. One of the primary merits of the history of ideas is that it helps us to become aware of certain problems that continue to draw our attention, certain issues that we encounter repeatedly at the centre of our societal discussions, issues that do not emerge out of nowhere but instead carry with them considerable historical baggage. From this perspective, the history of ideas facilitates our ability to see these problems more clearly, while offering the conceptual tools that enable us to form a more profoundly considered opinion.

Translation by Clorinda Donato

NOTES

1 Scholarly contributions about Cesare Beccaria and *On Crimes and Punishments* are legion. Let us recall here the exemplary studies by Maestro 1973, Burgio 2008, and Audegean 2010.

2 Letter to Morellet, in Beccaria 1994, 362.

3 See Christophe Cave's recent critical edition in Voltaire 2012.

4 Excluding the plates, publication of the *Encyclopédie* had actually been completed by July 1764, the same year that *Des délits et des peines* appeared in print. Thus it is not impossible that Voltaire's 1766 edition *Commentaire* had factored in the Chevalier de Jaucourt's article "Question" (i.e., torture), which was published in volume 13 of the *Encyclopédie* in 1765 (see Audegean 2010, 348, note 151).

5 The following pages develop in greater depth a number of the issues I touched upon previously in a more general work on Beccaria published in French, entitled *Droit et philosophie à la lumière de l'*Encyclopédie (see Delia 2015, 181–99).

6 Fortunato Bartolomeo De Felice (1723–1789) fully participated in the philosophical spirit of the age. He was a professor of philosophy in Rome from 1746 to 1753, after which he joined the circle of Antonio Genovesi in Naples before leaving for Switzerland in 1757. His legacy to the evolution of *lumières* can be found in a remarkable body of work that scholars have finally begun to examine systematically to determine the true parameters of its impact. Within the De Felice corpus we may count the Italian translation of Descartes' *Discours de la méthode*; his editorial acumen in publishing any number of what have become essential texts of enlightenment thought, such as the French translation of Beccaria's *Traité des délits et des peines*; and an edition of Jean-Jacques Burlamaqui's *Principes du droit naturel* (1747), replete with a set of copious notes from his own hand, making the Yverdon edition (1768) the most widely regarded. He also published an edition of Burlamaqui's *Principes du droit politique* (1751). He directed the impressive *Encyclopédie* d'Yverdon (1770–80), which reorganizes the system of knowledge along a new set of philosophical and cultural lines. De Felice also authored works on logic, justice, and education, not to mention his *Tableau philosophique de la religion chrétienne* (1779).

7 See Doig and Donato 1991, 141. Attorney general to the parlement of Grenoble, Paul-Joseph Vallet is the author of the *Discours sur l'administration de la justice criminelle*, published in 1766.

8 *Encyclopédie* d'Yverdon, art. "Carcan," vol. 7 (1771), 499b. Cf. 1751–72, *Encyclopédie ou Dictionnaire raisonné des sciences, des arts et des métiers* [...] (Paris: n.p.), art. "Carcan," 2:674b.

9 "M. de Montesquieu, in the *Esprit des lois*; the marquis of Beccaria, in *On Crimes and Their Punishments*; Servant, general lawyer; William Mérédith, and Phileon, lawyer in Besançon, have shown in their writings on the administration and reform of criminal justice, that the death penalty has always been, generally speaking, useless and harmful to the public good, and that the collar shackle, or a similar punishment, might advantageously replace the tortures of the cord, the wheel, and fire […]. If the condemnation were commensurate with the crime, and if the worst of tortures were limited to the collar shackle or to the jails on sea or land, then each of us would fulfil our duty of contributing to the restoration of public order, condemning all criminals appropriately and prosecuting them in a timely manner. (V. A. L.)" (*Encyclopédie* d'Yverdon, art. "Carcan," vol. 7 [1771], 499b).

10 From the founding of his publishing house in Yverdon in 1762, De Felice established himself as an important purveyor of works in the field of civil and penal legislation. At his Yverdon presses he published Jean-Jacques Burlamaqui's *Principes du droit de la nature et des gens* (1766–8) with copious notes that he himself penned, as well as the abbé Morellet's translation of Beccaria, with the addition of the term "treatise" and the false imprint of Philadelphia, *Traité des délits et des peines (1766) et le Discours sur l'administration de la justice criminelle* (1767) of Joseph-Michel-Antoine Servan.

11 The correspondence between De Felice and Beccaria, housed in Milan, can be consulted in the electronic edition of De Felice's *Correspondance* edited by Léonard Burnand, Université de Lausanne, 2013, accessed 21 April 2020, www.unil.ch/webdav/site/defelice/shared/DF_BECCARIA.pdf.

12 In this work Beccaria is also mentioned in the article "Infanticide" (*Médecine légale*), written by the medical examiner from Montpellier, Jean Lafosse (1742–75): "Il me suffit de dire avec un auteur ami de l'humanité, *qu'on ne peut appeler précisément juste ou nécessaire la punition d'un crime, tant que la loi n'a pas employé pour le prévenir les meilleurs moyens possibles.* Dei delitti e delle pene" (*Encyclopédie* d'Yverdon, 3:592) (Suffice it to say with an author who is a friend of humanity, that the punishment of a crime cannot be called precisely just or necessary until the law has employed the best possible means to prevent it. *On Crimes and Punishments*).

13 While Morellet attaches the issue of the inevitability of punishment to that of the punishment's mildness (§20), De Felice instead places it after the issue of the punishment's immediacy. The order preferred by De Felice in his assembling of Beccaria's content does not completely correspond to the one adopted by Morellet.

14 Letter from De Felice, 7 December 1770, in Perret 1981, 205.
15 De Felice, "Prospectus de l'Encyclopédie d'Yverdon," *Bibliothèque des sciences et des Beaux-Arts de la Haye*, vol. 30, July–September 1768, 229.
16 The succinct article "Assassinat" constitutes a curious exception. De Felice upholds a proposal that is also supported by those who support the strictest of punishments: "L'*assassinat*, dit-il, est un crime si atroce, qu'on a pu très bien, sans aucune ombre d'injustice, infliger les plus grandes peines à ceux qui s'en sont rendus coupables du moindre degré, ou qui en ont seulement formé le dessein" (Assassination, he says, is such an atrocious crime that beyond even a shadow of injustice it has been very easy to inflict the greatest of punishments upon those who are only minimally guilty of it or who have merely entertained the idea of committing it) (*Encyclopédie* d'Yverdon, 3:755).
17 Brissot de Warville would publish it in the first volume of his *Bibliothèque philosophique du Législateur, du Politique et du Jurisconsulte*, 1782–6.
18 *L'Esprit des journaux, français et étrangers*, December 1779, 414–18. The review appearing in the *Journal des Savants* 1778 (October), 2286, is enthusiastic.
19 This reference can be found in the Sowerby Catalogue, vol. 2 (Philosophy – Moral, chap. 16, "Law of Nature and Nation"), 73, of *Thomas Jefferson's Libraries*. The reference for the letter is LC 2533.
20 The first English translation was published in London in 1767. The translator remained anonymous. Beccaria's book influenced Blackstone, Godwin, and Bentham in England, while Franklin and Jefferson read the book in the edition of 1773 that accompanies Voltaire's *Commentaire*.
21 Beccaria's name also appears in the article "Torture" appearing in vol. 4: "The marquis Beccaria (chap. 16) with exquisite raillery proposes the problem: the force of the muscles and the sensibility of the nerves of an innocent person being given, it is required to find the degree of pain necessary to make him confess himself guilty of a given crime."
22 Briegel 2006, 312.
23 *Encyclopédie méthodique (Jurisprudence)*, art. "Assassin," vol. 1 (1782), 492a. Cf. Locke 1994, chap. 2, §11, 9–10.
24 "By removing the death penalty, it is not our intention to eliminate all punishment for the murderer. Let there be no mistake, death is not a punishment; and it is precisely because we want to deliver him to punishment, pain, shame, and hard labour, which is useful to society, that we wish to wrest him from death. The hanged man or the man tortured at the wheel is no longer good for anything. It would be therefore desirable

that the suffering and torments of those who have harmed society be good for something. That is the only way to repair the damages to a society whose order has been disrupted and whose interests have been betrayed. That cannot be done if they are not allowed to live. The usefulness of their suffering makes it all the more grand; the daily impression that it makes on others will be continually reinforced, making the resulting effects all the more certain and lasting" (*Encyclopédie méthodique* [*Jurisprudence*], art. "Assassinat [*jurisprudence criminelle*]," vol. 1 [1782], 494–5).

25 Beccaria 2010, §27 ("De la peine de mort"), 231.

26 See Beccaria 2010, 366–7, note 196.

27 "I have observed that he [Beccaria] renounces, and rightly so, his principle of tolerance and humanity with regard to the criminal. 'In chains, cowered by blows, and caged behind bars, despair does not end his evil ways, but merely initiates them.' That picture is more frightening than the wheel, and the torture it represents is actually crueler than the cruelest of deaths. But since 'it offers a regular and lasting example,' its effectiveness makes it preferable to capital punishment, which lasts only an instant and is the option preferred by certain criminals [...]. A hard and cruel enslavement is thus preferable to the death penalty, solely because it is more effective" (Diderot, *Notes sur le* Traité des délits et des peines, in Beccaria 1994, 403–4).

28 *Encyclopédie méthodique* (*Jurisprudence*), art. "Assassinat," vol. 1 (1782), 495a.

29 "[I]t is the punishment of an eye for an eye that touches the first principles of natural fairness the most closely. If, upon the loss of a citizen, one adds the death of another, the second death appears useful; it frees society of a perverse human being who no longer belongs to humanity anyway, as he has broken the bond of social conventions. Besides, the punishment of this murderer prevents new crimes that he might have committed, and his penalty becomes an important example against perversity" (*Encyclopédie méthodique* [*Jurisprudence*], art. "Peine de mort," vol. 6 [1786], 552b).

30 *De l'État naturel des peuples ou Essai sur les points les plus importants de la société civile, et de la société générale des nations*, 1786 (Paris: chez la veuve Hérissant), 3 vol. in-8°.

31 No critical assessment of this essay has been found.

32 "May the sovereigns, the legislators, and the magistrates meditate upon these important truths in the interest of the happiness of the people confided to their care, and may they hasten the reform of the penal codes, which should be the work of a century as enlightened as ours is!" (*Encyclopédie méthodique*, vol. 6 [1786]: 430b).

33 *Encyclopédie*, art. "*Encyclopédie* (*Philosophie*)," vol. 5 (1755), 642a.

Bibliography

Audegean, Philippe. 2010. *La philosophie de Beccaria. Savoir punir, savoir écrire, savoir produire.* Paris: Vrin.

Beccaria, Cesare. 1766 [1765]. *Traité des délits et des peines.* Edited by André Morellet. Philadelphie [Yverdon].

– 1984. *Dei delitti e delle pene,* vol. 2 of *Edizione nazionale delle opere di Cesare Beccaria.* Edited by Gianni Francioni. Milan: Mediobanca.

– 1994. *Dei delitti e delle pene.* Edited by Franco Venturi. Turin: Einaudi.

– 2008. *On Crimes and Punishments and Other Writings.* Edited by Aaron Thomas. Toronto: University of Toronto Press.

– 2010. *Des délits et des peines.* Edited by Philippe Audegean. Lyon: ENS Editions.

Briegel, Françoise. 2006. "Asservir les jugements à la lettre, c'est en bannir la justice." La jurisprudence de l'*Encyclopédie méthodique.*" In *L'Encyclopédie méthodique. Des Lumières au positivisme,* edited by Claude Blanckaert and Michel Porret, 311–39. Geneva: Droz.

Brissot de Warville, Jacques-Pierre. 1782–6. *Bibliothèque philosophique du Législateur, du Politique et du Jurisconsulte.* 10 vols., in-8°. Berlin and Paris.

Burgio, Alberto. 2008. "Introduction: Between Law and Politics – The Idea of Equality in On Crimes and Punishments". In Cesare Beccaria, *On Crimes and Punishments and Other Writings,* edited by Aaron Thomas, xxxiii–lii. Toronto: University of Toronto Press.

Castronuovo, Antonio. 2009. *La vedova allegra. Storia della ghigliottina.* Rome: Nuovi equilibri.

Diderot, Denis, and Jean le Rond d'Alembert, eds. 1751–80. *Encyclopédie, ou dictionnaire raisonnée des sciences, des arts et des métiers.* Paris, Neuchâtel: Briasson.

De Felice, Fortuné Barthélemy. 1770–80. *Encyclopédie* ou *Dictionnaire universel raisonné des connaissances humaines* (*Encyclopédie* d'Yverdon). 58 vols. Yverdon: dans l'Imprimerie de M. De Felice.

– 1778. *Code de l'Humanité, ou la Législation universelle, naturelle, civile et politique.* 13 vols. Yverdon: dans l'Imprimerie de M. De Felice.

– 2013. *Correspondance.* Edited by Léonard Burnand, Université de Lausanne. Accessed 21 April 2020. www.unil.ch/webdav/site/defelice/shared/DF _BECCARIA.pdf.

Delia, Luigi. 2012. "Justice des Lumières et guillotine: Un problème philosophique." *Lumières* 20: 121–34.

– 2015. *Droit et philosophie à la lumière de* l'Encyclopédie. Oxford: Voltaire Foundation.

Delia, Luigi, and Ethel Groffier. 2012. *La vision nouvelle de la société dans* l'Encyclopédie méthodique, vol. 1: Jurisprudence. Quebec City: Presses de l'Université Laval.

Diderot, Denis. 1994. "Notes sur le *Traité des délits et des peines*." In Cesare Beccaria, *Dei delitti e delle pene*, edited by Franco Venturi, 398–408. Turin: Einaudi.

Doig, Kathleen Hardesty. 1977. *The Supplément to the* Encyclopédie. Berlin: Springer.

Doig, Kathleen Hardesty, and Clorinda Donato. 1991. "Notices sur les auteurs des quarante-huit volumes de "discours" de l'*Encyclopédie* d'Yverdon." In *Recherches sur Diderot et sur l'Encyclopédie* 11: 133–41.

Draper, Anthony J. 2000. "Cesare Beccaria's Influence on English Discussions of Punishment, 1764–1789." *History of European Ideas* 26, nos. 3–4: 177–99.

Encyclopédie méthodique, Jurisprudence, 1782. Par une société de jurisconsultes. Paris: chez Panckoucke.

Esprit des journaux, français et étrangers, L'. December 1779. Vol. 12, An 8. Paris-Liège.

Gavoty de Berthe, Jean-François. 1786. *De l'état naturel des peuples, ou Essai sur les points les plus importants de la société civile, et de la société générale des nations.* 3 vols., in-8°. Paris: chez la veuve Hérissant.

Gerould, Daniel. 1992. *Guillotine: Its Legend and Lore.* New York: Blast Books.

Journal des Savants. October 1778. Paris: Bureau du journal de Paris.

Locke, John. 1994. *Traité du gouvernement civil.* Edited and translated by Jean-Fabien Spitz. Paris: Presses Universitaires de France.

Maestro, Marcello. 1973. *Cesare Beccaria and the Origins of Penal Reform.* Philadelphie: Temple University Press.

Perret, Jean-Pierre. 1981. *Les imprimeries d'Yverdon au XVIIe et au XVIIIe siècle.* Geneva and Paris: Slatkine.

Rousseau, Jean-Jacques, 1964 [1762]. *Contrat social.* In *Œuvres complètes*, vol. 3. Paris: Gallimard.

Vermeil, François-Michel. 1781. *Essai sur les réformes à faire dans la législation criminelle.* Paris: chez Demonville.

Voltaire. 2012. *Commentaire sur le livre Des délits et des peines.* In *Œuvres complètes de Voltaire*, edited by Christophe Cave, vol. 61A, 1766 (II). Oxford: Voltaire Foundation.

chapter eight

Translating Liberalism: Brockhaus's *Conversations-Lexikon* and the Development of an International European Constitutional Discourse*

IWAN-MICHELANGELO D'APRILE

The European constitutional period, beginning with the French Revolution and culminating with the revolutionary movements before 1848, marks the beginning of the formation of European nation states. In what follows, I will use the example of Brockhaus's *Conversations-Lexikon* to consider the extent to which these national and nationalistic developments took place in a public sphere marked by a distinct European and international character. In this way, internationalization and nationalization can be understood as two faces of the same process in the early nineteenth century. Just as constitutional movements were tied to nation state formation, so too did the European revolutions of France, Spain, Portugal, Italy, Belgium, and Greece occasion a growing European consciousness.[1] When we consider the relevance of and the manifold ties to North, Central, and Latin American independence movements and constitutions, the constitutional process thus comes into focus as a mutually dependent pan-European or even global occurrence.[2] Within the context of German constitutional movements, Brockhaus's *Conversations-Lexikon,* the most widely read book of the nineteenth century and second only to the Bible, plays an important role.

In the following three sections I first highlight the formal innovations that Brockhaus brought to the genre of the *Konversationslexikon,* turning it into one of the most important sources of political historiography.

* The title of this chapter was chosen in tribute to Fania Oz-Salzberger's *Translating the Enlightenment: Scottish Civic Discourse in Eighteenth-Century Germany* (Oxford: Clarendon Press, 1995).

Second, I trace the networks of liberals who were persecuted and exiled after the Congress of Vienna and discuss their central role in the global diffusion of the *Konversationslexikon*. Finally, I consider to what extent the immediate and extensive portrayal of the different European revolutionary movements contributed significantly to the emergence of a liberal and constitutional vocabulary in Germany. In terms of methodology, I shall start with media history and move through network analysis into the field of conceptual history.

The *Konversationslexikon* as a Medium of the Political Historiography of the Present

In his work on Zedler's *Universallexikon*, Ulrich Johannes Schneider has shown that encyclopedias, journals, and newspapers were closely related in the eighteenth century, sharing a number of traits, such as their claim to be current, their writing style, and the publishing process.[3] This is particularly true for the genre of the *Konversationslexicon*, which emerged around 1700 under the name of *Zeitungslexikon* (newspaper lexicon), with the name *Conversationslexicon* first appearing in 1709 as the subtitle of Hübner's *Zeitungslexikon*. The genre addressed itself primarily to political functionaries and merchants, who found within its pages the knowledge they needed for their travels and for understanding European newspapers. This knowledge included currencies and exchange rates, weights and measures, and geographical information as well as explanations of words of foreign origin.[4]

In the late eighteenth century, this merged with a growing interest in the history of the present – known as "histoire immédiate" in France in the wake of the French Revolution – and quickly spread to the German-speaking world (Bourdin 2008). This is clear from the surge of new historical-political journals with a contemporary focus and with titles such as *Geschichte der gegenwärtigen Zeit* (History of the present time; Strasbourg 1790–3), *Räsonnierendes Magazin des Wichtigsten an der Zeitgeschichte* (Reasoning journal on the most important issues of contemporary history; Salzburg 1791–2), and *Klio: Eine Monatsschrift für die französische Zeitgeschichte* (Klio: A monthly journal for French contemporary history; Leipzig 1795–6).[5] Besides these historical-political monthly journals the *Konversationslexicon* became an important medium of contemporary historical discourse. The Löbel-Franke *Konversationslexicon* that was founded in 1796 in Leipzig and taken over by Brockhaus in 1808 clearly proclaimed its programmatic focus on contemporary history in its title:

Conversationslexikon mit vorzüglicher Rücksicht auf die gegenwärtigen Zeiten (*Conversationslexicon* dealing above all with the present times).[6]

This field of contemporary historical journalism was where Friedrich Arnold Brockhaus's career as a publisher began.[7] After establishing his publishing house in 1801 in Amsterdam, he started out by publishing the political journal *De Ster* (The star) as well as eyewitness accounts from revolutionary France that were compiled by Karl Friedrich Cramer under the title of *Individualitäten aus Paris* (Remarkable occurrences from Paris) – in other words, a typical genre of *histoire immédiate.*[8] Among Brockhaus's first publications are Christian von Massenbach's reflections on the recent demise of the old Prussian state. As a Prussian officer, Massenbach had taken part in the battle of Jena/Auerstedt. In his book, he combined his analysis of military defeat with a thorough critique of Prussia's backwardness.[9]

Brockhaus's example most clearly exemplifies the interplay between the press and contemporary politico-economic trends. Before founding his publishing house, Brockhaus traded in English textile products. He shifted his dealings from cloth to paper only because his former commercial field had been blocked by the Napoleonic Continental System. In terms of media history, there is an immediate link between the mechanization of textile production and the mass production of paper that was still based on rags, as Lothar Müller has shown in his history of paper.[10] The first name of the publishing house, "Kunst- und Industrie-Comptoir," still evokes something of both commercial fields.

Brockhaus considered Amsterdam – an international centre of trade and finance – to be an ideal site for producing journals and other contemporary historical publications. In a letter to one of his authors, Karl Friedrich Cramer, he calls attention to Amsterdam's position as both a financial and news hub:

> Es gibt durchaus kein Land in der Welt, das ein größeres Interesse an dem Wechsel der Weltbegebenheiten nimmt, als das unsere, weil keines ist, das den großen Herren im Westen, Süden, Osten und Norden, so viel Geld geliehen als unsere Nation und wo in so großer Handel mit Staatspapieren getrieben wird als hier. Man liest also in Holland mit verschlingender Neugier alles, was nur wie eine Zeitung aussieht. (Brockhaus 1872, 1:63)

> (There is absolutely no other country in the world that takes a greater interest in current global events than ours, since there is no other country that has lent as much money to governments in every which way, and that has

such a flourishing trade in government stocks. That is also why anything that even resembles a newspaper in Holland is read with enormous curiosity.)[11]

In 1808, Brockhaus took over the Löbel-Franke *Konversationslexicon,* whose previous success had been rather lackluster and quickly transformed it into an unprecedented publication powerhouse.[12] Within a few years the *Konversationslexicon* had become his most important product, and later became synonymous with the publishing house itself under the name "Der Brockhaus" (The Brockhaus).[13] Within ten years its circulation figures rose dramatically: from two thousand copies in 1808 to thirty-two thousand copies in 1819 (fifth edition CL). Sixty thousand copies were sold in 1823, and the figures reached three hundred thousand in 1864.[14] This success was only possible because Brockhaus revolutionized the genre of the *Konversationslexicon* in at least two ways.

First, the entries changed radically compared to those found in the older *Zeitungslexika.* In the *Konversationslexicon,* there were fewer lexicon-type explanations of words or places; they were replaced by critical essays like those found in historical-political monthlies. The so-called geographical entries focused on current developments in political hot spots, while the articles on people primarily portrayed famous contemporaries. As Brockhaus had stipulated, these should be persons of "öffentlich historische Charaktere" (public character), that is, "Geschäftsmänner, Künstler und Literatoren aller Art" (all types of merchants, artists, and men of letters), as long as "ihre Wirksamkeit oder ihre Thätigkeit eine gewisse Öffentlichkeit und höhere Bedeutung erhalten (z.B. Banquiers, die große Staatsanleihen übernehmen, bedeutende Fabrikanten, ansehnliche Buchhändler) oder bei Schriftstellern, sobald sie durch Originalwerke den Beifall und die Aufmerksamkeit der Nation auf sich gezogen haben" (their impact or occupation reaches a certain level of publicity and heightened significance (e.g., bankers who buy large stocks of state bonds, major factory owners, and eminent booksellers), or for men of letters, as soon as their original works have been met with acclaim and received national attention) (*Conversations-Lexikon* 1822, 1:XL–XLI).

Second, and even more immediately related to his success, Brockhaus took the medium of the periodical as a model for his reworkings of the *Konversationslexicon* by publishing a rapid succession of new editions, a large number of supplements, and special issues of selected, individual articles. All these measures were meant to ensure that the articles were as up to date as possible. Thus, *Konversationslexicon* became a collective term that could denote a whole family of products. The seven revised editions appearing between 1808 and 1827 stand side by side with the *Neue Folge* (New series, 1822–6), the *Conversations-Lexikon der neuesten Zeit und Literatur* (*Conversationslexicon* of the most recent times and literature, 4 volumes in 1834), and the *Conversations-Lexikon der Gegenwart* (*Conversationslexicon* of the present, 1843). The series *Zeitgenossen: Ein biographisches Magazin für die Geschichte unserer Zeit* (Contemporaries: A biographical journal for the history of our time) assembles and amends biographical articles from the *Conversationslexicon* that deal with living personages. Finally, Brockhaus published his own *Monatsschrift zum Conversations-Lexikon* (Monthly journal accompanying the *Conversationslexicon*) in 1870 with the periodical *Unsere Zeit: Deutsche Revue der Gegenwart* (Our time: German journal of the present). The publication of this journal draws a definitive line between the medium of the *Konversationslexicon* as factual dictionary and the medium of the periodical with its reports and comments on current political occurrences.

Its function as both a dictionary and a periodical and the fact that it was distributed in numbered installments – to be bound together by readers themselves – contributed to the immense success of the *Konversationslexicon*. Given that it favoured up-to-date information, the alphabetical order of entries within an individual installment was very often broken up by essays about current political events. For example, the 1834 booklet contained, among its entries for the letter "Z," from "Zeitung" to "Zollverein," two extensive pieces on the newest political occurrences in Greece and Spain (*Conversations-Lexikon der neuesten Zeit und Literatur* 1834, 1084–137, 1193–222).

These interjections effectively confused censors of the *Konversationslexicon*, as can be gleaned from a report in the Berlin *Oberzensurkollegium* addressed to the Prussian king:

Ew. Majestät Eröffnung, daß die Verbote öfters zu spät kämen, wenn die betreffenden Schriften bereits im Publikum verbreitet wären, erscheint vorzugsweise begründet bei einer Art von Literatur, welche seit einiger Zeit üblich geworden ist. Es ist dies die sogenannte Heft-Literatur, durch welche umfassende Werke in einzelnen Lieferungen von mehreren Bogen, oft mit fortlaufender Seitenzahl, ohne daß die einzelnen Hefte einen besonderen Abschnitt des Werkes bildeten, allmählig ins Publikum gebracht werden. Das heftweise Erscheinen erleichtert den Abnehmern die Bezahlung, gestattet aber den kontrollierenden Behörden keine Uebersicht der Richtung des Werkes [...] Wir haben der Heftliteratur besonders seit der Zeit, wo auf diese Weise das Konversations-Lexikon von Brockhaus in einer ungemein großen Anzahl von Exemplaren verbreitet worden ist, nähere Aufmerksamkeit gewidmet."[15]

(Your majesty's reprimand, that bans often come too late, at a time when the works in question have already been circulated among the public, seems to be particularly pertinent to a certain kind of literature that has recently become common. It is the so-called booklet literature, which distributes substantial works to the public by means of independent installments of a few sheets each, often with continuous numbering, the single installments themselves not constituting any particular part of the work. This booklet-type publishing makes the work more affordable to the customers, but for the authorities it becomes impossible to see which direction the work is going [...] We have paid the booklet literature close attention especially since an enormous number of copies of the *Konversationslexicon* of Brockhaus has been distributed in this way.)

Similarly to Diderot and d'Alembert's *Encyclopédie*, the success of Brockhaus's *Konversationslexicon* can thus only be understood as a combination of deft and innovative publishing strategies and a particular political and critical purpose.[16] In the case of Diderot and d'Alembert, this critique was to serve the Enlightenment's purposes, which is why, for instance, the article "Holy Communion"/"Eucharistie" in the *Encyclopédie* refers to the article "Cannibalism." In the case of Brockhaus, the purpose was explicitly tied to the political aims of early liberalism. All his publications were devoted "purely to liberalism and its spread" and thus at the same time to "the fight against the aristocratic principle of servitude" (Brockhaus 1872, 3:115).

Liberal Networks of Exile and the International Diffusion of the *Konversationslexikon*

One indication of the success of the *Konversationslexicon* is the large number of German adaptations that were published in different principalities, among them lexica for particular audiences such as the *Damen-Conversations-Lexikon* (Ladies' *Conversationslexicon*, Adorf 1834–8), the *Conversations-Lexikon für die Jugend* (*Conversationslexicon* for Youth, Meissen 1840–3), the *Kinder-Conversations-Lexikon* (Children's *Conversationslexicon*, Dillingen 1849), the *Studentikoses Conversations-Lexikon* (Student *Conversationslexicon*, Leipzig 1825), or the *Conversations-Lexikon für Weintrinker und Weinhändler* (*Conversationslexicon* for wine drinkers and wine sellers, Magdeburg 1838).[17] What is even more crucial, though, is that Brockhaus's *Konversationslexicon* was translated into other European and extra-European languages, or tailored to other countries more often than any other nineteenth-century encyclopedia.

The international diffusion of the *Konversationslexicon* is well documented and well researched. A chronological list of its many adaptations follows:

- 1816–18 Danish version: *Conversations-Lexicon aller enyclopaedisk Haandbog*, 6 volumes (fragmentary, up to letter "L"), Copenhagen.
- 1820–9 Dutch version: *Algemeen woordenboek van kunsten en wetenschappen*, edited by G. Nieuwenhuis, 8 volumes, Zutphen.
- 1829–32 American version: *Encyclopaedia Americana: A Popular Dictionary of Arts, Sciences, Literature, History, Politics, and Biography*, edited by Francis Lieber, 13 volumes, Philadelphia.
- 1831–4 Hungarian version: *Közhasznu Edmeretek Tára*, edited by Otto Wigand, 12 volumes, Pest.
- 1833–44 French version: *Encyclopédie des gens du monde*, edited by Jean-Henri Schnitzler, 22 volumes, Paris.
- 1835–9 French version: *Dictionnaire de la conversation et de la lecture*, edited by William Duckett, 52 volumes, Paris.
- 1835–41 Russian version: *Entsiklopeditscheskii Leksikon*, edited by N.J. Gretsch, 17 volumes, St. Petersburg.
- 1837 Italian version: *Dizionario di conversazione*, Padua.
- 1841–50 British version: *The Popular Encyclopaedia or Conversations-Lexicon, being a general dictionary of useful knowledge*, 7 volumes, edited by William Blackie, Glasgow.
- 1860–70 British version: *Chambers's Encyclopaedia: A Dictionary of Universal Knowledge for the People*, edited by William and Robert Chambers, 10 volumes, Edinburgh. (Spree 2000; Review 1863)

Besides the *Encyclopedia Americana* there was an extra-European adaptation in Mexico (*Diccionario universal de historia y de la geografía*, 7 volumes, Mexico City, 1853–5) as well as in India, the Bengal *Encyclopedia Bengalensis* (9 volumes, Calcutta, 1846–8) (*Vollständiges Verzeichnis* 1905, 36).

Just as the European Republic of Letters was crucial to the international circulation of Diderot and d'Alembert's *Encyclopédie*, so too did the international networks of liberals in exile play a decisive role in the diffusion of the *Konversationslexicon*. In the increasingly repressive restoration period after the Congress of Vienna in 1815, the Carlsbad Decrees, and the so-called *Demagogenverfolgung*, thousands of liberals from Spain, Italy, Poland, and the German states were forced into exile. They then continued their journalistic work at their places of exile: Paris, Brussels, London, the United States, or Latin America. In Paris alone, for example, there were seven thousand German expatriates in 1830, growing to sixty thousand in 1848 – Heinrich Heine, Ludwig Börne, and Karl Marx being the best known among them.[18] The Spanish historian Juan Luis Simal has aptly called these liberal networks of exile a nineteenth-century update of the Enlightened Republic of Letters.[19]

The connection between these networks of exiles and the international adaptations of the *Konversationslexicon* is often visible when one looks at the editors of these adaptations. The most striking example is surely the editor of the American *Konversationslexicon*, Franz Lieber. Lieber was born in 1798 in Berlin. As a young man, he was a supporter of Friedrich Ludwig Jahn's nationalist gymnastics movement, and was repeatedly arrested by the Prussian government for this reason. In 1821, to avoid persecution, Lieber joined an international regiment fighting in the Greek war of independence and wrote an eyewitness account about this for Brockhaus. After spending time in London, where he was supported by John Stuart Mill and Jeremy Bentham among others, he went to the United States in 1827, where he published the thirteen-volume *Encyclopedia Americana* to great success. He later became a renowned expert in constitutional law and a professor at several American universities, as well as an advisor of Abraham Lincoln. Lieber died in 1872 in New York, highly esteemed and wealthy.[20]

The same kind of connections can be made with the editors of the Hungarian or French adaptations. The editor of the Hungarian *Konversationslexicon*, Otto Wigand (born in 1795 in Göttingen, died in 1870 in Leipzig), acted as a publisher in Pécs and Budapest before he fled to Saxonian Leipzig in 1833 to avoid persecution by the Metternich government. There he participated, along with Brockhaus, in the Solidarity Club for Poland (Leipziger Verein zur Unterstützung hilfebedürftiger Polen), one of the many associations practising solidarity with revolutionary Poland in Germany after 1830, and he became a member of the city assembly (Stadtverordnetenversammlung) as part of the Democratic group.[21]

The French *Konversationslexicon* was published under the title *Encyclopédie des gens du monde* by the Alsatian Jean-Henri Schnitzler (see also chapter 9 by Jeff Loveland in this volume). Born in Strasbourg in 1802, Schnitzler first worked as a journalist in Berlin in the 1820s, then in Paris. Before starting to work on the *Konversationslexicon* in 1833, he wrote political treatises on all subjects pertaining to contemporary European politics. These included the brochure *Griechenland und Spanien* (Greece and Spain; Strasbourg 1822); a "histoire immediate" of the French July revolution under the title *Bericht eines Augenzeugen über den letzten Auftritt der französischen Revolution Ende Julius 1830 erstattet* (Eyewitness report of the latest manifestation of the French Revolution at the end of July 1830; Stuttgart and Tübingen 1830); a continuation of the previous report under the title *Briefe aus Paris über die Jahressitzung von 1830 und die unmittelbaren Folgen der Juliusrevolution* (Letters from Paris about the annual meeting of 1830 and the immediate consequences of the July revolution; Stuttgart and Tübingen 1832); and the treatises within *Polen und Russland* (Poland and Russia; Paris 1831) and the work *Die deutsche Einheit oder über die Regeneration Deutschlands* (German unification, or on the regeneration of Germany, Strasbourg 1832).

Finally, the history of an important German-language derivative of the *Konversationslexicon*, Rotteck and Welcker's *Staats-Lexikon,* is directly linked to these networks of exile.[22] It was Friedrich List who, having been sentenced in Würzburg and banished to the United States, became acquainted with the American *Konversationslexicon.* When he returned from exile in 1834, he immediately proceeded to publish his own *Historisch-Politisches Konversationslexikon* (Historico-political *Converstionslexicon*), as his preliminary title read. Since he himself as an ex-convict could not serve formally as an editor, he asked the professors Karl von Rotteck and Carl Theodor Welcker to put the plan into practice. The ensuing *Staatslexikon oder Enzyklopädie der Staatswissenschaften* (Staatslexicon or encyclopedia of political science) was to become the most important forum of early German Liberalism.

The Internationalization of Constitutional Discourse in the *Konversationslexikon*

The case of the *Konversationslexicon* exemplifies more than most other works how crucial European entanglements and transfers were to the development of a liberal political vocabulary. From the beginning, Brockhaus himself programmatically declared how important the perception of other cultures was for the emergence of a national culture. In his very first circular letter on the establishment of the Amsterdam publishing house, he wrote that he wanted to create "a central juncture between national and foreign art and science for the Batavian Republic" by means of his publications, "thus fulfilling a long-felt and generally acknowledged need" (dass er mit seinen Publikationen "für die Batavische Republik einen Zentral- und Verbindungspunkt zwischen nationaler und fremder Kunst und Wissenschaft" bilden wolle, um "dadurch einem längst gefühlten und allgemein anerkannten Bedürfnis abzuhelfen").[23]

In fact, the articles on the different European revolutionary independence movements in opposition to the Vienna System make up the most extensive as well as the most interesting set of entries in the *Konversationslexicon*. Among the articles that stand out by virtue of their length alone we find the entry "Spaniens Neueste Geschichte" (Spain's newest history) with long passages on the revolution of 1820; "Griechenland: Befreiungskampf seit dem Jahr 1821" (Greece: struggle for liberation since the year 1821); or "Polnische Revolution" (Polish revolution). In addition, Brockhaus often published these articles, together with entries on related topics, as separate brochures immediately following the respective events. Examples are:

1820 Karl Friedrich Hartmann: *Die spanische Constitution der Cortes und die provisorische Constitution der Vereinigten Provinzen von Südamerika* (The Spanish constitution of the Cortes and the provisional Constitutions of the United Provinces of South America)

1820 Dominique de Pradt: *Die neueste Revolution in Spanien und ihre Folgen* (The most recent revolution in Spain and its consequences)

1821 Louis Bignon: *Du congrès de Troppau, ou Examen des prétentions des monarchies absolues à l'égard de la monarchie constitutionelle de Naples* (The congress of Troppau, or examination of the pretentions of the absolutist monarchies with regard to the constitutional monarchy of Naples)

1821 Wilhelm Traugott Krug: *Griechenlands Wiedergeburt* (Rebirth of Greece)

1821 August Heinrich Meisel: *Beiträge zur Geschichte der spanischen Revolution* (Contributions to the history of the Spanish Revolution)

1822 Wilhelm Traugott Krug: *Neuester Stand der griechischen Sache* (Recent state of the Greek affair)

1822 Christian Müller: *Reise durch Griechenland in den Monaten Junius, Julius und August 1821* (Travels through Greece in the months of June, July, and August 1821)

1823 Franz Lieber: *Tagebuch meines Aufenthaltes in Griechenland im Jahre 1822* (Diary of my stay in Greece in 1822)

In these articles, the depicted revolutionary events are always brought into relation with the situation at home and connected to generalizing and universalizing reflections on the causes and justifications for revolutionary and constitutional movements. To give just one example, consider Heinrich Meisel's August eyewitness account of the revolutionary days in Madrid in the year 1820 in which the Spanish Revolution is presented as the model of a "unblutigen fast mit theoretischer Umsicht geführten Staatsumwälzung" (political upheaval that is conducted in a nonviolent and almost theoretically discrete way). It is said to be a "moralische Naturnothwendigkeit" (moral imperative of nature) that had arisen out of the Spanish king's refusal to recognize the constitution. This then was the answer to the question "ob den Völkern ein Recht zustehe, sich zu revolutionieren" (whether peoples have a right to revolutionize themselves). Thus, it wasn't the liberal agitators who were responsible for revolutions but autocratic and backward-looking rulers who rigidly held on to outmoded political institutions and prevented the introduction of representational constitutions.[24]

Moreover, the article contains an extensive survey of the development of the two factions of the "liberals" or "constitutionalists" on the one side and the "royalists" or "absolutists" on the other. The term "liberal" in the German-speaking world before 1820 was primarily used as an adjective, signifying a cosmopolitan enlightened-philosophical worldview. Within this depiction of the Spanish revolutionary events, it took on its modern meaning as the denomination of a political party.[25] The same is true for the terms "royalism" and "absolutism" on the other side.

The extent to which this transfer of concepts was politically charged can best be understood by considering the censorship records of Brockhaus's *Konversationslexicon*. Brockhaus was the most persecuted publisher in the kingdoms of the two major anti-constitutional powers in the Vienna System: Prussia and Austria. In Prussia, for instance, Brockhaus's entire publishing house was subjected to a so-called re-censorship in 1822, which for all intents and purposes was the equivalent of a temporary publication ban. At the same time, the Prussian post refused to transport publications issued by the Brockhaus press (Kapp 1881, 218ff.). According to information imparted by his relatives, these measures were partly to blame for Brockhaus's early death in 1823 (Brockhaus 1872, 3:184–5). The censors found issue in particular with the above-mentioned articles on Spain, Naples, and Poland (Kapp 1881, 214).

The censorship instructions explicitly forbade the new usage of the term "liberal" in the sense of a faction or party. The relevant Prussian censorship instruction for the year 1822 states:

> Aus demselben Grunde werden Ew. Ex. nicht länger dulden, daß der Name Liberale zur Bezeichnung einer Faction mißbraucht werde, deren strafwürdige Bemühungen und verruchte Zwecke von ihren Mitgliedern selbst in Schriften und Reden enthüllt worden sind. Um das Publicum nicht länger in Täuschung zu erhalten, soll das Wort Liberale nicht ohne den Zusatz: die vorgegebenen oder die sich selbst so nennenden gebraucht werden. Wohlgesinnte Schriftsteller behandeln ohnehin diese Partei als Revolutionäre und werden sich dieser Benennung am Liebsten bedienen. (Kapp 1881: 216)

> (For the same reason your majesty will no longer suffer the name liberal to be misused as the designation of a faction whose punishable endeavours and infamous intentions have been revealed by its members themselves in their writings and speeches. In order to put an end to the deception of the public, the word liberal shall not be used without the addendum: the purported or self-professed. Well-intentioned writers treat this party as revolutionary anyway, and will prefer to use that term.)

All in all, the *Konversationslexicon* in the early nineteenth century became one of the most important institutions of political group formation prior to the emergence of political parties in Germany on the basis of three decisive developments: (1) the *Konversationslexicon*'s focus on the present and the corresponding formal convergence of encyclopedia and journal; (2) the international network of editors, authors, and readers; and (3) the emergence of a liberal political vocabulary by means of the reception of the different European revolutionary movements. This constitutional and early national orientation was not in conflict with the European perspective. On the contrary, the revolutions in France, Spain, Italy, or Greece are both portrayed in terms of their structural interdependence within the Vienna System and displayed as mirrors to one's own constitutional movements. Behind this stands the oft-repeated insight that the borders within Europe did not run between nations but rather between a "Europe of the princes" and a "Europe of the people."

NOTES

1 See Andreas Fahrmeir, 2010, *Revolutionen und Reformen: Europa 1789–1850* (Munich: C.H. Beck); Bernd Wunder, 2001, *Europäische Geschichte im Zeitalter der Französischen Revolution 1789–1815* (Stuttgart, Berlin, Cologne: W. Kohlhammer).

2 Wim Klooster, 2009, *Revolutions in the Atlantic World: A Comparative History* (New York: New York University Press).

3 Ulrich Johannes Schneider, 2013, *Die Erfindung des allgemeinen Wissens: Enzyklopädisches Schreiben im Zeitalter der Aufklärung* (Berlin: Akademie Verlag).

4 Anja zum Hingst, 1995, *Die Geschichte des Großen Brockhaus: Vom Conversationslexikon zur Enzyklopädie* (Wiesbaden: Harrassowitz), 21ff.

5 Iwan-Michelangelo D'Aprile, 2013, *Die Erfindung der Zeitgeschichte. Geschichtsschreibung und Journalismus zwischen Aufklärung und Vormärz* (Berlin: Akademie).

6 [Renatus Gottheld Löbel and Christian Wilhelm Franke], 1796, *Conversationslexikon mit vorzüglicher Rücksicht auf die gegenwärtigen Zeiten* (Leipzig: Leupold).

7 Heinrich Eduard Brockhaus, 1872–81, *Friedrich Arnold Brockhaus. Sein Leben und Wirken nach Briefen und anderen Aufzeichnungen geschildert von seinem Enkel Heinrich Eduard Brockhaus*, 3 vols. (Leipzig: Brockhaus); Thomas Keiderling, 2005, *F. A. Brockhaus 1905–2005*, 2 vols. (Mannheim: Brockhaus).

8 Zum Hingst 1995, 78ff.

9 Christian von Massenbach, 1809, *Memoiren über meine Verhältnisse zum preußischen Staat und insbesondere zum Herzog von Braunschweig*, 2 vols. (Amsterdam: Verlag des Kunst- und Industrie-Comptoirs).

10 Lothar Müller, 2012, *Weiße Magie. Die Epoche des Papiers* (Munich: Carl Hanser).

11 All translations are mine unless otherwise indicated.

12 Zum Hingst 1995; Ulrike Spree, 2000, *Das Streben nach Wissen. Eine vergleichende Gattungsgeschichte der populären Enzyklopädie in Deutschland und Großbritannien im 19. Jahrhundert* (Tübingen: De Gruyter).

13 Thomas Keiderling, 2012, "Der Brockhaus," in *Große Lexika und Wörterbücher Europas. Europäische Enzyklopädien und Wörterbücher in historischen Porträts*, ed. Ulrike Haß, (Berlin: De Gruyter), 193–210.

14 Zum Hingst 1995, 102ff.

15 "Bericht des preußischen Ober-Censur-Kollegiums vom 31. März 1836," in Friedrich Kapp, 1881, "Die preußische Preßgesetzgebung unter Friedrich Wilhelm III. (1815–1840). Nach den Akten im Königl. Preußischen Geh. Staatsarchiv," *Archiv für Geschichte des Deutschen Buchhandels* (Leipzig: n.p.), 6:244.

16 Robert Darnton, 1979, *The Business of Enlightenment: A Publishing History of the Encyclopedie 1775–1800* (Cambridge: Harvard University Press).

17 *Vollständiges Verzeichnis der von der Firma F. A. Brockhaus in Leipzig seit ihrer Gründung durch Friedrich Arnold Brockhaus im Jahre 1805 bis zu dessen hundertjährigem Geburtstage im Jahre 1872 verlegten Werke. In chronologischer Folge mit biographischen und literarhistorischen Notizen,* 1905, ed. Heinrich Brockhaus (Leipzig), 27ff.

18 Mareike König, 2003, "Brüche als gestaltendes Element: Die Deutschen in Paris im 19. Jahrhundert," in *Deutsche Handwerker, Arbeiter und Dienstmädchen in Paris,* ed. Mareike König (Munich: Oldenbourg), 9–26.

19 Juan Luis Simal, 2013, *Emigrados. España y el exilio internacional 1814–1834* (Madrid: Centro de Estudios Políticos y Constitucionales – Asociación de Historia Contemporánea), 15.

20 Gerhard Weiss, 2005, "The Americanization of Franz Lieber and the *Encyclopedia Americana,*" in *German Culture in Nineteenth-Century America: Reception, Adaptation, Transformation,* ed. Lynne Tatlock and Matt Erlin (New York: Camden), 286ff.

21 Gert Klitzke, 1973, "Zur gesellschaftlichen Stellung des Verlegers Heinrich Brockhaus, insbesondere im Vormärz und in der Revolution von 1848/49. Ein Beitrag zu seiner Biographie," in *Beiträge zur Geschichte des Buchwesens,* ed. Helmut Rötzsch and Karlheinz Selle on behalf of the Historischen Kommission des Börsenvereins der Deutschen Buchhändler zu Leipzig (Leipzig: VEB Fachbuchverlag), 6:9–52.

22 Hans Zehntner, 1929, *Das Staatslexikon von Rotteck und Welcker. Eine Studie zur Geschichte des deutschen Frühliberalismus* (Jena: Fischer).

23 See zum Hingst 1995, 82.

24 Jörg Ludwig, 2013, *Deutschland und die spanische Revolution 1820–1823* (Leipzig: Leipziger Universitätsverlag), 176–7.

25 On the change of the meaning of "liberalism" in Germany, see Dieter Langewiesche, 1988, *Liberalismus in Deutschland* (Frankfurt am Main: Suhrkamp); Fritz Valjavec, 1978 [1951], *Die Entstehung der politischen Strömungen in Deutschland 1770–1815,* ed. Jörn Garber (Düsseldorf: Athenäum); Jörn Leonhard, 2010, "Zur Semantik gleichzeitiger Ungleichzeitigkeit: Europäische Liberalismen im Vergleich," in *Rechtsstaat statt Revolution, Verrechtlichung statt Demokratie? Transdisziplinäre Analysen zum deutschen und spanischen Weg in die Moderne,* ed. Detlef Georgia Schulze, Sabine Berghahn, and Frieder Otto Wolf, 1:313–24 (Münster: Dampfboot).

Bibliography

Bourdin, Philippe, ed. 2008. *La Révolution 1789–1871. Écriture d'une Histoire immédiate.* Clermont-Ferrand: Presses de l'Université Blaise-Pascal.

Brockhaus, Heinrich Eduard. 1872–81. *Friedrich Arnold Brockhaus. Sein Leben und Wirken nach Briefen und anderen Aufzeichnungen geschildert von seinem Enkel Heinrich Eduard Brockhaus.* 3 vols. Leipzig: Brockhaus.

Conversations-Lexikon. Neue Folge. 1822. 2 vols. Leipzig: Brockhaus.

Conversations-Lexikon der neuesten Zeit und Literatur. Ein Supplementband zu allen frühern Auflagen des Conversations-Lexikons. 1834. Leipzig: Brockhaus.

D'Aprile, Iwan-Michelangelo. 2013. *Die Erfindung der Zeitgeschichte. Geschichtsschreibung und Journalismus zwischen Aufklärung und Vormärz.* Berlin: Akademie.

Darnton, Robert. 1979. *The Business of Enlightenment: A Publishing History of the Encyclopedie 1775–1800.* Cambridge: Harvard University Press.

Fahrmeir, Andreas. 2010. *Revolutionen und Reformen: Europa 1789–1850.* Munich: C.H. Beck.

Gosewinkel, Dieter, Johannes Masing, and Andreas Würschinger, eds. 2006. *Die Verfassungen in Europa 1789–1949.* Munich: C.H. Beck.

Grimm, Dieter. 1990. "Verfassung." In *Geschichtliche Grundbegriffe. Historisches Lexikon zur politisch-sozialen Sprache,* edited by Otto Brunner, Werner Conze, and Reinhart Koselleck, 6:831–99. Stuttgart: Klett-Cotta.

Grimm, Dieter, and Heinz Mohnhaupt. 1995. *Verfassung. Zur Geschichte des Begriffs von der Antike bis zur Gegenwart.* Berlin: Duncker und Humblot.

Haltern, Utz. 1976. "Politische Bildung und bürgerlicher Liberalismus. Zur Rolle des Konversationslexikons in Deutschland." *Historische Zeitschrift* 223: 61–97.

Handbuch der europäischen Verfassungsgeschichte im 19. Jahrhundert (vol. 1: *Um 1800;* vol. 2: *1815–1847*). 2006. Edited by Peter Brandt, Martin Kirsch, and Arthur Schlegelmilch on behalf of the Historischen Forschungszentrums der Friedrich-Ebert-Stiftung and the Instituts für europäische Verfassungswissenschaften der FernUniversität Hagen. Bonn.

Hingst, Anja zum. 1995. *Die Geschichte des Großen Brockhaus. Vom Conversationslexikon zur Enzyklopädie.* Wiesbaden: Harrassowitz.

Kapp, Friedrich. 1881. "Die preußische Preßgesetzgebung unter Friedrich Wilhelm III. (1815–1840). Nach den Akten im Königl. Preußischen Geh. Staatsarchiv." In *Archiv für Geschichte des Deutschen Buchhandels,* 6:185–249. Leipzig: n.p.

Keiderling, Thomas. 2005. *F. A. Brockhaus 1905–2005.* 2 vols. Mannheim: Brockhaus.

– 2012. "Der Brockhaus." In *Große Lexika und Wörterbücher Europas. Europäische Enzyklopädien und Wörterbücher in historischen Porträts*, edited by Ulrike Haß, 193–210. Berlin: De Gruyter.

Klitzke, Gert. 1973. "Zur gesellschaftlichen Stellung des Verlegers Heinrich Brockhaus, insbesondere im Vormärz und in der Revolution von 1848/49. Ein Beitrag zu seiner Biographie." In *Beiträge zur Geschichte des Buchwesens*, edited by Helmut Rötzsch and Karlheinz Selle on behalf of the Historischen Kommission des Börsenvereins der Deutschen Buchhändler zu Leipzig, 6:9–52. Leipzig: VEB Fachbuchverlag.

Klooster, Wim. 2009. *Revolutions in the Atlantic World: A Comparative History*. New York: New York University Press.

König, Mareike. 2003. "Brüche als gestaltendes Element: Die Deutschen in Paris im 19. Jahrhundert." In *Deutsche Handwerker, Arbeiter und Dienstmädchen in Paris*, edited by Mareike König, 9–26. Munich: Oldenbourg.

Langewiesche, Dieter. 1988. *Liberalismus in Deutschland*. Frankfurt am Main: Suhrkamp.

Leonhard, Jörn. 2010. "Zur Semantik gleichzeitiger Ungleichzeitigkeit: Europäische Liberalismen im Vergleich." In *Rechtsstaat statt Revolution, Verrechtlichung statt Demokratie? Transdisziplinäre Analysen zum deutschen und spanischen Weg in die Moderne*, edited by Detlef Georgia Schulze, Sabine Berghahn, and Frieder Otto Wolf, 1:313–24. Münster: Dampfboot.

[Löbel, Renatus Gottheld, and Christian Wilhelm Franke]. 1796. *Conversationslexikon mit vorzüglicher Rücksicht auf die gegenwärtigen Zeiten*. Leipzig: Leupold.

Ludwig, Jörg. 2013. *Deutschland und die spanische Revolution 1820–1823*. Leipzig: Leipziger Universitätsverlag.

Lüsebrink, Hans-Jürgen, Susanne Greilich, and Jean-Yves Mollier, eds. 2000. *Presse et événement: Journaux, Gazettes, Almanachs (XVIIIe–XIXe siècles)*. Bern, Berlin, Bruxelles: Lang.

Lüsebrink, Hans-Jürgen, and Jeremy Popkin, eds. 2004. *Enlightenment, Revolution and the Periodical Press*. Oxford: Voltaire Foundation.

Massenbach, Christian von. 1809. *Memoiren über meine Verhältnisse zum preußischen Staat und insbesondere zum Herzog von Braunschweig*. 2 vols. Amsterdam: Verlag des Kunst- und Industrie-Comptoirs.

Müller, Lothar. 2012. *Weiße Magie. Die Epoche des Papiers*. Munich: Carl Hanser.

Oz-Salzberger, Fania. 1995. *Translating the Enlightenment: Scottish Civic Discourse in Eighteenth-Century Germany*. Oxford: Oxford University Press.

Review 1863. "The English Cyclopaedia: A New Dictionary of Universal Knowledge." *Quarterly Review* 113: 354–87.

Schneider, Ulrich Johannes. 2013. *Die Erfindung des allgemeinen Wissens. Enzyklopädisches Schreiben im Zeitalter der Aufklärung*. Berlin: Akademie Verlag.

Simal, Juan Luis. 2013. *Emigrados. España y el exilio internacional 1814–1834.*
    Madrid: Centro de Estudios Políticos y Constitucionales – Asociación de
    Historia Contemporánea.
Spree, Ulrike. 2000. *Das Streben nach Wissen. Eine vergleichende Gattungsgeschichte
    der populären Enzyklopädie in Deutschland und Großbritannien im 19. Jahrhundert.*
    Tübingen: De Gruyter.
Steinmetz, Willibald. 2000. *Private Law and Social Inequality in the Industrial Age.*
    Oxford: Oxford University Press.
Valjavec, Fritz. 1978 [1951]. *Die Entstehung der politischen Strömungen in
    Deutschland 1770–1815.* Edited by Jörn Garber. Düsseldorf: Athenäum.
*Vollständiges Verzeichnis der von der Firma F. A. Brockhaus in Leipzig seit ihrer
    Gründung durch Friedrich Arnold Brockhaus im Jahre 1805 bis zu dessen
    hundertjährigem Geburtstage im Jahre 1872 verlegten Werke. In chronologischer Folge
    mit biographischen und literarhistorischen Notizen.* 1905. Edited by Heinrich
    Brockhaus. Leipzig.
Weiss, Gerhard 2005. "The Americanization of Franz Lieber and the
    Encyclopedia Americana." In *German Culture in Nineteenth-Century America:
    Reception, Adaptation, Transformation,* edited by Lynne Tatlock and Matt Erlin,
    273–87. New York: Camden.
Wunder, Bernd. 2001. *Europäische Geschichte im Zeitalter der Französischen
    Revolution 1789–1815.* Stuttgart, Berlin, Köln: W. Kohlhammer.
Zehntner, Hans. 1929. *Das Staatslexikon von Rotteck und Welcker. Eine Studie zur
    Geschichte des deutschen Frühliberalismus.* Jena: Fischer.

chapter nine

Two French *Konversationslexika* of the 1830s and 1840s: The *Dictionnaire de la conversation et de la lecture* and the *Encyclopédie des gens du monde*

JEFF LOVELAND

The years of the French Revolution, the Napoleonic era, and the early Bourbon Restoration were difficult for large French encyclopedias. These years were a time of crisis for the French book trade in general, but large titles were particularly affected. War and political instability increased demand for news and periodicals but discouraged investment in long-term literary projects. The gigantic *Encyclopédie méthodique* (1782–1832) managed to continue publication throughout the period, and a few huge works of reference were started and finished, notably the sixty-volume *Dictionnaire des sciences naturelles* (1816–30). Still, in this climate, multi-volume encyclopedias like Denis Diderot and Jean le Rond d'Alembert's *Encyclopédie* (1751–72) and the later editions of the *Dictionnaire de Trévoux* became rare.[1] The largest new general encyclopedia of the time was the twenty-four-volume *Encyclopédie moderne, ou dictionnaire abrégé des sciences, des lettres et des arts* (1823–32). By the number of volumes, it would seem to have been longer than the *Encyclopédie,* but by the early nineteenth century the volumes of encyclopedias had grown significantly smaller than in the previous century, the typical size dropping from folio to quarto or octavo.[2] Thus, the *Encyclopédie moderne* contained less than a third as many words as the *Encyclopédie.* Partially filling in for the period's largely absent encyclopedias were a number of short, variously encyclopedic dictionaries such as Pierre-Claude-Victor Boiste's two-volume *Dictionnaire universel de la langue française* (1800), which had gone through fourteen editions by 1857.[3]

In contrast, despite war and political turmoil in the German states, the three or four decades before 1830 were fertile ones in German-language encyclopedism. The ambitious but never finished *Allgemeine Encyclopädie der Wissenschaften und Künste* (1818–89), now associated with the names of the sometime editors Johann Samuel Ersch and Johann Gottfried Gruber, was conceived in 1813 and already comprised around thirty volumes by 1830. More important in the long run was the reformulation of the eighteenth-century German genre of the *Konversationslexikon*, or conversational dictionary, by Friedrich Arnold Brockhaus. In 1808 Brockhaus acquired rights to a *Conversationslexikon* (1796–1808) by Renatus Gotthelf Löbel and Christian Wilhelm Franke, just in time to have it finished and updated with a supplement. He then proceeded to issue new editions in quick succession, originally acting as an editor and contributor as well as the publisher. By the time of the fifth edition (1819–20), Brockhaus's *Konversationslexikon*, now called the *Allgemeine deutsche Real-Encyclopädie*, had become a carefully planned, broadly collaborative, and extraordinarily successful ten-volume compilation.[4] "Pirated" and imitated by other German-language publishers, it was also adapted for use in Danish (1816–18), Dutch (1820–9), English (1829–33), Hungarian (1831–4), and other languages.[5] Along with the *Encyclopaedia Britannica*, it was a model for encyclopedias worldwide in the nineteenth and twentieth centuries.

In France, a revival of large encyclopedias began with the *Encyclopédie moderne* in the 1820s and accelerated in the 1830s with the launching of such works as the *Encyclopédie nouvelle* (1833–48) and the *Encyclopédie du dix-neuvième siècle* (1836–53). As relatively "popular" encyclopedias, these works may have been inspired by the flowering of the *Konversationslexikon* in Germany.[6] Two of them, however, were explicitly indebted to the *Konversationslexikon*: the *Encyclopédie des gens du monde* (1833–44) and the *Dictionnaire de la conversation et de la lecture* (1832–39). Paul Rowe has written two articles on the *Encyclopédie des gens du monde*,[7] while Jean-Yves Mollier has illuminated the *Dictionnaire de la conversation et de la lecture* as a commercial enterprise.[8] Otherwise, neither of these French works has been studied much. In this article, building on the research of Rowe and Mollier, I will briefly characterize the two encyclopedias and then, having taken stock of what a *Konversationslexikon* was in the early nineteenth century, examine their adaptation of Brockhaus's invention for France. As encyclopedias, neither of the two French works examined here was distinguished in the way that, say, the *Encyclopédie* was: they were unambitious intellectually and only moderately successful as commodities. They are nonetheless worth studying to shed light on the business of encyclopedia-making in early nineteenth-century France and on the story of the *Konversationslexikon* as an international model.

The *Encyclopédie des gens du monde*

Brockhaus's achievements were brought to the attention of the French public upon his death in 1823, when obituaries in the francophone press noted his success as a maker of encyclopedias and of the *Konversationslexikon*.[9] Writing for the barely started and never finished *Encyclopédie progressive* (1826), the future French minister of education François-Pierre-Guillaume Guizot praised Brockhaus's *Konversationslexikon* as "la plus complète des encyclopédies populaires" (the most complete of popular encyclopedias) and as a major contributor to Germany's uniquely widespread culture of learning.[10] The first attempt to adapt Brockhaus's encyclopedia for the use of the French does not seem to have come until 1829, however. At this time, a prospectus and advertisements for a *Nouveau Dictionnaire encyclopédique à l'usage des gens du monde* to be adapted from the *Konversationslexikon* were issued by the publisher Treuttel and Würtz.

Why Treuttel and Würtz's project was delayed until 1833 is unclear. Two different causes were alleged in the *Encyclopédie des gens du monde*, as their encyclopedia was ultimately titled. First, the "Discours préliminaire" stated that they had originally planned to "réduire notre travail à une simple reproduction de l'ouvrage allemand en français, sauf les changements qui devaient naturellement résulter de la différence des besoins dans des lieux différents" (limit our work to a mere reproduction of the German work in French, except for changes that had to follow naturally from the difference in needs in different places), but that they had decided to expand the encyclopedia after drawing up the prospectus of 1829.[11] In fact, already in 1829 the prospectus insisted that the encyclopedia would be more than a "simple traduction" (mere translation) and that it would cover subjects ignored in Brockhaus's *Konversationslexikon*.[12] Furthermore, the editor Jean-Henri Schnitzler claimed that a team of distinguished "hommes de lettres et savants" (men of letters and scholars) had been recruited in 1829, a team that would hardly have been necessary for a translation.[13] Nor did the prospectus announce a markedly shorter work than the one that appeared. Specifically, in 1829 the *Nouveau Dictionnaire encyclopédique* was to comprise between fifteen to twenty volumes in octavo,[14] whereas the *Encyclopédie des gens du monde* was projected for twelve volumes in 1833 and then fifteen volumes in 1840,[15] though it ended up extending to twenty-two volumes. In the end, the "Discours préliminaire" exaggerated the extent of any expansion since 1829, presumably to discredit the rival *Dictionnaire de la conversation et de la lecture*, which was initially more dependent on mere translation. Second, in his article "Encyclopédie," Schnitzler blamed the delay in the publication of the *Encyclopédie des gens du monde* on the revolution of July 1830 without invoking a decision to expand the encyclopedia.[16] The summer of 1830 would have been a difficult time to launch an encyclopedia, but it is hard to imagine why the delay would have stretched into 1831 and 1832.

Instead, it may be that the project was abandoned and then resuscitated in response to the start of the *Dictionnaire de la conversation et de la lecture* in 1832. Certainly, comparison with the rival work was important in early advertising for the *Encyclopédie des gens du monde*, which allegedly included circulars shoved under every "porte cochère" (coach gate) in Paris.[17] Similarly, the change in title from "encyclopedic dictionary" to the more grandiose "encyclopedia" was perhaps meant to set the *Encyclopédie des gens du monde* apart from the *Dictionnaire de la conversation et de la lecture.*

Inspiration for the *Encyclopédie des gens du monde* probably came from the publisher, Treuttel and Würtz. The company was founded in Strasbourg in the 1770s and had risen to become one of Europe's biggest international publishers by the 1820s, with a main office in Paris and subsidiary ones in London and Strasbourg.[18] Familiar with the German market for books, and probably wiser in the ways of encyclopedia-making for their involvement as distributors of the failed *Encyclopédie progressive* of 1826,[19] the publishers must have concluded that the moment was right for a translation and adaptation of Brockhaus's *Konversationslexikon.* As editor, they selected Schnitzler, a young Alsatian Lutheran who had just returned from a trip to Russia in 1828 and was in the process of establishing himself as a historian, statistician, and liberal journalist; he would also become a German tutor for the ruling Orléans family.[20] It is possible, alternatively, that Schnitzler conceived the encyclopedia and then proposed it to Treuttel and Würtz. Fluent in German as well as French, he was surely familiar with Brockhaus's encyclopedia.

As noted above, contributors for the *Encyclopédie des gens du monde* were recruited from 1829 onward. By the conclusion of publication, some three hundred people had contributed. Many were journalists hailing from Paris, but the roster also included, most eminently, the linguist Julius Klaproth, the historian Jules Michelet, and the physiologist François Magendie.[21] Articles in the encyclopedia were signed with initials or acronyms, while the signatures "CL" and "CLm" were used to indicate translations and "modified" translations from Brockhaus's work.

The *Encyclopédie des gens du monde* was published in half-volume instalments of around four hundred pages, issued at a rate of about four per year and advertised as costing five francs each. This system was consistent with the prospectus of 1829 except that instalments had been promised there at a rate of one per month.[22] Encyclopedias had been published serially – that is, in instalments stretched over time – for more than a century. Serial publication was a logical choice for the makers of large encyclopedias especially: it mirrored what was usually a protracted schedule of compilation, it allowed capital-starved publishers to replenish their coffers from instalment to instalment, and it encouraged less affluent consumers to consider buying a work whose price might seem prohibitive in a single payment. Serialization by simple volumes was the norm in France through the late eighteenth century, whereas instalments of a hundred pages or fewer were common in Britain. Problems with censorship undoubtedly contributed to the later development of comparably fine-grained serialization in France,[23] and it is worth noting that the size of the half-volume instalments of the *Encyclopédie des gens du monde* was just sufficient to put it above what had once been a limit for pre-publication censorship: laws in place during the Restoration had mandated this censorship for publications of fewer than twenty printed sheets, the equivalent of 320 pages in octavo.[24] Still, some publishers evidently saw the advantages of slimmer instalments as outweighing the potential risk of pre-publication censorship, for the *Encyclopédie progressive*, the *Dictionnaire de la conversation et de la lecture*, and even the markedly leftist *Encyclopédie nouvelle* were all to be published in instalments of fewer than twenty leaves, specifically in instalments of around 250, 250, and 16 pages in octavo respectively.[25] Like the publisher of the *Dictionnaire de la conversation et de la lecture*, the publisher of the *Encyclopédie des gens du monde* could have defined its half-volume instalments as units to be bound separately rather than combined, but the resultant volumes might then have appeared less attractive, traditional, or authoritative.

The *Dictionnaire de la conversation et de la lecture*

The originator of the *Dictionnaire de la conversation et de la lecture* seems not to have been the Parisian publisher Auguste-Jean Belin-Mandar but rather the editor William Duckett, the son of an exiled Irish nationalist and professor of English of the same name. The future editor of the encyclopedia was born around 1803 when his parents settled in Paris. Roughly the same age as Schnitzler, he too was a journalist.[26] As a translator of German books from at least 1829 onward,[27] he was familiar with German culture and thus presumably with Brockhaus's encyclopedia. His son, also William, collaborated on a second edition (1852–8) of the *Dictionnaire de la conversation et de la lecture*. As editor of the first edition, Duckett chose the financially struggling writer and journalist Edme-Joachim Héreau. Coincidentally, Héreau, like Schnitzler, had spent time in Russia, as a secretary, a professor of French, and a political prisoner. He had also lived in Berlin and thus presumably had some knowledge of the German language and German culture.[28] Along with many other articles signed with his name, "EH," or simply "H," Héreau wrote "Encyclopédie," where he characterized the work's principles as exactness and "good faith"; the latter concept he explained as a kind of moral dispassionateness.[29] Héreau resigned in 1835, apparently overworked and on poor terms with Duckett, before committing suicide in 1836.[30] I have been unable to discover who edited the encyclopedia from the letter "E" onward.

An advertisement for the *Dictionnaire de la conversation et de la lecture* that appeared in the *Journal des connaissances utiles* in 1832 hints at the contents of the prospectus, which was pushed throughout France by travelling salesmen.[31] Here the *Dictionnaire* was characterized as a translation of an unnamed but widely disseminated German encyclopedia, and announced as consisting of twenty-four volumes to be delivered in forty-eight instalments extending to around 250 pages and costing two francs each. By 1836, the number of projected volumes had more than doubled to the definitive figure of fifty-two, while the price for subscribers had fallen to one franc eighty centimes per instalment.[32]

Above all, the advertisement dwelt on the names and titles of contributors. Indeed, in volume 1 alone, the *Dictionnaire de la conversation et de la lecture* listed a greater number of prestigious contributors than the *Encyclopédie des gens du monde* could have listed for all its volumes combined, including the physicist François Arago, the novelist Honoré de Balzac, the mathematician Augustin-Louis Cauchy, the novelist François-René de Chateaubriand, the philosopher Victor Cousin, the politician Édouard de Fitz-James, the naturalist Étienne Geoffroy Saint-Hilaire, the statesman Guizot, the writer Victor Hugo, the critic Charles Augustin Sainte-Beuve, and the economist Jean-Baptiste Say.[33]

In 1833, one reviewer suggested that the famous names in the prospectus were mainly for show, since few had contributed to the first four instalments.[34] Whether or not the advertised celebrities all wrote an article, they were undoubtedly not among the most prolific contributors.

Most articles were anonymous at the start of the encyclopedia, though the proportion of signed articles quickly rose, probably in response to the arrival of the *Encyclopédie des gens du monde*. In volume 1, for example, only around 10 per cent of articles were signed, whether with a name or variously ambiguous initials.[35] Furthermore, only around twenty-five people signed articles in volume 1. In particular, the contributors with the most articles to their credit in volume 1 were the statesman and writer Antoine Français de Nantes (with eleven articles), Héreau (eight), the botanist Claude Tollard the Elder (seven), a certain H. Audiffret (six),[36] the general Frédéric-François Guillaume de Vaudoncourt (five), Say (four), and the teacher and historian Charles Du Rozoir (four). By contrast, whereas the first signed article in the *Dictionnaire de la conversation et de la lecture* – "Ablécimof," by Héreau – occurred thirteen pages into volume 1, nine of the first ten articles in volume 9 (1833) were signed, a proportion roughly maintained in subsequent volumes.

When the *Encyclopédie des gens du monde* was revived in 1833, the backers of the *Dictionnaire de la conversation et de la lecture* accused Treuttel and Würtz of duplicitously advertising the names of contributors already writing for and loyal to their encyclopedia. Indeed, testimonials from two of the contributors in question – the general Étienne-Alexandre Bardin and the historian and politician Jacques Marquet de Montbreton de Norvins – indicate that certain people were solicited as contributors by Treuttel and Würtz in 1829 before committing, definitively, to the *Dictionnaire de la conversation et de la lecture*. Some were apparently surprised to see themselves identified as contributors in early advertisements for the *Encyclopédie des gens du monde*.[37] In any event, a handful of people ended up contributing to both encyclopedias, including the critic Jules Janin and the writer Pierre-Joseph Onésime Leroy. Perhaps prohibited by contract, they do not seem to have used any of the same material for both. In some instances, however, material from one or the other of the French encyclopedias was reused by contributors in their own publications, occasionally even contemporaneously: Amédée Prévost's article "Descartes" (1837) in the *Encyclopédie des gens du monde*, for example, reappeared in his introduction to the *Œuvres philosophiques de Descartes* (1838) the following year,[38] just as Pierre-Sébastien Laurentie's "Enseignement" (1835) in the *Dictionnaire de la conversation et de la lecture* reappeared in his *Histoire, morale et littérature* (1838) some three years later.[39] Whether by contract, tolerance, or simple ignorance, the publishers of the French encyclopedias were undoubtedly less opposed to such reuse than to sharing material with each other.

What Was a *Konversationslexikon* in 1830?

The first works of reference to be called *Konversationslexika* were editions and imitations of the *Reales Staats- und Zeitungs-Lexicon* (1704), compiled anonymously by Philip Balthasar Sinold von Schütz but associated with the name of the preface-writer, the rector and educator Johann Hübner. As of the third edition of 1708, this work's title was changed to *Reales Staats- Zeitungs- und Conversations-Lexicon*. The goal of the encyclopedia, which had gone through more than thirty official editions by the early nineteenth century, was to help people read periodicals and engage in conversation. In practice, we shall see, the eighteenth-century *Konversationslexikon* was dominated by geographical information.

The genre of the *Konversationslexikon* acquired greater generality and a new sense of purpose in the early nineteenth century. Already in the preface to his and Franke's *Conversationslexikon mit vorzüglicher Rücksicht auf die gegenwärtigen Zeiten* (1796–1808), Löbel criticized "Hübner's" work for its old-fashioned narrowness and claimed that his and Franke's would have an appropriately modern breadth for the period's readers and conversationalists.[40] Accordingly, whereas some two-thirds of the keywords in the opening pages of an edition of the *Reales Staats- Zeitungs- und Conversations-Lexicon* from 1735 were names of places or geographical features,[41] only a fifth were in the first fifty pages of Löbel and Franke's *Conversationslexikon*.[42] After Brockhaus acquired rights to the encyclopedia in 1808 and retitled it *Conversations-Lexicon oder kurzgefaßtes Handwörterbuch für die in der gesellschaftlichen Unterhaltung aus den Wissenschaften und Künsten vorkommenden Gegenstände*, he further advanced Löbel's goal of making the *Konversationslexikon* comprehensive and up to date, notably by stressing biographies of living people, which still remained rare in encyclopedias.[43]

As it went from edition to edition in the early nineteenth century, Brockhaus's *Konversationslexikon* changed considerably. It grew in size, though without approaching the size of such gigantic contemporary works as the *Encyclopédie méthodique* or Ersch and Gruber's *Allgemeine Encyclopädie*. It got more scholarly and objective in tone. Increasingly, it was written and reviewed by specialized contributors, not just compiled by Brockhaus or a few fellow generalists.[44] Another crucial shift took place between the sixth and seventh editions: after its sixth edition, the Brockhaus firm issued supplements that dealt with current events. The goal was to transform the *Konversationslexikon* itself into a repository of relatively stable knowledge and thus to facilitate future revisions. For this reason, according to Anja zum Hingst, the seventh edition deserves recognition as a decisive turning point towards modern conceptions of the *Konversationslexikon*.[45]

The seventh edition of Brockhaus's encyclopedia appeared in 1827 in twelve volumes under the title *Allgemeine deutsche Real-Encyklopädie für die gebildeten Stände (Conversations-Lexikon)* and then again in a reprint of 1830.[46] This was the work from which both of the French encyclopedias under study here took inspiration. Later, they were able to use material from the eighth edition, which appeared under the same title and with the same number of volumes from 1833 to 1837. Differences in alphabetization between French and German meant that recourse to the eighth edition would have had to be limited: by the time a given keyword was treated in the German work, it might have already been treated in the French works.

How Was the *Konversationslexikon* Transformed for Use in France?

Paul Rowe has noted two changes of format in the passage from Brockhaus's "sober" *Konversationslexikon* to the comparatively "elegant" *Encyclopédie des gens du monde*: the number of columns grew from one to two, while the layout became airier, with highlighted keywords.[47] The *Dictionnaire de la conversation et de la lecture* also featured two columns and highlighted keywords, though its margins were cramped. Multiple columns had been standard in eighteenth-century encyclopedias in both France and Germany, even in the *Reales Staats-, Zeitungs- und Conversations-Lexicon*. As a single-column design was common in periodicals, Brockhaus may have chosen it because of his encyclopedia's essay-like articles.[48] Perhaps in imitation, the *Encyclopédie moderne* was also presented in a single column per page, as was the *Encyclopédie progressive*, but the *Encyclopédie des gens du monde* and the *Dictionnaire de la conversation et de la lecture* both evidently succumbed to the allure of a time-honoured layout for French encyclopedias.

In contrast, both French encyclopedias followed Brockhaus's contemporary *Konversationslexikon* in including an alphabetical list of articles at the end of each volume, a kind of table of contents with a certain suitability for a collection of essay-like articles. Brockhaus finally furnished a general index for the eighth edition, but it came too late to inspire either French work. The absence of a general index limited the value of the French encyclopedias as works of reference, but it is worth noting that French encyclopedias had a poor record for indexing before this time. The *Encyclopédie*, for example, only acquired a general index belatedly, while the *Encyclopédie méthodique* was terminated without a promised "Vocabulaire universel."[49]

The price for a set of the *Encyclopédie des gens du monde* was around 220 francs, whereas the *Dictionnaire de la conversation et de la lecture* could be purchased for about 190 francs. By contrast, a set of the seventh edition of Brockhaus's *Konversationslexikon* sold for fifteen taler, though a deluxe edition on vellum went for over double that price; prices were similar for the eighth edition.[50] Since the taler was worth a little less than four francs,[51] the German encyclopedia cost roughly the equivalent of sixty francs and was thus far less expensive than either French encyclopedia. In part, the discrepancy was a matter of size: whereas Brockhaus's *Konversationslexikon* included around seven million words, the *Encyclopédie des gens du monde* included around twelve million and the *Dictionnaire de la conversation et de la lecture* around sixteen million.[52] In part as well, the volume of Brockhaus's sales and its reuse of material from previous editions allowed the company to set its prices at extraordinarily low levels.

Another factor allowing Brockhaus's encyclopedia to be sold for so little was its lack of illustrations. Ironically, despite their comparatively high prices and elegant appearances, neither French encyclopedia was illustrated in any significant measure, though the *Encyclopédie des gens du monde* included a portrait of one of its publishers at the head of the last volume, and though both encyclopedias included woodcuts within articles on rare occasions. The article "Géométrie" in the *Dictionnaire de la conversation et de la lecture*, for example, featured about ten crude woodcuts displaying geometrical objects, whereas "Géométrie" in the *Encyclopédie des gens du monde* was purely textual,[53] despite the continuing importance of diagrams for the discipline. Paul Rowe has speculated that intellectuals' disdain for the visual, along with cost, discouraged the originators of the *Encyclopédie des gens du monde* from investing in illustrations.[54] Certainly the only lavishly illustrated French encyclopedias of the preceding century, the *Encyclopédie* and the *Encyclopédie méthodique*, had been expensive, whereas scores of reputable French encyclopedias – for example, the final edition (1771) of the *Dictionnaire de Trévoux* – had maintained a tradition of purely textual encyclopedism. Still, in the early nineteenth century, the *Encyclopédie moderne* included a volume of copperplates interspersed with explanations, and this for a price of 216 francs, though the work was admittedly much smaller textually – at just four million words – than the ones studied here.[55] Line cuts, introduced to French encyclopedism with the *Encyclopédie nouvelle*, originally titled the *Encyclopédie pittoresque à deux sous*, would soon provide a cheap but still esthetically pleasing means of illustrating encyclopedias for those willing to brave scruples about pandering to the popular taste for the visual.[56]

Surveying the first instalment of volume 8 of the *Encyclopédie des gens du monde*, Paul Rowe has found that only around 6 per cent of articles were marked as wholly or partially translated from Brockhaus's encyclopedia. Shorter than most, these articles were frequently biographies of obscure Germans or treatments of subjects for which German erudition was renowned, notably antiquities and biblical history.[57]

Unfortunately, articles copied from the *Konversationslexikon* are not marked as such in the *Dictionnaire de la conversation et de la lecture*, at least early on. As noted above, only around 10 per cent of the articles in volume 1 are signed, yet not all of the others were from Brockhaus's encyclopedia. Even at the start of volume 1, many of the articles in the *Dictionnaire de la conversation et de la lecture* have no equivalent in Brockhaus's encyclopedia. Among the first forty articles, for example, the following are new with respect to that source: "Aalborg" (on a Danish diocese), "Aam" (on a Rhenish unit of measurement), "Aarhuus" (on a Danish diocese), "Aaron" (on Moses's brother), "Ab" (on a Hebrew month), "Abaoujvar" (on a Hungarian county), "Abaque" (on the abacus), "Abattoir" (on modern French slaughterhouses), "Abatucci" (on a French general), "Abazées" (on a celebration in Asia Minor), "Abbassides" (on an Arabic dynasty), "Abbesse" (on abbesses), "Abcès" (on abcesses), "Abdalonyme" (on an ancient king), "Abdérahme" (on a medieval Spanish ruler), "Abel" (on a recently deceased mathematician), "Aberdeen" (on a Scottish city), "Abernethy" (on a recently deceased surgeon), "Abesta" (on the sacred texts of Zoroastrianism), and "Abgar" (on ancient Syrian kings). Surprisingly, the more Germanic among these articles were apparently put together from a French source: "Aaarhuus" is identical to the article of the same name in the *Manuel encyclopédique*, the separately alphabetized subseries of short articles attached to the treatise-based *Encyclopédie progressive*, while "Aalborg" and "Aam" feature brief passages identical to those in articles of the same name in the *Manuel encyclopédique*. Regardless, these additions to the nomenclature of Brockhaus's encyclopedia point to the greater erudition of the *Dictionnaire de la conversation et de la lecture*. Furthermore, even articles with close equivalents in Brockhaus's encyclopedia were not necessarily copied. "A" (on the letter), "Abatis" (on a fortification), and "Aberration" (on the aberration of light), for example, bear little resemblance to "A" (on the letter), "Verhau" (on the abatis), or "Abirrung des Lichts" (on the aberration of light) in Brockhaus's encyclopedia.

In fact, of the first forty articles in the *Dictionnaire de la conversation et de la lecture*, only fifteen – or slightly less than 40 per cent – were wholly or partially copied from the *Konversationslexikon*. This copying was done in a range of manners. Ten of the articles were simply translated with few or no changes: "Abbt" (on a German philosopher), "Abdère" (on an ancient Greek city), "Abdication" (on the resignation of rulers), "Abdomen" (on the belly), "Abel" (on the Biblical figure), "Abélard" (on the scholastic philosopher), "Abélites" (on an ancient Christian sect), "Abensberg" (on a Bavarian city), "Ab intestat" (on a legal term), and "Abipons" (on a South American tribe). Significant additions were made to two other translated articles: an addition on French laws about bees in "Abeilles," and an addition on the British minister George-Hamilton Gordon of Aberdeen's policies since 1830 in "Aberdeen," especially regarding France.[58] Conversely, a few translated articles were shortened: a bibliography was dropped in "Abeilles," a bibliography and a brief assessment of the Swiss painter Johann Ludwig Aberli's influence were dropped in "Aberli," and an inventory of the Danish painter Nicolai Abraham Abildgaard's paintings and material on a controversy over his reputation were dropped from "Abildgaard."[59] Finally, the second half of the article "Abbot (Charles)" (on a British statesman) was translated from Brockhaus's encyclopedia,[60] whereas the first half was not, though the German work too had covered Abbot's early career.

Upon its inception, then, the *Dictionnaire de la conversation et de la lecture* owed more to Brockhaus's *Konversationslexikon* than did the *Encyclopédie des gens du monde*, as pointed out by contemporary observers.[61] Still, neither French work began – or ended – as a mere translation. In any event, the *Dictionnaire de la conversation et de la lecture* soon evolved towards less dependence on its German source, as even Schnitzler, the editor of the rival work, acknowledged in his article "Encyclopédie" of 1837.[62]

Independent of their copying, coverage in the French encyclopedias was both similar to and different from coverage in the seventh edition of Brockhaus's encyclopedia. Here, without pretending to exhaustiveness, I examine a similarity in their coverage of science and technology and a difference in their coverage of biography and language.

None of the three works treated science and technology with as much comprehensiveness or depth as the *Encyclopédie méthodique*, Ersch and Gruber's *Allgemeine Encyclopädie*, or contemporary British encyclopedias such as the seventh edition of the *Encyclopaedia Britannica* (1842) and the

Encyclopaedia Metropolitana (1845). The articles on botany in Brockhaus's seventh edition, the *Encyclopédie des gens du monde*, and the *Dictionnaire de la conversation et de la lecture* extended to seven pages, twelve pages, and sixteen pages respectively. By contrast, in the seventh edition of the *Encyclopaedia Britannica*, which was not much larger than the *Dictionnaire de la conversation et de la lecture*,[63] the article on botany was 112 pages long. Consistent with this example, Brockhaus's seventh edition was undoubtedly the weakest in its scientific and technical coverage, surely in part because of its small size.[64]

In a notice dated August 1834 published in volume 13, the "éditeurs" of the *Dictionnaire de la conversation et de la lecture* argued for the richness of their nomenclature relative to Brockhaus's. First, they claimed to have reduced the proportion of biographies, supposedly excessive in the *Konversationslexikon*, though their sample of 108 articles there was biased by its inclusion of 19 rulers named "Charles."[65] If they did in fact reduce the proportion of biographies, as appears likely, they did not do so drastically: in a sample of one hundred articles at the beginning of the letter "N," for example, around 30 per cent of the articles in both French encyclopedias dealt with real or mythological individuals, whereas even in the unfair sample of articles from the *Konversationslexikon* provided in the *Dictionnaire de la conversation et de la lecture*, less than 50 per cent did.[66] Second, the backers of the *Dictionnaire de la conversation et de la lecture* contended that Brockhaus's seventh edition was "plus pauvre en noms de choses les plus usuelles" (poorer in names for the most common things), citing seventeen articles absent from that work but present in theirs: "Charge" (on a military maneouvre), "Charges" (on administrative and juridical functions), "Charme, Charmes" (on charm), "Charrue" (on plows), "Chasteté" (on chastity), "Chat" (on the cat), "Chaudière" (on pots and boilers), "Chaudron" (on vats), "Chaume" (on thatch and thatched roofs), "Chaussée" (on causeways and roadways), "Chaussure" (on shoes), "Chauve-souris" (on the bat), "Chef" (on different meanings of a French word for chief or leader), "Chemin" (on paths and roads), "Cheminée" (on chimneys), "Chemise" (on undershirts), and "Chêne" (on oaks).[67] In its striving for completeness, the *Dictionnaire de la conversation et de la lecture* did outstrip the *Konversationslexikon* as well as the *Encyclopédie des gens du monde* in covering unspecialized terms. Indeed, at times, the *Dictionnaire de la conversation et de la lecture* verged on being a dictionary of language as well as an encyclopedia: among other things, it included articles on the demonstrative pronoun *ce* and the adjective *neuf*,[68] it frequently noted words' various meanings and uses,[69] and it carefully distinguished synonyms within certain articles.[70] In the article "Ce," the editor Héreau defended his attention to the word as following from the encyclopedia's title and genre: "que ceux qui jugeraient cependant que nous avons encore accordé trop de place à l'examen d'une question grammaticale […] veuillent bien réfléchir que nous faisons un *Dictionnaire*" (let those who nonetheless believe that we have given too much space to examining a grammatical matter […] remember that we are making a *Dictionary*).[71] Neither Brockhaus's seventh edition nor the *Encyclopédie des gens du monde* came as close to being a dictionary, but so-called encyclopedic dictionaries, combining the functions of the encyclopedia and dictionary, had been and would remain a common hybrid in France.

In one respect, both French encyclopedias ended up distancing themselves from the model of the *Konversationslexikon*: they allowed contributors to claim public credit for what they wrote. It would be wrong to present Brockhaus's encyclopedia as completely anonymous during this period, for a minority of articles are signed with initials or two-digit numbers. In the first one hundred pages of volume 12 of the seventh edition, for example, some 20 per cent of articles consisting of more than a cross-reference are signed in this manner. With effort, undoubtedly, some signatures could be identified as those of individual authors, since a list of contributors appears in volume 12, albeit without a key to the signatures.[72] By and large, however, Friedrich Arnold Brockhaus and his successors aimed to create a homogeneous encyclopedia, one in which submitted articles would be rewritten as needed by the editorial staff.[73] The *Encyclopédie des gens du monde* too was meant to be unified, but only in its adherence to the historical method of exploring subjects. According to the preface, contributors would be allowed to express their own opinions on the condition that they signed and thus took responsibility for their ideas.[74] Signed articles were hardly unusual in contemporary French encyclopedias, but the preface to the *Encyclopédie des gens du monde* stipulated, unusually, that all articles would be either signed or identified as borrowed from the *Konversationslexikon*, a promise that was kept to a remarkable extent. In fact, as the context of the promise in the preface suggests, the reason for identifying contributors with such scrupulousness seems to have been to demonstrate that the encyclopedia was not just being translated from Brockhaus's encyclopedia, as the preface argued that the *Dictionnaire de la conversation et de la lecture* was.[75] The latter work, in turn, was probably forced to a policy of pervasive signatures by accusations of excessive dependence on the *Konversationslexikon*. In this way, rivalry along with concern for responsible intellectual individualism pushed the two works away from the overall anonymity of Brockhaus's work and even of a broader tradition of German encyclopedism.[76]

In Paul Rowe's evaluation, the *Encyclopédie des gens du monde* was designed for a more educated audience than the *Konversationslexikon*: articles had longer bibliographies, for example, and the translators sometimes inserted phrases like "on sait" (it is known) to mark statements as belonging to common knowledge.[77] In mathematics, the *Encyclopédie des gens du monde* seems to have been written with more intellectual ambition than not only Brockhaus's *Konversationslexikon* but also the *Dictionnaire de la conversation et de la lecture*. In particular, the *Encyclopédie des gens du monde* was the only one of the three to deal with integral and differential calculus with any specificity or depth.[78] In the *Dictionnaire de la conversation et de la lecture*, "Différentiel" went so far as to state that algebra had been excluded from the encyclopedia, an exclusion that made a clear definition of differential calculus impossible.[79] Still, when compared with the most scholarly encyclopedias of the period, notably the *Encyclopédie méthodique* and Ersch and Gruber's *Allgemeine Encyclopädie*, the three works under scrutiny here were not so different from one another.

Structurally, too, the French encyclopedias were similar to Brockhaus's *Konversationslexikon*. On average, their articles were roughly the same length: whereas Brockhaus's seventh edition had some fourteen thousand articles averaging around five hundred words each, the *Encyclopédie des gens du monde* had roughly twenty-nine thousand articles averaging about four hundred words each, and the *Dictionnaire de la conversation et de la lecture* had some twenty-three thousand articles averaging around seven hundred words each.[80] More significantly, whereas scientific and technical articles were sometimes gigantic in other encyclopedias, the longest articles in these three were nearly all on European geographical regions. In Brockhaus's work, the only articles exceeding thirty pages were "Spanien" (on Spain, with 56 pages), "Sachsen" (on Saxony, with 36 pages), "Vereinigte Staaten" (on the United States, with 36 pages), "Frankreich" (on France, with 35 pages), "Rußland" (on Russia, with 32 pages), "England" (on England, with 31 pages), "Französische Literatur" (on French literature, with 31 pages), "Südamerikanische Revolution" (on recent uprisings in the Americas, 31 pages), and "Englische Literatur, Wissenschaft, Poesie, und Theater" (on English literature, science, poetry, and theater, with 30 pages), though all these were dwarfed by the complexes of separate articles devoted to different facets of western

Europe's states, above all to Germany (129 pages) and to France (121 pages).[81]

While preserving Brockhaus's generous treatment of Europe's regions, the two French adaptations differed from their model in distinct ways. Like the *Encyclopaedia Americana* (1829–33), Francis Lieber's American adaptation of the seventh edition of Brockhaus's *Konversationslexikon*, and like the Russian adaptation (1890–1906) of Brockhaus's thirteenth edition (1881–7) published by Il'ja Abramovič Efron,[82] the *Dictionnaire de la conversation et de la lecture* exhibited chauvinism in its allotment of space. The article "France" alone extended to 368 pages. It may have been the best article on the subject ever published in French, as one commentator suggested,[83] but at more than three times the length of "Allemagne" (on Germany, with 98 pages) and "Angleterre" (on England, with 76 pages), it created imbalance in the encyclopedia. Likewise, French biographies were disproportionately long in the *Dictionnaire de la conversation et de la lecture*. The French politician Narcisse-Achille de Salvandy undertook a biography of Napoléon, which appeared in instalments under three headings, the last in an appendix: "Bonaparte," "Consulat," and "Bonaparte" again. All told, the article spanned 199 pages and still left important episodes of Napoléon's life to other contributors.[84] Even less eminent French notables got ample coverage, especially political figures. At 14 and 17 pages respectively, for example, the articles on the recently deceased politician Jean-Denis Lanjuinais[85] and the seventeenth-century statesman Mathieu Molé were both longer than the articles on Johann Wolfgang von Goethe and Moses.

By contrast, articles in *Encyclopédie des gens du monde* varied much less in length, though the longest articles still tended to be on Europe's geographical regions. As in Brockhaus's *Konversationslexikon*, articles on nations in the *Encyclopédie des gens du monde* were broken up into separate articles on their various aspects, but the whole series on France occupied just 121 pages,[86] while the article on Napoléon occupied just 23 pages. With its shorter, more evenly planned articles, the *Encyclopédie des gens du monde* can be seen as advancing towards what the *Konversationslexikon* would become in the second half of the nineteenth century as expansion of the nomenclature forced a certain minimalism and briskness of style.[87]

Besides the length of its articles, the tone of Brockhaus's *Konversationslexikon* changed towards the middle of the nineteenth century, becoming less conversational, less overtly polemical, and less essayistic on the one hand and more objective on the other. Although many articles remained personal, diffuse, or essayistic, the process was already underway by the seventh edition.[88] In comparison, the two French adaptations under scrutiny here included a larger proportion of impassioned, polemical, essayistic, and simply quirky articles. Both works made more use of exclamations and rhetorical questions, for example. In the *Encyclopédie des gens du monde*, the editor Schnitzler evidently condoned both: his article "Abus," a moralistic six-page commentary on political, social, and other kinds of abuses, featured fifteen questions along with thirteen exclamations, among them the following: "fille du ciel, sainte religion! ne peux-tu toucher à la terre sans être souillée par le contact! Faut-il qu'éternellement la fange salisse ta robe d'éther!" (Daughter of heaven, holy religion! can you not touch earth without being sullied by the contact! Does mud have to besmirch your robe of ether eternally!).[89] In the *Dictionnaire de la conversation et de la lecture*, which had a larger number of patently non-objective articles than the *Encyclopédie des gens du monde*, Janin's article on Alphonse de Lamartine, "le plus grand poète de notre âge " (the greatest poet of our era),[90] offered thirteen exclamations on a single page.[91]

One reason for the difference with respect to Brockhaus's seventh edition was surely the French encyclopedias' policy of conferring responsibility for articles on specific contributors, thus granting them a certain freedom to express themselves. Janin, for example, brought to his articles in both encyclopedias the same opinionated, effusive, and playful style that made his reputation as a critic and journalist. His article on "Beaumarchais" in the *Encyclopédie des gens du monde* flippantly identified Jean-Jacques Rousseau as a "grand seigneur" (great lord), which drew a footnote disavowing responsibility for the article from the editor Schnitzler.[92] Likewise, his article "Baroque" in the same volume ended mockingly: "*baroque* est un de ces mots qui se sentent et qui s'expliquent tout seuls [… Ainsi] *baroque* est tout-à-fait un mot de la famille du *schick* et du *fion*. Pour définir le *baroque*, je n'ai ni *le fion*, ni *le schick*." (*Baroque* is one of these words that are felt and that explain themselves [… Thus] *baroque* is unquestionably a word in the family of *schick* and *fion* [two vague French neologisms indicating, respectively, a certain facility and a finishing touch]. To define *baroque*, I have neither the *fion* nor the *schick*).[93] Two of the more prolific contributors to the *Dictionnaire de la conversation et de la lecture* were also prone to playfulness and emphatic flourishes. As well as "compiling" a series of aspersions against compilers over the ages in his article on compilers ("Compilateur"),[94] Rozoir enriched his many articles with colourful anecdotes and digressions; he even threw in a joke about the business of encyclopedism in the conclusion to "Fouet," on the word "whip": "*fouetter* le cahier, signifie al[l]onger un écrit pour le plaisir de le faire. Malheur aux entrepreneurs de lexiques et d'encyclopédies qui ont à leur solde de pareils écrivains!" (to *whip* the booklet means to lengthen a piece of writing for the pleasure of doing so. Woe to those dictionary- and encyclopedia-makers who have such writers on their payroll!).[95] Likewise, Français de Nantes enlivened his numerous articles on agriculture and natural history with first-person pronouns, florid language, and elaborate comparisons: "Ainsi l'agriculture est un culte perpétuel, que l'espèce humaine rend au créateur en perfectionnant son oeuvre. Ce culte a ses dogmes, ses mystères, ses fêtes, ses solennités." (Thus agriculture is an everlasting worship, which the human species gives to the creator in perfecting his work. This religion has its dogmas, its mysteries, its holidays, its solemnities).[96] Regardless of such examples, the majority of articles in the *Dictionnaire de la conversation et de la lecture* as well as the *Encyclopédie des gens du monde* were written with as much dry informativeness as typical articles in Brockhaus's seventh edition.

Politically, Friedrich Arnold Brockhaus had been an exponent of liberalism, though he expressed his opinions with increasing subtlety in the *Konversationslexikon* towards the end of his life.[97] Otto Wigand, the publisher of a Hungarian adaptation of Brockhaus's encyclopedia from 1831 to 1834, was even more radical politically, so much so that he had to flee Budapest to continue publication of his *Konversationslexikon* in Leipzig.[98] Overall, according to Ulrike Spree, the genre of the *Konversationslexikon* was strongly associated with liberalism through the early 1830s.[99] The two French adaptions of Brockhaus's seventh edition were liberal in a broad sense, but their liberalism was defensive, pragmatic, and even conservative, presumably in part because a liberal constitutional monarchy had already been established in France as of 1830, and because many contributors were participants or stakeholders in the new government. Neither French encyclopedia risked getting repressed or censored in the way that the *Encyclopédie* had less than a century before, or even in the way that Brockhaus's *Konversationslexikon* regularly did before 1848.

In the *Encyclopédie des gens du monde*, Schnitzler expressed guarded support for the settlement of 1830 but criticized the earlier *Encyclopédie progressive* for being biased by "un *libéralisme* aujourd'hui dépassé" (a now outmoded *liberalism*).[100] His own article "Abus," on abuses of power, took pains to point out that freedom itself was subject to abuse, while the article "Privilège," on social and political privileges, defended existing inequalities in French society, including restrictions on those eligible to vote.[101] On the whole, despite the inclusion of articles representing divergent viewpoints, from which Schnitzler sometimes distanced himself in footnotes, and despite the work's favour for Protestantism, the *Encyclopédie des gens du monde* was the picture of polite centrism.[102]

Likewise, the preface to the *Dictionnaire de la conversation et de la lecture* positioned it between the extremes of works written by "de prétendus défenseurs exclusifs de la saine morale et de la religion" (those claiming a monopoly on the defence of healthy morals and religion) and those written by "écrivains qui vous parlent avec tant d'emphase au nom de l'humanité et de la philosophie" (writers who speak to you so emphatically in the name of humanity and philosophy).[103] One contributor linked with the latter group was Geoffroy Saint-Hilaire, whose "philosophical anatomy" was taken up enthusiastically on the political left.[104] In the *Dictionnaire de la conversation et de la lecture*, besides defending the methodology and results of his scientific work, his article on pantheistic heresies ("Hérésies panthéistiques") proposed a rehabilitation of pantheism – of which he was often accused – arguing that it was humanity's original religion, albeit different from any modern set of beliefs.[105] Still, the *Dictionnaire de la conversation et de la lecture* was hardly favourable to Geoffroy, as he bitterly recognized. He was criticized and accused of promoting atheism in "Geoffroi St-Hilaire," while his intellectual adversary, the naturalist Georges Cuvier, was lionized in a biography of thirty-seven pages.[106] In a way, Geoffroy's involvement with the *Dictionnaire de la conversation et de la lecture* corroborates the preface's contention that the "choc d'opinions [divergentes]" (clash of [divergent] opinions) between contributors on moral and political topics would allow readers to weigh both opinions and decide for themselves.[107] Still, as Pierre Larousse observed some thirty years later, the *Dictionnaire de la conversation et de la lecture* never realized its potential as a forum for debate, in part because contributors did not confront one another directly on the same topics. At the same time, in imagining the virtues of an article co-written by Guizot, the politician and socialist Pierre-Joseph Proudhon, and the ecclesiastic Félix-Antoine-Philibert Dupanloup – the first a contributor, the latter two not – Larousse hinted at a lack of range in contributors' viewpoints.[108]

Meanwhile, the article on liberalism ("Libéralisme") in the *Dictionnaire de la conversation et de la lecture* endorsed "liberal doctrines," doctrines predicated on gradual improvement, not sudden change, noting that the term "liberalism" had been discredited by its association with radicalism.[109] Similarly, among the many elected members of France's government who wrote for the encyclopedia, the authors of the articles on freedom of the press ("Presse") and the revolution of 1830 ("Révolution de 1830") upheld the accomplishments of the revolution but cautioned against extremism and utopianism.[110] In particular, the deputy Saint-Albin Berville used "Révolution de 1830" to prove that the revolution had given rise to the best result imaginable, since a republic, for example, would have been unlikely to succeed in "un pays de mouvement et d'émulation comme la France" (a country of action and emulation like France), and since neither Henri V nor Napoléon's son would have been an acceptable king.[111] Indeed, the July Monarchy was haunted on the right and left by the ideas of Bourbon legitimism and universal suffrage. At the same time, early forms of socialism, for example those proposed by Henri de Saint-Simon and Charles Fourier, were gathering converts. They even had a mouthpiece in the world of encyclopedias, the *Encyclopédie nouvelle*, edited by former disciples of Saint-Simon.[112] In opposition to this latter title, the *Dictionnaire de la conversation et de la lecture* stood for caution and scepticism about changes to society.

Belatedly, the *Dictionnaire de la conversation et de la lecture* nonetheless made a risky political gesture. In 1845, a technical article on cannons ("Canon") by Louis-Napoléon Bonaparte appeared in the supplement to the encyclopedia.[113] Regardless of its content, the article represented an act of political provocation insofar as Bonaparte was then in prison, having attempted to overthrow the French government on two occasions. Once Bonaparte was elected president in 1848, Duckett sought to capitalize on his early support for the former prisoner and exile, especially his publication of the article "Canon."[114] Here in the supplement, if not the main series, the *Dictionnaire de la conversation et de la lecture* exhibited a trace of the political subversiveness that made the *Encyclopédie* famous.

In the long term, one of the crucial innovations of Brockhaus's *Konversationslexikon* was its conception as an encyclopedia to be updated and continued. After the long-protracted first edition, Brockhaus turned at once to a second edition. Subsequently, he and his successors produced eight editions in just thirty-one years. In France, the nineteenth century saw little continuity in encyclopedia-making before the rise of the Larousse company after 1850, despite the example of the *Dictionnaire de Trévoux* in the previous century. The *Encyclopédie des gens du monde*, for example, never went into a second edition, though a two-volume *Nouvelle Encyclopédie des gens du monde* was published in Brussels in 1842, and though another Belgian work, the *Nouveau Dictionnaire de la conversation*, borrowed much of its content from the *Encyclopédie des gens du monde*, adding in Belgian and Dutch material as well as copperplates. Perhaps the encyclopedia was simply not a strong enough seller to warrant another edition in France; certainly unsold sets remained, for two Parisian publishers made an effort to liquidate them in 1857.[115] In Larousse's later assessment, the *Encyclopédie des gens du monde* was a better, more unified encyclopedia than the *Dictionnaire de la conversation et de la lecture*, though less complete, but it was doomed in being premised on a too scrupulous avoidance of bias and tendentiousness.[116]

As of 1833, the *Dictionnaire de la conversation et de la lecture* was rumoured to have ten thousand subscribers, a plausible and encouraging number, though still short of the sales attained by Brockhaus.[117] Like the *Encyclopédie moderne*,[118] the *Dictionnaire de la conversation et de la lecture* was also reworked and reissued on a limited scale. Indeed, the historian Jean-Yves Mollier has praised Duckett for his innovativeness in adapting the material of his encyclopedia to different formats and purposes.[119] In addition to being continued with a sixteen-volume supplement (1844–51), the encyclopedia was reissued, abridged and revised, as the ten-volume *Dictionnaire de conversation à l'usage des dames et des jeunes personnes* (1841). Then, from 1852 to 1858, a second edition appeared, followed by reprints through the late 1870s. Duckett himself launched the second edition and successfully defended his right do so against his former partner and creditor, the publisher Henri Plon, who also claimed to own the title.[120] As a journalist, however, Duckett was ill equipped to establish a company or dynasty. Instead, the *Dictionnaire de la conversation et de la lecture* expired around the same time that its originator did.

Conclusion

Projects for translating encyclopedias into alien contexts rarely ended up being as simple as planned or as might be imagined. In order to avoid complaints about foreignness like those that greeted the first volume of Efron's Russian adaptation of the *Konversationslexikon* in the late nineteenth century,[121] adjustments were almost inevitably made to the new local market, though occasionally the mere fact of producing an encyclopedia on native soil seems to have been perceived as sufficiently nationalistic to compensate for simple replication of a foreign text.[122] As a result, many encyclopedias that were originally conceived as translations ultimately developed an independent identity. Most famously, Diderot and d'Alembert's *Encyclopédie* grew out of a plan to translate Ephraim Chambers's *Cyclopaedia* (1728) into French. Departing even further from its origins as a translation was Johann Georg Krünitz and others' 242-volume *Oeconomisch-technologische Encyklopädie* (1773–1858), which started as a translation of a far smaller French encyclopedia, itself adapted from a string of earlier ones.[123]

Among the numerous works said to derive from Brockhaus's *Konversationslexikon*, the two French encyclopedias studied here were more independent than some, though the *Dictionnaire de la conversation et de la lecture* began as quite dependent. On the one hand, they seem to have borrowed less material from Brockhaus's encyclopedia than did the *Encyclopaedia Americana*,[124] Wigand's Hungarian *Konversationslexikon*,[125] or the Scottish *Popular Encyclopaedia* (1841), which borrowed from Brockhaus via the *Encyclopaedia Americana*.[126] On the other hand, they were perhaps roughly as indebted to the contents of Brockhaus's encyclopedia as *Chambers's Encyclopaedia* (1868): although the Scottish publishers William and Robert Chambers had bought the exclusive rights to translate Brockhaus's *Konversationslexikon* into English in 1852, borrowing from the German work was apparently never a dominant mode of composition, in part because of disagreements about articles' content, but also because the British preferred a less diffuse, less deductive, and less definitional approach to writing articles.[127]

One significant divergence of the two French encyclopedias from Brockhaus's *Konversationslexikon* concerned the related matters of size, price, and intended audience. As noted above, both works were initially advertised as being much smaller and cheaper than they ended up being. Their subsequent growth must have increased the amount of profit per set, since extra volumes were sold for the same price as the promised ones, but this increase undoubtedly came at the price of restricting their readership and making quick re-editions unwieldy; considerations such as these were behind the refusal of Brockhaus and the publishers of the contemporary *Encyclopaedia Britannica* to countenance dramatic expansions relative to plans.[128] Among adaptations of the *Konversationslexikon*, the *Encyclopaedia Americana*, Wigand's Hungarian *Konversationslexikon*, and *Chambers's Encyclopaedia* stuck closer to the size of the original. Their greater size and expanded nomenclatures also made the French works more erudite than Brockhaus's. Independently of their size and price, they were designed for a public more drawn to elegance than that of Brockhaus's *Konversationslexikon*, and the *Encyclopédie des gens du monde* in particular seems to have been written with more intellectual ambition.

Decisions here and elsewhere to break with the model of the *Konversationslexikon* reflected not only differences between the French and German societies, but also a French tradition of producing works of reference. In particular, citations in articles indicate that the editors and other contributors to both the *Encyclopédie des gens du monde* and the *Dictionnaire de la conversation et de la lecture* worked with sets of the *Encyclopédie*, the *Dictionnaire de l'Académie française*, and other French dictionaries and encyclopedias at hand.[129] More generally, contributors to both French encyclopedias were aware of encyclopedism as an international phenomenon that went well beyond Brockhaus's *Konversationslexikon*. In the *Dictionnaire de la conversation et de la lecture*, the anonymous biography of David Brewster noted that "nous puiserons quelquefois d'utiles matériaux pour notre *Dictionnaire*" (we will sometimes draw useful material for our *Dictionary*) from Brewster's *Edinburgh Encyclopaedia* (1830) as well as Abraham Rees's *Cyclopaedia* (1819) and the *Encyclopaedia Britannica*.[130] The *Encyclopédie des gens du monde*, for its part, frequently cited Ersch and Gruber's *Allgemeine Encyclopädie* and established a code in the front matter of volumes 11 and 13 for identifying borrowing from two encyclopedias in addition to Brockhaus's: the *Encyclopaedia Americana* and Austria's *Österreichische National-Encyclopädie* (1835–8). Such cosmopolitanism militated against simple imitation of Brockhaus's encyclopedia.

In the history of foreign adaptations of the *Konversationslexikon*, the *Encyclopédie des gens du monde* and the *Dictionnaire de la conversation et de la lecture* are especially distinctive in having been published for similar readers at the same time. In some respects, they offered readers and purchasers quite different materials. The *Encyclopédie des gens du monde* was favourable to Protestantism and probably somewhat more sophisticated, while the *Dictionnaire de la conversation et de la lecture* was more Franco-centric and concerned with linguistic matters. At the risk of over-generalizing, one can say that the former was addressed to a more cosmopolitan public, perhaps even an international one, while the latter concentrated on a more traditional, language-conscious French public without explicitly courting Catholics in the way that the roughly contemporary *Encyclopédie du dix-neuvième siècle* did.

Nevertheless, the two encyclopedias were remarkably alike in other respects, both edited by a French Russianist and journalist with knowledge of German, both boasting more than a hundred named contributors, both sold in half-volume instalments, and both significantly longer and costlier than Brockhaus's encyclopedia. Representative of the political balance of the July Monarchy, both encyclopedias were cautiously liberal but supportive of the government and opposed to any radicalism. In this sense, they contrasted sharply with the contemporary *Encyclopédie nouvelle*. Even beyond its politically and religiously audacious contents, the *Encyclopédie nouvelle* was radical in a way that other French encyclopedias of the 1830s were not: like the *Penny Cyclopaedia* (1833–43) in England, it was conceived and priced to be purchased by the less affluent.[131] The *Encyclopédie des gens du monde* and the *Dictionnaire de la conversation et de la lecture* were both addressed to a more well-to-do readership.

Ironically, competition between these two works seems to have pushed them towards more similarity: after the *Encyclopédie des gens du monde* vaunted its signed articles as a way of highlighting the copying in the *Dictionnaire de la conversation et de la lecture*, the latter work switched from mostly anonymous to mostly signed articles and reduced its borrowing from Brockhaus's encyclopedia. Without the spur to originality of a national rival, not to mention the richness of France's culture and heritage of encyclopedism, they might have ended up being closer kin to Brockhaus's *Konversationslexikon*. As it was, they can be roughly described as mere cousins to the German encyclopedia. At the same time, they developed as warring siblings within the confines of French encyclopedism, both promoting guarded liberalism and supplying accessible content to the privileged classes of the July Monarchy.

NOTES

1 See Kafker 2009, 304–5; Pruvost 2005, 56. I would like to thank Frank Kafker and Paul Rowe for their valuable suggestions for improving this chapter. Translations into English are my own.

2 Technically, the terms "folio," "quarto," and "octavo" refer to the way books are formed from sheets of paper, but they correlate roughly with size as well.

3 Pruvost 2005, 53–4.

4 Hingst 1995, 102–20.

5 Hingst 1995, 117–19; [Piltz] 1872–5, XXXII–XXXVI.

6 For this suggestion see [Piltz] 1872–5, XXXIV–XXXV.

7 Rowe 2005, 11–23; Rowe 2006, 433–48. A similarly titled encyclopedia had been published in 1770, the five-volume *Dictionnaire des gens du monde*.

8 Mollier 1997, 299–302; Mollier 1988, 104–10.

9 See for example Anonymous 1823a, 235–7, and 1823b, 734–6.

10 Guizot 1826, 22–3.

11 *Encyclopédie des gens du monde* (hereafter cited as *EGM*) 1833–44, 1:xi–xii. A similar explanation appears in Anonymous 1833b, 1.

12 *Prospectus* [1829], 2–3. An early advertisement can be found in Anonymous 1829, [552].

13 *EGM* 1833–44, 9:503.

14 *Prospectus* [1829], 4.

15 Anonymous 1833a, 381; Anonymous 1840, 124.

16 *EGM* 1833–44, 9:503.

17 See for example the exchanges in Anonymous 1833b, 1–2; Anonymous 1833c, 1–2; Anonymous 1833d, 2–3.

18 On the company see Barber 1968, 118–44.

19 The company is listed as an official distributor in the prospectus. See Prospectus 1826, [57].

20 Rowe 2006, 437; Paul 1999, 3514. The diplomat and historian Alexis-François Artaud de Montor is sometimes identified as the "directeur" of the *Encyclopédie des gens du monde*, perhaps because his name figures first in the alphabetical list of contributors in certain volumes, though not volume 1.

21 For the number of contributors see Rowe 2005, 13–14n. Klaproth, Michelet, and Magendie are first listed as contributors in volumes 1, 2, and 3 respectively. None were prolific contributors, but Michelet wrote "Arioviste" and Magendie "Bégaiement," for example. On Klaproth's contribution see Lehner 2008, 26–7.

22 Compare Anonymous 1833a, 381; *Prospectus* [1829], 4.

23 Loveland 2014.

24 See for example *Dictionnaire de la conversation et de la lecture* (hereafter cited as *DCL*) 1832–9, 23:223–4; Paccaud 1887, 30–4.

25 The *Encyclopédie progressive* was to be published in monthly instalments of 250 pages, whereas its accompanying subseries, the *Manuel encyclopédique*, was to be published every two months in instalments of 500 pages. See Prospectus 1826, [58]. Instalments of the *Encyclopédie nouvelle* were sold in weekly pairs of 16 pages each. See for example Anonymous 1833a, 717. On instalments of the *Dictionnaire de la conversation et de la lecture* see the following section.

26 On Duckett and his family see Alger and McCoy 2004, 17:39–40. Duckett is identified as the originator of the *Dictionnaire* in Mollier 1997, 299–301.

27 In that year he published translations of poetry by Louis I of Bavaria as well as Friedrich von Schlegel's *Geschichte der alten und neuen Litteratur* (1815).

28 Audiffret 1857, 264. Audiffret was also a contributor to the *Dictionnaire de la conversation et de la lecture*, but no biography of Héreau appeared in that encyclopedia, perhaps because of the latter's quarrels with Duckett.

29 *DCL* 1832–9, 24:280. The signature "H" was used for "Ablécimof" and "Abraham Palitsine," two of the earliest signed articles in the encyclopedia. Since both were biographies of Russians, with neither one covered in Brockhaus's seventh edition, the author was almost certainly the Russianist Héreau.

30 On his resignation and suicide see Audiffret 1857, 264.

31 Anonymous 1832, "Compte rendu d'octobre." Notice the comments on the prospectus in Review 1833a, 65; Review 1833b, 401. On the innovativeness of recourse to travelling salesmen see Mollier 1997, 300.

32 Anonymous 1836, 159.

33 The list of contributors in volume 1 seems to have been the only one published, despite assurance there that an updated one would appear in the final volume.

34 Review 1833b, 401.

35 For example, the articles "Aboukir," "Abstinence," and "Académie royale des inscriptions et belles-lettres" are signed "C," "F," and "H A***T" respectively. "F" was probably the professor of medicine Charles-Polydore Forget, since similar later articles were signed with his last name. "H A***T" was almost certainly H. Audiffret; so he began signing later on in volume 1. The identity of "C" is less apparent. In any event, ambiguous initials tended to be abandoned in favour of surnames or full names in the course of volume 1, though some persisted.

36 Audiffret signed the articles "Académie royale des inscriptions et belles-lettres," "Académie royale de musique," "Alides," "Almanzor," "Almowahides," and "Ambigu." A Hippolyte Audiffret is credited with the satirical *La Saint-Charles et la Saint-Louis, dissertation historique et critique, qui peut-être n'en est pas une* (1825).

37 Anonymous 1833c, 2.

38 Compare *EGM* 1833–44, 8:33–43; Prévost 1838, VII–XV.

39 Compare *DCL* 1832–9, 24:388–92; Laurentie 1838, 51–60. Larentie's *Histoire, morale et littérature* contains other articles borrowed from his contribution to the *Dictionnaire de la convesation et de la lecture* as well.

40 [Brockhaus] 1796–1808, 1:III–V.

41 Loveland 2013, 168.

42 I have ignored entries consisting of a cross-reference to another entry.

43 Hingst 1995, 108–9. Löbel and Franke's *Conversationslexikon* had already included such biographies from the beginning. The first general encyclopedia to do so was Johann Heinrich Zedler's *Grosses vollständiges Universal-Lexicon* (1732–54). See Schneider 2004, 84–9; Loveland 2021, 47–69.

44 Hingst 1995, 105, 110–13, 116–18.

45 Hingst 1995, 120–2, 190–1.

46 Hingst 1995, 126–9.

47 Rowe 2005, 17.

48 Notice the analysis of Brockhaus's adoption of two columns for the thirteenth edition (1881–7) in Hingst 1995, 145.

49 Lough 1971, 34; Doig 1992, 64–5.

50 Keiderling 2012, 198.

51 For exchanges of 3.7 and 3.9 francs to the taler, respectively, see Flügel 1834, 66, 144; Doursther 1840, 328.

52 By my estimation, Brockhaus's seventh edition comprised around ten thousand pages with about seven hundred words per page, while the *Encyclopédie des gens du monde* comprised roughly seventeen thousand pages with about seven hundred words per page, and the *Dictionnaire de la conversation et de la lecture* comprised around twenty-six thousand pages with about six hundred words per page.

53 Compare *DCL* 1832–9, 30:161–8; *EGM* 1833–44, 12:332–8. For woodcuts in the latter work see for example *EGM* 1833–44, 1:4, 3:666, 9:45, 15:33.

54 Rowe 2005, 17–18.

55 For the price of a set of the *Encyclopédie moderne* see *Almanach* 1827, 7. The *Encyclopédie moderne* comprised around fourteen thousand pages of text with around three hundred words per page.

56 Hupka 1989, 113.

57 Rowe 2005, 18.

58 Compare *DCL* 1832–9, 1:8, 12; [Brockhaus] 1830, 1:16, 878.

59 Compare *DCL* 1832–9, 1:8, 12, 13; [Brockhaus] 1830, 1:17, 26–7, 878.

60 Compare *DCL* 1832–9, 1:6; [Brockhaus] 1830, 1:5.

61 See for example Review 1834, 381.

62 *EGM* 1833–44, 9:503.

63 By my estimation, the seventh edition of the *Encyclopaedia Britannica* had around twenty-four million words.

64 Brockhaus's *Konversationslexikon* had significantly improved its coverage of science and technology by the thirteenth edition, but it had also expanded. See Belgum 2010, 99–100; Keiderling 2012, 198.

65 *DCL* 1832–9, 13: "Avis à nos souscripteurs." I have been unable to find an earlier comparison of the encyclopedias' nomenclatures, supposedly put out with the seventeenth instalment.

66 Without the entries on rulers named "Charles," the proportion of biographies in the printed sample from Brockhaus's *Konversationslexikon* would have fallen to around 30 per cent.

67 *DCL* 1832–9, 13: "Avis à nos souscripteurs."

68 *DCL* 1832–9, 12:1–4, 40:85–6.

69 See for example *DCL* 1832–9, 33:34, 34:384–5, 457–9.

70 See for example *DCL* 1832–9, 4:489–96, 40:11–12.

71 *DCL* 1832–9, 12:4.

72 On the similar lack of a key for interpreting signatures in Brockhaus's supplemental *Conversations-Lexikon der Gegenwart* (1838–41) see Meyer 1966,

70–1. On the firm's reluctance to disclose authors' names see Prodöhl 2011, 43–5.

73 Spree 2000, 94–5; Hingst 1995, 112–13; Meyer 1966, 49.

74 *EGM* 1833–44, 1:vii, xii.

75 *EGM* 1833–44, 1:xii.

76 On the tendency towards anonymity in German encyclopedism see Goetschel, Macleod, and Snyder 1994, 263; Spree 2000, 94–5.

77 Rowe 2006, 439; Rowe 2005, 19.

78 Compare *EGM* 1833–44, 4:475–84; *DCL* 1832–9, 9:496–8, 21:39–40, 33:121–2; [Brockhaus] 1830, 1:272–3, 5:530–1, 11:579.

79 *DCL* 1832–9, 21:39. Algebraic equations appear elsewhere, however, notably in "Algèbre." See *DCL* 1832–39, 1:293–9.

80 These estimates derive from the encyclopedias' tables of contents. For this calculation, I have included listed articles consisting only of a cross-reference but excluded subarticles, that is, explicitly marked divisions within an article on a unified subject. In the case of the French encyclopedias, I have counted the articles in four scattered volumes and extrapolated the results to the whole set.

81 For the articles on Germany, running from "Deutsche Baukunst" to "Deutschland," see [Brockhaus] 1830, 3:139–267. For the articles on France, running from "Frankreich" to "Frankreichs geographisch-statistischer Zustand" and then from "Französische Akademie" to "Französische Staatskunst," see [Brockhaus] 1830, 4:230–95, 302–56.

82 Müller-Vollmer 2007, 223; Hexelschneider 2005, 212–7.

83 Review 1837, [3].

84 For Salvandy's biography see *DCL* 1832–9, 7:89–192, 16:417–54, 52:499–555. On the composition of the article, and for cross-references to other articles on Napoléon, see *DCL* 1832–9, 52:498.

85 This article, like many, appeared out of alphabetical order. See *DCL* 1832–9, 39:275–88.

86 *EGM* 1833–44, 11:430–550.

87 See Hingst 1995, 141, 145, 148–9, 192.

88 See Belgum 2010, 97–8, 101; Hingst 1995, 54, 84–5, 110–11, 128–9, 151, 190–2; Spree 2000, 149–99, 224–6, 249–50, 272–83, 306, 327–8.

89 *EGM* 1833–44, 1:85–6. Most of Schnitzler's articles were sober and factual.

90 *DCL*, 1832–9, 36:152.

91 *DCL* 1832–9, 36:174.

92 *EGM* 1833–44, 3:218.

93 *EGM* 1833–44, 3:70. For other articles by Janin see for example *EGM* 1833–44, 1:667–8, 4:356–7, 8:424–8, 11:103–4; *DCL* 1832–9, 22:349–60; 34:198–201, 36:152–75; 39:313–16.

94 *DCL* 1832–9, 16:1.

95 *DCL* 1832–9, 28:25. For more of Rozoir's joking about encyclopedism see for example *DCL* 1832–9, 29:418, 433.

96 *DCL* 1832–9, 1:171.

97 Hingst 1995, 33, 110–11, 123.

98 Lipták 2005, 192–3.

99 Spree 2000, 64–5, 323.

100 *EGM* 1833–44, 9:496, 502–3.

101 *EGM* 1833–44, 1:88, 20:172.

102 Rowe 2005, 15–16.

103 *DCL* 1832–9, 1:1–3.

104 Burns 2004, 1:409; Appel 1987, 8–9, 173, 193–201.

105 *DCL* 1832–9, 31:484–9. See also Appel 1987, 183–4.

106 *DCL* 1832–9, 18:461–97, 30:121–6. On Geoffroy's efforts to elicit a sympathetic counterbiography in another work of reference see Griffiths 1965, 157–9.

107 *DCL* 1832–9, 1:3–4.

108 Larousse 1866, XXXVII–XXXVIII.

109 *DCL* 1832–9, 35:169–73.

110 *DCL* 1832–9, 45:179–89, 47:67–74.

111 *DCL* 1832–9, 47:73.

112 On the background and doctrines of the encyclopedia's editors see Forcina 1987; Griffiths 1965.

113 *DCL* 1844–51, 4:121–32.

114 Mollier 1988, 104, 106–7, 110.

115 Rowe 2005, 18.

116 Larousse 1866, XXXV–XXXVI.

117 Anonymous 1833e, "Compte rendu de juillet." Some twenty-six thousand sets of the seventh edition of Brockhaus's *Konversationslexikon* ended up being printed. See Hingst 1995, 127.

118 A second edition of this work was published in 1846–58, followed by a *Complément* (1856–62) and then a reprint (1877–84).

119 Mollier 1997, 295, 301–2.

120 Mollier 1988, 103–5, 108–10.

121 Hexelschneider 2005, 212–13.

122 Notice the example of the American (1789–1803) and Irish (1790–1801) editions of the *Encyclopaedia Britannica* in Archbold 2008, 187; Kafker and Loveland 2011, 138–9.

123 On these projects see Kafker and Loveland 2012, 197, 203–5; Fröhner 1994, 25–8; Donato 1997, 543–57.

124 See Weiss 2005, 286–7; Spree 2000, 297.

125 See Lipták 2005, 191, 194–5.

126 Spree 2000, 289–93, 297.

127 See Cooney 2005, 199–207; Spree 2000, 293–310.

128 See Loveland 2012, 244–50.

129 See for example *EGM* 1833–44, 4:61, 8:71, 13:82, 20:308; *DCL* 1832–9, 6:271–2, 15:277, 19:264–5, 27:240.

130 *DCL* 1832–9, 8:415.

131 Griffiths 1965, 124–7. On the *Penny Cyclopaedia* in this regard see Spree 2000, 43–4, 126–7.

Bibliography

Alger, J.G., and Gerard McCoy. 2004. "Duckett, William (1768–1841)." In *Oxford Dictionary of National Biography*, edited by H.C.G. Matthew and Brian Harrison, 17:39–40. Oxford: Oxford University Press.

Almanach royal, pour l'an M DCCC XXVII. 1827. Paris: A. Guyot et Scribe.

Anonymous. 1823a. *Le Musée des variétés littéraires*, 3 (November).

– 1823b. *Revue encyclopédique*, 19 (July).

– 1829. *Revue encyclopédique*, 44 (October–December).

– 1832. *Journal des connaissances utiles*, 2 (October).

– 1833a. *Bibliographie de la France*, 22 (5 January).

– 1833b. *Feuilleton du Journal de la librairie*, 17 (8 June).

– 1833c. *Feuilleton du Journal de la librairie*, 19 (22 June).

– 1833d. *Feuilleton du Journal de la librairie*, 20 (29 June).

– 1833e. *Journal des connaissances utiles*, 3 (July).

– 1836. *Bibliographie de la France*, 25 (2 January).

– 1840. *Bibliographie de la France*, 29 (4 January).

Appel, Toby A. 1987. *The Cuvier-Geoffroy Debate: French Biology in the Decades before Darwin.* Oxford: Oxford University Press.

Archbold, Johanna. 2008. "'The Most Expensive Literary Publication Ever Printed in Ireland': James Moore and the Publication of the *Encylopaedia Britannica* in Ireland, 1790–1800." In *Georgian Dublin*, edited by Gillian O'Brien and Finola O'Kane, 175–87. Dublin: Four Courts.

Audiffret, H. 1857. "Héreau (Edme-Joachim)." In *Biographie universelle (Michaud) ancienne et moderne*, new ed., 19:264–5. Paris: C. Desplaces.

Barber, Giles. 1968. "Treuttel and Würtz: Some Aspects of the Importation of Books from France, c. 1825." *The Library: The Transactions of the Bibliographical Society*, 5th ser., 23: 118–44.

Belgum, Kirsten. 2010. "Documenting the Zeitgeist: How the *Brockhaus* Recorded and Fashioned the World for Germans." In *Publishing Culture and* the "*Reading Nation*": *German Book History in the Long Nineteenth Century*, edited by Lynne Tatlock, 89–117. Rochester: Camden House.

[Brockhaus]. 1796–1808. *Conversationslexikon mit vorzüglicher Rücksicht auf die gegenwärtigen Zeiten*. First edition of Brockhaus's *Konversationslexikon*. 6 vols. Leipzig: publisher varies.

[Brockhaus]. 1830. *Allgemeine deutsche Real-Encyklopädie für die gebildeten Stände (Conversations-Lexikon)*. Seventh edition of Brockhaus's *Konversationslexikon*. Second printing. 12 vols. Leipzig: F.A. Brockhaus.

Burns, William. 2004. "Geoffroy Saint-Hilaire, Étienne, 1772–1884." In *Encyclopedia of the Romantic Era, 1760–1850*, vol. 1, edited by Christopher John Murray, 408–9. New York: Fitzroy Dearborn.

Cooney, Sondra Miley. 2005. "Die deutschen Wurzeln der 'Chambers' Enzyklopädie: Ein Wörterbuch des universalen Wissens für das Volk.'" In *F.A. Brockhaus, 1905–2005*, edited by Thomas Keiderling, 199–207. Leipzig: F.A. Brockhaus.

Dictionnaire de la conversation et de la lecture (DCL). 1832–9. 52 vols. Paris: Belin-Mandar.

– (*Supplément*). 1844–51. 16 vols. Paris: Garnier Frères.

Doig, Kathleen Hardesty. 1992. "L'*Encyclopédie méthodique* et l'organisation des connaissances." *Recherches sur Diderot et sur l'Encyclopédie* 12: 59–69.

Donato, Clorinda. 1997. "Übersetzung und Wandlung des enzyklopädischen Genres: Johnn Georg Krünitz' *Oeconomische Encyklopädie* (1771–1858) und ihre französischsprachigen Vorläufer." In *Kulturtransfer im Epochenumbruch: Frankreich-Deutschland, 1770 bis 1815*, edited by Hans-Jürgen Lüsebrink et al., 539–65. Leipzig: Universitätsverlag.

Doursther, Horace. 1840. *Dictionnaire universel des poids et mesures anciens et modernes*. Brussels: M. Hayez.

Encyclopédie des gens du monde, répertoire universel des sciences, des lettres et des arts; avec des notices sur les principales familles historiques et sur les personnages célèbres, morts et vivans; par une société de savans, de littérateurs et d'artistes, français et étrangers (EGM) 1833–44. 22 vols. Paris: Treuttel and Würtz.

Flügel, Georg Thomas. 1834. *The Merchant's Assistant*. Translated by Francis J. Grund. Boston: Hilliard, Gray, & Company.

Forcina, Marisa. 1987. *I diritti dell'esistente: La filosofia della "Encyclopédie nouvelle" (1833–1847)*. Lecce, Italy: Milella.

Fröhner, Annette. 1994. *Technologie und Enzyklopädismus im Übergang vom 18. zum 19. Jahrhundert: Johann Georg Krünitz (1728–1796) und seine oeconomisch-technologische Encyklopädie*. Mannheim: Palatium Verlag im J. and J. Verlag.

Goetschel, Willi, Catriona Macleod, and Emery Snyder. 1994. "The *Deutsche Encyclopädie*." In *Notable Encyclopedias of the Late Eighteenth Century: Eleven*

Successors of the Encyclopédie, edited by Frank A. Kafker, 257–333. Oxford: Voltaire Foundation.

Griffiths, David Albert. 1965. *Jean Reynaud, encyclopédiste de l'époque romantique, d'après sa correspondance inédite.* Paris: M. Rivière.

Guizot, François-Pierre-Guillaume. 1826. "Encyclopédie." In *Encyclopédie progressive,* 1–40. Paris: Bureau de l'Encyclopédie Progressive.

Hexelschneider, Erhard. 2005. "Der 'Brockhaus' erobert den russischen Markt: Zur Entstehungsgeschichte des 'Brockhaus-Efron.'" In *F. A. Brockhaus, 1905–2005,* edited by Thomas Keiderling, 207–18. Leipzig: F.A. Brockhaus.

Hingst, Anja zum. 1995. *Die Geschichte des Großen Brockhaus: Vom Conversationslexikon zur Enzyklopädie.* Wiesbaden: Harrassowitz.

Hupka, Werner. 1989. *Wort und Bild: Die Illustrationen in Wörterbüchern und Enzyklopädien.* Tübingen: Max Niemeyer.

Kafker, Frank A. 2009. "Epilogue: The Tortoise and the Hare: The Longevity of the *Encyclopaedia Britannica* and the *Encyclopédie* Compared." In *The Early Britannica: The Growth of an Outstanding Encyclopedia,* edited by Frank A. Kafker and Jeff Loveland, 299–307. Oxford: Voltaire Foundation.

Kafker, Frank A., and Jeff Loveland. 2011. "The Publisher James Moore and his Dublin Edition of the *Encyclopaedia Britannica,* a Notable Eighteenth-Century Irish Publication." *Eighteenth-Century Ireland* 26: 115–39.

– 2012. "La Vie agitée de l'abbé De Gua de Malves et sa direction de l'*Encyclopédie.*" *Recherches sur Diderot et sur l'Encyclopédie* 47: 187–203.

Keiderling, Thomas. 2012. "Der Brockhaus." In *Große Lexika und Wörterbücher Europas: Europäische Enzyzklopädien und Wörterbücher in historischen Porträts,* edited by Ulrike Haß, 193–210. Berlin: De Gruyter.

Larousse, Pierre. 1866. Introduction to vol. 1 of *Grand Dictionnaire universel du XIXe siècle,* V–LXXVI. Paris: [Larousse].

Laurentie, Pierre-Sébastien. 1838. *Histoire, morale et littérature, par M. Laurentie, ancien inspecteur général de l'université: Fragments.* Paris: Lagny Frères.

Lehner, Georg. 2008. "Le Savoir de l'Europe sur la Chine: Transferts franco-allemands au miroir des encyclopédies (1750–1850)." *Revue germanique internationale* 7: 21–31.

Lipták, Dorottya. 2005. "Die 'Sammlung gemeinnütziger Kenntnisse' von Otto Wigand: Zur Geschichte des ungarischen 'Brockhaus.'" In *F.A. Brockhaus, 1905–2005,* edited by Thomas Keiderling, 188–99. Leipzig: F.A. Brockhaus.

Lough, John. 1971. *The Encyclopédie.* London: Longman.

Loveland, Jeff. 2012. "Why Encyclopedias Got Bigger … and Smaller." *Information & Culture* 47: 233–54.

– 2013. "Encyclopaedias and Genre, 1670–1750." *Journal for Eighteenth-Century Studies* 36: 159–75.

– 2014. "How Serialisation Changed the Meanings of Encyclopaedias." In
From Text(s) to Book(s), edited by Nathalie Collé et al., 85–109. Nancy: Presses
Universitaires de Nancy, 2014.

– 2021. "When History Caught Up with Historians: Biographies of Contemporaries
in Encyclopedias." *Eighteenth-Century Life* 45: 47–74.

Meyer, Georg. 1966. "Das Konversations-Lexikon, eine Sonderform der
Enzyklopädie: Ein Beitrag zur Geschichte der Bildungsverbreitung in
Deutschland." PhD diss., Universität Göttingen.

Mollier, Jean-Yves. 1988. *L'Argent et les lettres: Histoire du capitalisme d'édition,
1880–1920*. Paris: Fayard.

– 1997. "Encyclopédie et commerce de la librairie du XVIIIe au XXe siècle." In
L'Entreprise encyclopédique, edited by Jean Bouffartigue and Françoise Mélonio,
10:295–310. Nanterre: Centre des Sciences de la Littérature, Université Paris
X - Nanterre.

Müller-Vollmer, Kurt. 2007. "How Brockhaus' *Conversations-Lexicon* Became
the *Encyclopaedia Americana*: A Fresh Look at Nineteenth-Century German-
American Cultural Transfer." In *Der Mnemosyne Träume: Festschrift zum 80.
Geburtstag von Joseph P. Strelka*, edited by Ilona Slawinski, Vahidin Preljevic,
and Robert Weige, 209–23. Tübingen: Francke.

Paccaud, Auguste. 1887. *Du régime de la presse en Europe et aux États-Unis*.
Lausanne: Aug. Pache.

Paul, Catherine. 1999. "Jean-Henri Schnitzler." In *Nouveau Dictionnaire de
biographie alsacienne*, vol. 34, edited by Charles Baechler, 3514. Strasbourg:
Fédération de Sociétés d'Histoire et d'Archéologie d'Alsace.

[Piltz, Anton Ernst Oskar]. 1872–5. "Zur Geschichte und Bibliographie der
enzyklopädischen Literatur insbesondere des Conversations-Lexikon." In
*F. A. Brockhaus in Leipzig: Vollständiges Verzeichniss der von der Firma F. A. Brockhaus
in Leipzig seit ihrer Gründung durch Friedrich Arnold Brockhaus im Jahre 1805 bis
zu dessen hundert-jährigem Geburtstage im Jahre 1872 verlegten Werke*, edited by
Heinrich Brockhaus, I–LXXII. Leipzig: F.A. Brockhaus.

Prévost, Amédée. 1838. "René Descartes: Sa Vie et ses ouvrages." In *Oeuvres
philosophiques de Descartes*, edited by Louis Aimé-Martin, V–XV. Paris: Auguste Desrez.

Prodöhl, Ines. 2011. *Die Politik des Wissens: Allgemeine deutsche Enzyklopädien
zwischen 1928 und 1956*. Berlin: Akademie.

Prospectus of the *Encyclopédie progressive*. 1826. Copy of the unpaginated
prospectus inserted in Alexandre-Jacques-François Bertrand, *Extase: De l'état
d'extase considéré comme une des causes des effets attribués au magnétisme animal*,
in *Encyclopédie progressive: Collection de traités sur l'histoire, l'état actuel et les
progrès des connaissances humaines*, [57]–[62]. Paris: Bureau de l'Encyclopédie
Progressive.

Prospectus: Nouveau Dictionnaire encyclopédique, à l'usage des gens du monde. [1829].
   Paris: Treuttel and Würtz. Copy of the separately paginated prospectus
   inserted in [Juan Bautista Cayetano Raxis de Flassan], *Histoire du congrès de
   Vienne*, vol. 3, [455]–[8]. Paris: Treuttel and Würtz.
Pruvost, Jean. 2005. "De Diderot à Pierre Larousse: Un paysage lexicographique
   prémonitoire." In *Les Dictionnaires Larousse: Genèse et evolution*, edited by
   Monique C. Cormier and Aline Francoeur, 41–62. Montreal: Presses de
   l'Université de Montréal.
Review of *Dictionnaire de la conversation et de la lecture*. 1833a. *L'Ami de la religion:
   Journal ecclésiastique, poltique et littéraire* 75 (12 February): 65–8.
– 1833b. *L'Ami de la religion: Journal ecclésiastique, poltique et littéraire* 75 (30
   March): 401–6.
– 1837. *Waldie's Select Circulating Library: The Journal of Belles Lettres* 9 (23 May):
   [3].
Review of *Encyclopédie des gens du monde*. 1834. *Museum of Foreign Literature,
   Science, and Art* (October): 381–4.
Rowe, Paul. 2005. "Tous les savoirs des gens du monde? Un précurseur du
   GDU." In *Voyages dans le Grand Larousse*, edited by Yannick Portebois and
   Maxime Prévost, 11–23. Toronto: Centre d'Études du XIXe Siècle Joseph
   Sablé.
– 2006. "Upwardly Mobile Footnotes: German References in the *Encyclopédie des
   gens du monde*." *Modern and Contemporary France* 14: 443–8.
Schneider, Ulrich Johannes. 2004. "Das Leben im Lexikon." *Gegenworte* 13:
   85–9.
Spree, Ulrike. 2000. *Das Streben nach Wissen: Eine vergleichende Gattungsgeschichte
   der populären Enzyklopädie in Deutschland und Großbritannien im 19. Jahrhundert.*
   Tübingen: Niemeyer.
Weiss, Gerhard. 2005. "The Americanization of Franz Lieber and the
   Encyclopedia Americana." In *German Culture in Nineteenth-Century America:
   Reception, Adaptation, Transformation*, edited by Lynne Tatlock and Matt Erlin,
   273–87. Rochester: Camden.

chapter ten

Compiling Based on Translations: Notes on Raynal's and Diderot's Work on the *Histoire des deux Indes*

SUSANNE GREILICH

Despite its generic denomination as a "histoire" (history), Raynal's work on European settlements and commerce in the "two Indies," published in three different editions between 1770 and 1780,[1] can be considered an encyclopedic compilation. The chronological account of the conquest of Mexico and Peru in books VI and VII, for example, alternates with ethnographic descriptions; treatises on the natural history of exotic plants and animals (such as cacao, vanilla, cinchona, indigo, lama, and cochineal) stand next to scientific essays on volcanism, the formation of mountains, and the qualities of platinum and quicksilver. In most cases, a "cue" is enough for Raynal or Diderot to start an elaborate digression on natural history. In book VII of the 1780 edition, for instance, the description of Quito in chapter 22 is linked to a disquisition on cinchona, written by Jussieu, by establishing a relatively simple connection between the two fields in the heading of chapter 23: "Le quinquina vient de la province de Quito. Considérations sur ce remède" (Raynal 2018, 176).[2] The synopsis of information is not subject to any alphabetical system or headwords. Instead – and in this other sense the text is also an "histoire" (story) – Raynal draws on an authorial narrator that leads the reader through the text, through time and space of the "histoire des établissements et du commerce des Européens dans les deux Indes": "Ici vont se développer des scènes plus terribles que celles qui nous ont fait si souvent frémir. Elles se répéteront sans interruption dans les immenses contrées qui nous restent à parcourir," declares the narrator at the beginning of book VII (Raynal 2018, 119).[3]

Still, the narrative coherence often turns out to be somewhat sparse. The work's compiled structure remains obvious. In book VII, for example, the narrator leads from Jussieu's treatise on cinchona (chap. 23) to an essay on the formation of mountains, penned by Diderot (chap. 24), by establishing a connection between the cultivation of cinchona, the attempts to improve the cultivation of cochineal and cinnamon, the corruption of manners, and La Condamine's expedition into the Peruvian highlands. For all this, Jussieu's life serves as the major link:

> Mais pour distraire notre imagination de tant de tableaux désolans qui nous ont peut-être trop occupés, perdons un moment de vue ces campagnes ensanglantées, & entrons dans le Pérou, en fixant d'abord nos regards sur ces monts effrayans, où de savans & courageux astronomes allèrent mesurer la figure de la terre. Livrons-nous aux sentimens qu'ils éprouvèrent sans doute & que doit éprouver le voyageur instruit ou ignorant, par-tout où la nature lui offre un pareil spectacle. Osons même nous permettre quelques conjectures générales sur la formation des montagnes. (Raynal 2018, 178)[4]

Such rhetorical twists can be read as an example of the compiler's lack of literary skill. Conversely, the work's fragmentary style emphasizes its encyclopedic structure and aim. The whole text appears like a collection of highly detailed articles on almost every subject regarding the Spanish possessions in Latin America. On the one hand, the chronological account, which ranges from the discovery of America to the conquest of Mexico and Peru and, further, to the eighteenth-century colonial present, is an integral part of this panorama. On the other hand, it works as a kind of base text, from which branch-offs – provoked by implicit headwords – lead to other relevant fields before the text returns, once again, to the historical account.

Histoire des deux Indes, *Encyclopédie*, and *Encyclopédie méthodique*: Transfers, Interferences, Differences

The *Histoire des deux Indes* is related in different ways to other major encyclopedic projects of the time, such as the *Encyclopédie*, the *Encyclopédie méthodique*, or Savary des Bruslons's *Dictionnaire universel de commerce*. Not only were some authors (such as Diderot, Naigeon, d'Holbach, and Deleyre) given the task of writing articles for both the *Histoire* and one or sometimes even two *Encyclopédies*, but direct text transfers between the *Histoire* and other encyclopedic compilations also took place. These reciprocal transfers of knowledge were possible after years of publishing works that were essentially interlaced.[5]

Raynal's obvious borrowing of information on vanilla in book VI of the 1770 and 1774 editions of the *Histoire* from the *Encyclopédie* article on that subject may support this thesis (emphasis added):

Encyclopédie , art. *Vanille* , 1764, 16:830–1	Raynal 1770, 3:54; 1774, 3:88
C'est *une petite gousse* presque ronde, un peu aplatie, *longue d'environ six pouces, large de quatre lignes, ridée,* roussâtre, *mollasse, huileuse, grasse,* cependant *cassante,* & comme coriace à l'extérieur. La *pulpe* qui est dedans, est *roussâtre,* remplie *d'une infinité de* petits grains, noirs, luisans; elle est *un peu âcre,* grasse, *aromatique* […]	Une *petite gousse longue d'environ six pouces, large de quatre lignes, ridée, molasse, huileuse, grasse* quoique *cassante;* peut être regardée comme le fruit de cette plante. L'intérieur de la gousse est tapissé d'une *pulpe rougeâtre, aromatique, un peu âcre, remplie d'une liqueur noirâtre, huileuse & balsamique, où nagent une infinité de grains noirs, luisans, & presque imperceptibles.*

The article in the *Encyclopédie* was composed by the Chevalier de Jaucourt, who had relied on information provided by Plumier, Labat, and the sixteenth-century Spanish physician and botanist Francisco Hernández de Toledo. Though de Jaucourt considers Hernández's treatise on Mexican vanilla to be not very reliable ("[La description] du botaniste françois [Plumier] est aussi bien détaillée que l'autre [celle d'Hernández] l'est mal"; *Encyclopédie*, 1764, 16:832),[6] he reproduces the Spaniard's considerations – in the absence of any alternative information.[7] Raynal, on the contrary, avoids taking Hernandez's treatise as a basis for his own chapter on vanilla. He slashes de Jaucourt's extensive article, leaving only a few passages that he considers to be scientifically unproblematic.

For the *Histoire*'s third edition, the French botanist Jussieu completely revised – as Cecil Courtney (1963) has shown – the aforementioned paragraphs, taking as a primary basis Plumier's description of the Dominican vanilla. With regard to the revised chapter, the *Histoire*'s narrator proudly remarks: "ces notions, tout-à-fait modernes, sont-elles dues à un naturaliste François" (Raynal 2018, 70).[8] In the whole third edition numerous examples can be found that show how Raynal (and Diderot) tried to update and correct information that had been provided before, resulting in the complete rejection of Spanish sources, which to a certain extent had once been considered reliable. In the third edition these sources are condemned as false, or even "chimerical":

Grace à l'ignorance des voyageurs & à la légéreté avec laquelle [les Espag-
nols] considèrent les productions de la nature dans tous les règnes, son

> histoire se remplit de faussetés qui passent d'un ouvrage dans un autre, &
> que des auteurs qui se copient successivement, transmettent d'âge en âge.
> On n'examine guère ce qu'on croit bien savoir; & c'est ainsi qu'après avoir
> propagé les erreurs, les témoignages qui retardent l'observation en prolon-
> gent encore la durée. (Raynal 2018, 73)[9]

The *Histoire*'s effort to bypass the Spanish botanist Hernández is therefore only logical.[10]

Raynal and Diderot endeavoured to put an end to out-of-date knowledge that had been transferred over the centuries from one author and
nation to another through translation. In the third edition this would
lead to a complete revision of the compilers' notion of the Aztec and
Inca empires. In this case, too, Diderot and Raynal corrected the previously written information, after having read recent European writings
on the subject. For that reason, the knowledge of the New World that
encyclopedic works such as the *Encyclopédie* and the *Histoire des deux Indes*
imparted to a rather broad readership differs on some relevant issues
from one compilation to another. In his article "Mexico, Ville de," published in the *Encyclopédie*'s tenth volume (1764, 479–80), de Jaucourt
describes the magnificence of the Aztec capital, joining the chorus of
such European authors as Prévost or Thomas Gage, who – subsequent
to Spanish historians such as Solís (1685, French translation 1759 in its
sixth edition), López de Gómara (1552, French translation 1584 in its
fifth edition), and Herrera (1601–15, French translation 1660–71) –
came to an opinion similar to that of de Jaucourt himself: "Cette ville
[…] offroit aux yeux le plus beau monument de l'industrie américaine"
(*Encyclopédie*, 1764, 10:480).[11]

In the 1770 edition, Raynal was of the same opinion, but four years
later his ideas on Tenochtitlan had completely changed. In the second
and third edition of the *Histoire* the narrator rejects the idea that Mexico
was the splendid capital of a (relatively) civilized nation:

> La fausseté de cette description pompeuse, tracée dans des momens de van-
> ité par un vainqueur naturellement porté à l'exagération, […] peut être mise
> aisément à la portée de tous les esprits. […] Il doit […] passer pour démon-
> tré que […] la célèbre Mexico n'étoit qu'une bourgade formée d'une multi-
> tude de cabanes rustiques. (Raynal 1774, 3:61–2; Raynal 2018, 53)[12]

These changes in perception with regard to Mexico and the Aztec empire
correspond with how Raynal and Diderot modified, in the 1774 edition,

the representation of the Inca empire in book VII. After having followed the descriptions of the Spanish historians Zárate (1555, French translation in 1700), López de Gómara, Herrera, and Garcilaso Inca de la Vega (1609/17, French translation in 1633) in the 1770 edition, the compilers totally changed their attitude in the second edition four years later. Influenced by La Condamine's (see Wolpe 1957, 39–40) and De Pauw's recent treatises,[13] all accounts on the wonders of the Inca empire were relegated to "fairyland" ("au rang des fables," Raynal 1774, 3:128–9).

Nevertheless, the article on Mexico in the 1777 supplement of the *Encyclopédie* still provides its readers with an almost enthusiastic description of Tenochtitlan's grandeur – though very different from the one in de Jaucourt's article. Its author did not doubt the validity of his account, though he must have been aware of Raynal's and Diderot's reservations on the subject: at the end of the article we find an explicit reference to the *Histoire*, more precisely to its description of Mexican trading goods and natural resources: "Les mines d'or, le cacao, la vanille, l'indigo, la cochenille, le riz, le coton, font une grande partie du commerce. *Hist. phil. & polit. du commerce des Indes*, 3ᵉ vol. 1773" (*Supplément*, 1777, 3:924).[14] It is remarkable that the *Histoire* seems to have drawn the *Encyclopédie*'s attention to Mexico's economy; in the articles published thirteen years before, this subject had been of no interest to de Jaucourt. In 1788, the *Encyclopédie méthodique* (3:598–601) would finally reproduce word by word the *Histoire*'s detailed facts and figures on the Peruvian mines. As we can see, Raynal's compilation had become a reliable source and an important reference in the context of encyclopedic projects in the Age of Enlightenment.

Transfer of Knowledge and Translation: Raynal's and Diderot's Work on Non-French Sources

The Histoire *and the Spanish Golden Age*

As stated earlier, Raynal and Diderot made some effort to detach from the information transferred by Spanish historians and naturalists of the *Siglo de Oro* and to replace this information by data deriving from modern, "enlightened" accounts on Spanish possessions in America. We can base this claim on a detailed study of all likely sources that Raynal and his co-authors might have used and a precise comparison of texts. Unlike some of his contemporaries, Raynal does not explicitly indicate his sources and is content to provide only ambiguous hints.

By contrast, the Abbé Prévost discusses at length the historical works he used when composing the twelfth volume of his *Histoire générale des voyages*, which also deals with the Spanish conquest of America. Prévost not only provides the full titles of the sources he referenced, but also provides information about the authors, comments on their literary style, and judges their credibility. Finally, he comments on the quality of the available French translations. In his opinion there are ten authors worth mentioning: Martyr d'Anghiera, Oviedo, López de Gómara, Benzoni, Herrera, Las Casas, Diaz del Castillo, Cortés, Solís, and Charlevoix. He singles out Herrera's *Décadas* as being the best of all historical works ("on ne connoît point de source plus abondante & plus pure"; Prévost 1754, ix),[15] rates the French translations of Benzoni (by Vrain Chauveton) and Herrera (by Nicolas de la Coste) as "assez bonne,"[16] and praises the literary qualities of Solís's *Historia* but finds the French translation – made by De Broë – leaves a lot to be desired ("fort inférieure à l'Original," Prévost 1754, xiij).[17]

Raynal definitely relied on information provided by the historians that Prévost mentions. He either knew these works in their French translations or he became familiar with them through Prévost's *Histoire générale des voyages*. Herrera, Gómara, Solís, Las Casas, the Italian author Benzoni, finally – where book VII is concerned – Zárate, and Garcilaso Inca de la Vega: passages from the French versions of all these texts can be found in the *Histoire philosophique et politique*. Almost none of these authors were mentioned by name. Instead we find general allusions to "the Spaniards," often accompanied by an undertone of scepticism: "si l'on croit les Espagnols,"[18] and other such sentiments. If there are explicit references to sources, it is about uncontested eighteenth-century experts in natural history belonging to the (inner) circle of philosophers and *encyclopédistes*: Jussieu, La Condamine, and Buffon are mentioned, also Lehmann, whose treatise on the formation of mountains had been translated from German into French by d'Holbach, who also used this text for his article "Montagne" in the *Encyclopédie*.[19] By name-dropping, Raynal was intending to show how up to date, valid, and exact his information was.

The only real exception to this rule is Herrera, who in book VI of the third edition is referred to five times. Bartolomé de Las Casas is mentioned by name in book VII, but he is described as a historical colonial figure because he was *encomendero* in the Cumana region. Las Casas's *Brevísima relación* remains unnamed, though Raynal definitely utilized several passages from one of the numerous French translations of this pamphlet. Finally, book VI comes up with the names of two Spanish *croni-stas* that are both noteworthy: Torquemada and Acosta. In chapter 13, section 2, in a short passage on the Chichemecas, Raynal refers to the Franciscan monk and historian Torquemada, author of *Monarchía indi-ana*.[20] The work's three volumes, published from 1613 to 1615 in Seville and re-edited in 1723 in Madrid, deal with the history of the middle American indigenous nations, their manners and customs, and finally with their acculturation (especially their religious conversion), as it was undertaken by the Spaniards. In book VI, chapter 20, Torquemada is mentioned once again, in the context of a short digression on sixteenth-century smallpox epidemics. Here, the Spanish historian is described – in a disrespectful way – as "exaggerating" and "credulous":

> L'introduction de la petite-vérole, accrut la dépopulation, qui fut encore bientôt après augmentée par les épidémies de 1545 & de 1576, dont la première coûta huit cens mille habitans à l'empire, & la seconde deux mil-lions, si l'on veut adopter les calculs du crédule, de l'exagérateur Torque-mada. (Raynal 2018, 80)[21]

The *Monarchía indiana* does actually give the number of two million dead people. The author draws it from a statistical investigation initi-ated by the Spanish vice-king Martin Enriquez a while after the epi-demic. However, it seems unlikely that Raynal slogged through three voluminous Spanish folios that had never been translated into any other European language just to find a precise number that he would reject as non-credible immediately thereafter. In any case, the effect result-ing from the reference to Torquemada is interesting: Raynal makes the readership believe he had even consulted texts that can be regarded as of minor importance compared to those of Herrera, Gómara, Solís, or Zárate, and that he read those texts in their original versions. Thus, he emphasizes the effort he made to give an exact and complete account. At the same time, he takes advantage of the situation and attacks – once again – the Catholic Church and its monks as well as the state of Span-ish sciences.

The reference to Acosta is hardly less interesting. In book VI, Acosta and Herrera are designated as the only Spanish authors that can be taken seriously. At the beginning of the chapter that deals with the cultiva-tion of cochineals, Raynal admits having made a mistake regarding his remarks on the subject in the 1770 and 1774 editions.[22] He singles out Acosta's scientific merits, only to blame in the same breath the other

Spanish *cronistas* and *naturalistas* for lack of accuracy and not being up
to date:

> J'avois avancé d'après les meilleurs auteurs, même Espagnols, que la nature
> de cette couleur étoit inconnue avant le commencement du siècle. En
> remontant aux originaux, j'ai trouvé qu'Acosta, en 1530, & Herrera, en
> 1601, l'avoient aussi bien décrite que nos modernes naturalistes. Je me
> retracte donc; & je suis bien fâché de ne m'être pas trompé plus souvent
> dans ce que j'ai écrit des Espagnols. (Raynal 2018, 73)[23]

Once again, Raynal gives the impression of having studied the original
Spanish Golden Age sources in detail. However, he makes a mistake on
the year of publication of Acosta's *Historia natural y moral de las Indias*, a
real howler for Raynal, who was obsessed with details and data: in fact,
Acosta's text was published in 1590 and was translated into French eight
years later.[24] The parallels he draws between the description of the cochineal by Acosta and Herrera on the one hand and those of "modernes
naturalistes" (modern naturalists) on the other are also astonishing. In
Herrera's *Décadas* one can find a short passage on the subject (see Herrera 1934, 256), but it is off the mark, where precision and degree of
detail are concerned, from the in-depth description of the cochineal
written by Jussieu – probably based on relevant treatises of Réaumur (see
Courtney 1963, 220), Thiéry de Menonville, and others.[25]

Although it is assumed that Raynal used Nicolas de la Coste's French
translation of Herrera's *Décadas*, which was "une assez bonne Traduction
pour le tems"[26] according to Prévost (1754, x), the French philosopher
gave the impression that he had used the original Spanish sources. Obviously, Raynal was not aware of how original texts and their French translations may differ.

The Power of Translation: Two Case Examples

Raynal habitually read French translations of Spanish chronicles instead
of the Spanish-language originals. This practice led to knowledge transfer that reflected the information contained in the translation rather
than the Spanish-language source texts. The following two examples of
this kind of transfer are worthy of note in the *Histoire des deux Indes*.

Solís's *Historia de la Conquista de México* provides the first example. The
text was translated into French by Samuel de Broë, the translator that
Prévost would criticize in his *Histoire des voyages* more than half a century

later. The *Histoire de la conquête du Mexique* was published in 1691, only six years after the Spanish original came out, and in 1759, the sixth edition of the book would be sold by the Parisian publishing house. In its original version, the account of Cortés's conquest of Mexico ends before the battle of Tenochtitlan, as the translator states with some regret in the preface.[27] De Broë, who a few years later would translate Zárate's *Historia del Perú*, thereby producing another eighteenth-century bestseller in the field of *conquista* literature, is of the opinion that he owes his audience a sequel to Solis's account: "C'est ce qu'on a crû être obligé de rapporter en peu de mots, & d'instruire en même-tems le lecteur du reste de la vie de ce Conquérant" (Solís 1691, n.p.).[28] Inspired by other Spanish accounts, such as those of Herrera or Gómara, De Broë sketches in his preface Cortés's further actions and points to the fact that even Cortés has to be accused of outrages:

> Cette dangereuse passion les poussa a commettre d'horribles cruautez, qui leur ont été reprochées par des Auteurs de leur Nation même. Cortez n'en fut pas éxempt, au moins par une foible complaisance qu'il eut pour le Trésorier Julien d'Alderete, que presque tous les Historiens chargent du crime d'avoir fait mettre sur des charbons ardens Guatimozin, & un de ses Favoris; afin de les obliger par cet horrible supplice, à découvrir les tresors de Motezuma, que l'on supposoit qu'ils avoient cachez. Ce fut en cette occasion, que le Prince entendant un cri que la douleur faisoit pousser à son Favori, luy dit, en le regardant fierement: *Et moy, suis-je sur un lit de roses?* Ce mot obligea l'Indien à marquer son respect jusques à la mort, qu'il souffroit sans le plaindre davantage, en cet effroïable torment. (Solís 1691)[29]

The described scene can be traced back to two well-known authors, Herrera and Montaigne, but a crucial point of the representation is due to the translator's own creative input. In the third book of his *Essais* (1588), Montaigne describes the Aztec king's torture, falling back, according to his own statement, on López de Gómara's account. For Montaigne, the scene serves as a starting point for a more general reflection on the category of "barbarism":

> Ce seigneur se trouvant forcé de la douleur, environné de braziers ardens, tourna sur la fin, piteusement sa veue vers son maistre, comme pour luy demander mercy, de ce qu'il ne pouvoit plus: Le Roy, plantant fierement et rigoureusement les yeux sur luy, pour reproche de sa lascheté et

244   Susanne Greilich

> pusillanimité, luy dict seulement des mots d'une voix rude et ferme: Et
> moy, suis-je dans un baing? suis-je pas plus à mon ayse que toy? (Montaigne
> 2007, 957)[30]

Gómara does indeed describe Cuauhtémoc as a courageous monarch,
but the sentence coming out of the Aztec's mouth was invented by Montaigne himself. Herrera, in his *Décadas*, blames Julián de Alderete as the
man in charge of Cuauhtémoc's torture; still, the dialogue between the
Aztec king and his favourite cannot be found in Herrera's account. Obviously, De Broë, in his sequel, was inspired by Herrera as well as by Montaigne, but he varied the Aztec king's laconic answer: the bath ("baing")
became a bed of roses ("lit de roses"). The translator made an effort
to imitate, in his preface, the elegant literary style of Solís – a highly
esteemed poet and dramatist of the Spanish Golden Age, disciple of
Calderón de la Barca – who in his *Historia de la conquista de México* sometimes puts lofty sentences and statements in his hero's mouth.

During the ensuing period, the Aztec king's sentence invented by De
Broë ("Et moi, suis-je sur un lit de roses?") would be as successful as the
French translation of Solís's *Historia* itself. Cuauhtémoc's last words can
be found in Rousseau's *Discours sur les sciences et les arts* (1750; see Rousseau 1966, 91), in Voltaire's *Essai sur les mœurs* (1756; see Voltaire 1962,
259), in Samuel Pufendorf's *Histoire moderne* (see Pufendorf and Bruzen
de la Martinière 1759, 406), in the *Encyclopédie* article on Mexico (see
Encyclopédie, 1764, 10:481) (de Jaucourt refers explicitly to Solís), and in
Marmontel's *Les Incas* (see Marmontel 1777, 1:84) as well as, of course,
in the *Histoire des deux Indes*. Only Prévost, in his *Histoire générale des voyages*, does not reproduce the sentence; this may be due to the fact that
the abbot, who worked much more precisely with original sources and
their translations, was aware of the translator's invention. It is very probable that the "roses theme" found its way into the *Histoire des deux Indes*
by way of De Broë's preface. This theme can also be found in Raynal's
École militaire, and in this case the author names Solís's *Historia* as being
a major source for his own text. In any case, Raynal obviously knew how
to measure up to his audience's expectations: in the last decades of the
eighteenth century, the representation of a face-off between the barbarian conquistador and the noble savage had become both a well-known
topos and a literary vogue.[31]

My second example is a short passage from Herrera's *Décadas*. In this
case, the inaccuracy of the French translation seems to have contributed
to hardening the topos of the noble savage in the *Histoire*. In book VI,

chapter 6, one can find a portrait of the customs and manners of the Haitian people. Of all the customs he could have described, it is the burial of the widows that Raynal has chosen in order to demonstrate the Haitian people's noble-mindedness. The funeral practice he describes recalls the East Indian sati, a practice that contemporary travel accounts were unanimous in condemning as a barbarian act:

> Aucune loi ne régloit chez eux le nombre des femmes. Ordinairement, une d'entr'elles avoit quelques privilèges, quelques distinctions; mais sans autorité sur les autres. C'étoit celle que le mari aimoit le plus, & dont il se croyoit le plus aimé. Quelquefois à la mort de cet époux, elle se faisoit enterrer avec lui. (Raynal 2018, 29)[32]

The paragraph on this Haitian practice is most likely from Herrera, who describes the custom in his *Décadas*. Nicolas de la Coste's French translation of the passage reads as follows: "celle qu'il avoit aimée le plus, s'enfermoit avecque luy, & y mouroit" (Herrera 1660–71, 1:180).[33] It is worth noting that the French translation differs from the Spanish original text in a significant aspect. Herrera writes: "Cuando moría algún cacique, le abrían y le secaban al fuego [...] y de las mujeres que tenía *la que quería mostrar que le había amado más*, se encerraba con él y allí moría, y algunas veces eran dos" (Herrera 1601–15, 2:229, emphasis added).[34] Herrera emphasizes the fact that the widow's auto-sacrifice was an act of demonstration due to a social convention, whereas de la Coste's translation – perhaps unintentionally – makes it appear that the widow's death was an act of pure love. Raynal even reinforces this interpretation by adding a comment that makes the image of the noble savage perfect: "Ce n'étoit point chez ce peuple un usage, un devoir, un point d'honneur; c'étoit dans la femme une impossibilité de survivre à ce que son cœur avoit de plus cher" (Raynal 2018, 29).[35]

Conclusion

Although Raynal and Diderot definitely relied on French translations of Spanish Golden Age historical works when compiling information for the *Histoire des deux Indes*, they rarely commented on these sources, nor did they reflect on their use of translated texts. Yet the intercultural dimensions, or rather the cultural specifics of original and translated texts, had been discussed by French authors even before the *Histoire* was published. In the middle of the century, Prévost had already commented on the subject several times in his *Histoire générale des voyages*, whose first ten volumes are based on translations of English texts. In a long preface to a supplementary volume of the *Histoire des voyages* (see Prévost 1761), the publishers showed themselves angered by the Dutch pirated editions that came out using the pretext of correcting mistakes in the Parisian version: "Le Traducteur leur a répondu, dans plusieurs de ses préfaces, qu'il s'étoit écarté volontairement du Texte Anglois, lorsqu'il avoit jugé ce changement nécessaire, pour l'intérêt même de la vérité, de l'ordre, de l'honnêteté, ou de la Religion" (Prévost 1761, iv).[36] Obviously, Prévost had his readership's cultural background and expectations in mind. So did the French translator De Broë when he added the preface to Solís's account on the conquest of Mexico. De Broë was aware of French readers' expectations; contrary to the public of the Spanish Golden Age, the French did not want to read about Cortés's exploits but rather about the conquistador's cruelty and avarice, characteristic elements of the so-called *leyenda negra*. By adopting the anecdote on Cuauhtémoc in book VI, Raynal leaves a decidedly French mark upon his representation of the Conquista, propagating a view in which the noble savage faces the barbaric European. In this respect, the *Histoire des deux Indes* can definitely be understood as a work in which knowledge of the colonial world assumed not only a practical but also a symbolic value. By keeping silent on the Spanish sources they used for their *histoire politique* – that is to say, the bestsellers belonging to the official Spanish historiography – and by substituting the information provided by Spanish Golden Age chroniclers such as Zárate, Gómara, and Solís for contemporary "enlightened" reports, the *Histoire des deux Indes* established a prerogative of interpretation on the New World that one has to comprehend in perspectives of nation (France vs. Spain), time ("modernity" vs. *Siglo de Oro*), and ideology (Enlightenment). The explicit references to Acosta, Herrera, and Torquemada do not contradict this finding. In fact, they are most probably not due to Raynal's and Diderot's sincere esteem of these historians, but are instead attributable to the intervention of Spanish secretary Ignacio Heredia with the French compilers of the *Histoire* after the first edition was published in 1770. With regard to the representation of Spain, Heredia suggested several amendments, and these suggestions proved partially successful (see Tietz 1991, 103–4; Lüsebrink 2003). Raynal's negligent handling of Acosta's *Historia* and his shameless attack on Fray Torquemada's credibility both attest to Raynal's and Diderot's reluctance to concede a part of their prerogative of interpretation to the Spaniards.

During the ensuing period, the latter would try in turn to shape the perception of Spanish colonial history according to their own will with the publication of two *apologías* against the *Histoire des deux Indes* (see Tietz 1983).[37] The Duke of Almodóvar, member of the enlightened Spanish elite under the rule of Charles III, undertook a revised Spanish translation of the *Histoire*, which had been banned by the Inquisition in its original version. The first five volumes of this adaptation, entitled *Historia política de los establecimientos ultramarinos de las naciones europeas*, were published under a pseudonym in Madrid from 1784 to 1790 (see Tietz 1991, 108ff). As Manfred Tietz has shown, the Spanish version of the *Histoire* was purged of all attacks on the Catholic Church and of those passages that qualified Spain as a felonious colonial power. Nevertheless, the Spanish edition was aimed at opening the eyes of the Spanish public to the urgent "American problem" (see Tietz 1983, 998). After the French revolution broke out, the edition stopped. Even a "clean" Raynal had become unacceptable, so that the *Histoire*'s specific view on colonial history would disseminate its effects in many European countries as well as in America, but was actually not discussed in Spain.

Notes

1 As for Raynal's co-authors, especially Diderot, see Lüsebrink 1984, Duchet 1978, and Goggi 1991.

2 "The bark [cinchona] comes from the province of Quito. Reflections upon this remedy" (Raynal 1783, 4:121). All French passages from the third (and final) edition of Raynal's work, published in 1780, are cited after the critical and commented edition 2018, vol. 2. All English translations follow the English version of Raynal's work: *A Philosophical and Political History of the Settlements and Trade of the Europeans in the East and West Indies*, 8 vols. (London: printed for W. Strahan; and T. Cadell, 1783). The extracts are taken from volumes 3 and 4.

3 "We are going to display scenes, still more terrible than those which have so often made us shudder. They will be uninterruptedly repeated in those immense regions which remain for us to go over" (Raynal 1783, 4:2).

4 "But, in order to relieve our imagination from such a number of distressing pictures, which, perhaps, have too much engaged our attention, let us, for a moment quit these bloody scenes, and let us enter into Peru, fixing our contemplation upon those frightful mountains, where learned and bold astronomers went to measure the figure of the earth. Let us indulge ourselves in those sensations which they undoubtedly experienced, and

which every traveller, learned or ignorant, must experience, wherever
nature presents him such a scene. Let us even be allowed to throw out some
general conjectures respecting the formation of mountains" (Raynal 1783,
4:113).

5 *Histoire des deux Indes*: 1770, 1774, 1780; *Encyclopédie*: 1751–65; *Supplément*:
1776–7; *Encyclopédie méthodique*: from 1782 on.

6 "The French botanist's description is as detailed as the other one is bad." All
translations into English are my own unless otherwise indicated.

7 With regard to the contemporary botany de Jaucourt has to admit: "Nous
n'avons point encore de description exacte de la plante qui fournit la
vanille du Méxique, de ses caracteres, & de ses especes" (*Encyclopédie*, 1764,
16:831) (We do not yet have an exact description of the plant that provides
the Mexican vanilla, of its characteristics and its species).

8 "[T]his information [...] is entirely modern, and owen [*sic*] to a French
naturalist" (Raynal 1783, 3:342).

9 "The ignorance of travellers, and the levity with which they consider the
productions of nature in all it's [*sic*] kingdom, is the reason that natural
history is so full of falsities, which pass from one work to another, and which
are transmitted from age to age, by authors who successively copy each
other. We scarce give ourselves the trouble to examine, what we think we
are well acquainted with; and thus it is, that after having propagated error,
the testimonies which delay inquiries prolong the duration of it still more"
(Raynal 1783, 3:349–50).

10 Other paragraphs dealing with the natural history of the West Indies, for
example the paragraphs on the coca plant (see Raynal 2018, 192) were also
revised by Jussieu for the third edition, while the 1770 and 1774 editions
had still relied on information given by the *Encyclopédie*. Jussieu obviously
uses new information provided by Ulloa's travel account (see Ulloa 1752,
1:291–2). As was the case for vanilla, de Jaucourt, in the *Encylopédie*, had
to admit: "Je suis fâché de ne pouvoir rien dire de plus d'une plante de
ce prix, de ne la connoître même par aucune description de botaniste,
mais seulement par des relations de voyageurs, qui se contredisent les
uns les autres, & qui paroissent ne s'être attachés qu'à nous en débiter
des contes hors de toute créance" (*Encyclopédie*, 1753, 3:557). (I am sorry/
angry that I cannot say anything more about a plant of this value, that I do
not even know it by any description of a botanist, but only by the relations
of travelers, who contradict each other and who seem to have attached
themselves only to debiting to us tales lacking all credibility).

11 "This city [...] offered to the eyes the most beautiful monument of
American arts."

12 "This is a pompous description, given in an instant of vanity by a conqueror naturally addicted to exaggeration, […] and the falsity of it may easily be made evident to every man's capacity. […] We must therefore take it for granted, […] that the celebrated Mexico was nothing more than a little town, composed of a multitude of rustic huts" (Raynal 1783, 3:302–3). This harsh judgment is all the more surprising since the Italian voyager Gemelli Careri – unsuspicious of Spanish haughtiness – had given, in *Giro del Mondo* (1699–1700, 16ff.; French translation 1719), such a positive description of the city of Mexico in 1697 that Prévost, in *Histoire générale des voyages*, felt compelled to place Mexico on the same level with the most beautiful cities of Italy: "On peut dire que Mexico le dispose aux meilleures Villes d'Italie, par les Edifices, & qu'il emporte, par la beauté des femmes" (Prévost 1754, 444). (It can be said that Mexico, by the buildings, competes with the best cities of Italy, and by the beauty of women, even surpasses it.) In Gemelli Careri's account it says: "Per la bontà degli edificj, ed Ornamenti delle Chiese può dirsi, che garregia colle migliori d'Italia; ma per la bellezza delle Dame le supera" (1699–1700, 30–1). (By the quality of the buildings and the ornaments of the churches, it competes with the best cities of Italy, but by the beauty of women, [Mexico] even surpasses it.)

13 See De Pauw 1771–4, 3:344–57: "De l'état des arts chez les Péruviens, au temps de la découverte de leur pays" (On the state of the arts among Peruvians, at the time of their country's discovery).

14 "The gold mines, cocoa, vanilla, indigo, cochineal, rice, and cotton make a big part of the commerce."

15 "We do not know any source that is more abundant and pure."

16 "Quite good."

17 "Highly inferior to its original."

18 "If we believe the Spaniards."

19 Johann Gottlob Lehmann, *Versuch einer Geschichte von Flötz-Gebürgen, betreffend deren Entstehung, Lage, darinnen befindliche Metallen, Mineralien und Foßilien* (Berlin 1756). In 1759, a French version of Lehmann's work was published in Paris (at Jean-Thomas Hérissant), entitled *L'art des mines ou introduction aux connoissances nécessaires pour l'exploitation des mines métalliques*. The third volume, translated by d'Holbach and entitled *Traités de physique, d'histoire naturelle, de minéralogie et de métallurgie* contains a translation of *Versuch einer Geschichte von Flötz-Gebürgen*.

20 Fray Juan de Torquemada, c. 1557–1624, not to be confused with the cardinal and uncle of the inquisitor Tómas de Torquemada of the same name, who lived in the fifteenth century. "C'étoient, si l'on en croit Herrera & Torquemada, les peuples qui occupoient les meilleures plaines de la

contrée avant l'arrivée des Mexicains" (Raynal 2018, 60). (If we give credit to Herrera and Torquemada, these were the people who occupied the best parts of the country before the arrival of the Mexicans) (Raynal 1783, 3:319).

21 "The introduction of small-pox, increased the depopulation, which was still augmented soon after by the epidemic diseases of 1545 and 1576, the first deprived the empire of eight hundred thousand inhabitants, and the second, of two millions, if we chuse [*sic*] to adopt the calculations of the credulous and exaggerating Torquemada" (Raynal 1783, 3:366–7).

22 Raynal 1770, 3:59–60 and 1774, 3:95: "La nature de la cochenille, sans laquelle on ne pourroit faire ni pourpre ni écarlate, & qui ne se trouve que dans le Mexique, a été long-tems inconnue même aux nations qui en faisoient le plus d'usage. Les Espagnols naturellement réservés, & qui deviennent mystérieux, quand il s'agit de leur colonies, garderent un secret que tout leur faisoit croire important." (The nature of the cochenille, without which it would not be possible to make either purple nor scarlet and which is found only in Mexico, has long been unknown even to the nations that used it most. The Spaniards, who are naturally reserved, and who become mysterious when it comes to their colonies, kept a secret that everything made them believe important.)

23 "I had asserted, from the testimony even of the best writers, that the nature of this colour was not know'n [*sic*] before the beginning of this century. Upon searching into the originals, I find, that Acosta, in 1530, and Herrera, in 1601, had described it, as well as our modern naturalists. I therefore retract, and wish I could have an opportunity of doing the same with regard to many other things I have written of the Spaniards" (Raynal 1783, 3:349).

24 The article on cochineal may be found in Acosta 1590, 254–5.

25 Réaumur, *Mémoires pour servir à l'histoire des insectes*, 1734–42, 6 vols. in-4°. Nicolas Joseph Thiéry de Ménonville (1739–1780), author of *Traité de la culture du nopal, et de l'éducation de la cochenille dans les colonies françaises de l'Amérique; Précédé d'un Voyage a Guaxaca*, stole some Mexican cochineals in order to open a plantation in St. Domingo. It seems that Jussieu also consulted Melchior De Ruusscher's *Histoire naturelle de la cochenille* (1729) as well as Hartsoeker's *Essai de dioptrique*, Paris 1694, in-4° (see Courtney 1963, 220).

26 "[A] quite good translation at the time."

27 "[N]ôtre Auteur […] s'est arrêté précisément à la Conquête du Mexique; craignant sans doute que la suite de cette Conquête ne l'engageât dans un fâcheux démêlé, entre le respect qu'on doit à la vérité, & l'inclination qu'il avoit pour son Heros. Il sçavoit que la prise de Mexique eut quelques

circonstances peu favorables à la gloire de Cortez, dont il ne vouloit point ternir le lustre" (Solís 1691, n.p.) (our author [...] has stopped precisely at the conquest of Mexico, fearing that the continuation of this conquest might lead him into an unfortunate conflict between the respect due to the truth and the inclination he had for his hero. He knew that the capture of Mexico City had some circumstances unfavourable to the glory of Cortés, whose lustre he did not want to tarnish.)

28 "That's why we felt obliged to report briefly and to inform the reader at the same time on the rest of this conqueror's life."

29 "This dangerous passion pushed them to commit horrible cruelties, for which writers of their own nation have reproached them. Cortés was not exempt from that, at least he showed a weak indulgence for Julian of Alderete, the treasurer that almost all historians make responsible for having put Guatimozin and one of his favourites onto burning coals, in order to force them to reveal Motezuma's hidden treasures. It was on this occasion that the prince heard a scream that the pain made his favourite let out, and that he told him, looking proudly at him: 'And me? Am I on a bed of roses?' This remark made the Indian show respect until he died of the dreadful torment, without complaining anymore."

30 "The Prince, environed round with hot burning coales, being ouercome with the exceeding torment, at last in most pittious sort turning his dreary eyes toward his Master, as if hee asked mercy of him for he could endure no longer; The king fixing rigorously and fiercely his lookes upon him, seeming to upbraide him with his remisnesse and pusilanimity, with a sterne and setled voyce uttered these few wordes unto him; *What? Supposest thou I am in a colde bath? am I at more ease then thou art?*" (Montaigne 1613, 514).

31 See Greilich 2013.

32 "They had no law that limited the number of their wives. It was common for one of them to have some privileges and distinctions allotted to her; but these gave her no authority over the rest. She was the one whom the husband loved the best, and by whom he thought himself best beloved. On the death of her husband, she sometimes caused herself to be buried in the same grave with him" (Raynal 1783, 3:256).

33 "[T]he one whom he loved the best, shut herself away [in the grave] with him and died there."

34 "When a chief died [...], of all his wives, the one that wanted to show that she had loved him best shut herself away [in the grave] with him and died there, and sometimes two of them did so."

35 "This was not a custom, a duty, or a point of honor, among these people; but the wife found it impossible to survive the object of her tenderest

affection" (Raynal 1783, 3:256–7). Raynal's contemporaries are less sympathetic to the subject. De Pauw, in his *Recherches philosophiques sur les Américains*, compares the Haitian custom to the Indian sati, emphasizing that in most cases the widows were forced to sacrifice themselves, either by law, by the influence of priests, or by use of intoxicants (see De Pauw 1771, 2:183f: "De quelques usages bizarres, communs aux deux continents" [On strange habits, common to both continents] (my translation). Prévost (1754, 221) is also much more reluctant than Raynal, though he assures, as does Charlevoix (1733, 1:59–60), that self-sacrifices "étoient rares et volontaires" (were rare and willing).

36 "The translator has answered them, in many of his prefaces, that he voluntarily differed from the English text, because he found the changes necessary, for reasons of truth, order, honesty, or religion."

37 Juan Nuix y Perpiña, *Riflessioni sopra l'umanità degli Spagnuoli nell'Indie contro i pretesi filosofi e politici, per servire di lume alle storie dei signori Raynal e Robertson* (Venice 1780) (Spanish translation: *Reflexiones imparciales sobra la humanidad de los españoles en las Indias contra los pretendidos filósofos y políticos. Para ilustrar las historias de MM. Raynal y Robertson. Escritas en italiano por el abate Don Juan Nuix y traducidas con algunas notas por Don Pedro Varela y Ulloa, del Consejo de S.M. su Secretario* [Madrid 1782; Cervera 1783]); Juan de Escoiquiz, *Mexico conquistada. Poema heroico* (Madrid 1797), 3 vols.

Bibliography

Acosta, José de. 1590. *Historia natural y moral de las Indias*. Sevilla: Juan de Leon.

– 1598. *Histoire naturelle et morale des Indes tant Orientalles qu'Occidentalles, composée en Castillan par Ioseph Acosta, & traduite en François par Robert Regnault Cauxois*. In-8°. Paris: Chez Marc Orry,.

Charlevoix, Pierre-François-Xavier de. 1733. *L'histoire de l'Ile espagnole ou de St. Domingue. Écrite particulièrement sur des mémoires manuscrits du P. Jean-Baptiste Le Pers* [...]. 2 vol. in-4°. Amsterdam: Honoré.

Courtney, Cecil Patrick. 1963. "Antoine-Laurent de Jussieu collaborateur de l'abbé Raynal. Documents inédits." *Revue d'histoire littéraire de la France* 63: 217–27.

De Pauw, Cornelius. 1771–4. *Recherches philosophiques sur les Américains, ou mémoires intéressantes pour servir à l'histoire de l'espèce humaine*. London, 3 vols. including the *Défense des Recherches philosophiques*. (Other edition: Berlin: Decker, 1768–9, 2 vols. in-8°.)

Duchet, Michèle. 1978. *Diderot et L'Histoire des deux Indes ou l'écriture fragmentaire*. Paris: Nizet.

Encyclopédie méthodique ou par ordres de matières. 1782–1832. 166 vols. in-4°. Paris: Panckoucke et al.

Encyclopédie ou dictionnaire raisonné des sciences, des arts et des métiers. 1751–77. Paris, 17 vols. and 11 vols. of plates in-fol. (1751–71); supplements: 1776–7.

Garcilaso Inca de la Vega. 1609. *Comentarios reales.* Lisboa.

– 1617. *Comentarios reales,* part 2: *Historia del Perú.* Córdoba.

– 1633. *Le commentaire royal, ou l'Histoire des Yncas, rois du Péru* [...] escritte en langue péruvienne par l'Ynca Garcilasso de la Vega [...] et fidellement traduitte sur la version espagnolle par J. Baudoin. Paris: A. Courbé.

Gemelli Careri, Giovanni Francesco. 1699–1700. *Giro del Mondo.* 6 vols.

– 1719. *Voyage du tour du monde, traduit de l'Iitalien De Gemelli Careri Par M. L. N.* [i.e., Louis Francois DuBois de Saint-Gelais]. Paris: Ganeau. (Also: Paris 1727 as "Nouvelle Edition augmentée sur la derniere de l'Italien, & enrichie de nouvelles Figures.")

Goggi, Gianluigi. 1991. "Quelques remarques sur la collaboration de Diderot à la première édition de l'*Histoire des deux Indes.*" In *Lectures de Raynal: L'"Histoire des deux Indes" en Europe et en Amérique au XVIIIe siècle. Actes du Colloque de Wolfenbüttel, SVEC* 286, edited by Hans-Jürgen Lüsebrink and Manfred Tietz, 17–52. Oxford: Voltaire Foundation.

Greilich, Susanne. 2013. "'L'entrevue des deux mondes' – Vertextungen des indianischen und spanischen Anderen in Buch 6 und 7 der *Histoire des deux Indes* Guillaume-Thomas Raynals." In *"Das Andere Schreiben" – Diskursivierungen von Alterität in Texten der Romania (16.–19. Jahrhundert),* edited by Susanne Greilich and Karen Struve, 87–102. Würzburg: Königshausen & Neumann.

Herrera [y Tordesillas], Antonio de. 1601–15. *Historia de los Hechos de los castellanos en las islas i tierra firme del mar océano [Décadas].* Madrid: n.p.

– 1660–71. *Histoire géneralle des voyages* [...] *dans les isles* [...] *des Indes occidentales, trad. de l'Espagnol D'Antoine d'Herrera ... Par N[icolas] de la Coste.* Paris: Chez Nicolas & Iean de la Coste.

– 1934. *Historia general de los hechos castellanos en las islas y tierrafirme del mar océano.* Edited by Academía de la Historia. Madrid: n.p.

López de Gómara, Francisco. 1552. *Historia general de las Indias y Conquista de México y de la Nueva España.* Saragossa (also: Anvers: Nucio 1554): n.p.

– 1584. *Histoire génералle des Indes occidentales et terres neuves qui jusques à présent ont esté descouvertes, augmentée en ceste 5e édition de la description de la Nouvelle Espagne et de la grande ville de Mexicque autrement nommée Tenuctilan, composée en espagnol par François López de Gómara et traduite en français par le S. de Genille, Mart[in] Fumée,* 5th ed. Paris: M. Sonnius, in-8°. (1st ed.: Paris 1569, but without the description of Tenochtitlan; also: Paris/Basle 1587; 1606 in its 6th ed.)

Lüsebrink, Hans-Jürgen. 1984. "'Le livre qui fait naître des Brutus …' Zur
Verhüllung und sukzessiven Aufdeckung der Autorschaft Diderots an
der *Histoire des deux Indes*." In *Denis Diderot 1713–1784. Zeit, Werk, Wirkung.
Zehn Beiträge*, edited by Titus Heydenreich, 107–26. Erlangen: Univ. Bund
Erlangen-Nürnberg.
– 2003. "La critique de la colonisation espagnole dans l'*Histoire des deux Indes
– discours, enjeux, intertexte.*" In *Studies on Voltaire and the Eighteenth Century* 7:
203–13.
Marmontel, Jean-François. 1777. *Les Incas, ou La destruction de l'empire du Pérou*.
Berne/Lausanne: chez la Société typographique.
Montaigne, Michel de. 1613. *Essays vvritten by Michael Lord of Montaigne* [...]
done into English, according to the last French edition, by Iohn Florio [...]. N.p.:
n.p.
– 2007. *Les Essais*. Edited by J. Balsamo, M. Magnien, and C. Magnien-Simonin.
Paris: Gallimard (Bibliothèque de la Pléiade).
Prévost d'Exiles, Antoine-François, ed. 1754. *Histoire générale des voyages, ou
nouvelle collection de toutes les relations de voyages par mer et par terre, qui ont été
publiées jusqu'à présent dans les différentes langues de toutes les nations connues*. Vol.
12. Paris: Didot.
– 1761. Suite *de l'Histoire générale des voiages, ou nouvelle collection de toutes les
relations de voiages par mer et par terre … contenant les restitutions & les additions
de l'édition de Hollande pour servir de supplement à l'édition de Paris*. Vol. 17.
Amsterdam: Arkstée et Merkus.
Pufendorf, Samuel, and Bruzen de la Martinière. 1759. *Introduction à l'histoire
moderne, générale et politique de l'Univers, commencée par le baron de Pufendorf,
augmentée et continuée jusqu'en mil sept cent cinquante par M. De Grâce*. Vol. 8.
Paris: n.p.
Raynal, Guillaume-Thomas. 1770. *Histoire philosophique et politique des
établissements et du commerce des Européens dans les deux Indes*. 6 vols. in-8°.
Amsterdam: n.p.
– 1774. *Histoire philosophique et politique des établissements et du commerce des
Européens dans les deux Indes*. 7 vols. in-8°. La Haye: Gosse fils.
– 1780. *Histoire philosophique et politique des établissements et du commerce des
Européens dans les deux Indes*. 4 vols. and atlas in-4°. Genève: Pellet.
– 1783. *A Philosophical and Political History of the Settlements and Trade of the
Europeans in the East and West Indies*. 8 vols. London: printed for W. Strahan;
and T. Cadell.
– 2018. *Histoire philosophique et politique des établissements et du commerce des
Européens dans les deux Indes*. Vol. 2, edited by A. Brown and H.-J. Lüsebrink.
Ferney-Voltaire: Centre International d'Étude du XVIIIe siècle.

Rousseau, Jean-Jacques. 1966. *Œuvres complètes.* Vol. 3, edited by B. Gagnebien and M. Raymond. Paris: Gallimard (Bibliothèque de la Pléiade).

Solís [y Rivadeneyra], Antonio de. 1685. *Historia de la conquista de México, población y progresos de la América septentrional, conocida con el nombre de Nueva España.* Madrid: n.p.

— 1691. *Histoire de la conquête du Mexique ou de la Nouvelle Espagne par Fernando Cortez. Traduite de l'Espagnol de Don Antoine de Solis, par l'Auteur du Triumvirat* [Samuel de Broë, seigneur de Citry et de La Guette]. Paris: chez Maurice Villery. (Also: La Haye: chez Adrian Moetjens, 1692; 6th ed. Paris: Compagnie des Libraires, 1759, 2 vols. in-12°.)

Tietz, Manfred. 1983. "Amerika vor der spanischen Öffentlichkeit des 18. Jahrhunderts: zwei Repliken auf de Pauw und Raynal: die 'Reflexiones imparciales' von Juan Nuix y Perpiña und die 'México conquistada' von Juan Escoiquiz." In *Lateinamerika-Studien* 13(2): 989–1016.

— 1991. "L'Espagne et l'*Histoire des deux Indes* de l'abbé Raynal." In *Lectures de Raynal: L'"Histoire des deux Indes" en Europe et en Amérique au XVIIIe siècle. Actes du Colloque de Wolfenbüttel, SVEC* 286, edited by Hans-Jürgen Lüsebrink and Manfred Tietz, 99–130. Oxford: Voltaire Foundation.

Torquemada, Juan de. 1613–15. *Primera (-tercera) parte de los veinte i un libros rituales i Monarchía indiana, distribuidos en tres tomos, compuesto por F. Juan de Torquemada.* Sevilla: M. Clavijo (new ed.: Madrid 1723, no French translations).

Ulloa, Antoine de. 1752. *Voyage historique de l'Amérique méridionale fait* [...] *par Don George Juan* [...] *et Don Antoine de Ulloa* [...] *qui contient une histoire des Yncas du Pérou* [...]. 2 vols. in-4°. Paris: Chez Charles-Antoine Jombert.

Voltaire. 1962. *Essai sur les mœurs et l'esprit des nations.* Edited by Jacqueline Marchand. Paris: Éditions Sociales.

Wolpe, Hans. 1957. *Raynal et sa machine de guerre. L'"Histoire des deux Indes" et ses perfectionnements.* Stanford/Paris: n.p.

Zárate, Agustin de. 1555. *Historia del descubrimiento y conquista del Perú, con las cosas naturales que señaladamente allí se hallan, y los sucessos que ha avido.* Anvers (also: Sevilla 1577).

— 1700. *Histoire de la découverte et de la conquête du Pérou,* traduite de l'Espagnol D'Augustin De Zarate, Par S. D. C. [i.e., Samuel de Broë, seigneur de Citry et de La Guette]. 2 vols. in-12°. Amsterdam: Lorme. (Other editions: Amsterdam [2]1717; Paris: chez M. Clousier, 1706, 2 vols. in-12; Paris: Compagnie des Libraires, 1716, 1742, 1774, 2 vols. in-8°.)

chapter eleven

Encyclopedic Writing

ULRICH JOHANNES SCHNEIDER

When the second edition of the *Encyclopaedia Britannica* came out in 1777 it differed from the first edition of 1768 in content as well as form. There were ten quarto volumes instead of three, and there was less discrepancy between longer and shorter articles. While the first edition featured thirty essay-long articles, which in the case of "Medicine" ran to a staggering 111 pages, the second edition dispensed with general essays altogether.[1] The system of cross-references was modified accordingly. Individual species of plants within "Botany" or of animals within "Zoology" were dealt with in separate articles, rather than in their respective general essays. In the second edition, cross-references became more precise and hence more helpful. Differences in article length did not disappear altogether, yet essay-long texts had already vanished from the *Encyclopaedia Britannica* in the eighteenth century, never to resurface in encyclopedic writing again.

The thesis I want to put forward in the following is this: modern encyclopedic writing was first practised in the eighteenth century, and its main feature was the careful editing of information that was already extant. (I hold this to be basically true today as well. One of the recurrent problems of articles contributed to Wikipedia is excessive length.) Encyclopedic writing is not so much about new knowledge, but about how to best circulate available knowledge of recent discoveries, technological innovations, and historical information of all kinds. Encyclopedic writing is about editing text into a condensed format. Hence the design and the inner structure of an article are major concerns for authors and editors. How can one select information from different sources in an effective way? Should there be guidelines for vetting sources? The requirements for rewriting extant bits of information to make them fit into the format of an article are manifold.

An encyclopedic article provides knowledge and structure, with regard to both content and form. In addition, it is important for any encyclopedic enterprise to reach a large readership. Since the eighteenth century (when general encyclopedias started to cater to ever-larger audiences) publishers have aimed to conquer a market beyond the one that existed for books of specialized genres of knowledge designed for the initiated. But how does one successfully cater to a public with different interests and reading habits? On the one hand, authors, editors, and publishers producing encyclopedias are obliged to provide correct information. On the other hand, they have to present information that is accessible to a general audience. This means that they do not have a very clear picture of who their readers really are, and therefore have a difficult time writing to a specific audience. The editors of many failed encyclopedias testify to the challenge of marketing (I believe this continues true today). Producing an encyclopedia means anticipating the reader in the very mode employed in the writing of articles.

The example of the first editions of the oldest and longest-running encyclopedia to date, the *Encyclopaedia Britannica*, allows us to encounter and problematize encyclopedic writing: it is all about getting it right in view of the reader. Being truthful and reliable are important virtues of encyclopedic writing, but so are being brief and understandable. Diderot once observed that a degree of humour cannot be avoided when an article on theology is followed by one on technology.[2] This is no less true than d'Alembert's remark about alphabetical order essentially being no order at all.[3] When the eminent French philosophers compare encyclopedic writing with philosophical and scientific writing, the deficiencies are obvious. Yet their comparison does not address the main concern of general encyclopedias, which is communicating knowledge to the public at large. Encyclopedias aim at being relevant to their readers. The huge commercial and intellectual success of general encyclopedias since the eighteenth century[4] shows that readers cherish these books, and that authors and editors have found ways to satisfy the curiosity of the wider public.

There is a date we can put on the emergence of encyclopedic writing, and that is the year 1732 when the German *Universal-Lexicon* (Universal dictionary) started to appear. By the end, in 1754, it comprised sixty-eight folio volumes with text four times the length of the French *Encyclopédie*, whose first volume was published in 1751 just when the Leipzig publisher had come to the end of the alphabet. In terms of quantity its approximately 284,000 articles compare to about 71,000 articles organized by

Diderot. It is by far the largest encyclopedia of the eighteenth century, and for that matter, the first one of its kind. However, the sheer size of the *Universal-Lexicon* has proven to be an obstacle to detailed studies. There is no archive left, and we know neither the names of the contributors (of whom there must have been at least two hundred) nor the subscribers (recruited by the publisher in order to start his monumental enterprise in 1732).

In what is truly the first general encyclopedia we find modern features like anonymous editing and subscription funding. For the first time different kinds of information (scientific, technical, medical, as well as biographical and geographical) are gathered into one work rather than being treated separately. Moreover, the *Universal-Lexicon* tried to adopt the perspective of its readers through rather unusual means, not only in the very way that articles were defined and written but also by soliciting texts from its readership. The *Universal-Lexicon* is a model of encyclopedic writing even where it fails to meet standards of excellence. It is a true forerunner of the "conversational dictionaries" (*Konversationslexika*) that dominated the genre of general encyclopedias from the nineteenth century onwards.

There is no other encyclopedia prior to the *Universal-Lexicon* that unites all sorts of knowledge to create a truly "general," all-encompassing dictionary (*vollstaendig* is the German word used on the title page). Successful contemporary encyclopedias like Chambers's *Cyclopaedia* (first published in 1728, then re-edited and translated)[5] or Diderot's *Encyclopédie* (from 1751) aimed at scientific and technical knowledge, but steered away from information concerning the political, historical, and biographical spheres. Chambers just ignored biography and geography, while Diderot explicitly excluded biography and tried to limit the number of geographical articles.[6] For the vast area of non-scientific and non-technological knowledge there was the very successful dictionary of Louis Moréri. His *Dictionnaire historique* (first published in one volume in 1674) was republished and enlarged many times all over Europe, until a final edition in ten folio volumes appeared in 1759.

Like Moréri's dictionary, the *Universal-Lexicon* included biographical entries: more than 120,000 of them. It is by far the largest biographical dictionary of the eighteenth century, as many *dix-huitiémistes* know. The *Universal-Lexicon* also attempted to include much of the known world in more than 72,000 articles about continents, countries, towns, and villages. Many of those articles were innovative, surpassing their sources in form and content, articulating what seems today a modern worldview, where everything is put into perspective – Germanocentric for better or for worse in the case of the *Universal-Lexicon.*

The remainder of this chapter summarizes the findings of ten years of investigation into the *Universal-Lexicon.*[7] There are three sections. The first explains the unique concern that the makers of the *Universal-Lexicon* exhibited towards their readers. In the second section, a sample of geographical entries highlights the inevitable conflict between serving a regionally defined audience and communicating knowledge about other cultures. In conclusion, a third section presents some thoughts on the cultural effects of encyclopedic writing.

The Reader Within

When the publisher Johann Heinrich Zedler announced in 1730 that he was going to produce an eight-volume encyclopedia, he provoked outrage among many of the established Leipzig publishers who specialized in subject encyclopedias. Zedler was then twenty-four years old, but he had already produced a multivolume edition of Luther and to all appearances was undaunted by the task he had given himself.[8] Other publishers in Leipzig feared he would simply copy their books. They forced him to withdraw from the 1731 Leipzig book fair where he was to present the first volume of the *Universal-Lexicon.* In 1732 Zedler was back again, printing (so he said) in neighboring Halle (which was Prussian), thus circumventing the Leipzig restrictions (which belonged to Saxony). In 1738 he was broke; his *Universal-Lexicon* had to be saved by a merchant who miraculously provided for its almost unaltered continuation, picking up from the letter "L" in volume 19. The reasons for his financial difficulties are unknown. Most likely some subscribers were discouraged by the cost of two Reichstaler a volume, since the encyclopedia was obviously becoming much more compendious than the eight volumes originally announced. Little did they know that it would only reach the end of the alphabet with volume 64 in 1750 (four supplement volumes would follow by 1754).

During his time of crisis in 1738, Zedler hired a new editor-in-chief, Carl Günther Ludovici, then a renowned philosophy professor at Leipzig University. Ludovici was the author of books on the German philosophers Gottfried Wilhelm Leibniz and Christian Wolff. He stopped writing on philosophical matters after taking on this new job. Ludovici made some crucial changes to the *Universal-Lexicon;* one of them was opening up the dictionary to articles on living people. This was unheard of

for an encyclopedia. When Christian Gottlieb Jöcher, also a professor
at Leipzig University, published his four-volume dictionary of scholars
(*Allgemeines Gelehrtenlexikon*) in 1750–51 he stuck to dead people, trying
only to include the most recently deceased among his roughly sixty thousand entries.[9]

Judging by later publications from the second half of the eighteenth
century, the task of covering contemporaries was taken over by more jour-
nalistically oriented publications. The best known in Germany is Johann
Georg Meusel's *Gelehrtes Teutschland,* a review-like publication with regular
updates, starting in 1774 and running well into the nineteenth century.[10]
Meusel made it his exclusive concern to track academic careers. In some
ways, the *Universal-Lexicon* anticipated this in its attempt to represent as
many "well-known" people as possible. What editor-in-chief Ludovici and
publisher Zedler had in mind when including contemporaries in their
encyclopedia was made clear in the prefaces to volumes 19, 21, and 23.
They encouraged readers to provide information on individual or family
biographies, societies, or town histories, for the purpose of bringing the
dictionary increasingly up to date. Whether this invitation worked, we do
not know for sure. Little research has been done so far on the more than
120,000 biographical articles in the *Universal-Lexicon,* but two of them
were clearly provided by readers.

There is the article on a family named "Marschall" (vol. 19, cols.
1702–15), of Scottish descent, and held in high regard by the Prussian
king. The article not only includes text but reproduces documents like
a Latin "patent" and letters of recommendation by Prussian noblemen
and archivists. Also reprinted is a declaration by Friedrich Wilhelm I. of
Prussia, dated 11 August 1736. It looks as if the article was designed to
argue the case of the Marschalls in some unnamed dispute. Then there is
an article on an individual, *Reichsgraf* "Schmettau, Samuel" (vol. 35, cols.
347–61), which is obviously a self-advertising piece of text. The "diploma"
that made Schmettau a count is reproduced verbatim, followed by a list
of gifts given by the German emperor to Schmettau, who had won twenty-
eight battles and endured thirty-two sieges in his service. Schmettau went
on to become curator at the Berlin Academy of Sciences, but this happened after the publication of his biographical article in the *Universal-
Lexicon.* Both articles, the one on the Marschall family and the one on
Schmettau, appear to be departures from the other biographical articles,
if only by virtue of their subjective style and transparent self-interest.

There may be other cases where texts were handed over to the editor
and published without much – if any – revision, but the search for them

has only begun. A tendency to please the noble world, which may be inferred from the two examples given, is also reflected in the fact that at the beginning of each volume, by way of a dedication, a noble person was portrayed and addressed in a poem. There are altogether sixty "sponsors" placed within the *Universal-Lexicon* in this way, among them kings and tsars but mostly members of the German imperial nobility. Being involved with the nobility as a major support group of his dictionary was a specific aim of the publisher, as is plainly stated in the entry "Zedler, Johann Heinrich" in the *Universal-Lexicon* itself (vol. 61, cols. 309–11). The whole process of producing the *Universal-Lexicon* may be seen as an attempt to foster relations between the publisher, the editors, the authors, and the public at large in a new way. Other elements of this endeavour are the – then rather innovative – subscription run before the start of the *Universal-Lexicon*, the strategic system of dedications, the policy of seeking out the readers as contributors, and the prefaces in which the publisher professed his devotion to his audience.

When looking for articles that may actually have been provided by readers we must also consider texts on societies and on towns. There is an entry about the small town of "Wurzen" (near Leipzig; vol. 60, cols. 259–487) that was probably written by a local historian, since it is rather long and detailed.[11] The unknown author of this text sometimes talks about "our town," which may indicate a writer outside of the *Universal-Lexicon*. It may also just be a formulation left over from an original source by some careless editor.

In view of the scarce evidence assembled so far, it may be said that the editor and the publisher of the *Universal-Lexicon* risked including biased and poorly written articles when inviting their readers to contribute. Yet they clearly hoped to be close to their readers and to establish a rapport with them in the interest of making the *Universal-Lexicon* a mirror of contemporary society, even at the cost of substandard writing of uneven quality.

Overall, the *Universal-Lexicon* provides for a very mixed reading experience. But there are quite a few articles, especially biographical ones, that were well researched and compiled with constant reference to a great variety of sources. If we take biographical articles at random, for instance all 101 entries on persons named "Wagner,"[12] we can easily see what the *Universal-Lexicon*'s policy of information construction amounted to beyond cases that simply consisted of the copying of source material. Indeed, some eighty-nine different printed sources were used for compiling information about the Wagners in the *Universal-Lexicon*. When we examine the entries more closely, it turns out that half of them reported on people who were still alive, for these articles are rather brief and mention no date of death. Instead they cite a recent publication or some new career change. One may ask what the value of this kind of incomplete information was, especially when considering the laborious preparatory work involved. Did the encyclopedia want to say "these are the people living among us who are worthy of being included in this very book"? At any rate, it is clear that the *Universal-Lexicon* strove to be a book both written by and for its readers.

This pertains not only to form, but also to content. There is additional evidence of a strong inclination towards the reader in some of the medical entries. They clearly show that sharing the reader's perspective was indeed the intents of the *Universal-Lexicon.* While contemporary professional encyclopedias like Robert James's *Medicinal Dictionary,*[13] in both its original English and its French translation, served the medical community and indulged in technical terms, the *Universal-Lexicon* displays a decidedly pragmatic approach. Much like the French *Encyclopédie,* the *Universal-Lexicon* rewrites received medical knowledge from the patient's point of view. So "bloodletting" (Aderlass) is addressed foremost as a kind of general cure to fortify the body, and cutting an artery is recognized as part of a therapy. (In James's professional view, the prime definition of cutting an artery was that of the surgeon's error – only later did he mention its therapeutic use.)[14] For eighteenth-century patients, bloodletting was a well-known and widely practised cure that for the most part was still performed according to symbolic readings of the human body. Certain illnesses required the cutting of blood vessels at certain points on the body and not others. However, after the discovery of blood circulation, bloodletting could be explained in an enlightened way, for it had become clear that doctors could extract blood from anywhere on the body.

As a result, the French *Encyclopédie* tells its readers that they should listen to the doctors and trust their judgment. It was important for doctors and intellectuals to point out that the medieval art of bloodletting – cutting according to the illness – was nonsense. It actually made no difference if nose, arm, hand, or foot were chosen. The *Encyclopédie* relates precisely this information, an example of enlightenment at its best, adding practical value to new insights.

The *Universal-Lexicon* took the same tack as the French *Encyclopédie* by explaining modern medical knowledge to its readers. Yet it goes one step further: since in medical terms it does not really matter where a blood vessel is cut, the doctor is free to follow the patient's wish for a specific place on the body: "In order to please the common man" (dem gemeinen Mann zu gefallen), the doctor should recognize that doctor-patient collaboration is therapeutic, however badly informed the choice may be.[15] This is enlightenment in the second degree, or of a pragmatic kind, not sticking to truth at all costs but insisting on helpful applications.

The almost seventeen thousand medical articles in the *Universal-Lexicon* have not yet been studied in detail, and thus there is no way to tell if the linking of readers and patients is a consistent feature of medical article writing throughout the dictionary. Some indications point to a certain emphasis on instructiveness. First, a great number of pharmaceutical recipes that could be prepared without much training (mostly plasters and ointments) have been included. Additionally, there is a persistent concern to conclude non-medical articles on plants, animals, and minerals with a recipe, most of which seem to include medical applications, while others include culinary recipies, with some articles containing both. And last but not least, the chance discovery of the likely author of many medical articles in the *Universal-Lexicon* supports the hunch that applicability was part of an article's design: in the biographical article "Heinrich Winkler," Winkler is said to have written "most of the medical articles in this very dictionary."[16] Winkler was a town physician in Leipzig for whom being helpful in practical ways was, to use a modern phrase, "part of his job description."

The Reader's View of the World

The *Universal-Lexicon* could only assume such gigantic proportions over the relatively short period of eighteen years' time by relying heavily on other encyclopedias. Four thousand folio pages every year (on average) could not have been filled otherwise; there was most certainly not enough time for much original writing. And indeed, thirty works from other publishers have already been identified as sources for quoted passages, partial copying, or complete adoption in the *Universal-Lexicon*.[17] Among those are foreign encyclopedias like Nicolas Lemery's *Dictionnaire universel des drogues simples*, which appeared in 1721 in a German translation. This work was copied into the *Universal-Lexicon* in its entirety (without proper citations, which happened with other sources as well, but not consistently). With Lemery's text, copying became an art; his text was not just taken over article by article. Talking about the vanilla plant, Lemery, the celebrated French chemist and natural historian, gives botanical information and indicates medical applications. His dictionary was, after all, a work that included plants only in as much as they could be used by pharmacists and doctors. It was a specialized dictionary like many other dictionaries that were copied, one way or another, into the *Universal-Lexicon*: Walther on music, Wolff on mathematics, Hunger on the Bible, Fleming on hunting, and so on. Each covered a single discipline or area of knowledge. In combining these dictionaries, the *Universal-Lexicon* became another kind of work altogether: it became a universal or general encyclopedia, encompassing around seventy-two different areas of knowledge.[18]

Importing printed information was done in many different ways that still have to be studied. It was by no means always done by simply copying entries. The case of Lemery provides an instructive view of what it meant to turn the information from a specialized encyclopedia into an entry for a wider audience. The article "Vanilla" in the *Universal-Lexicon* (vol. 46, cols. 517–19) was copied word for word from the German translation of Lemery's prose, with no changes whatsoever, not even corrections to the two typographical errors. Yet the article was enhanced considerably by additional text inserted at four different places. The first instance gives additional general references, the second adds a travel report from 1702, the third gives specialized references to plant books, and the fourth adds a recipe on how to prepare hot chocolate with vanilla. Where these additional additions of one to five lines are taken from is not known, yet it becomes clear what the editor had in mind: he wanted to turn a specialized article on a plant and its specific usages into a general article dealing with whatever you want to know about a plant like vanilla, including where it was discovered, what it is called in other languages, and what its practical uses are besides its medicinal value.

Encyclopedic writing is different from specialized or disciplinary writing in that it does not cater to experts, but rather to the public at large. An author of an encyclopedic article is an editor of texts already extant but not yet linked to one another. Producing an encyclopedia means writing in the form of rewriting, adjusting the point of view, not the information itself. There are bad and good examples of rewriting in the *Universal-Lexicon*, especially among the articles grouped under "geography." The challenging part of this recasting was not so much related to natural geography (mountains, rivers, landscapes, etc.) but cultural geography, that is, countries, towns, and villages.

There is a rather sloppy article about Spain in the *Universal-Lexicon*, and a rather excellent article on Russia. The text about Spain ("Spanien," vol.

38, cols. 1107–64) relies on one source only, the German translation of a travel report by a French woman. When Madame d'Aulnoy describes Madrid as having, on the particular day of her arrival, rainy weather, and observes that Spanish women she met seemed a little diffident that first night, the article in the *Universal-Lexicon* turns this into general features: the weather in Madrid is often rainy and the women there are noticeably diffident.[19]

Transforming selective observation into national clichés happens quite often in the eighteenth century, though the *Universal-Lexicon* is certainly not the only work at fault. What it says about the peoples of India, China, or Japan is mostly eclectic and dismissive. It seems that the shorter the text, the more of a stereotype it becomes, as if there was little interest in being critical of the sources that had provided these stereotypes. It also seems that the farther away a country was, the shorter its article would be in the *Universal-Lexicon*. But perspective is hardly a mechanical calculation, depending instead on the availability of specific literature. The better the travel reports, the better the article in the *Universal-Lexicon*, as is the case for the entry on Siberia ("Siberien," vol. 37, cols. 852–60). No travel reports were used for the articles on France (vol. 9, cols. 1727–37) or Italy (vol. 14, cols. 1425–30), so they give minimal information on the history, sequence of rulers, geography, and religion.

An example of another high-quality article is the one devoted to Russia ("Russland," vol. 32, cols. 1907–74). Many reports, books, and journals were used for this article, which is intensively researched and clearly written with the aim of balancing the available information. There are a lot of interesting features, starting with the practice of subheadings, which were rarely used in the *Universal-Lexicon*. (Moréri's *Dictionnaire historique* had subheadings articulating the complexity of countries by different categories. In the *Universal-Lexicon* they are found only after Ludovici took over as editor-in-chief in 1738.) The 35-folio-page-long article is composed of twenty-fice subheadings; these include "Frontiers," "Titles," "Customs and Ways of Life," "Forms of Government," "Russian Sea-Power," and "Religion, Sects, and History." Information about Russia is divided into sections organized without any clear logic or consequence other than the structure itself. What is at work here and in other geographical articles is the presentation of cultural and historical knowledge as a kaleidoscope of different subject areas. Probably for the first time in literary history, encyclopedic writing has produced a text on a country that cannot be compared to travel reports, commercial handbooks, or historical essays. Whatever the source material, encyclopedic writing transforms it radically into a text for its own specific purpose of drawing a complete and condensed picture for the eyes of its readers.

An article on Russia in a general encyclopedia is a novel thing in the eighteenth century, answering mixed curiosities and unspecific demands for information related to a particular country. The importance of the long and well-structured article on Russia becomes even clearer when compared with the other approximately one hundred articles in the *Universal-Lexicon* referring to something "Russian" or "Moscovite."[20] There seems to have been a conscious choice about what to place in the main article and what to address elsewhere.

The sources for the article on Russia vary greatly. From the many books and reports published on Russia in the first half of the eighteenth century, the *Universal-Lexicon* quotes some directly, like Friedrich Christian Weber's *Das veränderte Rußland*, and others not, like *Die Europäische Fama*, from which text has been taken without acknowledgment.[21] Overall, the text of the *Universal-Lexicon* article can be traced back to a variety of sources that have been reworked into the encyclopedic format. One example is the popular practice of the Russian sauna. Weber talks about this over several pages, whereas the *Universal-Lexicon* has only one paragraph on the topic. The same happens with the description of the river Neva in Petersburg. Selecting and editing information amounts to transforming expert texts into concise and succinct textual pieces for the public at large.

Interestingly enough, in the final part of the article on Russia there is a passage that clearly indicates reader orientation, yet seems to be at odds with the aim of laboriously editing information out of books or reports: a journalistic piece of text. When the article on Russia appeared in 1742, it hastened to include an account of how Elizabeth I came to power as empress in 1741. The letter "E" of the *Universal-Lexicon* was long gone, and even though the article on Russia was only partly concerned with the government, the opportunity to provide the reader with up-to-date information from Petersburg could not be missed. However, what information to provide was unclear or controversial (maybe because it was too fresh), so the *Universal-Lexicon* decided to offer two different versions of the story. Version one says that a council of high-ranking noblemen elected Elizabeth, the daughter of Peter the Great, and begged her to rule the country. Version two says that Elizabeth wanted to become empress and aligned herself with the military to help her make her way into the palace by force. Version two is introduced by the words "Der andere Bericht von dieser merckwürdigen Revolution lautet also" (The other report of this noticeable revolution goes like this), confronting the reader with a description that is incompatible with the other version of the same event. Here encyclopedic writing comes closest to journalistic writing, which indeed was the source for both versions. More importantly, judgment on the chain of events is suspended and handed over to the reader. The *Universal-Lexicon* presents itself as an impartial observer, providing elements of historical facts, but no definitive interpretation.

The article on Russia in the *Universal-Lexicon* was not taken up by other writers on the subject. When, in 1795, Christoph Meiners reviewed sixty-five major texts published on Russia since 1740, he did not mention the *Universal-Lexicon*.[22] Meiners only lists works by authors, not anonymously published texts like encyclopedias. Already in the eighteenth century, it was common for encyclopedic texts to circulate outside of scientific communities and perhaps also outside acknowledged channels of higher education. The aim of informing the reader in a way that is, in the best of cases, critical of sources and pragmatic about using parts of them, is incompatible with the forms of writing and reading established in academia or in schools. Encyclopedic writing provides an end-format for texts, and is not likely to provide the basis for other studies. This is why new editions of encyclopedias require updates, often needing to start afresh with most of their entries. They are also culturally short lived and easily forgotten once they are out of print, since they are then also out of touch with their audience.

The Cultural Effects of Encyclopedic Writing

Considering encyclopedias from the point of view of encyclopedic writing takes them out of the history of ideas, where books are judged by learned intentions expressed by their authors or editors. Seeing encyclopedias as a writing exercise, or rather as an exercise in rewriting, makes them part of a wide range of cultural activities that relate not to individual intentions but to conventions and practices, as well as to the communications of ideas. The French literary historian Jacques Proust, an expert on the *Encyclopédie*, in 1995 suggested undertaking an analysis of encyclopedic writing ("écriture encyclopédique"). Proust names three qualifications for this kind of writing: it is a rewriting ("réécriture") with regard to its sources, it is a dialogue with contemporary authors as well as with the source material it transforms, and it is fragmentary ("écriture fragmentaire") because it recontextualizes pieces of text, thereby changing their meaning.[23] Also in 1995 Georges Benrekassa, commenting on Diderot and the *Encyclopédie*, proposed distinguishing encyclopedic writing ("écriture encyclopédique") from book writing ("écriture livresque"), because an encyclopedia should be seen as an interface, a place where book knowledge and individual knowledge meet.[24]

Encyclopedic writing as a practice is difficult to define, not only because of the ongoing prevalence of the history of ideas and traditional literary criticism, both of which understand text primarily in relation to authorship. The difficulty resides also in a well-established historical prejudice that one could call "Diderot's lenses." Diderot and the group of writers he engaged in producing the widely successful and influential *Encyclopédie* are well-known figureheads of the French enlightenment. What they produced was for a long time seen only through the claims of Diderot, d'Alembert, and others who wanted the *Encyclopédie* to be an instrument of some sort of intellectual avant-garde. Even if this claim is supported by excellent articles, as a whole the *Encyclopédie* was an encyclopedia like many others, reproducing knowledge, editing existing information, and making the perspective of the reader paramount in style and content. A good number of recent studies focusing on the vital contribution of the Chevalier de Jaucourt and closely analysing content by querying its digitized version have shown the *Encyclopédie* to be a very well written encyclopedia, though not a work that radically redefined encyclopedic writing.

Looking back, we may find a short window of opportunity for encyclopedias concentrating on scientific and technical knowledge alone, and that window was probably opened by Chambers in 1728 and closed with the last run of the quarto edition of the *Encyclopédie* in 1778. Before and after, encyclopedias have included geographical and biographical knowledge, and with the *Universal-Lexicon*, this knowledge is amalgamated with the rest. When in 1778 a German enterprise, the *Deutsche Enzyklopädie*, tried to emulate the *Encyclopédie*, it failed, most likely in part because of its exclusion of biographical articles: The last volume (no. 23) appeared in 1807 and ended at the letter "K."

Already in the eighteenth century, going beyond scientific and technological areas of knowledge really meant situating the general encyclopedia within a new genre of writing, one that was part of a cultural dialogue within society. When encyclopedic writing does more than summarize and popularize – as is the case in scientific matters – it is about inventing and editing articles for readers, and envisioning the subject matter from the reader's point of view. Chances are that writing an article about Newton or Newtonianism was never a considerable problem, but there were real challenges in writing about the sixteenth-century Reformation. Moréri's very Catholic articles on Luther and Calvin failed to meet the demands of a European audience and had to be rewritten. Writing about the ongoing Swedish-Russian war or social issues like slavery was also problematic. The *Universal-Lexicon* adopted a critical point of view and included a new article on American massacres in the first supplementary volume (1751; "Amerikanische Massaker," suppl. vol. 1, col. 1337). Thus encyclopedic writing is part of a social process of communication and has to continually be adapted in form and content. (Even today, describing a town or a country proves to be much more controversial than characterizing an invention or reporting a discovery.)

Analysing encyclopedic writing in the form specific to the *Universal-Lexicon* helps us understand the undoubtedly Eurocentric and Germanocentric choices of articles when it comes to towns and villages. Foreign cities are represented less, and even then with shorter texts, than German cities or even Saxon villages: all one hundred of them with over 202 inhabitants are included in the *Universal-Lexicon*. While Moréri's *Dictionnaire historique* (in its 1731 edition) shows a similar concern for extensiveness and detail, there is obviously a different perspective at work: the places readers might be able to travel to themselves get more text than distant cities. In the *Universal-Lexicon*, "Waldheim" near Leipzig has two columns, "Peking" in China three, "Delhi" in India just one.[25] Further research on the cultural biases of geographical articles could help with comparative studies of general encyclopedias and dictionaries of commerce where pragmatism is of the essence. Travelling by imagination is probably closely linked to real travel, as the importance of travel reports for encyclopedic articles also suggests.

In the examination of general encyclopedias, the emphasis should be on the practice of writing, including all aspects of articulating knowledge in a text for the general public: the use of terminology, the insertions of subheadings, the politics of cross-references – all of this constitutes encyclopedic writing. When an article is too long to hold the reader's attention, information is lost. When an article misleads by not representing all relevant points of view, it is equally problematic, not least because the level of complexity is reduced beyond a reasonable level. Even if some encyclopedias became famous for the excellence of some of their articles – this is true for the French *Encyclopédie* in the eighteenth century and for the *Encyclopaedia Britannica* in the late nineteenth century – this is not what they were primarily about or what constituted their success: that success existed independently of the quality of individual articles.

Encyclopedic writing is about a text finding its audience, not about the text as such.

NOTES

1 Frank A. Kafker, 1994, "William Smellie's Edition of the Encyclopaedia Britannica," in *Notable Encyclopaedias of the Late Eighteenth Century: Eleven Successors of the Encyclopédie*, ed. Frank A. Kafker (Oxford: Voltaire Foundation), 151; Jeff Loveland, 2010, *An Alternative Encyclopedia? Dennis de Coetlogon's Universal History of Arts and Sciences (1745)* (Oxford: Voltaire Foundation), 140–5.

2 Denis Diderot, 1755, "Encyclopédie," in *Encyclopédie, ou dictionnaire raisonnée des sciences, des arts et des métiers* (Paris, Neuchâtel: Briasson), 5:642: "L'ordre alphabétique donneroit à tout moment des contrastes burlesques; un article de Théologie se trouveroit relégué tout au-travers des arts méchaniques." (Alphabetic order would constantly cause comical contrasts; a theological article would be plunked down in the middle of the mechanical arts; English translation http://hdl.handle.net/2027/spo.did2222.0000.004).

3 Jean le Rond d'Alembert, 1955, *Discours préliminaire de l'Encyclopédie/ Einleitung zur Enzyklopädie (1751)* (Hamburg: Meiner), 82–3.

4 One may argue that encyclopedias were popular ever since printing began in Europe, although the term "encyclopedia" was absent and the books practising encyclopedic writing were specialized; see U.J. Schneider, ed., 2006, *Seine Welt wissen. Enzyklopädien in der Frühen Neuzeit* (Darmstadt: Primus).

5 Ephraim Chambers, 1728, *Cyclopædia; or An Universal Dictionary of Arts and Sciences* (London: Knapton); further editions with various numbers of volumes were published in 1738, 1740, 1741, and 1751.

6 See Johannes Dörflinger, 1967, *Die Geographie in der "Encyclopédie." Eine wissenschaftsgeschichtliche Studie* (Vienna: Österreichische Akademie der Wissenschaften).

7 Ulrich Johannes Schneider, 2013, *Die Erfindung des allgemeinen Wissens. Enzyklopädisches Schreiben im Zeitalter der Aufklärung* (Berlin: Akademie Verlag).

8 Gerd Quedenbaum, 1977, *Der Verleger und Buchhändler Johann Heinrich Zedler 1706–1751. Ein Buchunternehmer in den Zwängen seiner Zeit. Ein Beitrag zur Geschichte des deutschen Buchhandels im 18. Jahrhundert* (Hildesheim/New York: Olms).

9 Christian Gottlieb Jöcher, 1750–1, *Allgemeines Gelehrten-Lexicon*, 4 vols. (Leipzig: Gleditsch); see *Jöchers 60.000: Ein Mann – eine Mission – ein Lexikon,*

2008, ed. Ulrich Johannes Schneider (exhibition catalogue) (Leipzig: Universitätsbibliothek Leipzig).

10 Johann Georg Meusel, 1774, *Das gelehrte Teutschland, oder Lexikon der jetzt lebende teutschen Schriftsteller* (Lemgo: Meier), followed by many revisions and additions, last edition 1796–1834.

11 "Wurzen" (vol. 60, cols. 259–487) has 226 columns, much more than Leipzig. The author could be the historian Christian Schöttgen, who in 1717 published a history of this town.

12 The 101 articles on persons named "Wagner" are to be found in vol. 52 (1747), cols. 638–89.

13 Robert James, 1743–5, *A medicinal dictionary, including physic, surgery, anatomy, chymistry, and botany*, 3 vols. (London 1743–5); translated into French as *Dictionnaire universel de medecine, de chirurgie, de chymie, de botanique, d'anatomie, De pharmacie, d'histoire naturelle, &c. Précédé d'un Discours Historique sur l'origine & les progres de la Medecine. Traduit de l'Anglois de M. [Robert] James, Par Mrs [Denis] Diderot, [Marc-Antoine] Eidous & [François Vincent] Toussaint. Revue, corrigé & augmenté par M. Julien Busson, Docteur-Régent de la Faculté de Medecine de Paris*, 1746–8, 6 vols. (Paris: Briasson, David, Durand).

14 James 1746: "Phlébotomie" (vol. 5, cols. 508–1026), "Oeil" (vol. 5, col. 23), and "Artériotomie" (vol. 2, cols. 464–8); *Encyclopédie* 1751: "Artériotomie" (vol. 1, 720f.), "Phlébotomie, Aneurysme" (vol. 1, 454–7), "Saignée" (vol. 14 [1765], 501–16); Zedler 1732: "Aderlass, Aderlässe, Blutlassung" (vol. 1, cols. 493–5).

15 Vol. 1, col. 494: "Zuweilen kan man auch wol dem gemeinen Mann zu gefallen und damit sie ihr Vertrauen auf den Aderlass nicht gantz und gar verwerffen, andere nehmen." (At times, to please the common man, and so that they do not totally abandon their faith in bloodletting, one may well take/choose others.) All translations are mine unless otherwise stated.

16 Zedler 1732: "Winckler, Heinrich" (vol. 57, cols. 509–10).

17 Schneider 2013, 81 (table 2).

18 According to the category search on www.zedler-lexikon.de there are seventy-two areas of knowledge. The *Universal-Lexicon* itself lists thirty-three fields or disciplines on its title page. Peter von Ludewig, the Prussian historian prefacing the *Universal-Lexicon*, says in a text advertising it in 1731 that it would replace "22 other dictionaries" (Hallesche Nachrichten 1731, quoted by Quedenbaum 1977, 58); see Schneider 2013, 77–9.

19 See Ulrike Hönsch, 2000, *Von der Schwarzen Legende zum Hesperischen Zaubergarten: Wege des Spanienbildes in Deutschland des 18. Jahrhunderts* (Tübingen: Max Niemeyer).

20 See Schneider 2013, 134–5.

21　Editions of the *Fama* (first publication in 1702) from 1728 through 1732 are used in cols. 1944–59.

22　Christoph Meiners, 1798, *Vergleichung des ältern, und neuern Rußlandes. In Rücksicht auf die natürlichen Beschaffenheiten der Einwohner, ihrer Cultur, Sitten, Lebensart und Gebräuche, so wie auf die Verfassung und Verwaltung des Reichs, nach Anleitung älterer und neuerer Reisebeschreiber* (Leipzig: Fleischer), 1:34–42, esp. 38.

23　Jacques Proust, 1962, *Diderot et l'Encyclopédie* (Paris: Albin Michel), 3rd ed. 1995, xiv (Préface à la troisième édition).

24　Georges Benrekassa, 1995, "De l'*Encyclopédie* aux encyclopédies: Proposer et communiquer un état du savoir," *Recherches sur Diderot et sur l'Encyclopédie* 18–19: 159, 162.

25　Cf. Schneider 2013, 123–6.

Bibliography

Primary Sources

Chambers, Ephraim. 1728. *Cyclopædia; or An Universal dictionary of arts and sciences; containing the Definitions of the Terms; and the Accounts of the Things signisy'd thereby, in the several Arts, both Liberal and Mechanical, and the several Sciences, Human and Divine: the Figures, Kinds, Properties, Productions, Preparations, and Uses, of Things Natural and Artificial, the Rise, Progress, and State of Things Ecclesiastical, Civil, Military and Commercial: with the several Systems, Sects, Opinions, &c. Mong Philosophers, Divines, Mathematicians, Physicians, Antiquaries, Antiquaries, Criticks, &c. 2 vols., in-fol.* London: Knapton

d'Alembert, Jean le Rond. 1955. *Discours préliminaire de l'Encyclopédie/Einleitung zur Enzyklopädie (1751)*. Hamburg: Meiner.

Diderot, Denis, and d'Alembert, Jean le Rond, eds. 1755. *Encyclopédie, ou Dictionnaire raisonné des sciences, des arts et des métiers.* 28 vols. [1751–72]. Paris, Neuchâtel: Briasson.

James, Robert. 1743–5. *A Medicinal Dictionary, including physic, surgery, anatomy, chymistry, and botany.* 3 vols. London 1743–5. Translated into French as *Dictionnaire universel de medecine, de chirurgie, de chymie, de botanique, d'anatomie, de pharmacie, d'histoire naturelle, &c. Précédé d'un Discours Historique sur l'origine & les progres de la Medecine. Traduit de l'Anglois de M. [Robert] James, Par Mrs [Denis] Diderot, [Marc-Antoine] Eidous & [François Vincent] Toussaint. Revue, corrigé & augmenté par M. Julien Busson, Docteur-Régent de la Faculté de Medecine de Paris.* 1746–8. 6 vols. Paris: Briasson, David, Durand.

Jöcher, Christian Gottlieb. 1750–1. *Allgemeines Gelehrten-Lexicon.* 4 vols. Leipzig: Gleditsch

Meiners, Christoph. 1798. *Vergleichung des ältern, und neuern Rußlandes. In Rücksicht auf die natürlichen Beschaffenheiten der Einwohner, ihrer Cultur, Sitten, Lebensart und Gebräuche, so wie auf die Verfassung und Verwaltung des Reichs, nach Anleitung älterer und neuerer Reisebeschreiber.* 2 vols. Leipzig: Fleischer.

Meusel, Johann Georg. 1774. *Das gelehrte Teutschland, oder Lexikon der jetzt lebende teutschen Schriftsteller.* Lemgo: Meier

Zedler, Johann Heinrich. 1731–54. *Grosses vollständiges Universal-Lexicon aller Wissenschafften und Künste, welche bisher durch menschlichen Verstand und Witz erfunden und verbessert werden.* Halle and Leipzig: Zedler.

Secondary Sources

Benrekassa, Georges. 1995. "De l'*Encyclopédie* aux encyclopédies: Proposer et communiquer un état du savoir." *Recherches sur Diderot et sur l'Encyclopédie* 18–19: 157–69.

Dörflinger, Johannes. 1967. *Die Geographie in der "Encyclopédie." Eine wissenschaftsgeschichtliche Studie.* Vienna: Österreichische Akademie der Wissenschaften.

Hönsch, Ulrike. 2000. *Von der Schwarzen Legende zum Hesperischen Zaubergarten. Wege des Spanienbildes in Deutschland des 18. Jahrhunderts.* Tübingen: Max Niemeyer.

Kafker, Frank A. 1994. "William Smellie's Edition of the Encyclopaedia Britannica." In *Notable Encyclopaedias of the Late Eighteenth Century: Eleven Successors of the Encyclopédie,* edited by Frank A. Kafker, 145–82. Oxford: Voltaire Foundation.

Loveland, Jeff. 2010. *An Alternative Encyclopedia? Dennis de Coetlogon's Universal History of Arts and Sciences (1745).* Oxford: Voltaire Foundation.

Proust, Jacques. 1962. *Diderot et l'Encyclopédie.* 3rd ed. 1995. Paris: Albin Michel.

Quedenbaum, Gerd. 1977. *Der Verleger und Buchhändler Johann Heinrich Zedler 1706–1751. Ein Buchunternehmer in den Zwängen seiner Zeit. Ein Beitrag zur Geschichte des deutschen Buchhandels im 18. Jahrhundert.* Hildesheim/New York: Olms.

Schneider, Ulrich Johannes, ed. 2006. *Seine Welt wissen. Enzyklopädien in der Frühen Neuzeit.* Darmstadt: Primus.

– 2013. *Die Erfindung des allgemeinen Wissens. Enzyklopädisches Schreiben im Zeitalter der Aufklärung.* Berlin: Akademie Verlag.

– 2019. "Des transferts savants en format encyclopédique. Le 'Dictionnaire Historique' (1674–1759)." In *Les échanges savants franco-allemands au XVIIIe siècle,* edited by Claire Gantet, Markus Meumann, 119–38. Presses universitaires de Rennes.

chapter twelve

Barbarians in the Archive: Transfer of Knowledge of the Colonial Other in the *Encyclopédie* of Diderot and d'Alembert

KAREN STRUVE

Knowledge of medicine and architecture, of Africa and Asia, of "primitive peoples" and fantastic beings; all these fields of human knowledge are united in the famous *Encyclopédie, ou Dictionnaire raisonné des sciences, des arts et des métiers* (1750–72), edited by Denis Diderot and Jean-Baptiste le Rond d'Alembert. This key work of French (or even European) enlightenment aimed to collect, categorize, and represent the entire span of knowledge, up to and including the eighteenth century. Its intention was to logically and factually unite all fields of knowledge ("l'ordre & l'enchaînement des connoissances humaines" [the order & the connection between human knowledge])[1] in order to become an actual reference book, a *Dictionnaire*, so as to educate and enlighten the public by presenting the amount of knowledge available at that time.

The transfer and transformation of knowledge constitute basic functional mechanisms in Diderot's and d'Alembert's *Encyclopédie*, with translational, intertextual, and discursive transfer elements. The *Encyclopédie* was, first and foremost, a project of transfer in that it began as a literal translation of Chambers's famous *Cyclopaedia* (1728), but it very quickly expanded due to a need to update the evolution of knowledge in the some twenty-five years separating the two works, but also in order to add new knowledge fields now considered pertinent. In addition to its beginnings as a form of translational transfer, it was a project of intertextual transfer, since the implementation and, moreover, the rewriting of external text sources were fundamental to the encyclopedic text. Thus, it can genuinely be considered as an opus that transferred knowledge: from different disciplines (although not completely differentiated at that time) and from different authors. Finally, it was also shaped by a kind of discursive transfer of "foreign but Europeanized" knowledge because information about the colonial world entered the *Encyclopédie* and posed specific challenges to the encyclopedists themselves.

In this article, I focus precisely on this discursive knowledge about the colonial Other in the *Encyclopédie*. I do this on three levels. Following a short overview of conceptions of knowledge in the *Encyclopédie*, I examine first how this knowledge about the colonial Other is categorized and represented, emphasizing the role of the noble savage/*bon sauvage* and his counterpart "the fierce savage," and how they influenced the contemporary European's self-image and the image of the colonial Other. I also investigate the veracity of the encyclopedic texts and use examples of known falsehoods to uncover why the *Encyclopédie* occasionally reports untruths. I then examine whether the colonial Other might be seen not only as a mere addition to our knowledge base, in terms of a unidirectional transfer from colonial peripheries to European epistemological systems, but moreover as a fundamental dimension of the *philosophe*, as for example Walter Mignolo would argue. Finally, I analyse knowledge transfer as poetic transformation by focusing on the narratological, architextual, and intertextual literary strategies to describe the colonial Other. Focusing on this discursive knowledge paves the way to analysing the role of the colonial Other as a powerful transformation of information and poetics.

Knowledge about the Colonial Other Enters the *Encyclopédie*: Transfer of Knowledge as Implementation of Knowledge

Before analysing the encyclopedic knowledge about the colonial Other, one has to consider the composition and concept of the *Encyclopédie* as knowledge collection and systematization by recalling (1) what knowledge meant to Diderot and d'Alembert, (2) what the main claims about it were, and (3) where the producer of knowledge placed himself.

(1) Encyclopedic knowledge or "connaissances humaines" (human knowledge), as Diderot and d'Alembert described it, is in their view both individual and collective, both practical and textual, and both factual and fictional. The *Encyclopédie* is written by experts assembled in an imagined community called "société des gens de lettres" (society of philosophers), essentially a collective project assembling individual expertise. Diderot emphasizes this collective dimension of the project explicitly ("ce ne peut être l'ouvrage d'un seul homme" [this can't be the work of a single

human]) by explaining that a universal project needs the expertise and time of many people.

What is new to the project is it includes not only the scientific findings and insights of academic philosophers from various disciplines (mathematics, music, philosophy, etc.) but also practical knowledge. The practical dimension of the knowledge represented in the *Encyclopédie* comes from the technical "know-how" of architects and craftsmen.[2] This is crucial for the *Encyclopédie* as a key project of French enlightenment: knowledge is not only generated by scientific institutions or academic societies but is defined as both conceptional/abstract and practical/operational. Bitterli emphasizes this interrelation between theoretical and practical knowledge by narrating how the circulation of knowledge took place between autodidacts, academic circles, and amateurs, and even transcended national or social barriers.[3] Beyond the practical, the textuality of knowledge is obvious because, as a written text (except for the *Planches*, which are an important part of the *Encyclopédie* but cannot be taken into account in this chapter), it is textual itself and feeds from textual sources such as scientific surveys, reference books, and other cyclopedias.

The factual and fictional aspects of the contemporary knowledge about the colonial Other come from two different sources. The presence of the colonial world and especially of its peoples is generally emerging from the reports produced by exploration expeditions, such as those of Cook, La Pérouse, and Bougainville to name only a few, and from the new methods of collecting and compiling knowledge (cartography, soil science, the surveying sector, etc.).[4] In addition to these erudite sources, the encyclopedists also use myths, travelogues, letters, and even fictional stories to explain and define their objects. Knowledge is therefore both factual and fictional – an aspect that plays a decisive role in the analysis of the colonial Other.

(2) The main claim of the *Encyclopédie* is universal. It was intended that all the knowledge of that time would be represented in it, providing an all-embracing, truly global dimension. This dimension is both geographical ("de rassembler les connoissances éparses sur la surface de la terre" [to collect knowledge disseminated around the globe; CTPUML])[5] and historical, since it aims at global knowledge of the past, present, and even future ("d'en exposer le système général aux hommes avec qui nous vivons, & de le transmettre aux hommes qui viendront après nous; afin que les travaux des siècles passés n'aient pas été des travaux inutiles pour les siècles qui succéderont" [to set forth its general system to the men with whom we live, and transmit it to those who will come after us, so that

the work of preceding centuries will not become useless to the centuries to come; CTPUML]). This universal basic principle is accompanied by an ethical and, in a certain way, utopic connotation. Diderot explains the aim of the enlightenment as that of wanting to make people more educated, and consequently more virtuous and happier: "que nos neveux, devenant plus instruits, deviennent en même tems plus vertueux & plus heureux, & que nous ne mourions pas sans avoir bien mérité du genre humain" (and so that our offspring, becoming better instructed, will at the same time become more virtuous and happy, and that we should not die without having rendered a service to the human race; CTPUML).

(3) These prospective aims are closely linked to a superior enlightenment self-positioning of the encyclopedist. The "reach" of the *Encyclopédie* is global, and moreover, as d'Alembert puts it in his *Discours préliminaire*, the position of the *philosophe* is a distant and sovereign one. The *philosophe* is situated "au-dessus de ce vaste labyrinthe dans un point de vûe fort élevé d'où il puisse apercevoir à la fois les Sciences & les Arts principaux" [1955, 84, 86] (high above this vast labyrinth, whence he can perceive the principal sciences and the arts simultaneously; CTPUML). He manages to illuminate and to link knowledge fields as if they were visible on a map of the world (see. 1955, 84, 86).

The metaphors of the labyrinth and the world map lead us directly to the question of the colonial Other. Aside from their specific epistemological connotations, these metaphors allude to the question of the interrelation between enlightenment and discovery. Metaphors such as world maps, routes, and travellers can illustrate what Lüsebrink calls the simultaneous "exotischer Faszination und philosophischem Denkimpetus" (exotic fascination and philosophical impetus of thinking)[6] or what postcolonial studies call the powerful discursive strategy of colonial "naming" and "mapping."[7] The projects of collecting and describing all knowledge of that time and of European colonialism did not coincide by accident. The gesture of categorizing, universalizing, and "Europeanizing" in the two is the same. This interrelation between the expansion and seizure of knowledge as one of the main characteristics of the *Encyclopédie* has already been emphasized by Bitterli: expansion, discovery, and conservation were closely linked and all information should be poured into the *Encyclopédie*.[8]

In this regard, the colonial world is – at first sight – a small part of the encyclopedic universe. Accounts of the colonial world and of the colonial Other do not totally pervade Diderot's and d'Alembert's *Encyclopédie*, but they certainly represent a sizeable body of the work overall. Implicit information regarding the colonial world can be found on almost every page. Explicitly, there are more than one thousand references for terms such as "Africa"/"Afrique" (1,287 mentions), "America"/"Amérique" (1,339 mentions), or "India"/"Indes" (1,231 mentions), although only fourteen entries explicitly deal with the African continent.[9]

It is obvious that a corpus like the *Encyclopédie* unites different, if not to say disparate, discourses about the colonial Other. One can find a broad spectrum of representations of colonial alterity and traces of the challenges (or even the provocation)[10] it brought to the European *philosophe*: from the demoniac cannibal to the gentle "bon sauvage" (noble savage). The latter is one pole of the representation of (colonial) alterity in the *Encyclopédie* – even though it may be a marginal one. For the case of the "noble savage," the colonial Other (in the sense of Rousseau's "noble savage/bon sauvage" or "natural man/homme naturel")[11] is known to be the positive foil for the self-image of the European, who is now distorted and criticized as a civilizing, socially self-alienated person. In this regard, it is instructive to consider those entries that are not obviously part of the natural history or geography/"histoire naturelle ou la géographie" of the colonial world but that deal with human attributes, or even those values that French enlightenment and particularly the *Encylopédie* are supposed to defend and promote. The entry "Hospitalité" by de Jaucourt, for example, is clearly written in a Rousseauian manner: the Indians are full of compassion to the extent that they even treat their slaves like themselves ("ce peuple compatissant, qui traitoit les esclaves comme eux-mêmes" [this compassionate people who treated their slaves like themselves; CTPUML]). Their hospitality even extends to installing institutions to accommodate and even bury travellers: "ils allerent jusqu'à établir, & des hospices, & des magistrats particuliers, pour leur fournir les choses nécessaires à la vie, & prendre soin des funérailles de ceux qui mouroi-ent dans leurs pays" (they went so far as to establish hospices and specific magistracies for furnishing travelers with life's necessities and taking care of the funerals of those who died on their land; CTPUML). De Jaucourt defines hospitality as a human virtue performed by nearly all people in the past ("Je viens de prouver suffisamment, qu'autrefois l'hospitalité étoit exercée par presque tous les peuples du monde" [I have sufficiently demonstrated that in earlier times hospitality was exercised by almost all peoples around the world; CTPUML]), which has gotten lost during the processes of so-called civilization.

The other pole of the discourse about colonial alterity is the "fierce savage,'" who plays a much more prominent role in the *Encyclopédie* than his gentle brother the "bon sauvage." In order to analyse the encyclopedic construction of the colonial Other, let us take as a starting point two entries that, at first sight, are not necessarily located in the colonies but in ancient times. The entries "Barbares" and "Sauvages" seem to be basic, both in form and content. In "Barbares," barbarians are described as those at a great distance from the Greeks, who define as barbarian all those who are positioned at the extreme opposite with respect to themselves: "pour marquer l'extrème opposition qui se trouvoit entr'eux & les autres nations" (to distinguish the extreme opposition existant between them and other nations; CTPUML). Barbarians are characterized as uncultivated since they do not participate in the "progrès de l'esprit humain" (progress of the human mind); they lack a certain "politesse" (politesse); they are primitive, still afflicted by a "rudesse des premiers siècles" (harshness of the first centuries), and they do not know the language of the modern Greeks. Representing aspects of a phylogenetic preliminary phase as well as those of savageness and linguistic underdevelopment, the barbarians thus represent the paradigmatically antithetical character of civilization. Consequently, the term "barbarian" is easily transferred from the antithetical figure of the Greeks to one that enables the encyclopedist to describe those who differ from the French and their customs ("tout ce qui s'eloigne de nos usages" [everything that is distant from our own practices; CTPUML]).

This antithesis implies a significant power difference, which can be shown in the pejorative lexis ("rudesse" [harshness]) and by constructions of the Other again *ex negativo* ("ni la politesse des Grecs, ni une langue aussi pure, aussi féconde, aussi harmonieuse que celle de ses peuples" [neither the politesse of the Greeks, nor a language as pure, as fertile, and as harmonious; CTPUML]). The Greeks – and the French of the time – generate themselves as a level of comparison and even more as a standard of civilization. The characteristics of the Other therefore arise from this reciprocal relationship between different peoples.[12] To put it briefly: the European seems to be advanced, modern, civilized, and perhaps also enlightened to such an extent that he himself can generate the colonial Other as his respective antithesis.

The attributes of this ancient figure of the Other are often transferred to the colonial Other. Thus, in "Sauvages," the barbarian characteristics are attributed to the savages, who populate most of America. Rhetorically phrased *ex negativo*, the savages are lawless barbarian people, without religion and homestead: "peuples barbares qui vivent sans loix, sans police, sans religion, & qui n'ont point d'habitation fixe" (barbarous peoples who live without law, without governance [police], without religion, and who have no fixed habitation; CTPUML). They are furthermore apostrophized as fierce cannibals ("Une grande partie de l'Amérique est peuplée de *sauvages*, la plûpart encore féroces, & qui se nourrissent de chair humaine. *Voyez* ANTHROPOPHAGES" [A large part of America is peopled by savages, the majority of whom are still fierce and feed upon human flesh. *See* Cannibals; CTPUML]).

These xenophobic attributes of the barbarian savages – superstition, an incomprehensible language or aphasia, bad character and cannibalism – can be transferred to and used in various articles about the colonial Other. Within America, this transfer is employed, for instance, for the "Eskimaux," to whom are attributed the characteristics of the savages and barbarians but to an extreme degree, as "savages of the savages," not tameable and even inhuman: "Ce sont les sauvages des sauvages, & les seuls de l'Amérique qu'on n'a jamais pû apprivoiser; petits, blancs, gros, & vrais antropophages. On voit chez les autres peuples des manieres humaines, quoiqu'extraordinaires, mais dans ceux-ci tout est féroce & presqu'incroyable" (These are the savages of the savages and the only ones of America that could never be domesticated; small, white, thick, and real cannibals. One can observe human manners, although extraordinary, in the other peoples, but concerning them, everything is ferocious and nearly unbelievable). Subsequently, they are reduced to the status of untameable animals, with criticism of their diet ("Ils mangent tout crud, racines, viande, & poisson"; Everything they eat is raw: roots, flesh, and fish), their living quarters and their mobility, as they have no fire and live in holes ("des trous soûterrains, où ils entrent à quatre pattes"; underground holes where they enter on all fours), and their clothes and nursing techniques ("Les femmes portent leurs petits-enfans sur leur dos, entre les deux tuniques, & tirent ces pauvres innocens par-dessous le bras ou par-dessus l'épaule pour leur donner le téton" [The women carry their babies on the back between two smocks and they pull these poor innocents under the arm or under the shoulder in order to breast-feed them]).

Turning to Africa, one of the entries that most shows the transfer of barbarian or savage attributes to foreign and, not by accident, colonial people is d'Holbach's entry "Jagas."[13] This African people is fierce, fearsome, and martial, nomadic and cannibalistic, the most cruel, superstitious, and inhuman people ever seen: "nulle nation n'a porté si loin la cruauté & la superstition: en effet, ils nous présentent le phénomene étrange de l'inhumanité la plus atroce" (no nation has taken so far cruelty and superstition; indeed, they represent the strange phenomenon of the most terrible inhumanity). Pitiless, they attack their neighbours to take prisoners and eat them. They even have public meat markets for human meat. In his article d'Holbach recounts the legend of one of their ancient queens who made an unguent out of her only son that she spread over her body while ensuring that all of her soldiers imitated her. In doing so, she wanted to give the most barbarian example, "comme des chefs-d'œuvre de la barbarie, de la dépravation, & du délire des hommes [...] l'exemple de la barbarie la plus horrible" (like masterpieces of barbarity, of depravity, and human delusion [...] the example of the most horrible barbarity), aiming at eliminating all natural, human, and familial feelings ("en détruisant en eux les liens de la nature & du sang" [by destroying the links of nature and blood in them]).

This drastic antithetical figure of the savage is still closely linked to the European and makes the latter's superior position even more striking: the more savage is his view of the colonial Other, the more civilized becomes his image of himself as European. In comparison to the Jagas, the European *philosophe* comes out as human, reasonable, empathetic and civilized, mindful of family. It turns out that the aim of these drastic constructions of colonial alterity is not primarily the description of the Other but – on the contrary – a self-description and self-assurance of the European. In Hayden White's words: "The notion of 'wildness' (or, in its Latin form, 'savagery') belongs to a set of culturally self-authenticating devices which includes, among many others, the ideas of 'madness' and 'heresy' as well. These terms are used not merely to designate a specific condition or state of being but also to confirm the value of their dialectical antitheses 'civilization,' 'sanity,' and 'orthodoxy,' respectively" (1978, 151).

To return to the cannibalistic attribution of the colonial Other, it is remarkable that information about a foreign, cannibalistic people is often accompanied by the caveat that it is doubtful because of the uncertainty of the source (interestingly, this is not the case with the extreme description of the Jagas, in which the testimonials of travellers and missionaries are, on the contrary, labelled as "unanime" (unanimous). That is also the case in the entry about the Cafres ("Cafrerie"), where the author, N.N., admits that he has little information about them but that they are said to be cannibalistic: "Ce pays est peu connu des Européens, qui n'ont point encore pû y entrer bien avant: cependant on accuse les peuples qui l'habitent d'être anthropophages" (This country is little known by the Europeans who have not even been able yet to enter it well before).

The link between the barbarian attributes and the uncertainty of information is even more explicit in Diderot's entry about the African kingdom Ansico. It is purportedly inhabited by cannibalistic people eating
their relatives, having public human meat markets, and enjoying human
flesh in royal banquets: "les habitans s'y nourrissent de chair humaine;
qu'ils ont des boucheries publiques [...] ils mangent leurs peres, meres,
freres & soeurs, aussi-tôt qu'ils sont morts; & qu'on tue deux cens hommes par jour, pour être servis à la table du *grand Macoco,* c'est le nom de
leur monarque" (their inhabitants feed on human flesh; that they have
public butcher's shops [...] they eat their fathers, mothers, brothers & sisters as soon as they are dead; & that two hundred humans a day are killed
in order to be served at the table of the great Macoco, which is the name
of their monarch). This information seems very dubious to Diderot: "Plus
ces circonstances sont extraordinaires, plus il faudra de témoins pour les
faire croire. Y a-t-il sous la ligne un royaume appellé *Ansico?* les habitans
d'*Ansico* sont-ils de la barbarie dont on nous les peint, & sert-on deux
cens hommes par jour dans le palais du *Macoco?*" (The more these circumstances are extraordinary, the more witnesses are necessary to make
them believable. Is there a kingdom called Ansico under the line? Are the
inhabitants of Ansico as barbaric as they are drawn to us, and do they serve
two hundred humans by day in the palace of Macoco?)
Diderot uses the purported customs of the inhabitants of Ansico as
an opportunity to reflect on the reliability of travellers or "ordinary historians." He assumes that one has to distrust those people, as they tend
to exaggerate and tell fairy tales ("Il faut soupçonner en général tout
voyageur & tout historien ordinaire d'enfler un peu les choses, à moins
qu'on ne veuille s'exposer à croire les fables les plus absurdes" [You have
to distrust every traveller & every ordinary historian in general that they
swell things a bit, unless one does not expose oneself to believe in the
most absurd fables]). Diderot deeply doubts his sources, explaining that
the reason for telling these stories is that no one wants to tell what every-
body already knows – in other words, that the traveller tends to exoti-
cize. Consequently, Diderot refuses to believe what he himself has given
as information about cannibalistic customs in Ansico. But, surprisingly,
he does not rule out cannibalism; he only doubts the reported amount
of two hundred humans eaten by the king every day: "j'oserois presque
assûrer que le grand *Macoco* ne mange pas tant d'hommes qu'on dit:
à deux cens par jour, ce seroit environ soixante & treize mille par an;
quel mangeur d'hommes!" (I would nearly dare to insure that the great
Macoco does not eat so many humans as they say: at two hundred by

day, it would be about seventy-three thousand per year; what an eater of humans!) Whereas Diderot is not willing to believe in the number of human ingredients in the king's meal, he is willing to believe in "prejudices" about a cannibalism that is justified by honour in being eaten by a king ("Si toutefois [...] le préjugé de la nation fût qu'il y a beaucoup d'honneur à être mangé par son souverain, nous rencontrerions dans l'histoire des faits appuyés sur le préjugé, & assez extraordinaires pour donner quelque vraisemblance à celui dont il s'agit ici" [If, however, the prejudice of the people was that it was a great honour to be eaten by their sovereign, we encounter in this story facts based on this prejudice and being so extraordinary that we can concede some plausibility to the very one alluded to here]).

For Diderot, this justification through honour is related to the belief in self-sacrifice, another custom he invokes to strengthen the argument that follows. Interestingly, he uses here the practice of sati, a famous example popular both in exotistic literature in the eighteenth and nineteenth centuries and in postcolonial studies.[14] Diderot reasons that if women, as the weak sex, are so brave as to sacrifice themselves for their husbands (whom they even hated), there is no reason to disbelieve that people sacrifice themselves for honour:

S'il y a des contrées où des femmes se brûlent courageusement sur le bûcher d'un mari qu'elles détestoient; si le préjugé donne tant de courage à un sexe naturellement foible & timide; si ce préjugé, tout cruel qu'il est, subsiste malgré les précautions qu'on a pû prendre pour le détruire, pour-quoi dans une autre contrée les hommes entêtés du faux honneur d'être servis sur la table de leur monarque, n'iroient-ils pas en foule & gaiment présenter leur gorge à couper dans ses boucheries royales?"

(If there are regions where women burn themselves courageously on the funeral pyres of a husband they hated; if the prejudice gives such a courage to a naturally weak and shy sex; if the prejudice remains, as cruel as it is and despite all the precautions that might have been taken to destroy it; why can't men of other regions who are obstinate with the false honour to be served at their monarch's table join the crowd and present cheerfully their throats to be cut in public butcher's shops?)

Also suspicious to Diderot is information in the entry "Humaine Espece" about the islands Mindoro and Formose, where humans are sup-posed to have tails. This is information that Diderot deems dubious, "ce fait est suspect" (this fact is suspect; CTPUML), but he does not give any further explanations.

The colonial Other apparently justifies judging the related sources and information as anything from inaccurate to pure fiction. In the entry "Tinagogo," describing an idol of the Indians, de Jaucourt clarifies how this has obviously been invented by Fernand Mendez Pinto, whose "contes" (tales) possibly form one of the least truthful articles in the *Dictionnaire de Trévoux*. Rather than using this entry solely to describe an aspect of the colonial world, De Jaucourt uses it to attack the Jesuits' rival compilation project. And not only the fictional character of Pinto's argumentation is striking ("Toutes les fictions du récit de Pinto sautent aux yeux" [All the fictions of de Pinto's story jump out]). De Jaucourt carries on his argument by describing how even the location is imagined ("le lieu même de la scène est imaginaire"). He points out that the geographers know neither the city Meydur nor the kingdom Brama and that no European has ever entered this part of Asia. But he gives, again surprisingly, information about a group of people living there, the Brama, who are human and gentle. Interestingly, the data provided by de Jaucourt are by no means any more accurate; on the contrary, he names as a source two Jesuit travellers without explaining why their descriptions are more reliable than those of others.

Despite the unreliability of his sources, de Jaucourt has the power to determine that certain information is more credible and therefore, in a certain way, more encyclopedic. In another entry, he also strongly condemns Lahontan's reports about Eskimos, which are, in his opinion, pure fiction – this time clearly meant in the sense of invention. De Jaucourt warns the reader to be sceptical about the sources, for example, Lahontan's travelogues, because these texts are "que des fictions" (only fictions) and there is no other source from a traveller who knew the area (see de Jaucourt, "Eskimaux"). The same is true for the "peuples fabuleux" (mythical people) of the pygmies (de Jaucourt, "Pygmées"). De Jaucourt's entry "Raisin Barbu" (Bearded Grape) nonchalantly describes the source as ridiculous supposition and an imaginary fact, which is an astonishing oxymoron ("en un mot Borel a expliqué par une ridicule supposition un fait imaginaire" [in a word Borel explained an imaginary fact by a ridiculous supposition]).

After all these examples, which constitute a mere sampling, two questions arise: Why do we find such dubious information in the *Encyclopédie* when in fact it is meant to be a project of proven knowledge? What is the function of these descriptions?

It might be surprising that information an author deems unreliable or sometimes even impossible is ultimately included, rather than excluded. This unreliable knowledge actually functions at diverse levels. First and foremost, it allows the encyclopedist to powerfully define himself or to defame competing encyclopedic projects. The encyclopedist demonstrates that by reflecting on and commenting on the work used as a source; he still pulls the strings, thus retaining the (Eurocentric) power to define and to decide between truth and lies. It becomes a performance of European rationality's ability to systematize the world and to judge what information belongs to reality and what to fantasy.[15] However, these fictional textual elements are also part of the encyclopedic project, its inner logic and aesthetics. I will return to this specific poetology of knowledge in the third section of this chapter.

With regard to the colonial Other, what remains at first sight is its self-referential or elliptical status. Whether the savage is considered from above as a cannibalistic, stammering kind of human or whether he is presumed to hold a mirror up to the European at eye level as the happy pre-stage ancestor, his function is that of reassuring the European *philosophe*. The Other is always constructed according to a colonial, Eurocentric and egocentric discursive logic. He opens up ways of imagining the self or, according to Spivak, is the native informant who presents "the imagined and impossible perspective."[16] The colonial Other is the antithetic Other (positive or negative) who can be generated as the "alter ego" of the *philosophe*[17] without any contradiction. But is discursive submission the only possible diagnosis?

Knowledge about the Colonial Other in the *Encyclopédie*: Supplement or Fundament?

A closer look to the constructions of colonial alterity and European self-conceptions in the *Encyclopédie* raises some doubts about this unequivocal function of the colonial Other. If the encyclopedist is forced to think about the factuality of colonial information based on available sources to be avowed or disavowed, if the colonial Other is compared to something that is familiar to the European but cannot be described by European categories, this is not a pure sign of submission. The colonial Other exposes the relation between fact and fiction, between reliable explanation und unreliable narration, and thus becomes simultaneously a topic and a problem. The colonial Other questions the border between a

European "us" and the foreign "them" and consequently challenges the
self-concept of the European *philosophe.*

If the colonial Other has a deep impact on European concepts of the
self, of knowledge, and of the *Encyclopédie* as the "machine de guerre" of
French enlightenment, could it be considered as (only) one topic among
others in the *Encyclopédie?* Are the discourses about the colonial Other in
the *Encyclopédie* a simple supplement, or are they rather playing a role as
an (irritating) fundament?

From the perspective of these questions, a close reading of the
encyclopedic articles makes it appear as if the Other, in the Other's
difference, is indeed marked, but cannot really be kept in antithetical distance as initially assumed. One can find this deep impact on
European concepts in the *Encyclopédie* in those textual passages where
authors encounter some difficulties in defining what European is. The
definition of barbarians as those who are the extreme opposite of the
Greeks, and of the French, shows how the European defines himself[18]
as barbarian antithesis. However, other entries using the barbarian
attribute obscure this differentiation, so that even the European position is no longer secure. "L'Occident étoit barbare du tems d'Aristote"
(The Occident was barbaric in times of Aristotle), Voltaire explains
in his entry "Eloquence." The supposedly genuine European achievements are of other provenance: astronomy stems from the Chaldeans,
geometry from the Egyptians, and the art of writing from the Phoeni-
cians. Here, in the service of European sciences and arts, the Other
is indeed revaluated – yet on a de-individualized and abstract level
of science and with regard to historically advanced civilizations that,
without exception, have been positively connoted. Nevertheless, this
implication of the Other also avoids the possibility of essentialization
and self-reflection from a Eurocentric perspective. The Other is not
external to but implemented in European achievements.

To give another striking example as an opposite to these epistemological achievements, one can analyse the entry about the African "Galles."
De Jaucourt makes an interesting and daring comparison between the
cannibalistic people of the African Galles and the European/Eurasian
Huns, Goths, or Tartarians: "C'est ainsi qu'on vit autrefois les Huns, les
Avares, les Goths, les Vandales, les Normands, répandre la terreur chez
les nations policées de l'Europe, & les Tartares orientaux se rendre maî-
tres de la Chine" (That is how we saw in the past the Huns, the Avares, the
Goths, the Vandals, the Normans terrorize the other civilized European
peoples, and how the oriental Tartars became masters of China). The

martial and cannibalistic character can no longer be confined to Africa or the New World but has already become part of European history – even though still as the antithetical figure to the civilized ("nations policées" [polite nations]). Consequently, discourses about the colonial Other are not necessarily intelligible by means of dialectics of the self and the Other, of Europe and the colonies or the New World, of centre and periphery, of the philosopher/*philosophe* and the savage/*sauvage*, they are far more complicated, entangled, and complex.

Hence, knowledge about the colonial Other cannot be seen as an object of unproblematic transfer of knowledge in the sense of implementation. The transfer of colonial knowledge leads to an epistemological transformation and deeply irritates the notion of knowledge itself. Knowledge cannot be understood as European (nor as ratio, either), since already the description of the colonial Other forces the encyclopedist to rethink notions of truth and reliability, of humanness and civilization. This disturbance might be described by the idea of "entangled knowledge," as Hock and Mackenthun put it.[19] Their work as encyclopedists finds them operating at the interstices of cultural exchange and knowledge production at the beginning of the modern age in ways that are similar to the processes outlined by the scholars mentioned above. Their point is, however, that knowledge cannot be conceptualized as specifically European since this cultural-scientific interrelation means that it is always "infected" by foreign, especially colonial, knowledge.[20]

It is in this direction that postcolonial and decolonial studies consider colonialism as a fundamental aspect within and for European discourse and knowledge. Studies in the field of "Postcolonial Enlightenment"[21] underscore the influence of the colonial Other on European representations by investigating two different aspects. First, influence is regarded not as an implementation but as a transformation – basically the influence of the universalistic claim of European enlightenment. "With global expansion," Festa and Carey state, "the test cases for universalism changed. The encounter with new populations radically altered concepts of human nature [...] generating more elastic and plural ideas of humanity."[22] From this perspective, the colonial Other cannot be seen as an epistemological addendum; instead the Other is already deeply implemented in the knowledge of the European.

Here it is important to consider two prominent positions within this discourse: postcolonial and decolonial. The studies by Sala-Molins provide a certain counter-history for the enlightenment, and their focus is the aporia of colonialism in terms of the inhuman slave trade.[23] Sala-Molins attacks Eurocentrism and the power imbalance in the texts of the enlightenment, in which the universalistic body of thought on liberty, equality, and fortune is limited to France, and at best Europe. His studies aim to develop a counter-history of the enlightenment by means of colonial discursive analyses. He evaluates the presence of the colonial as a challenge within the perspective of slavery: "Clearly, the crucial test case for the Enlightenment is the slave trade and slavery."[24] He then becomes even more radical and states in polemic escalation that, to detect the "Misères des Lumières," the enlightenment could *only* be understood by means of the project of slavery: "How can the Enlightenment be interpreted? Only with the *Code Noir* in hand."[25] Consequently, according to Sala-Molins, slavery plays a decisive role in European enlightenment. Both generalizing and radicalizing this line of argument, Mignolo and his decolonial theory go beyond this idea.[26] Mignolo considers that the colonial Other is not somehow part of the European enlightenment but that colonialism is fundamental to European modernity: "there is no modernity without coloniality."[27]

Second, the transfer of knowledge, no longer linear or unidirectional, has become more complex.[28] There is no longer a European centre of enlightenment, spreading out ideas in the world and incorporating ideas of the world within. The hypothesis is that the colonial world is not outside European territory and thinking, but is already right in the centre of it.

Nevertheless, this entanglement cannot only be interpreted as simply part of the enlightenment project. If the encyclopedist sees the colonial Other in himself, this is not a simple or sovereign gesture of self-critique. It is, rather, an enormous effort to construct and reconstruct the colonial binaries of the self and the Other – by means of eroticization, exoticization, animalization, stereotyping, of tropes and prejudices, exaggeration and imagination. This effort can be seen in the diverse constructions of the colonial Other, which no longer appear natural, objective, or universal. Deconstructive postcolonial analyses go beyond that, believing that dialectics can be overcome by in-between, uncertain, scary, or even indescribable figures.

I will further consider deconstructive postcolonial analysis below, but will first reflect on the formal-aesthetic dimension of the encyclopedia entries in the interest of delineating the constitutional elements of their construction of the Other.

Narrating the Knowledge: Poetic Transformations in the *Encyclopédie*

The representation of the colonial Other presents the encyclopedist with a challenge as far as key concepts of the European enlightenment (e.g., reason, humanness) are concerned. But it is also – and maybe in the first instance – a challenge with regard to the mode of representation. How can the colonial Other be described, narrated, and portrayed in a convincing way? Is reproducing myths producing truth? A glance at the textual analysis presented above shows to what extent knowledge about the colonial world is not simply represented but deeply constructed.

The reports and travelogues that have already been referred to show how poetics already plays a special role in the *Encyclopédie* with regard to the narrating mode of the articles and to the ontological status of the text. The fictiousness or factuality, if one were to use these terms *avant la lettre*, refers to the reliability of information in the articles to be reflected on, as mentioned above. But it is also obvious that the encyclopedist has to argue, to persuade his audience, and to do this, he develops various strategies.

In the following, I focus on the formal-aesthetical dimension of narrating the colonial Other. We have already encountered rhetorical strategies such as the "ni ... ni" rhetorics *ex negative* that aim to keep him at a distance and to downgrade him in comparison to the European *philosophe.* Two further omnipresent and expectable rhetorics in relation to the colonial Other are exoticizing and eroticizing. The exoticizing strategies using cannibalistic, monstrous images of the colonial Other have been explored above. But very often, exoticizing textual elements are accompanied by eroticizing ones. Promiscuity and lasciviousness are referred to in several articles, mostly regarding women's sexual behaviour. In Diderot's article about humankind ("Humaine Espece"), for example, he argues that Bengali women are "les plus lascives de l'Inde" (the most lascivious of India), or that men from the "Naires de Calicut" are only allowed to have one wife; women on the contrary may have as many husbands as they desire. Women of the African "Jalofes" are described as "gaies, vives, & très-portées à l'amour" (cheerful, agile, and promiscuous). In colonial contact, the male Jalofes even support this behaviour by offering their wives, daughters, and sisters to white Europeans: "Elles ont du goût pour tous les hommes, & particulierement pour les blancs, auxquels elles se livrent pour quelque présent d'Europe, dont elles sont fort curieuses; d'ailleurs leurs maris ne s'opposent point à leur goût pour les étrangers, & même ils leur offrent leurs femmes, leurs filles & leurs sœurs" (They have a taste for all men, especially for whites, to whom they give themselves up for some presents from Europe that they are very curious about; and their husbands do not oppose their taste for strangers, and even offer them their wives, their daughters and their sisters) (De Jaucourt, "Jalofes"). One can easily depict the fascination and dystopian nightmare the encyclopedist invokes by describing these customs, which certainly do not just relate information, but also attract the reader. This intentional effect on the readership is even more relevant for textual strategies on the narrative level. For the narration of the colonial Other, this is especially the case when the encyclopedist devises fictitious speech situations with indirect speech in a narrative or dramatic mode, in line with the narratology of Genette (1980).

The voice of the Other can be explicitly heard in several encyclopedic articles. The encyclopedist uses popular poetic strategies of the eighteenth century, similar to famous texts such as Diderot's *Supplément au voyage de Bougainville*, Montesquieu's *Lettres Persanes*, de Graffigny's *Lettres d'une Péruvienne*, and in doing so brings the (noble) savage to the fore in the *Encyclopédie* as well. A very explicit example can surprisingly be found in an entry that at first sight has nothing in common with the colonial world. In the article about wool, the perspective of the savages towards the efforts of the European is imagined and even culminates in fictitious talk. Savage men walk around a wool manufacture and cannot help but find what they see as quite unnecessary:

Ils [les hommes sauvages] regardent en pitié les peines que nous prenons pour obtenir de notre industrie un secours moins sûr & moins prompt que celui que la bonté de la nature leur offre contre l'inclémence des saisons. Ils nous diroient volontiers: *Tu as apporté en naissant le vêtement qu'il te faut en été, & tu as sous ta main celui qui t'est nécessaire en hiver. Laisse à la brebis sa toison. Vois-tu cet animal fourré. Prend ta fleche, tue-le, sa chair te nourrira, & sa peau te vêtira sans apprêt.* [...] On raconte qu'un sauvage transporté de son pays dans le nôtre, & promené dans nos atteliers, regarda avec assez d'indifférence tous nos travaux. Nos manufactures de couvertures en *laine* parurent seules arrêter un moment son attention. Il sourit à la vue de cette sorte d'ouvrage. Il prit une couverture, il la jetta sur ses épaules, fit quelques tours; & rendant avec dédain cette enveloppe artificielle au manufacturier: *en vérité*, lui dit-il, *cela est presqu'aussi bon qu'une peau de bête.*

(They [the savages] look with pity on the efforts we make to get from our industries a help less secure and rapid than the one that is offered to them by nature's kindness against the inclemency of the seasons. They would tell us willingly: *Being born, you have the clothes you need in summertime, you have at hand what you need in wintertime. Leave the coat to the ewe. Do you see this furred animal. Take your arrow, kill it, its flesh will feed you, and its hide will dress you naturally.* [...] One tells the story that a savage who was transported from his country to ours, and taken for a walk in our workshops, looked without interest at all of our work. Only our manufactories of wool blankets seemed to arrest his attention for a while. He smiled when seeing this kind of work. He took a blanket, he threw it over his shoulders, turned around a bit, and gave this artificial covering back to the fabricant with contempt: *in fact,* he told him, *this is nearly as good as an animal's hide.*) (N.N., "Laine, Manufacture en Laine, *ou* Draperie")

This is not only a readoption of the literary tradition of the noble savage but also the orchestration and staging of a speech act. The encyclopedist uses the dramatic mode and direct speech of the savage. The intent is obvious: to involve, to convince, and perhaps even to touch the readership by speaking directly to the reader and by using a striking rhetoric of "we" and "us" ("le nôtre" [ours], "tous nos travaux" [all of our work], "nos manufactures" [our manufactories], etc.), in dialectical opposition to "them" or "him" ("ils regardent" [they look], "ils nous diroient" [they would tell us], "il sourit" [he smiled], "il prit" [he took], "il la jetta" [he threw it], etc.). Doing so opens a window for criticism of the French or European by means of an imagined noble savage. Interestingly, the encyclopedist has obviously left behind the strategy of referring to reliable, erudite sources. He visualizes his invention of a situation and a speaker. This, certainly, lies beyond the stated encyclopedic purpose of collecting, categorizing, and representing knowledge. The enlightenment critique becomes visible here – not only through the content but also through the aesthetic strategy the author uses.

A second example of imagined speech is provided by the entry "Insensibilité" (Insensibility), authored by N.N. We are no longer in a European setting, but rather among Iroquois women. The author explains that Iroquois women do not scream during childbirth, and that doing so would be considered shameful for them. To present this custom or – as he qualifies it – this superstition, he lets a woman speak directly:

Aujourd'hui dans le pays des Iroquois la gloire des femmes est d'accoucher sans se plaindre; & c'est une très grosse injure parmi elles que de dire, *tu as crié quand tu étois en travail d'enfant;* tant ont de force le préjugé &

la coutume! Je crois que cet usage ne sera pas aisément transplanté en Europe; & quelque passion que les femmes en France aient pour les modes nouvelles, je doute que celle de mettre au monde les enfans sans crier ait jamais cours parmi elles.

(In the land of the Iroquois the glory of women is today to give birth without complaining, and it is a great insult amongst them to say: *You have screamed when you were in labour*; that is how powerful prejudices and customs are! I think this custom will not be easily transferred to Europe; and even though women in France are passionate for new styles, I doubt that giving birth without screaming could ever be admissible for them.)

Direct speech is used as in the previous example, and is typographically marked by italics. But in this case the imagined words of the Iroquois woman are directly followed by the author's comment that this custom could never be transferred to Europe (alluding to the statement that European women are not capable of silence in this situation).

This is an example where the author invents the savage's speech not only to criticize European society but also to make the narration of the virtue of insensibility more nuanced and interesting. Leaving aside whether this is turn-taking, or rather turn allocation,[29] I note an interesting hypothesis articulated by Garraway, who shows in her analysis of Diderot's fictional works that the simulated debates between the savage and the European had two effects.[30] First, they gave space to the absent discussion about colonial power at the European centre. "By figuring a critique of French colonial power through fictionalized colonized subjects," Garraway maintains, "Enlightenment thinkers anticipated as well the consent of those imagined colonized peoples to the reform proposals implied within the critique itself."[31] Second, the imagined dialogues supported the colonial project by instrumentalizing the colonial Other.

Coming back to the formal-aesthetical strategies used to evoke the colonial Other, we can recognize a specific inter- and archi-textuality. On the intertextual level, strictly speaking, references are involved. They are, as indicated above, not only sources of supply for studies and scholarly analyses, but also explicitly commented on as "les fables les plus absurdes" (the most absurd fables), "contes" (tales), and "fictions" (fictions). On the architextual level, there is a mixture of genres and meaning that are needed for the description of knowledge in general and the colonial Other specifically. As already explained above, identifying certain statements as "fabuleux," "imaginaire," or "merveilleux" by no means prevents their inclusion as entries in the *Encyclopédie*. This inclusion of falsehoods serves, on the one hand and as seen above, in a defamation of other knowledge projects and the evaluation of quoted sources with regard to their credibility. On the other hand, however – and this seems to be a crucial point – this mixture of genres as forms of knowledge in the sense of a poetology of knowledge[32] is also a genuine part of the *Encylopédie*.[33]

The functioning of the generic and intertextual transgressions as well as the play with the narrative authority indicate that the threshold between "raison" and "imagination" must be openly addressed in the descriptions of the indescribable colonial Other. This is not a phenomenon that is limited to the construction of the colonial Other. It can be explained by the contemporary meaning of "lettres," which includes both scientific and literary texts and the interrelation between "raison" and "imagination" as shown in the famous system of human knowledge in d'Alembert.[34] Furthermore, it can be explained by the rhetorics of knowledge itself.

Therefore, the study of the "poetology of knowledge,"[35] of the colonial Other, seems worthwhile when analysing constructions of otherness in the *Encyclopédie*. Vogl's interest is not primarily in knowledge itself but rather in both its conditions and the requirements for what can be referred to as knowledge and its rhetorical constructedness. In line with Vogl, the representations of the colonial Other in the *Encyclopédie* could easily be focused within the perspective of their poetological dimensions. A poetology of knowledge of the colonial Other captures the appearance of new knowledge objects and areas of knowledge as a form of orchestration.[36] That such knowledge is not only innocently compiled and described in the *Encyclopédie* but also deeply constructed, invented, and staged was described in the previous explanations concerning the savage and barbarian Other.

But by "constructed," I do not mean an intended strategy of orchestration that makes up information on purpose, nor do I aim at the unconscious, personal phantasms that are inscribed into a text by the author. My observations, rather, target textual strategies that are pervaded by different discourses intentionally used to downgrade or upgrade the colonial Other, or that perhaps contain elements of all of the above – proof of the "unauthority" of the *philosophe*. The entries always show both knowledge and the margins of knowledge as an ascertainable non-knowledge. And they let something shine through that arises from the basis of the *Encyclopédie* and the multiplicity of authors: unconscious knowledge and the collective unconscious.[37] Focusing on the "staging dimensions and performative practices" ("die inszenatorischen Dimensionen und performativen Praktiken")[38] of knowledge of the colonial Other means, contemporaneously, the intentional and unintentional aspects of textual phenomena.

As described in the convincing works of Gipper,[39] the articles refer to a specific poetics of the *Encyclopédie*, which does not primarily (and innocently) represent circumstances and facts in "distance to rhetorics,"[40] but instead shows, virtually constructs, and aestheticizes objects of knowledge. Gipper illustrates how the aesthetic of the spectacular and the marvellous is part and parcel of the articles in the *Encyclopédie*, even though this has been denied within the *Encyclopédie* itself.[41] This is the "reverse side of the powerful anti-rhetorics" ("die Rückseite der machtvollen Antirhetorik").[42] My hypothesis is that this reverse side comes to light particularly when describing the colonial Other as the (impossible) reverse side of the *philosophe*. It is noticeable that entries in the *Encyclopédie* repeatedly use persuasive strategies of argumentation – Vogl calls this the "performative power."[43]

The striking textual dimension of narrative staging of the colonial Other might indicate the necessity to speak about the colonial Other in a very specific way. The colonial Other is not a simple object of knowledge that can be shunted into European or universal categories by simple definition. The transfer of knowledge about the colonial Other demands a transformation of the encyclopedic text. Encyclopedists need to narrate, to invent, to imagine, and to "skate around" the colonial Other. The transfer of knowledge about the colonial Other has a feedback effect on the European who is questioning European self-conception, European ways of thinking, and European expressions of the self.

NOTES

1 Jean le Rond d'Alembert, 1955 [1751], *Discours préliminaire de l'Encyclopédie (1751). Einleitung zur Enzyklopädie von 1751*, ed. Erich Köhler (Hamburg: Felix Meiner), 12. All translations not otherwise attributed are mine.
2 See basic research by Frank A. Kafker and Serena L. Kafker, 1988, *The Encyclopedists as Individuals: A Biographical Dictionary of the Authors of the* Encyclopédie (Oxford: Voltaire Foundation); Frank A. Kafker, 1996, *The Encyclopedists as a Group: A Collective Biography of the Authors of the* Encyclopédie (Oxford: Voltaire Foundation).

3 See Urs Bitterli, 2004, *Die Wilden und die Zivilisierten. Grundzüge einer Geistes-und Kulturgeschichte der europäisch-überseeischen Begegnung* (Munich: Beck), 223.

4 See Hans-Jürgen Lüsebrink, 2004, "Wissen und außereuropäische Erfahrung im 18. Jahrhundert," in *Macht des Wissens: die Entstehung der modernen Wissensgesellschaft,* ed. Richard van Dülmen and Sina Rauschenbach (Cologne: Böhlau), 636; Philippe Despoix, 2005, *Le monde mesuré: Dispositifs de l'exploration à l'âge des Lumières* (Geneva: Droz).

5 The translations into English marked with "CTPUML" are taken from the Collaborative Translation Project of the University of Michigan Library: http://quod.lib.umich.edu/d/did/.

6 Hans-Jürgen Lüsebrink, 2006, "Von der Faszination zur Wissenssystematisierung: die koloniale Welt im Diskurs der europäischen Aufklärung," in *Das Europa der Aufklärung und die außereuropäische koloniale Welt,* ed. Hans-Jürgen Lüsebrink (Göttingen: Wallstein Verlag), 10.

7 See Bill Ashcroft, Gareth Griffiths, and Helen Tiffin, 2007, *Post-Colonial Studies: The Key Concepts,* 2nd ed. (New York: Routledge, 28ff).

8 See Bitterli, *Die Wilden und die Zivilisierten,* 223.

9 Ute Fendler and Susanne Greilich, 2006, "Afrika in deutschen und französischen Enzyklopädien des 18. Jahrhunderts," in *Das Europa der Aufklärung und die außereuropäische koloniale Welt,* ed. Hans-Jürgen Lüsebrink (Göttingen: Wallstein Verlag), 118.

10 See Lüsebrink, "Wissen und außereuropäische Erfahrung im 18. Jahrhundert," 629.

11 The difference between "homme naturel" and "bon sauvage" is that the former requires historical thinking, comparison, and self-reflexion as well as the verification of the social way of life; "bon sauvage" is pure exotization and the projection of one's own desires (see Bitterli, *Die Wilden und die Zivilisierten,* 283). My research initially concludes that the topos of the "bon sauvage," as understood in this sense and compared to the "homme naturel," is actually under-represented in the *Encyclopédie* (see Struve, *Wildes Wissen,* 428). As a consequence, its self-reflexive function seems to be much more relevant than the escapist exotization of the colonial Other. This would support the idea that the colonial Other serves, on the one hand, as a self-affirmation of the *philosophe* by self-criticism. On the other hand, and as an encyclopedic moment, the externalization of unfulfilled wishes and desires becomes impossible since the colonial Other is already part of the European enlightenment.

12 See Susanne Greilich and Karen Struve, eds., 2013, *"Das Andere Schreiben." Diskursivierungen von Alterität in Texten der Romania (16–19. Jahrhundert)* (Würzburg: Königshausen & Neumann).

13 The encyclopedist Cornelius de Pauw mentions this article in his *Recherches philosophiques sur les Américains* of 1771. He is astonished that the author has not realized that all the information about the Jagas has already been provided in the entry "Galles" (223).

14 See Gayatri C. Spivak, 1995, "Can the Subaltern Speak?" in *The Post-Colonial Studies Reader*, ed. Bill Ashcroft, Gareth Griffiths, and Helen Tiffin (London: Routledge), 24–8.

15 See Ottmar Ette, 2012, *TransArea. Eine literarische Globalisierungsgeschichte* (Berlin: De Gruyter, 111).

16 Gayatri C. Spivak, 2000, *A Critique of Postcolonial Reason: Toward a History of the Vanishing Present* (Cambridge, MA: Harvard University Press), 9.

17 Julia Kristeva, 1988, *Étrangers à nous-mêmes* (Paris: Fayard), 196.

18 The use of the male pronoun seems to me to be advisable because of the dominance of male voices, authors, and philosophers at that time.

19 See Klaus Hock and Gesa Mackenthun, eds., 2012, *Entangled Knowledge: Scientific Discourses and Cultural Difference* (Münster: Waxmann).

20 Hock and Mackenthun, *Entangled Knowledge*, 9–10.

21 See for example Daniel Carey and Lynn Festa, 2009, "Introduction: Some Answers to the Question: 'What Is Postcolonial Enlightenment?'" in *The Postcolonial Enlightenment: Eighteenth-Century Colonialism and Postcolonial Theory*, ed. Daniel Carey and Lynn Festa (Oxford: Oxford University Press), 1–33.

22 Carey and Festa, "Introduction," 21.

23 See Louis Sala-Molins, 1992, *Les misères des Lumières. Sous la raison, l'outrage …* (Paris: Robert Laffon).

24 Louis Sala-Molins, 2006, *Dark Side of the Light: Slavery and the French Enlightenment* (Minneapolis: University of Minnesota Press), 8.

25 Sala-Molins, *Dark Side of the Light*, 9.

26 Walter D. Mignolo, 2011, *The Darker Side of Western Modernity: Global Futures, Decolonial Options* (Durham: Duke University Press).

27 Mignolo, *The Darker Side of Western Modernity*, 3.

28 See e.g. Ette, *TransArea*, 120; see also Santiago Castro Gómez, 2006, "Aufklärung als kolonialer Diskurs. Humanwissenschaften und kreolische Kultur in Neu Granada am Ende des 18. Jahrhunderts," PhD diss., Universität Frankfurt am Main, http://publikationen.ub.uni-frankfurt.de/files/2152/CastroGomezSantiago.pdf; Wolfgang Hardtwig, 2010, *Die Aufklärung und ihre Weltwirkung* (Göttingen: Vandenhoeck & Ruprecht).

29 See Lüsebrink, "Wissen und außereuropäische Erfahrung im 18. Jahrhundert," 632.

30 See Doris L. Garraway, 2009, "Of Speaking Natives and Hybrid
    Philosophers: Lahontan, Diderot, and the French Enlightenment Critique
    of Colonialism," in *The Postcolonial Enlightenment: Eighteenth-Century
    Colonialism and Postcolonial Theory*, ed. Daniel Carey and Lynn Festa (Oxford:
    Oxford University Press), 207–39.

31 Garraway, "Of Speaking Natives," 210.

32 See Gunhild Berg, ed., 2014, *Wissenstexturen. Literarische Gattungen als
    Organisationsformen von Wissen* (Frankfurt am Main: Peter Lang).

33 See Andreas Gipper, 2002, *Wunderbare Wissenschaft. Literarische Strategien
    naturwissenschaftlicher Vulgarisierung in Frankreich. Von Cyrano de Bergerac bis
    zur* Encyclopédie (Munich: Fink), 329.

34 See d'Alembert, *Discours préliminaire de l'Encyclopédie (1751)*.

35 Joseph Vogl, 2010, *Poetologien des Wissens um 1800* (Munich: Fink Verlag);
    Daniel Fulda, 2008, "Poetologien des Wissens. Probleme und Chancen am
    Beispiel des historischen Wissens und seiner Formen," www.simonewinko
    .de/fulda_text.htm.

36 See Vogl, *Poetologien des Wissens um 1800*, 13.

37 See Hannelore Bublitz, 1999, *Foucaults Archäologie des kulturellen Unbewußten.
    Zum Wissensarchiv und Wissensbegehren moderner Gesellschaften* (Frankfurt am
    Main: Campus Verlag).

38 Ralf Klausnitzer, 2008, *Literatur und Wissen. Zugänge, Modelle, Analysen*
    (Berlin: De Gruyter), 154.

39 See Gipper, 2002, *Wunderbare Wissenschaft*; Gipper, 2006, "Logik der
    Sammlung und Ästhetik der Curiositas in Diderots *Encyclopédie*," in
    Frühneuzeitliche Sammlungspraxis und Literatur, ed. Robert Felfe and Angelika
    Lozar (Berlin: Lukas), 233–48.

40 See Klaus Semsch, 1999, *Abstand von der Rhetorik. Strukturen und Funktionen
    ästhetischer Distanznahme von der "ars rhetorica" bei den französischen
    Enzyklopädisten* (Hamburg: Meiner).

41 See Gipper. "Logik der Sammlung und Ästhetik der Curiositas," 234.

42 Gipper, "Logik der Sammlung und Ästhetik der Curiositas," 235.

43 Vogl, *Poetologien des Wissens um 1800*, 13.

Bibliography

Ashcroft, Bill, Gareth Griffiths, and Helen Tiffin. 2007. "Cartography (Maps
    and Mapping)." In *Post-Colonial Studies: The Key Concepts*, 2nd ed., edited
    by Bill Ashcroft, Gareth Griffiths, and Helen Tiffin, 28–30. New York:
    Routledge.

– 2007. *Post-Colonial Studies: The Key Concepts*. 2nd ed. New York: Routledge.

Berg, Gunhild, ed. 2014. *Wissenstexturen. Literarische Gattungen als Organisationsformen von Wissen.* Frankfurt am Main: Peter Lang.

Bhabha, Homi K. 2011. *Our Neighbours, Ourselves: Contemporary Reflections on Survival.* Berlin: Walter de Gruyter. E-book.

Bitterli, Urs. 2004 [1976]. *Die Wilden und die Zivilisierten. Grundzüge einer Geistes- und Kulturgeschichte der europäisch-überseeischen Begegnung.* Munich: Beck.

Blanchard, Gilles, and Mark Olsen. 2002. "Le système de renvoi dans l'Encyclopédie. Une cartographie des structures de connaissances au XVIIIe siècle." *Recherches sur Diderot et sur l'Encyclopédie* 31–2: 45–70.

Bublitz, Hannelore. 1999. *Foucaults Archäologie des kulturellen Unbewußten. Zum Wissensarchiv und Wissensbegehren moderner Gesellschaften.* Frankfurt am Main: Campus Verlag.

Carey, Daniel, and Lynn Festa. 2009. "Introduction: Some Answers to the Question: 'What Is Postcolonial Enlightenment?'" In *The Postcolonial Enlightenment: Eighteenth-Century Colonialism and Postcolonial Theory*, ed. Daniel Carey and Lynn Festa, 1–33. Oxford: Oxford University Press.

Castro Gómez, Santiago. 2006. "Aufklärung als kolonialer Diskurs. Humanwissenschaften und kreolische Kultur in Neu Granada am Ende des 18. Jahrhunderts." PhD diss., Universität Frankfurt am Main. Accessed 11 November 2012. http://publikationen.ub.uni-frankfurt.de/files/2152/CastroGomezSantiago.pdf

d'Alembert, Jean le Rond. 1955 [1751]. *Discours préliminaire de l'*Encyclopédie *(1751).* In *Einleitung zur Enzyklopädie von 1751*, edited by Erich Köhler. Hamburg: Felix Meiner.

Diderot, Denis, and d'Alembert, Jean le Rond, eds. 2000 [1750–72]. *Encyclopédie, ou Dictionnaire raisonné des sciences, des arts et des métiers.* Marsanne: Redon CD-ROM.

Derrida, Jacques. 1997 [1995]. *Dem Archiv verschrieben.* Berlin: Brinkmann + Bose.

Despoix, Philippe. 2005. *Le monde mesuré: Dispositifs de l'exploration à l'âge des Lumières.* Geneva: Droz.

Diderot, Denis. 2000 [1750–72]. "Ansico." In Diderot and d'Alembert, *Encyclopédie.*

– 2000 [1750–72]. "Humaine Espece." In Diderot and d'Alembert, *Encyclopédie.*

Ebeling, Knut, and Stephan Günzel, eds. 2009. *Archivologie: Theorien des Archivs in Wissenschaften, Medien und Künsten.* Berlin: Kadmos, 2009.

Ette, Ottmar. 2012. *TransArea. Eine literarische Globalisierungsgeschichte.* Berlin: De Gruyter.

Fendler, Ute, and Susanne Greilich. 2006. "Afrika in deutschen und französischen Enzyklopädien des 18. Jahrhunderts." In *Das Europa der*

Aufklärung und die außereuropäische koloniale Welt, ed. Hans-Jürgen Lüsebrink, 113–37. Göttingen: Wallstein Verlag.

Formey, M. 2000 [1750–72]. "Negre." In Diderot and d'Alembert, *Encyclopédie*.

Fulda, Daniel. 2008. "Poetologien des Wissens. Probleme und Chancen am Beispiel des historischen Wissens und seiner Formen." Accessed 17 December 2020. www.simonewinko.de/fulda_text.htm.

Garraway, Doris L. 2009. "Of Speaking Natives and Hybrid Philosophers: Lahontan, Diderot, and the French Enlightenment Critique of Colonialism." In *The Postcolonial Enlightenment: Eighteenth-Century Colonialism and Postcolonial Theory*, ed. Daniel Carey and Lynn Festa, 207–39. Oxford: Oxford University Press.

Genette, Gérard. 1980 [1972]. *Narrative Discourse*. Oxford: Blackwell.

Gipper, Andreas. 2002. *Wunderbare Wissenschaft. Literarische Strategien naturwissenschaftlicher Vulgarisierung in Frankreich. Von Cyrano de Bergerac bis zur* Encyclopédie. Munich: Fink.

– 2006. "Logik der Sammlung und Ästhetik der Curiositas in Diderots *Encyclopédie*." In *Frühneuzeitliche Sammlungspraxis und Literatur*, edited by Robert Felfe and Angelika Lozar, 233–48. Berlin: Lukas.

Greilich, Susanne, and Karen Struve, eds. 2013. *"Das Andere Schreiben." Diskursivierungen von Alterität in Texten der Romania (16.–19. Jahrhundert)*. Würzburg: Königshausen & Neumann.

Hardtwig, Wolfgang. 2010. *Die Aufklärung und ihre Weltwirkung*. Göttingen: Vandenhoeck & Ruprecht.

Hock, Klaus, and Gesa Mackenthun, eds. 2012. *Entangled Knowledge: Scientific Discourses and Cultural Difference*. Münster: Waxmann.

Hofmann, Sabine. 2001. *Die Konstruktion kolonialer Wirklichkeit. Eine diskursanalytische Untersuchung französischer Karibiktexte des frühen 17. Jahrhunderts*. Frankfurt am Main: Campus.

d'Holbach, Paul-Henri Thiry. 2000 [1750–72]. "Jagas, Giagas ou Giagues." In Diderot and d'Alembert, *Encyclopédie*.

Jaucourt, Louis Chevalier de. 2000 [1750–72]. "Eskimaux." In Diderot and d'Alembert, *Encyclopédie*.

– 2000 [1750–72]. "Galles." In Diderot and d'Alembert, *Encyclopédie*.

– 2000 [1750–72]. "Hottentots." In Diderot and d'Alembert, *Encyclopédie*.

– 2000 [1750–72]. "Hurons." In Diderot and d'Alembert, *Encyclopédie*.

– 2000 [1750–72]. "Pygmees." In Diderot and d'Alembert, *Encyclopédie*.

– 2000 [1750–72]. "Raisin Barbu." In Diderot and d'Alembert, *Encyclopédie*.

– 2000 [1750–72]. "Sauvage." In Diderot and d'Alembert, *Encyclopédie*.

– 2000 [1750–72]. "Tinagogo." In Diderot and d'Alembert, *Encyclopédie*.

Kafker, Frank A. 1996. *The Encyclopedists as a Group: A Collective Biography of the Authors of the* Encyclopédie. Oxford: Voltaire Foundation.

Kafker, Frank A., and Serena L. Kafker. 1988. *The Encyclopedists as Individuals: A Biographical Dictionary of the Authors of the* Encyclopédie. Oxford: Voltaire Foundation.

Klausnitzer, Ralf. 2008. *Literatur und Wissen. Zugänge, Modelle, Analysen.* Berlin: De Gruyter.

Kristeva, Julia. 1988. *Étrangers à nous-mêmes.* Paris: Fayard.

Lüsebrink, Hans-Jürgen. 2004. "Wissen und außereuropäische Erfahrung im 18. Jahrhundert." In *Macht des Wissens: die Entstehung der modernen Wissensgesellschaft,* edited by Richard van Dülmen and Sina Rauschenbach, 629–53. Cologne: Böhlau.

– 2006. "Von der Faszination zur Wissenssystematisierung: Die koloniale Welt im Diskurs der europäischen Aufklärung." In *Das Europa der Aufklärung und die außereuropäische koloniale Welt,* edited by Hans-Jürgen Lüsebrink, 9–18. Göttingen: Wallstein Verlag.

– 2013. "Enzyklopädismus und Kulturtransfer." In *Epoche und Projekt. Perspektiven der Aufklärungsforschung,* edited by Stefanie Stockhorst, 263–84. Göttingen: Wallstein Verlag.

Mallet, Edmé-François. 2000 [1750–72]. "Anthropophages." In Diderot and d'Alembert, *Encyclopédie.*

Mignolo, Walter D. 2011. *The Darker Side of Western Modernity: Global Futures, Decolonial Options.* Durham: Duke University Press.

N.N. 2000 [1750–72]. "Cafrerie." In Diderot and d'Alembert, *Encyclopédie.*

– 2000 [1750–72]. "Infidelite (*Gram. & Morale*)." In Diderot and d'Alembert, *Encyclopédie.*

– 2000 [1750–72]. "Innombrable." In Diderot and d'Alembert, *Encyclopédie.*

– 2000 [1750–72]. "Jagos." In Diderot and d'Alembert, *Encyclopédie.*

– 2000 [1750–72]. "Laine, Manufacture en Laine, *ou* Draperie." In Diderot and d'Alembert, *Encyclopédie.*

Pauw, Cornelius de. 1771. *Recherches philosophiques sur les Américains, ou Mémoires intéressants Pour servir à l'Histoire de l'Espèce humaine.* Berlin: n.p.

Said, Edward W. 1994. *Culture and Imperialism.* London: Vintage.

Sala-Molins, Louis. 1992. *Les misères des Lumières. Sous la raison, l'outrage . ..* Paris: Robert Laffon.

– 2006. *Dark Side of the Light: Slavery and the French Enlightenment.* Minneapolis: University of Minnesota Press.

Semsch, Klaus. 1999. *Abstand von der Rhetorik. Strukturen und Funktionen ästhetischer Distanznahme von der "ars rhetorica" bei den französischen Enzyklopädisten.* Hamburg: Meiner.

Spivak, Gayatri C. 1995 [1988]. "Can the Subaltern Speak?" In *The Post-Colonial Studies Reader*, edited by Bill Ashcroft, Gareth Griffiths, and Helen Tiffin, 24–8. London: Routledge.

– 2000. *A Critique of Postcolonial Reason: Toward a History of the Vanishing Present.* Cambridge, MA: Harvard University Press.

Struve, Karen. 2020. *Wildes Wissen in der "Encyclopédie." Koloniale Alterität, Wissen und Narration in der französischen Aufklärung.* Berlin/Boston: de Gruyter.

Vogl, Joseph. 2010. *Poetologien des Wissens um 1800.* Munich: Fink Verlag.

White, Hayden. 1978. *Tropics of Discourse: Essays in Cultural Criticism.* Baltimore: Johns Hopkins University Press.

Yvon, Toussaint. 2000 [1750–72]. "Barbares." In Diderot and d'Alembert, *Encyclopédie.*

chapter thirteen

The Last *Encyclopédie*

ARIANNE BAGGERMAN AND CLORINDA DONATO

When Willem Holtrop (figure 13.1) announced his *Nederduitsche encyclopedie* in 1786, he had every reason to expect an enthusiastic response from subscribers. He was an experienced publisher belonging to the upper ranks of his profession in the Dutch Republic, well aware of changing sentiments and tastes among Dutch readers.[1] His proposal was exciting and creative, so much so that it moved none other than the prominent and notorious Swiss publisher Fortunato Bartolomeo De Felice (figure 13.2), the editor of the *Encyclopédie* d'Yverdon, to seek a part in the venture. Had Holtrop's project actually materialized, his publishing legacy would have included a new sort of encyclopedia, universal in scope but culturally and nationally specific in provenance and vision. But alas, the venture failed, in circumstances of disappointing opacity and tantalizing complexity.

Holtrop entered the market for encyclopedias at a moment when publishers everywhere were being forced to abandon one of the staples that had sustained them for decades: revised, recast, abridged, excerpted, and sometimes even pirated editions of French-language works, among them encyclopedias and compendia of every type.[2] Publishers in Holland and Switzerland, unfettered by the censorship that occasionally hindered production of these works in their country of origin, Ancien régime France, had been especially active in this niche market, as the catalogues of the semi-annual Leipzig book fairs reveal: offerings by the Dutch stand out in the first half of the eighteenth century, while those of the Swiss dominate in the second half, with peak production between 1765 and 1780.[3] Relations of competition between Dutch and Swiss publishers had been complemented in many cases by relations of cooperation and interdependence, as both worked to satisfy the needs and demands

13.1. Portrait of Willem Holtrop (1751–1835) by D. Sluyter to a design by H. Langeveld. Photograph Iconographic Bureau, The Hague.

13.2. Portrait of Fortunato Bartolomeo De Felice (1723–1789), artist unknown, Accademia Roveretana degli Agiati.

of Protestant readers for works presenting the wealth of enlightenment ideas coming out of Catholic France.[4] But quite suddenly, after 1780, the French-language book market had collapsed, apparently glutted by offerings from the Swiss. In these conditions, the viability of encyclopedias and compendia had been heavily compromised, and publishers of these genres consequently began developing and testing new models, rethinking the essential goals and functions of such publications, in order to revitalize old markets and create new ones.[5]

The conditions associated with the glut are no better reflected than in the fortunes of Charles-Joseph Panckoucke, whose 264-volume *Encyclopédie méthodique* is an excellent example of one of these new models: a strictly utilitarian work, with volumes defined by specific disciplinary subject matter and articles shorn of philosophical allusions or implications.[6] Panckoucke was not only trying to find a new niche market within the broader boundaries of the encyclopedia genre, he was also hoping to avoid controversies of the type that had been generated for Diderot and d'Alembert on account of their decision to embed the practical articles of their *Encyclopédie* with subversive "philosophical" content.[7] For historians, Panckoucke's compilation signals a new era in the configuration of encyclopedic works. Even more, the fate of his publication attests to the grim reality of the glutted international market: Swiss publishing houses in 1783 were so overstocked with encyclopedic works, and so lacking in the financial means necessary for underwriting a pirated French-language edition of Panckoucke's innovative work, that no Swiss-produced French edition appeared, something unthinkable just a few years earlier. It is telling that the only projects to be spun off from the *Encyclopédie méthodique* were to be aimed at specialized national markets. One was a translation from the original French into Spanish edited by Antonio de Sancha; the second, a French edition made for the Italian and broader European markets edited by Giovanni Coi in the Republic of Venice. These two editions are discussed in detail in Clorinda Donato's contribution to this collection of essays.

The practice of translating works and adapting them in some way to specialized readers was certainly not new, but was acquiring greater appeal as a survival strategy in the market conditions of the later eighteenth century. An excellent example of this practice and its promise for publishers comes from Holland, in the form of Jacques Alexandre de Chalmot's 1778 *Huishoudelijk Woordenboek*.[8] Chalmot created his very successful work by translating De Felice's Swiss *Encyclopédie oeconomique*, and then infusing the translation with a substantial amount of specifically Dutch material.

But De Felice's work was itself derivative, having been developed by adding new material to an early eighteenth-century French work, Noël Chomel's 1709 *Dictionnaire œconomique*.[9] Each permutation of the original French publication adapted the practical content to local conditions: thus, for example, Chalmot's version contains agricultural information and advice geared to the requirements for and practices of farming and other horticulture in Holland.[10] Marketed as a "domestic" dictionary, the work covers topics ranging from gardening to cooking to sewing to animal husbandry, avoiding the controversial subjects with philosophical, political, or religious content that would have appeared in a "universal" encyclopedia and focusing instead on rural self-sufficiency and production strategies, "safe" and practical topics. Compilations along these lines were extremely desirable and ultimately would prove more durable as encyclopedic commodities in local markets than the grand universal encyclopedias brought out earlier by Diderot and d'Alembert in France, and by their competitor De Felice in Switzerland. Holtrop certainly must have taken Chalmot's success into account as he formulated his own encyclopedia proposal, but rather than offer yet another practical, Dutch-language compilation, he proposed a work that harked back to the grander, more comprehensive model, embellished with a national twist.

Holtrop conceived the *Nederduitsche encyclopedie* as a "Vaderlandsche" encyclopedia, a fusion of practical knowledge with national content that would lead readers to reflect in philosophical mode on the Dutch character and spirit. He planned to focus heavily on the seventeenth-century era of empire and wealth, the Dutch Golden Age, as the ideal to which the Dutch should aspire.[11] His published announcements, which appeared in 1786 in Dutch periodicals and in a formal prospectus distributed internationally, promised his potential subscribers forty quarto-volumes, each of about 460 pages, a work so complete that "het grootste getal der bezitteren geene andere boeken volstrekt noodig hebben" (most readers would need no other book).[12] Holtrop definitely was not proposing a commonplace eighteenth-century translation, amalgamation, or abridgment: "Niet geheel-en-al vreemdeling zijnde in de Engelsche, Fransche en Hoogduitsche Encyclopédieën, durve ik beweeren, dat eene bloote Nederduitsche vertaaling van een of meer derzelven, een zeer onvoldoende arbeid en voor ons altoos gebrekkig werk zoude zijn en blijven" (Not being an entire stranger to the English, French, and German Encyclopedia, I dare declare that a simple translation of these works would be an unsatisfactory undertaking and would be and remain insufficient for us all). Rather, he was offering a work entirely rewritten from scratch by Dutch contributors and illustrated by "de beroemdste en meest ervaaren kunstenaaren in ons Vaderland, als: Buys, Vinkeles, Bogerts, Brasser, Philips, Brouwer, de Wit, Saliet, Bendorp, van Jagen, Schenk, Kloekhoff, en anderen" (the most famous and experienced artists of our homeland, such as: Buys, Vinkeles, Bogerts, Brasser, Philips, Brouwer, De Wit, Saliet, Bendorp, van Jagen, Schenk, Kloekhoff, and others). Nevertheless, Dutch works were not his sole model; as a point of reference for prospective subscribers who were curious about the format of the volumes and its plates, Holtrop cited the physical appearance of a Swiss publication, De Felice's grand encyclopedia: "Het aantal der plaaten is vooraf onmooglijk te bepaalen; allen echter zullen geheel nieuw zijn, en elk deel derzelven dikte hebben van die, welke tot de Yverdonsche editie der Encyclopedie behooren" (The number of plates is impossible to predict beforehand; however, all will be entirely new, with each volume of plates the same thickness as those of the Yverdon edition of the *Encyclopédie*).

Nothing about Holtrop's choice of the Yverdon *Encyclopédie* as a positive comparative model is unusual given either the mutual dependence of the Dutch and Swiss book trades or the specific history of De Felice's publication and its ready availability in Holland. The Yverdon *Encyclopédie* had actually been underwritten in a fashion by the Dutch firm Gosse and Pinet, which had not only advertised the work in Dutch periodicals but had also purchased three-quarters of the total print run of sixteen hundred, for distribution in Holland and other Protestant states.[13] This investment is all the more interesting when read in the light of the firm's primary function in the French-language book trade, as purchaser of pirated French works. Over its thirty years of experience, it habitually had purchased anywhere from five hundred to fifteen hundred copies of pirated French editions. In the case of the Yverdon *Encyclopédie*, however, the firm claimed an expanded role, presenting itself in its advertisement as a full collaborator on the project rather than a mere distributor providing a service. Indeed, the origins of the *Encyclopédie* d'Yverdon leave one wondering whether from the financial perspective the work might not have been better dubbed the *Encyclopédie* de La Haye. Given this history of cooperation with the Dutch, it should not surprise us that shortly after he saw Holtrop's prospectus, De Felice proposed to Holtrop that the *Nederduitsche Encyclopedie* be transformed into a sort of joint Dutch-Swiss enterprise.[14]

De Felice understood the vagaries of the encyclopedia and compendium business very well. His *Encyclopédie œconomique*, which as we noted above was an expansion of Chomel's *Dictionnaire œconomique*, had been successful in part because it had required the assistance of just a few members of the Economic Society of Berne, who had been chosen for their knowledge based on "constant experience." Working "in-house" for this project, De Felice had brought out sixteen octavo-volumes between 1770 and 1771, which had sold readily as a set and, moreover, had been easy for the likes of a Chalmot in Holland or a Krünitz in Leipzig to translate and adapt to other markets. But the Yverdon *Encyclopédie* had been a different story. It had been launched in 1768 as a revision of Diderot's and d'Alembert's *Encyclopédie*, oriented specifically towards Protestant French-language readers.[15] With its 1769 announcement of the Yverdon *Encyclopédie*, the firm of Gosse and Pinet set in motion one of the most fruitful and sustained joint ventures of the eighteenth century between Swiss and Dutch publishing houses; however, its ambition immediately embroiled De Felice in controversy. The announcement in the *Gazette de Leyde* had boasted that Swiss luminaries with European reputations would be contributing, naming Daniel Bernouilli, Charles Bonnet, Samuel Gessner, Samuel Auguste Tissot, and Albrecht von Haller, alongside second-tier figures such as Elie Bertrand, Frédéric Samuel Ostervald, and De Felice himself. Unfortunately, the advertisement was printed before De Felice had actually secured the participation of the promised Swiss scholars. Angered by the unauthorized use of his name to draw buyers, Bonnet, for one, had disavowed his participation in a retraction sent to the *Gazette de Leyde* and had engaged Haller in an exchange on the matter.[16] He had also written to De Felice, expressing both his discontent and his doubts that the project ought to be undertaken: "Je ne sçaurais donc vous encourager le moins du monde à tenter une entreprise qui ruinerait votre santé et vos affaires" (Under no circumstances would I encourage you to attempt an enterprise that would ruin your health and your finances).[17] Bonnet's public disavowal had cooled Gessner, Haller, and Tissot on the enterprise, leaving De Felice to scramble to find replacements for them.[18] De Felice would successfully resolve these controversies, but, as we shall see, the experience left him wounded and wary.

De Felice had worked on both publications, the *Encyclopédie œconomique* and the *Encyclopédie* d'Yverdon, at the same time, and he was keenly aware that the universal encyclopedia model was the more difficult of the two models to bring to adequate fruition. As his subsequent history with Holtrop reveals, he was more than willing to share that awareness so long as he could benefit in the process. Thus, when his agent Pierre Giraud alerted him to Holtrop's plans, De Felice decided to send Holtrop a bit of unsolicited advice.[19] This advice tells us something of one publisher's thinking about possibilities in the years that we know, from hindsight, would end in revolution and war. Holtrop's silence in response tells us perhaps as much as De Felice's words, or at least suggests possible hypotheses for additional research. Together, the letters and other evidence related to Holtrop's enterprise, directly and indirectly, expand our knowledge of the possibilities and difficulties that faced aspiring encyclopedia publishers as they wound their way through the labyrinth of unclear paths and prospects at the close of the eighteenth century.

De Felice's Involvement

When agent Giraud came across Holtrop's prospectus, he clearly saw an opportunity for his employer to shore up his crumbling fortunes by acting as senior consultant to the projected Dutch venture. De Felice had hired Giraud in 1786, giving him power of attorney to travel on his behalf in Italy, Germany, and Holland, in order to sell off his remaining stock of books in the most advantageous way possible and to settle accounts with his debtors by the most suitable of methods.[20] The French-language book market had collapsed just after De Felice, director of the Yverdon publishing house and chief editor of all of its publications, produced the last volume of plates of his Yverdon encyclopedia. In 1781 he was staring at a backlog of orders. De Felice had resorted to tried and true strategies in order to bolster his flagging enterprise, but to no avail. With the help of loans, he had managed to publish a few of his own works, as well as a few successful titles from the Italian market, present and past, although it is not clear how he sold them, or if he actually did. But in 1782 he had begun having difficulties collecting from his debtors, among them Pierre Gosse.[21] De Felice was to be engaged in attempts to collect from debtors that continued until his death in 1789. Given this background, it is not difficult to see the reasons for Giraud's decision to notify De Felice; he was right in thinking that his employer would see the prospectus as a potential opportunity for productive collaboration once again in Holland. De Felice jumped at the prospect of reclaiming a piece of his fading publishing glory. He may have seen the waxing and waning of his career in the pages of Holtrop's prospectus, or perhaps he saw only a business opportunity; perhaps he saw some combination of both. We do not know. What is certain is that De Felice understood enough of Holtrop's Dutch prospectus to feel confident about approaching the Amsterdam publisher with advice – "voici, Monsieur, à ce qu'il me semble, la manière de la conduire" (this, Sir, is the way I believe you should proceed)[22] – and a few business proposals. And thus he sent off his still unpublished letter of 19 October 1786 to his Dutch counterpart and competitor.

De Felice begins his letter with a series of compliments on Holtrop's proposal, only broaching the true purpose of his communication on the second page, at which point he makes a business proposition. For only five thousand Louis d'or, he offers the Dutch publisher his notes for a revised edition of the Yverdon *Encyclopédie*, a substantial corpus of medical notes, and the notes left by the late Albrecht von Haller, "qui était lui même une Encyclopédie vivante" (who was a veritable walking encyclopedia).[23] To sweeten the deal, De Felice throws in his personal editorial services, free of charge, pointing out the enormous benefits that his substantial experience in such enterprises could bring. Were Holtrop to accept this proposal, he would have only to hire a translator and a few Dutch authors to add specific Dutch content to the translated text. Additionally, De Felice offers to spare Holtrop the tremendous expense of creating new plates, since the Yverdon *Encyclopédie* plates, each still good for fifteen hundred to two thousand impressions, could be made available, thereby reducing the price of each plate for Holtrop to only one Louis d'or, a quarter of the cost of new plates.[24] In other words, De Felice proposes that the Dutch project be altered to fit the more common translation-adaptation model, which had proved so profitable for his *Encyclopédie méthodique* and for Chalmot's *Huishoudelijk Woordenboek*.

In keeping with his focus on financial issues, De Felice stresses that the translation-adaptation model would expedite production. Large-scale alphabetically organized encyclopedias dependent on numerous authors entail much risk for their publishers, not least because these projects are not really complete until the final volume appears. Unless the entire set is marketed speedily, chances increase that subscribers will die, lose their money, or find other reasons to walk away from their commitments. Though De Felice does not specifically mention his own troubles, it is easy to "read" in his lines evidence of his earlier experience as the editor of the *Encyclopédie* d'Yverdon. Driven by extreme perfectionism and by his promise to surpass the achievement of Diderot and d'Alembert, De Felice had simply taken too long to complete his enterprise. He had discovered, in the process, that the public cared more about price than content; he had actually lost a large part of his market to Panckoucke's cheaper quarto- and octavo- editions of Diderot's *Encyclopédie*. Furthermore, he had seen a large percentage of his subscriptions cancelled after he announced to subscribers that he was expanding the enterprise to fifty-eight volumes. De Felice's greatest public triumph, his Yverdon *Encyclopédie*, had, in the end, actually been his worst private financial defeat.

De Felice further elaborates his overriding concern with production schedules in a lengthy postscript, penned after a full translation of Holtrop's prospectus had clarified its contents for him. The postscript expresses the opinion that Holtrop's focus on contributions by Dutch authors for this new encyclopedia would expose the Dutch publisher to too great a risk. To substantiate his point, De Felice relates that he had expected to tap a vast pool of intellectual talent from all over Europe for his encyclopedia, but that the glory that had come with this dream had been short lived. In its place had come a daily grind brought about by the realities of supervising the contributors. Many writers had dropped out or failed to deliver on their promises, leaving him with the difficult task of reassigning articles, all the while trying to preserve continuity in point of view and content. As a stick for motivating delinquent writers his only recourse was the threat of withholding their fees, but even that had not been enough to bring the project to completion in a timely fashion. De Felice notes that he had succeeded in publishing the forty-eight volumes of text in five years only because he had actually written a good portion of the articles himself; he lamented the fact that had he relied wholly on his collaborating authors "Je n'aurois pas fini l'impression du texte dans 15 ou 20 ans" (not even fifteen or twenty years would have been enough time to finish printing the text volumes).[25] As for the plates, De Felice opines that Holtrop's promise to work with only Dutch engravers would compromise both the quality of the illustrations and their production time. He then reiterates his earlier point about the cost of plates.

In closing, the Swiss publisher offers some opinions on the controversial subject of religious content. "Votre titre porte *des Sciences humaines*. Il semble par là que vous voulez exclure de votre Encyclopédie les matières théologiques. Le clergé en Hollande est nombreux et en état d'acheter votre encyclopédie, et il y seroit plus encouragé s'il espéroit y trouver les sciences théologiques bien traitées." (Your title carries within it *the Social Sciences*. From this it seems that you wish to exclude theological material from your encyclopedia. There are many clergymen in Holland who have the means to buy your encyclopedia and they would be more encouraged to do so if they hoped to find the theological sciences well developed within.)[26] But De Felice knows only too well that articles touching on certain aspects of doctrine or superstition could endanger publishers, or at least cause them grave troubles. Therefore, he suggests

a way to frame the planned work that would appeal to the clerically dominated Dutch market without triggering negative reactions: Holtrop, he
thinks, ought to be able to find a Dutch theologian prepared to limit his
focus to religious ritual, a safe way to present material on the many varieties of religion, then of interest, without getting into subject matter that
could bring charges of apostasy or heresy, or embroil publishers and editors in scandal.[27] We note the success and multiple editions of Bernard
Picart and Jean-Frédéric Bernard's *Cérémonies et coutumes religieuses de tous
les peuples du monde,* on the religions of the world and their rituals, fully
illustrated, first published in Amsterdam in 1723.

Here De Felice feels compelled to discuss his own troubles in handling
theological content. He had intended to edit and shape his encyclopedia
so that its religious content would not offend his readers or censors in
Protestant nations; he had not wanted a repetition of the outrage from
religious circles that had greeted Diderot and d'Alembert's great work.
He acknowledges to Holtrop that his encyclopedia was, despite his best
efforts, still deficient in the area of religion, ascribing the problem to
his choice of contributors, one of whom was a zealot and the other very
liberal.[28] Alexandre Chavannes was the zealot and pastor Gabriel Mingard the liberal theologian. The writings of both had been problematic
in different ways. Chavannes represented the old guard of unenlight-
ened religion and had supplied articles on theology and *histoire sacrée*
whose distinguishing feature was their orthodoxy. His work was pedan-
tic and limited. Mingard, on the other hand, with whom De Felice had
a profound intellectual affinity, represented a theology so liberal and
heterodox that his contributions had caused problems with the censors.
Signed with the initials G.M., his articles had covered the domains of
theology and philosophy. The signature clearly belonged to Gabriel Mingard, which became a problem for both Mingard and De Felice, due to
the controversial nature of his articles. De Felice would eventually assign
him another set of initials, M.D.B., to conceal to the extent possible content that might spark the censors' ire. De Felice revealed this strategic
change to subscribers in an *Avis de l'éditeur* placed at the end of the tenth
volume of plates. To Holtrop, De Felice declares that he would have preferred writing the theological contributions himself had he not been
constrained by time. Still, he notes that the theological articles became
one of the strongest selling points of the Yverdon edition, despite their
deficiencies and inconsistencies, which included oscillation between
extreme orthodoxy and quasi-heresy. And while these articles posed a
significant challenge to him as editor, the success of theological articles

convinced him that their inclusion in an encyclopedic enterprise constituted an important marketing strategy.

Holtrop's proposed title, *Nederduitsche encyclopedie, of Algemeen beredeneerd woordenboek van alle menschelyke kundigheden,* certainly lacked theological connotations, but the prospectus itself contained many references to religion in general, and to the Dutch Reformed Church in particular. De Felice's misunderstanding may have been the result of a faulty and somehow misleading translation of the prospectus. It is more likely that De Felice, the one-time Catholic Franciscan monk converted to Calvinist Protestantism, understood the prospectus very well, and that, reading between the lines, he was alarmed by the impartiality on religious matters professed therein. Holtrop's prospectus actually states that religious subjects will be treated as objectively as possible because it "noch met den aart van het werk zelve, en veel minder met onze oogmerken strooke, om samenstellen te vormen, of dezelven te verdeedigen" (does not fit the nature of the work itself, and even less our intentions, to take a stance or defend a particular belief). He promised a thorough and objective coverage of all world religions, even citing in the prospectus the cooperation of "etlijke Rabbijnen" (several rabbis) and thus signaling a certain radicalism within a climate dominated by the Reformed Church. Acknowledging that all encyclopedias had failed in the area of religious impartiality, he suggested that Holland was the best place to attempt to rectify the matter because one must admit that "de uitvoering van alle zulke zaaken in geen land veiliger geschieden kunne, dan in ons vrije Vaderland" (the bringing forth of such issues cannot take place in a safer manner than in our own free Homeland.)[29] He had found many "voortreffelijke en beroemde mannen" (excellent and famous men) of the "heerschende kerk" (reigning church), "zo wel als die van andere Godsdienstige gezindheden, in ons land" (as well as those of other religious backgrounds in our country) who were prepared to contribute articles on the practices of their specific churches.[30] With these words, Holtrop was trying to dispel any notion that his encyclopedia might contain the sort of controversial ideas about theology and religion contained in earlier eighteenth-century works of reference. In other words, he was going to take a neutral position on confessional and doctrinal matters. His statement certainly could have made many a clergyman fear the worst – indifference towards religion – as De Felice clearly recognized.

How might Holtrop have viewed De Felice's proposal? The latter's Yverdon *Encyclopédie* was, of course, well known to the Dutch public, and it is likely that Holtrop's prospectus had referred to it as a model for that very reason. Numerous copies of the work were still available for purchase in the 1780s, making it a serious probable competitor with Holtrop's proposed venture. Holtrop might well have welcomed the opportunity to eliminate that competition by agreeing to De Felice's proposal. That fact cannot have escaped De Felice. It also does not seem unreasonable to think that Holtrop might have been interested in the Swiss publisher's advice. But De Felice was also a notorious figure in the enlightenment world of letters, anything but unsullied in reputation, business or personal.

Thus when Gosse and Pinet had announced the Yverdon *Encyclopédie*, they had taken the unusual step of defending De Felice's intellectual and moral rectitude, even though he was, at that time, unknown, formally at least, to the Dutch public. The Gosse and Pinet flyer declared that De Felice is "[g]énéralement connu, dans la République des lettres et dans l'Europe entière, pour un parfait honnête homme, incapable d'en imposer ou de manquer au public [...] tous les autres avis et accusations contre la personne et la candeur du Professeur de Felice, sont également un tissu de mensonges et de faussetés" (generally known in the Republic of Letters and throughout Europe as a perfectly upright man, incapable of imposing himself on the public or letting the public down [...] all other opinions or accusations against the person and the candour of Professor De Felice are by the same token a fabrication of lies and falsehoods).[31] Their statements suggest that they were not a little concerned that De Felice's past would cast doubts on his integrity, especially in a world shaped both by Calvinist mores and the anticlerical sensibilities of the Enlightenment. An intellectual and religious exile, De Felice had a reputation in learned circles, especially those of the most prominent *philosophes*, as a sort of rogue, one of those scandal-creating refugees from Catholicism whose intellectual credentials had been tainted by corrupt mores. His "adventure" with a Roman countess whom he had helped escape from a convent while he was still a Franciscan had provided ample grist to the *philosophes'* anticlerical mill. In their eyes, De Felice was nothing more than an *abbé galant*, despite his conversion to Protestantism. Joseph Gorani had immortalized the scandal with the countess in a sensationalistic biographical sketch, *Aventures d'un homme célèbre*, which had provided Europe with the theatricalized story.[32]

Having earned the ire of the *philosophes*, De Felice might well have seemed a liability as the editor of an encyclopedia aimed at enlightened readers, but Gosse and Pinet seem to have recognized that the *philosophes'* ire was inflamed as much by fear in the face of a credible competitor as by substantive critiques of De Felice's past and intellectual positions. De Felice was indeed, in the fullest sense, a competitor to the *philosophes*, especially to Diderot and d'Alembert, whose *Encyclopédie* had begun to appear dated by the 1770s. De Felice was able to pilfer what he liked for the Yverdon project, recycling, rewriting, revising, or removing articles as he saw fit. In the competitive market conditions that already surrounded encyclopedia production, the *philosophes* simply could not pass up the chance to use a salacious *histoire* to their own advantage. Voltaire also had ample reason to disdain De Felice, who had published a 1767 pamphlet, *Etrennes aux desœuvrés, ou lettre d'un Quaker à ses frères et à un grand docteur*, directed against him. De Felice had further offended Voltaire by overseeing the commissioning of a series of articles providing caustic commentary on the most *outré* entries of Voltaire's *Dictionnaire philosophique*.[33] These critiques had appeared in seventeen consecutive issues of the *Journal helvétique*, of which De Felice was a managing editor in 1768–9, and in whose pages his Yverdon *Encyclopédie* was already being announced. To put it simply, whatever his enlightened ideas and actions, De Felice was simply "the enemy" to powerful *philosophes*. Reading between the lines of Gosse's and Pinet's announcement, we can discern the thoughts that might have caused them to see in De Felice the kind of intellectual and commercial ally worth betting on. In the aftermath of the Paris *Encyclopédie*, he was promising a second wave of the encyclopedic venture designed to address the needs, both practical and religious, of the ever-growing constituency of the Protestant Enlightenment.[34] Perhaps they thought that an enlightened *abbé galant*, converted to Calvinism and cleansed of frivolity, would best be able to translate enlightened positions on religion into ideas digestible to that constituency without lapsing into unacceptable neutrality, indifference, or atheism.

Given his personal history, De Felice knew very well the problems that could bedevil an editor with the best of intentions, especially if his personal religious affiliations and integrity could in any way be questioned. For this reason alone, Holtrop might have done well to accept De Felice's warnings, even though the elder Swiss editor had misread Holtrop's intentions. Holtrop himself was not above suspicion in orthodox circles. Already in 1786 he was associated with radical theological positions through his involvement with freemasonry. On this issue, all that is known at present is that Holtrop served as master of the Amsterdam masonic lodge La Charité from 1791 to 1835. The subject deserves further exploration.[35]

Whether masonic affiliation actually caused trouble for Holtrop we do not know, but we do know that for some reason the public failed to warm to his Dutch encyclopedia proposal. Perhaps potential subscribers simply mistrusted his promise to deliver a work penned by Dutch intellectuals. A footnote in the prospectus suggests that Holtrop anticipated troubles on this account: "Let nobody think that this statement is exaggerated, or beside the truth. More than *fifty* intellectuals in our homeland have promised their contributions and given permission to announce their names publicly. However, an even larger amount, regardless of repeated requests, has chosen not to. Instead of supplying a partial list of these *Maecenas*, we have chosen not to mention any names."[36] Holtrop's claim sounds like a bluff, and readers may have taken it as such. They may have been disturbed by his refusal to reveal names, or perhaps by the scale he was projecting for his promised work.[37] Whatever the cause, after an announcement on 25 November 1786 giving prospective buyers until the end of the month to subscribe, nothing was heard again of this Dutch encyclopedia.

Ultimately, Holtrop was probably stymied by the high cost of the encyclopedia and the small size of the Dutch Republic. There were relatively few of his compatriots who could afford the expense of such a work at the phenomenal price of at least 240, and many of those wealthy enough to subscribe to such a project had already done so with the Yverdon *Encyclopédie*. The latter fact is probably one of the reasons that Holtrop never reacted to the suggestions made by De Felice. Even the optimistic Holtrop would not have expected to find a market for the revision of the Yverdon *Encyclopédie* when copies of the original edition were still readily available. Besides, Holtrop had already advertised a wholly new work.[38] Indeed, he was targeting a new readership, newcomers to the book market, connoisseurs who wanted to enhance their libraries and their status by supplementing their ownership of a French-language encyclopedia with the purchase of a thoroughly Dutch one, an important point for the wealthy who were not fluent in French. Holtrop may have been trying to capture some of the same market that had made Chalmot's *Algemeen huishoudelijk-, natuur-, rekenkundig- en kunstwoordenboek* such a success. If so, he seems not to have considered the possibility that Chalmot's work might already have exhausted the market for Dutch-language compilations, whatever the differences in their design and purpose. Perhaps he thought he could compete directly with Chalmot, who had announced in 1785 and 1786 the printing of supplements to his popular dictionary.[39] Here too, it appears that Holtrop miscalculated or underestimated his savvy competitor. Chalmot had released the first sections of the sequel in a preliminary volume, which had received a rave review in *the Algemeene Vaderlandsche Letteroeffeningen*. In this way he seems to have secured public confidence in his undertaking; buyers proved more inclined to purchase Chalmot's supplements than to subscribe to Holtrop's new encyclopedia. Perhaps, in the tight market conditions of the 1780s, purchasers simply stayed with the familiar, passing up the opportunities and risks that would have come with buying a new model reference work.[40]

Chalmot's strategy reinforces the wisdom of De Felice's remarks about publication timelines. Indeed, a review in September 1786, upon completion of the first volume of the *Sequel*, remarks that Chalmot's "diligence, backed up by his patrons [...,] [give] a favourable prognosis that this work [a complete Low German encyclopedia] will soon be brought to fruition."[41] Critics were in fact signalling that Chalmot's work was likely to come out in timely fashion, simply because he was writing it himself, with assistance from only three associates. The problems that had delayed the finalization of De Felice's Yverdon *Encyclopédie* simply could not occur in such circumstances: one more sign that the market for vast cooperative intellectual enterprises had evaporated. In fact, however, the market even for these more circumscribed works was disappearing. Chalmot did not fare very well with his sequel. His supplement attracted only 375 subscribers, while his first edition had attracted 1,000 subscribers for a press run of fifteen hundred. More than twenty years later he would complain to the German publisher Heinemeyer about the lack of demand for dictionaries and encyclopedias.[42] Chalmot's fate only reinforces our contention that Holtrop's ambition to bring a piece of work to the market that would measure up to the French example and surpass Chalmot's sales figures was simply too grand for the small Dutch Republic.[43]

If Willem Holtrop had been a newcomer to the publishing business, or an eccentric figure whose projects had revealed signs of megalomania, then his error in judgment would need no further comment, but he was neither, as we have noted earlier. We must look elsewhere for explanations of his failure.[44] The little that we know suggests that the explanations in the end will be complex, constructed of personal, political, and economic elements playing out within the specific context of the Dutch Republic in an error of upheaval.

To begin, we must note that part of the answer may be found in the political, in the way that Holtrop's political convictions and affiliations may have structured his perceptions of possibilities. Holtrop was not a neutral publisher, having published several works with political implications. Without exception, these publications expressed a reformist Patriotic opinion. It was Holtrop's Patriot convictions that may have brought about his error in judgment, especially in the context of an unfolding revolution, however brief its duration.

The fact that Holtrop's ambitious plans were formed in 1786, the year in which the Patriots took hold of political power, is no coincidence. After the stadtholder was publicly humiliated in March 1786, and several councilmen had set out to replace the old oligarchy with newcomers, the impossible seemed possible. Among publishers, democratic dreams and a certain confidence that national Dutch pride could be translated into Dutch readers may have been the stimulus behind the several proposals for new Dutch encyclopedic projects floated not only by Holtrop but also by his fellow Patriot Chalmot and by his former master Pieter Blussé.[45] When, in 1787, the Orangists regained power with foreign aid, this would not merely put an end to Holtrop's encyclopedia but also bring about an end to the Patriotic euphoria. While in the seventeenth century and the first half of the eighteenth century the republic was able to give refuge to and actually seek out French intellectuals, it was now up to the French to give asylum to a large group of Dutch radicals.

Holtrop's error in judgment could also have been caused by an obscured view of economic realities at the end of the eighteenth century. Many of his contemporaries were troubled by what they perceived as that reality. Disappointed by the relative economic decline during this period, some were hoping to resurrect Dutch greatness in the markets by reinvigorating the nation's spirit, that is, by fostering a "return" to the seventeenth-century Dutch Golden Age when the Dutch had been a moral nation of hardworking Patriots.[46] De Oeconomische Tak van de Hollandse Maatschappij der Wetenschappen, an economic reform movement that favoured mercantilist politics – economic self-sufficiency, the purchase of Dutch rather than foreign goods – was the key to revival and restoration. The methods for reaching these goals were pragmatic: convincing wealthy citizens to invest their capital in native industries.[47] Unfortunately their interpretation of the problems facing the Dutch Republic relied on the erroneous presupposition that the cause of the economic decline was internal. People forgot that the Dutch Golden Age, when the republic had flourished as an export country, had been dependent on external factors. The seventeenth century across much of Europe had been an era of internal confessional strife, political struggles and civil wars, and large-scale international wars, all of which had allowed the peaceful Dutch Republic not only to develop into an important sanctuary for intellectuals but also to become the central European transit port for goods. The Dutch book market had profited handsomely from the production of books that, for whatever reason, could not be published elsewhere. The conditions that had allowed the Dutch to attain such prominence, of course, had disappeared in the later seventeenth century, and with them the Dutch Golden Age. During the eighteenth century markets were more restricted and turned inward, and the book market, at least by the later decades of the eighteenth century, was no exception. Large international firms such as Elzevier and Blaeu made way for a new group of so-called Dutch publishers, among whom Holtrop and Chalmot figured prominently.[48]

Within this framework, Holtrop's forays into the Dutch encyclopedia market can be best understood as those of a new type of publisher exploring the boundaries of a market of unclear configuration, based on consumers whose interests and needs were difficult to assess. He was probably not only misled but also beguiled by ideas such as those expressed by the Oeconomische Tak. This movement was growing rapidly – it had three thousand members in 1777 and its membership peaked in the 1780s, the point at which Holtrop tried to launch his encyclopedia. Holtrop may have been pitching his encyclopedia to precisely the types most likely to belong to the Oeconomische Tak or to support its policies; specifically, he might have been gambling on the willingness of the wealthier members of this group to invest in homespun cultural heritage by buying a reference work that was explicitly *not* a reworking of famous English, French, German, or Swiss predecessors. If this supposition is true, then it is probably no coincidence that Holtrop stresses the Dutch origins of his encyclopedia in his prospectus, or that he emphasizes that his writers would all be Dutch; these actions would be part of a conscious strategy to touch on nationalistic sentiments.

And what about De Felice and the Swiss book trade? When we review the success of the publishing industry in the Suisse romande, what stands out, as in the Dutch case, is the occurrence of unfavourable religious and political situations elsewhere, which transformed Switzerland into a place of refuge for exiles and, by extension, into an intellectual capital. De Felice, himself, had entered Switzerland as a religious exile and had built his reputation and wealth on his ability to operate as a cultural broker and producer. During the years in which the Swiss book trade flourished, the Yverdon Press as well as the Société Typographique de Neuchâtel depended heavily on book dealers from other countries for its success, Holland being perhaps the most important locus for distribution.

Once market conditions changed, however, a classic case of domino effect began to occur. With no more market, booksellers were left with excess inventory, publishers could not interest them in new ventures, and the whole trade gradually slowed. De Felice's appeal to Holtrop in 1786 amounts to a last-ditch effort to stay alive and underscores the extent to which De Felice depended on his relationship with Dutch book dealers. Between 1770 and 1780 his publishing house had known great prosperity and his books had spread the name of Yverdon throughout Europe, but much of that success had depended on the distribution services provided by Pierre Gosse. Gosse, continuing his tendency to think of the Yverdon *Encyclopédie* as his publication, had actually reserved for himself the continuing sale of its volumes after 1773 when his son, Pierre Frédéric Gosse, took over the activity that was formerly that of Gosse and Pinet. As late as 1777, Pierre Frédéric Gosse informed the Société Typographique de Neuchâtel that he was not in the market for their abridged *Encyclopédie* in-quarto, as he was still engaged in the Yverdon edition, which is "very well received, and which I consider preferable to all others" (p. 241).[49] Although he claimed that only a few sets still existed, he was committed to exhausting his supply of Yverdon encyclopedias before investing in another compilation. It is possible that Gosse was bluffing here, especially since he was not technically involved with selling the Yverdon *Encyclopédie* volumes at all, per his agreement with his father. Overall his book sales may not have been bad; he may simply have wanted to avoid further commitments to compendia and encyclopedias. Periodicals prove that Gosse and Pinet and later Gosse junior continued to purchase books from De Felice, indicating that good relations prevailed into the early part of the 1780s. However, at the end of De Felice's career, from 1782 to 1789, the picture had changed drastically.

Neither De Felice nor Holtrop would see the production of what would have been the last great encyclopedia of the eighteenth-century enlightenment, and it is unlikely that it could have ever been produced. What their joint stories tell is the extent to which the grandeur of the *Encyclopédie* model still was fueling national, financial, and personal ambition in the book trade, even after the conditions for the success of such an enterprise had disappeared.

By the beginning of the nineteenth century, Holtrop has significantly adjusted his reach. He advertises his new venture, the three-volume household dictionary *Algemeen nuttig en noodzaaklyk stad- en land- huishoudkundig woordenboek voor het daaglyksch leven* (Useful and necessary dictionary of general knowledge for daily life in urban and rural households), of "more than two thousand pages, densely printed in large 12pt" that for "veelen" (many) would compensate for "het gemis […] van het zeer uitgebreid Huishoudelijk Woordenboek van Chomel, welk hier als in het kleen gevonden wordt" (the absence of Chomel's comprehensive Huishoudelijk Woordenboek, of which one will find this to be a reduced version).[50] In an earlier advertisement he takes care to stress the compactness and favourable relationship between price and quality of his new publication:

> Indien stedeling en landman, indien huisvader en huismoeder, voor weinig gelds – want het gantsche werk kost niet meer dan 2, – ieder deel – veel, ja genoegzaam alles, begeeren te weeten, wat hun noodig zij ter gemaklijke, aangename en voordeelige waarneming van ambt, beroep, bedrijf, handwerk en huishouding; dan koopen zij zig dit boek, waarvan nu na genoeg 3000 exemplaaren verkogt zijn.[51]

> (If the city dweller and country man, if the father of the family and the mistress of the house, want to know more, yes, practically everything that is needed to attain simple, convenient, and efficient performance in their office, profession, business, handicraft, and household, then for just a bit of money – because the entire work costs no more than 2 – per volume – they can purchase this book, of which now nearly three thousand copies have been sold.

Holtrop's vision had adapted to the market.

NOTES

1 Willem Holtrop (1751–1835), born in Dordrecht, was one of the leading booksellers and publishers in the Dutch Republic. His father, John Holtrop, was the official translator for the city and translated for various publishing houses, including A. Blussé & Son. Both he and Blussé had encyclopedic ambitions, which are amply covered in this collection of essays.
2 As we know from Robert Darnton, 1979, *The Business of Enlightenment: A Publishing History of the* Encyclopédie (Cambridge, MA: Harvard University Press), 465, a French-proficient European reading public willingly purchased encyclopedias at least up until the 1780s.
3 Typographical societies in Geneva, Berne, Neuchâtel, and Lausanne, as well as book dealers throughout Europe (including the Dutch firm Gosse and Pinet, which figures prominently in the present chapter) made more money

from these encyclopedias and compendia than from any other type of publication. An anecdote from the life of Sophia van der Meulen (1745–1781) illustrates the widespread availability of Diderot's *Encyclopédie* in the Dutch Republic. Before her marriage, van der Meulen regularly bought volumes of the French encyclopedia. Storage of the folio tomes proved more daunting than the purchase price, and shortly after her wedding her new husband, Jan Jacob de Malapert, systematically sold off all volumes of her diligently collected piece of cultural heritage. On this issue, see J. Hokke, 1987, '"Mijn alderliefste Jantielief.' Vrouw en gezin in de Republiek. Regentenvrouwen en hun relaties," *Jaarboek voor vrouwengeschiedenis* 8: 69.

4 A major source of information on relations between the Swiss and Dutch in the matter of book publishing is the correspondence of the Société Typographique de Neuchâtel with various Dutch book dealers, among them the firm of Gosse and Pinet. These unpublished letters may be found at the Bibliothèque Publique et Universitaire de Neuchâtel.

5 See, on this general subject, Darnton, *The Business of Enlightenment.* For an overview of the eighteenth-century Dutch book trade, see Arianne Baggerman, 2001, *Een lot uit de loterij. Het wel en wee van een uitgeversfamilie in de achttiende eeuw*, 2nd ed. (The Hague: SDU), published in English as *Life's Lottery: Family Policy and Marketing Strategy of a Distinguished Eighteenth-Century Dutch Publishing Company (A. Blussé and Son 1745–1823)* (Leiden: Brill, 2007). On the Swiss books at the Leipzig book fair, see Clorinda Donato, 1994, "From Switzerland to Europe through Leipzig: The Swiss Book Trade and the Leipziger Messe 1765–1785," *Leipziger Jahrbuch zur Buchgeschichte* 4: 103–34.

6 See Kathleen Hardesty Doig and Christabel P. Braunrot, 1995, "The *Encyclopédie méthodique*: An Introduction," *Studies on Voltaire and the Eighteenth Century* 327: 1–152.

7 For a discussion of cross-references in the *Encyclopédie*, see G. Blanchard and M. Olsen, 2002, "Le système des renvois dans l'*Encyclopédie*: Une cartographie des structures de connaissance au XVIIIème siècle," *Recherches sur Diderot et l'Encyclopédie* 31–2: 45–70; and Benoît Melançon, 2002, "Sommes-nous les premiers lecteurs de l'*Encyclopédie*?" in *The Future of Web Publishing: Hyper-reading, Cybertexts, and Metapublishing, Interdisciplines*, accessed 24 April 2020, https://archivesic.ccsd.cnrs.fr/sic_00000269/document.

8 *Algemeen huishoudelijk-, natuur-, zedekundig- en konst- woordenboek*, 1778, ed. J.A. De Chalmot, 2nd printing (Leyden [etc.]: Johan Le Maire [etc.]).

9 For a discussion of one of the evolutionary lines of eighteenth-century encyclopedism that traces the several adaptations and expansions of Chomel's *Dictionnaire œconomique*, see Clorinda Donato, 1997, "Übersetzung

und Wandlung des enzyklopädischen Genres: Johann Georg Krünitz' *Oeconomische Encyclopädie* (1771–1858) und ihre französischsprachigen Vorläufer," in *Kulturtransfer im Epochenumbruch Frankreich-Deutschland 1770 bis 1815* (Leipzig: Leipziger Universitätsverlag), 539–67.

10 Jacques Alexandre de Chalmot's 1778 *Huishoudelijk Woordenboek* was also published in Japanese, with specifically Japanese agricultural content. See Jacques Proust, 2002, *Europe through the Prism of Japan: Sixteenth to Eighteenth Centuries,* trans. Elizabeth Bell (Notre Dame: University of Notre Dame Press).

11 All quotations in this paragraph come from the subscription announcement included in the magazine *Algemeene genees- natuur- en huishoudkundige jaarboeken* published by Holtrop and Pieter Blussé Dordrecht [etc.], 1786, vol. 3, 1st piece, 92. The price per volume was 6 for those who signed up. This amounts to 240 for the entire encyclopedia, but does not include the separate volumes containing the plates.

12 Holtrop announced the encyclopedia for several months in 1786, first in the *Algemeene genees- natuur- en huishoudkundige jaarboeken,* later in several journals, among them the *Rotterdamsche Courant* and the *Oprechte Haerlemse Courant.* All translations are the authors' unless otherwise indicated.

13 On Gosse and Pinet, see Jean-Pierre Perret, 1981 [1945], *Les imprimeries d'Yverdon au XVIIe et au XVIIIe siècle* (Geneva: Slatkine). Perret has pointed out that the Yverdon *Encyclopédie* was first announced in a Dutch newspaper by Gosse and Pinet, who refer to themselves in the first person as they describe the recruitment of Swiss scholars for what they consider their own enterprise.

14 This unusual move by De Felice has, until now, escaped the attention of historians. On De Felice's financial position at the end of his life, see Eugène Maccabez, *F. B. De Felice 1723–1789 et son "Encyclopédie"* (Basel, 1903).

15 The Yverdon *Encyclopédie* acquired its name on account of its place of publication, the small city of Yverdon-les-Bains, locus of the presses responsible for three-quarters of the publications sponsored by the Société Typographique de Berne. See Darnton, *The Business of Enlightenment,* 19–20.

16 See *The Correspondence between Albrecht von Haller and Charles Bonnet,* 1983, ed. Otto Sonntag (Berne: Hans Huber Verlag), esp. 807–9, Bonnet to Haller, 24 March 1769: "Le Protégé de votre République à Yverdon, Mr Felice, m'avoit écrit deux fois en Janvier & Février dernier, pour me presser de concourir avec lui à une sorte de *refonte* de l'immense *Encyclopédie.* Vous comprenés, mon Illustre Ami, si une pareille Proposition étoit faite pour un Homme dont la Santé lui permet à peine d'achever ses propres Ouvrages. Je répondis donc au *Refondeur,* qu'il m'étoit impossible de m'engager dans un pareil travail. Je fis plus; je cherchai à l'en détourner lui même, en lui

représentant qu'il courroit le risque de ruiner sa Santé & ses Affaires, &c. Quelle n'a donc point été ma surprise, quand on m'a informé, que j'étois annoncé au Public dans la *Gazette de Leide* pour un des Entrepreneurs de la nouvelle Edition de l'*Encyclopédie!* Voici, mon excellent Ami, la Copie fidèle de l'*Avis* inséré dans cette Gazette. Vous verrés qu'on vous place à la Tête des Travailleurs, et je pense bien que c'est sans plus de fondement que moi. J'ai écrit aussi tôt à un Ami de Leide pour le prier d'insèrer dans la Gazette un *Contre-Avis,* où je désavoue hautement ce qu'on ose m'attribuer. Vous connoissés Felice, & vous sçaves si ses forces intellectuelles répondent à un travail de ce genre. J'ai lu la plume à la main près de 200 Articles de ce Vaste Dictionnaire, & c'en étoit bien assés pour porter un Jugement solide sur la manière dont il a été éxécuté. J'ai choisi ces Articles dans presque tous les Genres, & partout j'ai trouvé des fautes d'*omission* ou de *commission* Je ne parle point de cette multitude de choses dangereuses qui y sont répanduës, et qu'on rencontre souvent lors qu'on s'y attend le moins. Il s'y trouve pourtant d'excellents morceaux en divers genres, et la partie des *Arts & Métiers* est incontestablement la plus précieuse. L'Extrait le mieux fait de cette immense Compilation ne suffiroit point: il faudroit la refondre en entier. Il s'en faut bien que les Auteurs ayent toujours puisé dans les meilleures sources. &c &c."

(Mr. Felice, who enjoys protected status in your Republic in Yverdon, had written to me twice last January and February to urge me to collaborate with him on some sort of revised edition of the immense *Encyclopédie.* You do understand, my illustrious friend, that such a proposal has been made to a man whose health hardly makes it possible for him to realize his own books. I therefore answered the *Revisor* himself, that it would be impossible for me to become involved in a similar undertaking. I even went further and tried to change his mind about it by telling him that he ran the risk of ruining his health and his business, etc. Imagine, then, my surprise when I was informed that my name was announced as one of the entrepreneurs of this new edition of the *Encyclopédie* in the *Gazette de Leide!* Here, my excellent friend, is the exact copy of the *Avis* inserted in this gazette. You will see that your name appears at the top of the list of the contributors, and I believe that your name has been used with the same lack of consultation as mine was. As soon as I saw it I wrote to a friend in Leiden to ask him to insert a *Contre-Avis* in the *Gazette* where I strongly disclaim what has been attributed to me. You know Felice & you will know if his intellectual energy corresponds to an undertaking of this kind. Pen in hand, I read some two hundred articles of this vast dictionary, & that was indeed enough to

form a solid judgment about how it has been carried out. I selected some
articles from almost every discipline, and throughout, I have found errors
of *omission* if not of *commission*. I'm hardly talking about that multitude
of dangerous things that you often encounter in its pages when you least
expect it. Here and there, nonetheless, you find a few excellent bits in a
variety of disciplines, and the section on the *Arts & Métiers* is without a
doubt the most valuable. The best sampling from this huge compilation
wouldn't save it: the work has to be completely recast. The Authors have to
always make sure that they are drawing from the best sources, but this is not
the case. &c &c.) Bonnet's correspondence with Haller on this contentious
point illuminates both the strong ties between the Swiss and Dutch
scientists and publishers and the general apprehension scholars felt about
encyclopedia projects that might fail due to the enormity of the task.

17 For this remark, see Bonnet to Felice, 21 January 1769, Bibliothèque
    publique et universitaire de Genève, Inv. 740, fol. 31 verso.

18 Perret, *Les imprimeries d'Yverdon*, 112. Haller, of course, eventually came
    on board, but only after the publication was well underway and its success
    guaranteed. According to Perret, Haller contributed assiduously to the
    Encyclopédie d'Yverdon from volume 15 on. He signed his name to 125
    articles in the categories of medicine and the sciences. The number of
    articles was calculated through means of an electronic database. See
    Clorinda Donato, "Inventaire de l'*Encyclopédie* d'Yverdon," http://c18.net
    /ey/ for database information.

19 Giraud outlines his discovery of the prospectus in a letter to Holtrop dated
    3 March 1787 (The Hague, Royal Library: 133 L 29).

20 F.B. de Felice, letter to W. Holtrop, 19 December 1786, accessed 24 April
    2020, www.unil.ch/defelice/files/live/sites/defelice/files/shared/DF
    _HOLTROP.pdf. The original letter is in The Hague, Royal Library: 133 L 29.

21 In 1787, De Felice hired Cornelis van der Cocq, a lawyer in The Hague, to
    try to collect the funds he was owed by Pierre Gosse. The attempt to collect
    from Gosse failed, and Gosse actually refused to pay for the last volume
    of Yverdon *Encyclopédie* plates. De Felice pursued the matter in court but
    died in 1789 before the case could be resolved. In 1791, his estate was still
    fighting for its due.

22 F.B. de Felice, letter to W. Holtrop, 19 December 1786.

23 Albrecht von Haller's relationship with the *Encyclopédie* was conflicted.
    He contributed unsigned articles, but stopped furnishing them once the
    controversial nature of the work became apparent. His correspondence
    with Charles Bonnet, however, reveals an active interest in writing for an
    encyclopedic work and achieving recognition for it. In his letter of 15

October 1772, Haller reveals that he has revised the entries "A–E" and had written three hundred pages thus far. He became a contributor to the Yverdon *Encyclopédie* around this time, but the manuscript for articles "A–E" was never published. He had been planning to publish a dictionary of medicine with De Felice at the time of his death in 1777. These are the papers that De Felice refers to here, knowing they would make an impact due to Haller's reputation in the Netherlands and abroad. See *Correspondence between Albrecht von Haller and Charles Bonnet*, ed. Sonntag, 1049.

24 In the letter he says: "Ils peuvent en donner encore 1500 a 2000 sans être retoucher" (They are still good for 1500 to 2000 impressions without needing refurbishing). F.B. de Felice, letter to W. Holtrop, 19 December 1786.

25 Ibid. De Felice wrote 849 articles according to our inventory; it is difficult to know the exact numbers, as his style and content are also recognizable in a number of unsigned articles.

26 Ibid.

27 See John Lough, 1963, "The *Encyclopédie:* Two Unsolved Problems," *French Studies* 17, no. 2: 121–35. According to Luneau de Boisjermain, a disgruntled subscriber and Paris book dealer, Diderot in 1768 expressed reservations to Catherine the Great over the handling of the categories of religion and geography in the *Encyclopédie*. Whether the reference is apocryphal or not, it was widely recognized that the articles on these subjects needed thorough revamping, particularly if success in markets outside of France was the goal.

28 "C'est la seule branche qui m'a manqué dans la mienne, j'ai eu d'abord un bigot et ensuite un théologien a gros grains." (It's the only discipline missing from my encyclopedia. The first contributor I had for this branch was a zealot, and the one after him was a theologian in name only.) For a study of Mingard, see Etienne Hofmann, 1996, "Le Pasteur Gabriel Mingard Collaborateur de l'*Encyclopédie* d'Yverdon. Matériaux pour l'étude de sa pensée," in *Le goût de l'histoire, des idées et des hommes. Mélanges offerts au professeur Jean-Pierre Aguet*, ed. Alain Clarien and Bertrand Müller, 77–106 (Lausanne: Editions de l'Aire).

29 *Algemeene genees- natuur- en huishoudkundige jaarboeken*, vol. 3, 1st piece, 92.

30 Ibid. "Dan dat elke geleerde met zijne toestemming gerekend worde bekrachtigd te hebben, dat gene, het welk volkoomen met zijne begrippen strooke, of met het stelsel zijner kerke overeenkoome, en alle overige ten vollen te laaten voor rekening van den steller." (Then, that each intellectual, having sanctioned with his approval that which entirely conformed to his standards, or corresponds with the system of his church, and that all else is fully left to the editor).

31 Perret, *Les imprimeries d'Yverdon*, 239.
32 Joseph Gorani, "Aventures d'un homme célèbre," *Memoires secrets et critiques des cours*, 1: 321–8. As we gain greater insight into De Felice's views of women, as well as the world of eighteenth-century convents, especially the houses for the "malmaritate" or unhappily married women, De Felice's act of liberation of the countess can be read as an enlightened gesture rather than the sign of a salacious affair. On this see Clorinda Donato, 1992, "An Intellectual Exile in the 18th-Century: Fortunato Bartolomeo de Felice in Switzerland," *Romance Languages Annual*, 243–7.
33 Clorinda Donato, 2007, "L'Abbé Bergier et le *Journal helvétique*: Dix-sept articles contre Voltaire et le *Dictionnaire philosophique*," in *Critique, critiques*, ed. Malcolm Cook (Oxford: Peter Lang), 127–37.
34 For a thorough discussion of the inner workings of publishers and book dealers in the business of pirating, gauging, and creating markets in the French book trade outside of France in the eighteenth century, see Robert Darnton, 2003, "The Science of Piracy: A Crucial Ingredient in Eighteenth-Century Publishing," *Studies on Voltaire and the Eighteenth Century*, 2003, 12: 3–29.
35 See *De nagedachtenis van wijlen Willem Holtrop, Reg. Mr. van de A. Loge La Chartié, gevestigd in het O. van Amsterdam. Plegtig gevierd den 10.D der 7M. 1853* (Amsterdam [1835]), 36. See also "Religion et lumières en Italie, 1745–1775: Le choix protestant de Fortunato Bartolomeo De Felice," in *Une Encyclopédie à vocation européenne: Le Dictionnaire universel raisonné des connaissances humaines de F.-B. De Felice (1770–1780)*, ed. Jean-Daniel Candaux, Alain Cernuschi, Clorinda Donato, and Jens Häseler (Geneva: Slatkine, 2005). The freemasonry connection linking Swiss and Dutch publishers is worth exploring, as De Felice was originally brought to Berne through connections between his mentor in Naples, Raimondo di Sangro, the prince of San Severo, head of the Grand Lodge, and the Bernese patrician Vincenz Bernard von Tscharner. San Severo had close ties with Holland and his wife was Dutch. Freemasons promoted the creation of encyclopedic works, as stipulated in Andrew Michael Ramsay's "Oration" delivered to the new initiates in the "Louis d'Argent" Lodge in Paris on 20 March 1737: "All the Grand Masters in Germany, England, Italy, and elsewhere, exhort all the learned men and all the artisans of the Fraternity to unite to furnish the materials for a Universal Dictionary of the liberal arts and useful sciences, excepting only theology and politics. The work has already been commenced in London, and by means of the union of our brothers it may be carried to a conclusion in a few years. Not only are technical words and their etymology explained, but the history of each art and science, its principles and operations, are described."

36 *Boekzaal,* October 1786, message of subscription, 8.

37 De Felice used only thirty-five contributors. Diderot had recourse to one hundred thirty-five.

38 It is possible that he had weighed this option well and decided to wait until his previous plans had ebbed from Dutch readers' memories before suggesting the completely different and far cheaper De Felice setup. If those plans indeed existed they were halted by the death of De Felice on 13 February 1789.

39 The first part of the first volume was published in 1785 (see AVLO 1785, 608 and RC 16–2–1786). Subscription possibility ended in November 1786 (RC 9–11–1786).

40 The fact that the buyers of this cheaper encyclopedia also belonged to the wealthier part of the community could be proven by research on book ownership in the inventory of estates in The Hague and research on the books belonging to customers of bookshop Tijl in Zwolle. Among these estates, two owners of Chalmot's *Huishoudelyk* [...] *woordenboek* were found: Countess Anna Boud, widow of Willem Jan van Hogendorp, buried at the second highest rate, and Dominicus Cornelis Roosmale, buried at the highest rate. Book dealer Tijl sold this title to eight different customers in the period 1778–83. Half of these belonged to the aristocracy, two to the upper classes, one to the upper-middle class, and one to a middle-class citizen. (Thanks are due to José de Kruijf, who allowed consultation of her research files on the eighteenth century, The Hague estate inventories, and Han Brouwer, who allowed viewing of his data from the Tijl customer books.)

41 The fact that this work was, to a large extent, the undertaking of one man (he only had three employees – "his patrons") would have raised confidence that the work would indeed be realized, especially since, according to his message of subscription, he had collected his supply with diligence for many years, and still was, and had others working on it with fervour. One might wonder if this restricted team of employees was a conscious choice, or if De Chalmot had encountered problems in recruiting suitable writers, as was foreseen by De Felice for Holtrop. In the preface to the first seven volumes of his *Huishoudkundig woordenboek* he closes with an introduction of his employees – Petrus Camper, Augustus Sterk, and J.H. Knot – and some snide comments: "Apart from these Gentlemen [...] there has not been one person who has been of help in this weighty undertaking, with exclusion of the subjects of Notary Public, Substitution, Testament." De Vries, "De Oeconomisch-Patriottische beweging," *De Nieuwe Stem* 7, no. 12: 729.

42 His letter to Heinemeyer, a German who was working on a Dutch
    biographical work of reference, is indicative with its detail about Dutch
    readers' lack of interest in this type of reference work: "I cannot do anything
    but appreciate your plans to bring forth a dictionary of intellectuals and
    writers of our Confederation [...]. The circumstances of this time, however,
    and particularly the lack of encouragement one finds in such an undertaking,
    cause me to fear that the demand here for it will be meagre." University
    Library Leiden, Ltk 1001, letter of Chalmot to Heinemeyer, d.d. 26-8-1800.

43 This corroborates the conclusions drawn by G.J. Johannes, who judged that
    the Dutch magazines were bound to a general formula because the small
    market did not allow for specialization or polarization, based on his study
    of the market for magazines in the second half of the eighteenth century.
    See his *De barometer van de smaak. Tijdschriften in Nederland 1770–1830* (The
    Hague: Sdu Uitgevers, 1995), 194–9.

44 After receiving his education in Dordrecht from the esteemed publisher
    A. Blussé and Son, Holtrop left for Amsterdam in 1772, where he became
    a partner in the publishing firm De weduwe Van Esveldt & Holtrop by
    marrying the daughter of book salesman Steven van Esveldt. After 1779
    this firm continued under the name Uitgeverij Willem Holtrop. Hereafter
    Holtrop soon ascended to the higher echelons of the booksellers and
    publishers within the Republic. Among other things, this is apparent by
    the frequency with which his name appeared on stocklists, as well as the
    number of titles that were marketed by him. On average he marketed
    eleven titles per year from 1777 to 1787, ranging from fiction such as
    the anonymous *De Soldaat van fortuin*, to dictionaries such as the then
    standard work of John Holtrop's English dictionary, to magazines such as
    the bimonthly appearing *Natuur, genees- en huishoudkundige jaarboeken*, to
    translations of famous enlightened scientific works such as Montesqueieu's
    The Spirit of the Laws (De geest der wetten).

45 C.N. Fehrmann, "De drukker, uitgever en auteur Jacques Alexandre de
    Chalmot (Leeuwarden 1734–Kampen 1801)," *Kamper Almanak* 1964,
    Kampen 1964, 249.

46 See J.J. Kloek, 1987, "Letteren en landsbelang," in *Voor vaderland en vrijheid*,
    ed. F. Grijzenhout, W.W. Mijnhardt, and N.C.F. van Sas (Amsterdam: De
    Bataafsche Leeuw), 81–95.

47 See Johannes de Vries, 1968, *De economische achteruitgang der Republiek
    in de achttiende eeuw*, 2nd printing (Leiden: n.p.); de Vries, 1952, "De
    Oeconomisch-patriottische beweging," *De Nieuwe Stem*, vol. 7, nr 12, 723–30;
    J. Bierens de Haan, 1952, *Van Oeconomische Tak tot Nederlandsche Maatschappij
    voor Nijverheid en Handel 1777–1952* (Haarlem: Tjeenk Willink).

48 It is a fact that the internationally operating book trade in the Republic was
    dealt a few blows in the second half of the eighteenth century. See J.J. Kloek,
    1993, "1 januari 1790: A.B. Saakes start de 'Lijst van nieuw uitgekomen
    boeken' – De modernisering van het boekbedrijf," in *Nederlandse literatuur.
    Een geschiedenis*, ed. M.A. Schenkeveld-van der Dussen (Groningen:
    Noordhoff Uitgevers), 388–95; W.W. Mijnhardt, 1983, "De geschiedschrijving
    over de ideengeschiedenis van de 17e- en 18e-eeuwse Republiek," in
    Kantelend geschiedbeeld. Nederlandse historiografie sinds 1945, ed. Mijnhardt
    (Utrecht: n.p.), 175; G.C. Gibbs, 1971, "The Role of the Dutch Republic
    as the Intellectual Entrepôt of Europe in the Seventeenth and Eighteenth
    Centuries," *Bijdragen en Mededelingen betreffende de geschiedenis der Nederlanden*
    86: 323–49.
49 Jean-Pierre Perret, 1981 [1945], *Les imprimeries d'Yverdon au XVIIe et au XVIIIe
    siècle* (Geneva: Slatkine), 241.
50 *Oeconomische Courant*, 3–12–1800 nr. 174, 143.
51 *Oeconomische Courant*, 20–8–1800 nr. 159, 23.

Bibliography

Primary Sources

1778. *Algemeen huishoudelijk-, natuur-, zedekundig- en konst- woordenboek*. Edited by
    J.A. de Chalmot. 2nd printing. Leyden [etc.]: Johan Le Maire [etc.].
1786. *Algemeene genees- natuur- en huishoudkundige jaarboeken*. Published by
    Holtrop and Pieter Blussé. Vol. 3, 1st piece. Dordrecht [etc.]: A. Blussé en
    Zoon [etc].
Boekzaal. October 1786. Message of subscription, 8.
Bonnet, letter to Felice, 21 January 1769. Bibliothèque publique et universitaire
    de Genève, Inv. 740, fol. 31 verso.
De nagedachtenis van wijlen Willem Holtrop, Reg. Mr. van de A. Loge La
    Chartié, gevestigd in het O. van Amsterdam. Plegtig gevierd den 10.D der
    7M. 1853. Amsterdam [1835].
F.B. de Felice, letter to W. Holtrop, 19 December 1786. Accessed 24 April 2020.
    www.unil.ch/defelice/files/live/sites/defelice/files/shared/DF_HOLTROP
    .pdf. (Original letter: The Hague, Royal Library: 133 L 29.)

Secondary Sources

Baggerman, Arianne. 2001. *Een lot uit de loterij. Het wel en wee van een
    uitgeversfamilie in de achttiende eeuw*. 2nd ed. Den Haag: SDU. Published in

English as *Life's Lottery: Family Policy and Marketing Strategy of a Distinguished Eighteenth-Century Dutch Publishing Company (A. Blussé and Son 1745–1823)*, Leiden: Brill, 2007.

Bierens de Haan, J. 1952. *Van Oeconomische Tak tot Nederlandsche Maatschappij voor Nijverheid en Handel 1777–1952*. Haarlem: Tjeenk Willink.

Blanchard, G., and M. Olsen. 2002. "Le système des renvois dans l'*Encyclopédie*: Une cartographie des structures de connaissance au XVIIIème siècle." *Recherches sur Diderot et l'Encyclopédie* 31–2: 45–70.

The Correspondence between Albrecht von Haller and Charles Bonnet. 1983. Edited by Otto Sonntag. Bern: Hans Huber Verlag.

Darnton, Robert. 1979. *The Business of Enlightenment: A Publishing History of the* Encyclopédie. Cambridge, MA: Harvard University Press.

– 2003. "The Science of Piracy: A Crucial Ingredient in Eighteenth-Century Publishing." *SVEC* 2: 3–29.

Doig, Kathleen Hardesty, and Christabel P. Braunrot. 1995. "The *Encyclopédie méthodique*: An Introduction." *Studies on Voltaire and the Eighteenth Century* 327: 1–152.

Donato, Clorinda. 1992. "An Intellectual Exile in the 18th Century: Fortunato Bartolomeo de Felice in Switzerland." *Romance Languages Annual*, 243–7.

– 1994. "From Switzerland to Europe through Leipzig: The Swiss Book Trade and the Leipziger Messe 1765–1785." *Leipziger Jahrbuch zur Buchgeschichte* 4: 103–34.

– 1997. "Übersetzung und Wandlung des enzyklopädischen Genres: Johann Georg Krünitz' *Oeconomische Encyclopädie* (1771–1858) und ihre französischsprachigen Vorläufer." In *Kulturtransfer im Epochenumbruch Frankreich-Deutschland 1770 bis 1815*, eds. Hans-Jürgen Lüsebrink and Rolf Reichardt. Leipzig: Leipziger Universitätsverlag. Vol. 2: 539–65.

– 2007. "L'Abbé Bergier et le *Journal helvétique*: Dix-sept articles contre Voltaire et le *Dictionnaire philosophique*." In *Critique, critiques*, edited by Malcolm Cook, 127–37. Peter Lang: n.p.

Gibbs, G.C. 1971. "The Role of the Dutch Republic as the Intellectual Entrepôt of Europe in the Seventeenth and Eighteenth Centuries." *Bijdragen en Mededelingen betreffende de geschiedenis der Nederlanden* 86: 323–49.

Gorani, Joseph. n.d. "Aventures d'un homme célèbre." *Memoires secrets et critiques des cours* (xxx), 1: 321–8.

Hofmann, Etienne. 1996. "Le Pasteur Gabriel Mingard Collaborateur de l'*Encyclopédie* d'Yverdon. Matériaux pour l'étude de sa pensée." In *Le goût de l'histoire, des idées et des hommes. Mélanges offerts au professeur Jean-Pierre Aguet*, edited by Alain Clarien and Bertrand Müller, 77–106. Lausanne: Editions de l'Aire.

Hokke, J. 1987. "'Mijn alderliefste Jantielief.' Vrouw en gezin in de Republiek. Regentenvrouwen en hun relaties." *Jaarboek voor vrouwengeschiedenis* 8: 69.

Kloek, J.J. 1987. "Letteren en landsbelang." In *Voor vaderland en vrijheid*, edited by F. Grijzenhout, W.W. Mijnhardt, and N.C.F. van Sas, 81–95. Amsterdam: De Bataafsche Leeuw.

– 1993. "1 januari 1790: A.B. Saakes start de 'Lijst van nieuw uitgekomen boeken' – De modernisering van het boekbedrijf." In *Nederlandse literatuur. Een geschiedenis*, edited by M.A. Schenkeveld-van der Dussen, 388–95. Groningen: Noordhoff Uitgevers.

Lough, John. 1963. "The *Encyclopédie:* Two Unsolved Problems." *French Studies* 17, no. 2: 121–35.

Maccabez, E. 1903. *F. B. de Felice 1723–1789 et son "Encyclopédie."* Basel: n.p.

Melançon, Benoît. 2002. "Sommes-nous les premiers lecteurs de l'*Encyclopédie?*" In *The Future of Web Publishing: Hyper-reading, Cybertexts, and Metapublishing, Interdisciplines*. Accessed 24 April 2020. https://archivesic.ccsd.cnrs.fr/sic_00000269/document.

Mijnhardt, Wijnand W. 1983. "De geschiedschrijving over de ideengeschiedenis van de 17e- en 18e-eeuwse Republiek." In *Kantelend geschiedbeeld. Nederlandse historiografie sinds 1945*, edited by Wijnand W. Mijnhardt, 162–206. Utrecht: Het Spectrum.

Perret, Jean-Pierre. 1981 [1945]. *Les imprimeries d'Yverdon au XVIIe et au XVIIIe siècle.* Geneva: Slatkine.

Proust, Jacques. 2002. *Europe through the Prism of Japan: Sixteenth to Eighteenth Centuries.* Translated by Elizabeth Bell. Notre Dame: University of Notre Dame Press.

"Religion et lumières en Italie, 1745–1775: Le choix protestant de Fortunato Bartolomeo De Felice." 2005. In *Une Encyclopédie à vocation européenne: Le Dictionnaire universel raisonné des connaissances humaines de F.-B. De Felice (1770–1780)*, edited by Jean-Daniel Candaux, Alain Cernuschi, Clorinda Donato, and Jens Häseler. Geneva: Slatkine.

Vries, Johannes de. 1952. "De Oeconomisch-patriottische beweging." *De Nieuwe Stem* 7, no. 12: 723–30.

– 1968. *De economische achteruitgang der Republiek in de achttiende eeuw.* 2nd printing. Leiden: Stenfert Kroese.

Cited Encyclopedias and Translations/Adaptations

Bayle, Pierre. 1697. *Dictionnaire Historique et Critique,* 4 vols., in-folio. Rotterdam: Reinier Leers.

Translations/Adaptations

Dutch

1733. *Groot algemeen historisch, geographisch, genealogisch en oordeelkundig woordenboek, behelzende het vornaamste, dat vervat is in de Woordenbook van Moreri, Bayle; Buddeus, enz. ...,* ed. by David van Hoogstraten, and Jan Lodewyk Schuër. 10 vols., in-folio. Amsterdam, Pierre Brunel et al.

English

Bayle, Peter. 1734–41. *A General Dictionary Historical and Critical: in Which A New and Accurate Translation of the Celebrated Mr. Bayle, with the Corrections and Observations printed in the late Edition at Paris, is included* ... By the Reverend Mr. John Peter Bernard; The Reverend Mr. Thomas Birch; Mr. John Lockman; and other Hands ... 10 vols., in-2°. London: Printed by James Bettenham, for G. Strahan.

Bayle, Pierre, and Pierre Des Maiseaux. 1734–8. *The Dictionary Historical and Critical of Mr Peter Bayle.* 2nd ed. 5 vols. London: Printed for J.J. and P. Knapton (1st edition in 1710).

French

Chauffepié, Jacques-Georges de. 1750–6. *Nouveau Dictionnaire historique et critique pour servir de Supplément ou de continuation au Dictionnaire historique et critique de Mr. Pierre Bayle, par Jacques-Georges de Chauffepié.* 4 vols., in-40 cm. Amsterdam: Pierre de Hondt.

German

Moréri, Louis. 1709–14. *Allgemeines Historisches Lexicon* …, ed. by Johann Franz Buddeus, 4 vols. Suppl., in-folio. Leipzig/Frankfurt: Thomas Fritsch.

Iselin, Jacob Christoph. 1726–7. *Neu-vermehrtes historisch und geographisches allgemeines Lexicon* … 6 vols., in-37 cm. Basel: Johann Brandmüller (partially based on Bayle).

Blussé, Pieter. 1729–95. *Volledige Beschrijving van alle konsten, ambachten, handwerken, fabrieken, trafieken, derzelver werkhuizen, gereedschappen enz.* … 24 vols., in-8°. Dordrecht: Blussé.

[Brockhaus, Friedrich Arnold, Renatus Gottheld Löbel, and Christian Wilhelm Franke]. 1796–1808. *Conversationslexikon mit vorzüglicher Rücksicht auf die gegenwärtigen Zeiten.* 6 vols., in-8°. Leipzig: Leupold.

– 1812–20. *Conversations-Lexikon oder encyclopädisches Handwörterbuch für gebildete Stände*, 1st–5th. ed. 10 vols. Leipzig: Brockhaus.

– 1822. *Conversations-Lexikon.* Neue Folge. 2 vols. Leipzig: Brockhaus.

– 1830. *Allgemeine deutsche Real-Encyklopädie für die gebildeten Stände (Conversations-Lexikon).* 7th ed. 2nd printing, 12 vols. Leipzig: Brockhaus.

– 1834. *Conversations-Lexikon der neuesten Zeit und Literatur,* 4 vols. Leipzig: Brockhaus. (Supplement to 7th ed.)

Translations/Adaptations

Danish

1816–18. *Conversations-Lexicon aller enyclopaedisk Haandbog.* 6 vols. Copenhagen: s.p. (fragmentary, up to letter "L").

Dutch

1820–9. *Algemeen woordenboek van kunsten en wetenschappen*, ed. by Gerrit Nieuwenhuis, 7 vols. Thieme: Zutphen.

English

1830–3. *Encyclopaedia Americana, a popular Dictionary of arts, sciences, literature, history, politics, and biography*, ed. by Francis Lieber, 13 vols., in-24cm. Philadelphia: Carey and Lea.

1841–50. *The popular Encyclopaedia being a general dictionary of arts, sciences, literature, biography, history, and political economy. Reprinted from the American ed. of the "Conversations lexicon,"* …, ed. by William Blackie, 7 vols., in-26 cm. Glasgow: Blackie.

1860–70. *Chambers's Encyclopaedia. A Dictionary of universal knowledge for the people*, ed. by William and Robert Chambers, 10 vols., in-27cm. Edinburgh.

French

1833–44. *Encyclopédie des gens du monde*, ed. by Jean-Henri Schnitzler, 22 vols. Paris: Treuttel and Würtz.

1832–9. *Dictionnaire de la conversation et de la lecture*, ed. by William Duckett. 52 vols., in-8°. Paris: Belin-Mandar.

– 1844–51. (*Supplément*). 16 vols. Paris: Garnier Frères.

Italian

1837. *Dizionario di conversazione*. 1 vol., in-8°. Padova: Coi tipi della Minerva.

Hungarian

1831–4. *Közhasznu Edmeretek Tára*, ed. by Otto Wigand, 12 vols. Pest: n.p.

Russian

1835–41. *Entsiklopeditscheskii Leksikon*, ed. by N.J. Gretsch, 17 vols. St. Petersburg: n.p.

Spanish

1853–5. *Diccionario universal de historia y de la geografia*, ed. by Lucas Alamán. 7 vols. Mexico: De Rafael.

Chambers, Ephraim. 1728. *Cyclopædia; or An Universal dictionary of arts and sciences ...*, 2 vols., in-folio. London: Knapton.

Chomel, Noël. 1709. *Dictionnaire œconomique*. 2 vols., in-folio. Lyon: Pierre Thened.

Translations/Adaptations

Dutch

1778–93. *Algemeen huishoudelijk-, natuur-, zedekundig- en konst-woordenboek*, ed. by Jacques Alexandre de Chalmot. 2nd printing. 7 vols., in-4°. Leyden: Le Maire.

Chomel, Noël, Jan Lodewyk Schuër, and Arnold Heinrich Westerhoff. 1743. *Huishoudelyk woordboek, vervattende vele middelen om zyn goed te vermeerderen, en zyne gezondheid te behouden ...*, *door M. Noel Chomel ...* 2 vols., in-4°. Leiden, Amsterdam: Luchtmans, Uytwerf.

English

Chomel, Noël, and Richard Bradley. 1725. *Dictionnaire Oeconomique: Or, the Family Dictionary.* London: Printed for D. Midwinter.

French

De Felice, Fortunato Bartolomeo. 1770–1. *Encyclopédie œconomique, ou, Système général, ...* 16 vols., in-18 cm. Yverdon : s.p.

Japanese

1811–45. Baba Sadayoshi and Otsuki Gentaku, *Kosei Shinpen* 厚生新編, translated from the Dutch of Chalmot (more than 100 manuscript volumes).

Corneille, Thomas. 1708. *Dictionnaire Universel, Géographique et Historique* ... 3 vols., in-4°. Paris: Coignard.

Translations/Adaptations

Dutch

Buys, Egbert. 1769–78. *Nieuw En Volkomen Woordenboek van Konsten en Weetenschappen* ... 10 vols. Amsterdam: Baalde (also partially based on Chambers's *Cyclopædia* and Diderot's and d'Alembert's *Encyclopédie*).

Diderot, Denis, and Jean-Baptiste le Rond d'Alembert, eds. 1751–77. *Encyclopédie ou dictionnaire raisonnée des sciences, des arts et des métiers.* 17 vols. and 11 vols. of plates., in-folio. Paris: Briasson.

Translations/Adaptations

English

Croker, Temple Henry, Thomas Williams, and Samuel Clark. 1764–6. *The Complete Dictionary of Arts and Sciences.* 3 vols., in-folio. London: J. Wilson and others.

French

De Felice, Fortunato Bartolomeo. 1770–80. *Encyclopédie, ou Dictionnaire universel raisonné des connoissances humaines.* 58 vols., in-4°. Yverdon: n.p. 1782–1832. *Encyclopédie méthodique.* 203 vols., in-4°. Paris: Panckoucke.

Italian

Diodati, Giovanni. 1758–76. *Encyclopédie, ou Dictionnaire raisonné des sciences, des arts et des métiers.* 2nd ed. 28 vols. Lucques: Giuntini.
Aubert, Giuseppe. 1770–9. *Encyclopédie, ou Dictionnaire raisonné des sciences, des arts et des métiers.* 3rd ed. 33 vols. Livourne: Imprimerie de la Société.

1782–1832. ***Encyclopédie méthodique.*** 203 vols., in-4°. Paris: Panckoucke.

Translations/Adaptations

Italian

1785–91. *Encyclopédie méthodique nouvelle édition enrichie de remarques dédiée à la sérénissime République de Venise* ... 4°-in. Padova: Seminario di Padova.

Spanish

Sancha, Antonio de. 1788–94. *Encyclopedia metódica.* 10 vols., in-2°. Madrid: Por Antonio de Sancha.

Furetière, Antoine. 1690. *Dictionnaire universel, contenant généralement tous les mots françois.* The Hague, Rotterdam: Leers.
– 1727. *Corr. et augm. par Henri Basnage de Beauval. Nouvelle éd. revû corr. et considérablement augm. par Jean Baptiste Brutel de la Rivière.* 4 vols. The Hague: n.p.

Herbelot, Barthélemy d'. 1697. *Bibliothèque orientale ou dictionnaire universel* ... 1 vol., in-folio. Paris: Compagnie des Libraires.

Hübner, Johann. 1704. *Reales Staats- und Zeitungslexicon* ... Leipzig: Johann Friedrich Gleditsch.

Translations/Adaptations

Dutch

Hübner, Johann. 1732–4. *De staats- en koeranten-tolk of woordenboek der geleerden en ongeleernden* ... 2 vols., in-4°. Leiden: Samuel Luchtmans et al.

Hübner, Johann. 1727. *Lexicon Genealogicum Portatile, Das ist: Ein Verzeichnis aller itzt-lebenden Hohen Häupter in der gantzen Welt, Welches man allezeit bey sich tragen kann.* In-8°. Hamburg: Felginer.

Translations/Adaptations

Dutch

Hübner, Johann de Jonge. 1727. *Beknopt genealogisch woordenboek … Uit het Hoogduitsch overgezet, en uit de overgezondene berechten van … Johan Hubner … en eigene aantekeningen tot dezen tydt vervolgt.* Trans. by Jan Lodewijk. 1 vol., in-8°. Amsterdam: Bos.

Köster, Heinrich Martin Gottfried, and Ludwig Julius Friedrich Höpfner. 1778–1804. *Deutsche Encyclopädie oder allgemeines Real-Wörterbuch aller Künste und Wissenschaften*, 23 vols., in-31 cm. Frankfurt am Main: Bey Varrentrapp und Wenner.

Marperger, Paul Jacob. 1712. *Curieuses Natur- Kunst- Gewerk- und Handlungs-Lexicon*, ed. by Johann Hübner. 1 vol., in-8°. Leipzig: Gleditsch.

Translations/Adaptations

Dutch

Westerhoff, Arnold Heinrich. 1732. *De Staats- en Koeranten-Tolk of Woordenboek der Geleerden en Ongeleerden … in het Hoogduitsch uytgegeven en met een Voorede verzelt door den Heer Johan Hubner …* 2 vols. Leiden.

Moréri, Louis. 1674. *Le grand dictionaire historique, ou le mélange curieux de l'histoire sainte et profane […].* In-folio. Lyon: Jean Girin, Barthélémy Rivière.

Moréri, Louis, and Jean Le Clerc. 1702. *Neuvième Édition où l'on a mis le Supplément dans le même ordre Alphabetique …* 4 vols., in-folio. Amsterdam, La Compagnie des Librairies.

Translations/Adaptations

Dutch

Hoogstraten, David van, Matthæus Brouërius van Nidek, and Jan Lodewyk Schuër. 1725–33. *Groot algemeen historisch, geographisch, genealogisch en oordeelkundig woordenboek, behelzende het vornaamste, dat vervat is in de Woordenbook van Moreri, Bayle; Buddeus, enz. ...*, ed. by David van Hoogstraten and Jan Lodewyk Schuër. 10 vols., in-folio. Amsterdam: Pierre Brunel et al.

Luïscius, Abraham George. 1724–37. *Het Algemeen Historisch, Geographisch, en Genealogisch Woordenboek ...* 8 vols., in-45 cm. The Hague, Delft: Husson, Boitet.

English

Moréri, Louis and Edmund Bohun. 1694. *The great historical, geographical and poetical dictionary ...* London: Printed for Henry Rhodes ... [and 3 others].

German

Moréri, Louis. 1709–14. *Allgemeines Historisches Lexicon ...*, ed. by Johann Franz Buddeus. 4 vols. + suppl. Leipzig, Frankfurt: Thomas Fritsch.

– 1722. *Allgemeines Historisches Lexicon... andere und vermehrte Auflage.* 4 vols. + suppl., in-folio. Leipzig: Thomas Fritsch.

Iselin, Jacob Christoph. 1726–7. *Neu-vermehrtes historisch und geographisches allgemeines Lexicon [...].* 6 vols., in-37 cm. Basel: Johann Brandmüller.

French

Bernard, Jacques. 1716. *Supplément Aux Anciennes Editions Du Grand Dictionnaire Historique De Mre. Louis Moreri ...* 2 vols., in-folio. Amsterdam: Pierre Brunel, R. & G. Wetstein, David Mortier, Pierre De Coup; The Hague: Adrian Moetjens, L. & H. Van Dole; Utrecht: Guillaume van de Water.

Spanish

Moréri, Louis. 1753. *El gran diccionario historico, o Miscellanea curiosa de la historia sagrada y profana ...* por Don Joseph de Miravel y Casadevante ... In-folio. Paris, Leon: Hermanos de Tournes.

Peuchet, Jacques. 1789–99. *Dictionnaire universel de la géographie commerçante ...* 5 vols., in-4°. Paris: Blanchon.

Translations/Adaptations

Greek

Papadhópoulos, Nicolas, ed. *Hermès the God of Profit or commercial En-cylopedia* [translation of the Greek title], 1815–17, 3rd vol. [partial translation, combined with a partial translation of Savary Des Brus-lons' Dictionnaire].

Raynal, Guillaume-Thomas. 1770. *Histoire philosophique et politique des établissemens et du commerce des Européens dans les deux Indes.* 6 vols., in-8°. Amsterdam: n.p.
– 1774. 7 vols. in-8°. La Haye: Gosse fils.
– 1780. 4 vols. + atlas, in-4°. Genève: Pellet.
– 1820–1. 12 vols. + atlas, in-22cm. Paris: A. Costes.

Translations/Adaptations

English

Raynal, Guillaume-Thomas. 1783. *A Philosophical and Political History of the Settlements and Trade of the Europeans in the East and West Indies.* 8 vols. London: Printed for W. Strahan and T. Cadell.

Robert, James. 1743–5. *A Medicinal Dictionary, including physic, surgery, anatomy, chymistry, and botany.* 3 vols., in-folio. London: T. Osborne.

Translations/Adaptations

French

1746–8. *Dictionnaire universel de médecine, de Chirurgie, de Chymie, de Botanique, d'Anatomie, de Pharmacie, d'Histoire Naturelle, &c.* Traduit de l'Anglois de M. [Robert] James. Par Mrs. [Denis] Diderot, [Marc-Antoine] Eldous & [François Vincent] Toussaint. Revue, corrigé & augmenté par M. Julien Busson, Docteur Régent de la Faculté de Médecine de Paris … 6 vols., in-folio. Paris: Briasson, David, Durand.

Savary des Bruslons, Jacques, and Philémon-Louis Savary. 1759–65. *Dictionnaire universel de commerce* … 3 vols., in-folio. Copenhague: Chez les Frères Cl. and Ant. Philibert.

Translations/Adaptations

German

1763. "Aufrichtige und vollständige Beschreibung der Art, wie die Zitsen in Indien gemacht warden (et)c. Aus der Herren Savary *Dictionnaire universel de Commerce*. Th. IV, S. 789 u.f. der neuesten Genever Ausgabe," in *Gemeinnütziges Natur- und Kunstmagazin oder Abhandlungen zur Beförderung der Naturkunde, der Künste, Manufacturen und Fabriken*. 1(1): 29–47. Berlin: Arnold Wever.

1763. "Die Art das ungarische Leder zuzurichten: aus der Herren Savary *Dictionnaire universel de Commerce*. Th. 1, S. 1290 u.f. der neuesten Genever Ausgabe," in *Gemeinnütziges Natur- und Kunstmagazin oder Abhandlungen zur Beförderung der Naturkunde, der Künste, Manufacturen und Fabriken*. 1(1): 100–4. Berlin: Arnold Wever.

1763. "Historische Nachricht von den Spiegelglasmanufakturen in Frankreich. Aus der Herren Savary Dictionnaire universel de Commerce. Th. II,. S. 658 u.f. übersetzt," in *Gemeinnütziges Natur- und Kunstmagazin oder Abhandlungen zur Beförderung der Naturkunde, der Künste, Manufacturen und Fabriken*. 1(1): 100–4. Berlin: Arnold Wever.

Ludovici, Carl Günther. 1741–3. *Allgemeine Schatz-Kammer der Kauffmannschaft, oder vollständiges Lexikon aller Handlungen und Gewerbe, sowohl in Deutschland als auswaertigen Königreichen und Ländern*. in-36cm. Leipzig: Heinsius.

Ludovici, Carl Günther. 1752–6. *Eröffnete Academie der Kaufleute: oder vollständiges Kaufmanns-Lexicon*. 5 vols., in-22cm. Leipzig: B.C. Breitkopf.

Israel, Moses, Friedrich Heusinger, and Casar Ihling. 1809. *Universal-Lexicon der Handlungswissenschaften, bearbeitet nach Savary*. 1 vol., in-4°. Leipzig: Heinrich Gräff.

English

Postlethwayt, Malachy. 1751–5. *The Universal Dictionary of Trade and Commerce. Translated from the French of the Celebrated Monsieur Savary* … 2 vols., in-folio. London: Knapton (2nd edition 1766, 3rd edition 1774).

Rolt, Richard. 1756. *A New Dictionary of Trade and Commerce, compiled from the information of the most eminent merchants*, 1 vol., London (2nd edition 1761).

Mortimer, Thomas. 1766. *A New and complete dictionary of trade and commerce containing a distinct explanation of the general principles of commerce, an accurate definition of its terms ... 2 vols., in-folio.* London: The author, printed by S. Crowder, J. Coote, J. Fletcher.

Greek

Papadhópoulos, Nicolas. *Hermès the God of Profit or commercial Encylopedia,* 1815–17, 4 vols. vols. 1–2 [partial translation, combined with a partial translation of Peuchet's *Dictionnaire*].

Italian

1770–1. *Dizionario di commercio dei signori fratelli Savary, ... Accrescituo di varj importantissimi Articoli, tratti dall'Enciclopedia, e dalle Memorie dell'accuratissimo Mr. Garcin, ec. Edizione prima italiana.* 4 vols., in-26 cm. Venezia: Press Giambatista Pasquali.

Portuguese

Sales, Alberto Jacqueri de. *Diccionario do commercio* [manuscript], 4 vols., enc., in-34 cm (unpublished).

Russian

Savary des Bruslons, Jacques. 1747. *Экстракт Савариева лексикона о комерции,* ed. by Sergei Savvich Volchkov. in-4°. St. Petersburg: Akademie der Wissenschaft.

Savary des Bruslons, Jacques. 1787–92. *Словарь коммерческий* [...], ed. by Levshin, Vasily Alekseevich. 4 vols., in-8°. Moskau: Тип. Комп. типогр.

Smellie, William. 1768–71. *Encyclopaedia Britannica; or a Dictionary of Arts and Sciences, ...* 3 vols., in-29 cm. Edinburgh: Bell and Macfarqhuar.

Zedler, Johann Heinrich. 1731–54. *Grosses vollständiges Universal-Lexicon aller Wissenschafften und Künste, welche bisher durch menschlichen Verstand und Witz erfunden und verbessert werden.* 64 vols. + 4 suppl., in-34/36 cm. Halle, Leipzig: Zedler.

Contributors

Arianne Baggerman is a professor of the history of publishing and book trade at the University of Amsterdam and teaches history at Erasmus University Rotterdam. Her study on publishing and the book trade, *Een lot uit de loterij. Familiebelangen en uitgeverspolitiek in de Dordtse firma A. Blusse en zoon 1745–1823* (2000), has also appeared in English translation as *The Fortunes of a Dutch Publishing House in the 18th and Early 19th Centuries* (2014). With Rolf Dekker, she published *Child of the Enlightenment: Revolutionary Europe Reflected in a Boyhood Diary* (2009) and co-edited *Controlling Time and Shaping the Self* (2011).

Alain Cernuschi is a maître d'enseignement et de recherche at the Faculty of lettres, University of Lausanne. He is the co-director of l'*Edition numérique collaborative et critique de l'Encyclopédie* (ENCCRE), online since 2017. A specialist in the history of enlightenment encyclopedias, his recent publications include a co-edited volume, *Oser l'*Encyclopédie. *Un combat des Lumières* (2017), and "'Une espèce d'ouvrage cosmopolite.' Variations énonciatives dans les articles encyclopédiques des Lumières, de Chambers à l'*Encyclopédie*," *Travaux neuchâtelois de linguistique* (2018).

Iwan-Michelangelo D'Aprile holds the Cultures of the Enlightenment professorship chair at the Faculty of Arts, University of Potsdam, where he is the director of the Research Center Sanssouci (RECS). D'Aprile's book publications include *Das 18. Jahrhundert. Das Zeitalter der Aufklärung* (2008), *Berlins 19. Jahrhundert. Ein Metropolenkompendium* (2011), *Die Erfindung der Zeitgeschichte. Geschichtsschreibung und Journalismus zwischen Aufklärung und Vormärz* (2013), and *Fontane. Ein Jahrhundert in Bewegung* (2018).

Luigi Delia is a CNRS associate researcher at the Centre Jean Pépin, Villejuif. A graduate from the Collegio Superiore, University of Bologna, he was a Swiss National Science Foundation postdoctoral researcher at the University of Geneva (2016–19). His publications include *Panckoucke et l'Encyclopédie méthodique. Ordre de matières et transversalité* (2019, with Martine Groult); *Le Moment Beccaria. Naissance du droit pénal moderne (1764–1810)* (2018, with Philippe Audegean); and *Droit et philosophie à la lumière de l'Encyclopédie* (2015).

Clorinda Donato is a professor of French and Italian at California State University, Long Beach, where she directs the Clorinda Donato Center for Global Romance Languages and Translation Studies. Recent publications include *Fanny Hill Now*, a special issue of *Eighteenth-Century Life* (co-edited in 2019 with Nicholas Nace); *The "Encyclopédie Méthodique" in Spain* (2015, with Riccardo Lopez); *Gender, Science and Sensationalism in Eighteenth-Century Italy and England: The Life and Legend of Catterina Vizzani* (2020); and *John Fante's ASK THE DUST: A Gathering of Voices*, co-edited with Stephen Cooper (2020).

Susanne Greilich is an assistant professor of French and Spanish, Department of Romance Languages and Literatures, University of Regensburg. She heads the DFG-Research Project "French Encyclopedism and Its Translational Dimensions in the Age of Enlightenment (1680–1800): Knowledge Transfer, Intermediary Figures, Intercultural Processes of Adaptation" (with H.-J. Lüsebrink). Recent publications include *L'encyclopédisme, du XVIIIe siècle à nos jours*, co-edited with H.-J. Lüsebrink (2020), and *Clash culturel et communauté du rire: L'humour interculturel dans les sociétés francophones contemporaines*, co-edited with D. Schmelzer (2020).

Kathleen Hardesty Doig is a professor of French emerita, Department of World Languages and Cultures, Georgia State University. With Dorothy Medlin, she published a critical edition of the *Mémoires de l'abbé Morellet* (2013); with Felicia Sturzer, Doig edited a collection of essays, *Women, Gender and Disease in Eighteenth-Century England and France* (2014). Her *From Encyclopédie to Encyclopédie méthodique: Revision and Expansion* appeared in 2013. She continues her studies on the *Méthodique* in a recent article, "Ébauche d'une étude transversale: Le *Dictionnaire de Physique*," in Groult and Delia, with Claire Fauvergue, *Panckoucke et l'Encyclopédie méthodique. Ordre de matières et transversalité* (2019).

Jeff Loveland is a professor in the Department of Romance and Arabic Languages and Literatures at the University of Cincinnati. In addition to articles and book chapters, he has written three books: *Rhetoric and Natural History: Buffon in Polemical and Literary Context* (2001), *An Alternative Encyclopedia? Dennis de Coetlogon's Universal History of Arts and Sciences* (2010), and *The European Encyclopedia from 1650 to the Twenty-First Century* (2019). He also co-edited *The Early Britannica: The Growth of an Outstanding Encyclopedia* (2009) and is currently co-editing a book on specialized encyclopedias.

Hans-Jürgen Lüsebrink is Senior Professor of Romance Cultural Studies and Intercultural Communication at Saarland University in Germany. He holds a PhD in romance philology (Bayreuth, Germany) and in history (EHESS, France) and is a founding member of the International Research Training Group "Diversity: Mediating Difference in Transcultural Spaces" of the universities of Trier, Montreal, and Saarbrücken. Recent volumes include *Écrire l'encyclopédisme. Du XVIIIe siècle à nos jours,* co-edited with Susanne Greilich (2020), and *Cultural Transfers Reconsidered,* co-edited with Steen Bille Jorgensen (2021). Together with S. Greilich he heads the DFG research project "The Translational Dimension of the French Encyclopedism in the Age of Enlightenment."

Ina Ulrike Paul is Apl. Professor at the Friedrich-Meinecke-Institute of History, Department of History and Cultural Studies, Freie Universität Berlin. Recent publications include *Weltwissen. Das Eigene und das Andere in enzyklopädischen Lexika des langen 18. Jahrhunderts* (2020); "Paul Anton de Lagarde und 'die Juden,'" in *Der Nachlaß Paul de Lagarde. Orientalistische Netzwerke und antisemitische Verflechtungen,*" ed. by Heike Behlmer et al. (2020); and "Charles-Frédéric, comte Reinhard (1761–1837): Diplomate et homme de lettres," in *L'identité du diplomate (Moyen Âge–XIXe siècle): Métier ou noble loisir?,* ed. by Indravati Félicité (2020).

Ulrich Johannes Schneider, PhD, has been Director of Leipzig University Library since 2006, Professor of Philosophy at Leipzig University since 2004, and since 2007 has taught at the Institute for Cultural Studies at that university. His most recent publications include *Die Erfindung des allgemeinen Wissens. Enzyklopädisches Schreiben im Zeitalter der Aufklärung* (2013); *Les arts du texte. La révolution du livre autour de 1500* (2016); and *Der Finger im Buch. Die unterbrochene Lektüre im Bild* (2020).

Karen Struve is a substitute professor for French Literature and Cultural Studies at Technische Universität Dresden and PI of the "Anxiety Culture" research project (a cooperation between Columbia University and Christian-Albrechts-University of Kiel). Recent publications include *Wildes Wissen in der "Encyclopédie." Koloniale Alterität, Wissen und Narration in der französischen Aufklärung* (2020) and co-editor, with K. Harbrecht, E. Tüting, and G. Febel, of *Die un-sichtbare Stadt. Urbane Perspektiven, alternative Räume und Randfiguren in Literatur und Film* (2020).

Index

THE UCLA CLARK MEMORIAL LIBRARY SERIES